T0382811

"Over the past three decades, scholarship of networks has grown substantially. However, scholars still need to address major challenges around conceptual, theoretical, and methodological concerns in network scholarship. This volume, edited by leading scholars, is a great contribution to methods and methodological issues in networks and network governance, which includes diverse methodological perspectives discussed by authors that have also applied them in their network research."

— *Naim Kapucu, Pegasus Professor and Director at the School of Public Administration, University of Central Florida, Orlando, USA*

"The editors have brought together an invaluable collection of many of the methodological approaches to network and collaboration commonly used in public administration research. The chapters include descriptions of methods as diverse as case studies and narrative inquiry, surveys, social network analysis, and agent-based modelling. Combined with the integrative and forward-looking final chapters, this book provides an excellent resource for researchers and public managers alike."

— *Jenny M. Lewis, Professor of Public Policy at the University of Melbourne, Australia, and President of the International Research Society for Public Management*

"Despite the vast and growing literature on governance networks and collaboration, until now a text presenting a comprehensive overview of methods and methodology of network research was missing. This book fills the gap. It discusses the nuts and bolts of well-established as well as new contemporary methods and their potentials given current and future research contexts. An essential guidebook for everyone interested in network and collaboration research: students, practitioners, early career *and* established researchers."

— *Joop Koppenjan, Professor of Public Administration at Erasmus University Rotterdam, Netherlands*

Networks and Collaboration in the Public Sector

Networks and other collaborations are central to the public sector's ability to respond to their diverse responsibilities, from international development and regional governance, to policy development and service provision. Great strides have been made toward understanding their formation, governance and management, but more opportunities to explore methodologies and measures is required to ensure they are properly understood.

This volume showcases an array of selected research methods and analytics tools currently used by scholars and practitioners in network and collaboration research, as well as emerging styles of empirical investigation. Although it cannot attempt to capture all technical details for each one, this book provides a unique catalogue of compelling methods for researchers and practitioners, which are illustrated extensively with applications in the public and non-profit sector.

By bringing together leading and upcoming scholars in network research, the book will be of enormous assistance in guiding students and scholars in public management to study collaboration and networks empirically by demonstrating the core research approaches and tools for investigating and evaluating these crucially important arrangements.

Joris Voets is an associate professor in the Department of Public Governance and Management at the Faculty of Economics and Business Administration, Ghent University, Belgium.

Robyn Keast is a professor in the School of Business and Tourism, Southern Cross University, Australia.

Christopher Koliba is a professor in the Community Development and Applied Economics Department at University of Vermont, USA, Co-Director of the Social Ecological Gaming and Simulation (SEGS) Lab and fellow at the Gund Institute on the Environment.

Routledge Critical Studies in Public Management

Series editor: Stephen Osborne

The study and practice of public management has undergone profound changes across the world. Over the last quarter century, we have seen

- increasing criticism of public administration as the over-arching framework for the provision of public services,
- the rise (and critical appraisal) of the 'New Public Management as an emergent paradigm for the provision of public services,
- the transformation of the 'public sector' into the cross-sectoral provision of public services, and
- the growth of the governance of inter-organizational relationship as an essential element in the provision of public services.

In reality these trends have not so much replaced each other as elided or co-existed together – the public policy processes has not gone away as a legitimate topic of study, intra-organizational management continue to be essential to the efficient provision of public services, whilst the governance of inter-organizational and inter-sectoral relationships is now essential to the effective provision of these services.

Further, whilst the study of public management has been enriched by contribution of a range of insights from the 'mainstream' management literature it has also contributed to this literature in such areas as networks and inter-organizational collaboration, innovation and stakeholder theory.

This series is dedicated to presenting and critiquing this important body of theory and empirical study. It will publish books that both explore and evaluate the emergent and developing nature of public administration, management and governance (in theory and practice) and examine the relationship with and contribution to the over-arching disciplines of management and organizational sociology.

Books in the series will be of interest to academics and researchers in this field, students undertaking advanced studies of it as part of their undergraduate or postgraduate degree and reflective policy makers and practitioners.

Ethics Management in the Public Service
A Sensory-based Strategy
Liz Ireni-Saban and Galit Berdugo

Critical Perspectives on the Management and Organization of Emergency Services
Edited by Paresh Wankhade, Leo McCann, and Pete Murphy

Public Service Management and Asylum
Co-production, Inclusion and Citizenship
Kirsty Strokosch

Networks and Collaboration in the Public Sector
Essential Research Approaches, Methodologies and Analytic Tools
Edited by Joris Voets, Robyn Keast and Christopher Koliba

For more information about this series, please visit: www.routledge.com/Routledge-Critical-Studies-in-Public-Management/book-series/RSPM

Networks and Collaboration in the Public Sector

Essential Research Approaches,
Methodologies and Analytic Tools

Edited by
Joris Voets, Robyn Keast
and Christopher Koliba

Routledge
Taylor & Francis Group

LONDON AND NEW YORK

First published 2020
by Routledge
2 Park Square, Milton Park, Abingdon, Oxon OX14 4RN

and by Routledge
605 Third Avenue, New York, NY 10017

First issued in paperback 2021

Routledge is an imprint of the Taylor & Francis Group, an informa business

British Library Cataloguing-in-Publication Data
A catalogue record for this book is available from the British Library

Library of Congress Cataloging-in-Publication Data
A catalog record for this book has been requested

ISBN 13: 978-0-367-78443-0 (pbk)
ISBN 13: 978-1-138-68272-6 (hbk)

Typeset in Bembo
by Apex CoVantage, LLC.

To Myrna P. Mandel

It can be said that as researchers we have been able to see further and advance knowledge by standing on the shoulders of the giants who have come before us. In the study of networks and collaboration, one such giant – in thinking if not stature – is Myrna Mandell.

Myrna was one of the very early network researchers and has influenced the research careers of all three editors of this volume, and likely most of the chapter contributors, through her mentorship, collegiality and championing of network and collaboration research. However, her impact is much broader and reaches out into the cohort of early career researchers with whom she has shared her time, her encouragement and, most of all, the knowledge accumulated over a celebrated career, which in 2016 was acknowledged with the Routledge Prize for Outstanding Contribution to Public Management Research.

In recognition and appreciation of her scholarly contribution and her friendship we dedicate this volume to our friend and colleague Myrna Mandell.

Contents

Figures

Tables

Acknowledgements

We want to thank the Routledge team – Jacqueline Curthoys, Laura Hussey and Jess Harrison – for their enthusiasm, support and patience in getting this volume published. We are also indebted to Hannah Murphy, whose help was invaluable in editing and submitting the final manuscript. Finally, we want to extent our gratitude to all authors who have done a marvellous job in writing the chapters as we envisaged them from the outset – an excellent collaborative result, drawing on the scholarly networks on networks and collaboration.

Joris Voets, Robyn Keast and Christopher Koliba

Abbreviations

ABM	Agent-based model
AI	Artificial intelligence
AOT	Agency of Transportation
CSB	Common source bias
ERGM	Exponential random graph modelling
HCBS	Home and Community-Based Services
ICMA	International City/County Management Association
NAO	Network administrative organization
NGO	Non-governmental organization
ODD	Overview, design concepts, details protocol
OLS	Ordinary least squares
OSU	Ohio State University
QAP	Quadratic Assignment Procedure
QCA	Qualitative comparative analysis
NPM	New Public Management
PA	Public administration
PAR	Participatory action research
PCA	Principal Components Factor Analysis
RO-AR	Research oriented action research
SAOMS	Stochastic actor-oriented models
SEM	Structural equation modelling
SES	Socioeconomic status
SNA	Social network analysis
TCA	Theory of collaborative advantage
TPP	Transportation project prioritization
UK	United Kingdom
US	United States

Contributors

Robert Agranoff is Professor Emeritus in the School of Public and Environmental Affairs at Indiana University Bloomington, USA, and is affiliated with the Instituto Universitario Ortega y Gasset in Madrid, Spain. His areas of expertise include collaborative public management, intergovernmental relations and management, public administration, economic and community development, and federalism.

Denita Cepiku is an associate professor in public management at the University of Rome 'Tor Vergata', Italy, where she coordinates the PhD program track in Public Management and Governance. Her main research interests are in the areas of collaborative governance, cutback management, and strategic performance management. In 2017 she edited the *Routledge handbook of global public policy and administration*. She has been board member of the IRSPM (2011–2017) and is chair of the EURAM SIG on Public Management (since 2009). She is a member of the editorial committee for journals in Public Management and the Public Sector.

Dan Chamberlain is a Research Fellow in Social Network Analysis in Disease Prevention, with the Australian Prevention Partnership Centre, and the Department of Public Health at La Trobe University, Australia. He holds a PhD in Sociology from the School of Arts at Griffith University. Dan's research is focused on applications of social network analysis, and he teaches and provides methodological expertise on the design, conduct and analysis of network research. He has applied network analysis to a variety of trans-disciplinary projects, including research in sociology, criminology, education, public policy, management and public health.

Ming Cheng is a joint PhD candidate at the School of Political Science and Public Administration in China University of Political Science and Law, China, as well as the Faculty of Economics and Business Administration in Ghent University, Belgium. His fields of expertise cover the development of meta-governance in different contexts and the function of state power in various governance modes, especially networks and collaborative arrangements. In the doctoral program, he is further exploring the power dynamics of collaborative environmental governance in China.

Daniela Cristofoli is research fellow at the University of Milano-Bicocca, Italy. Her main research interests involve network governance, network management and public leadership. She is co-chair of the XIX EGPA Permanent Study Group on 'network policy and management'.

Jennifer Dodge is an associate professor in the Department of Public Administration and Policy at Rockefeller College, University at Albany, USA, and Co-Editor of *Critical Policy Studies*. She holds a PhD from New York University. Drawing on interpretive and qualitative methodologies, her research focuses on the interpretation of policy conflict and the role of civil society organizations and networks in supporting citizen participation in policy discourse, most recently related to fracking and climate change. She seeks to explain how policy conflict affects decision-making and policy formulation, and how conflict can be used productively to create more just and sustainable policy.

Jurian Edelenbos is a professor of Interactive Governance at the Department of Public Administration and Sociology, Erasmus University Rotterdam, the Netherlands. He has published in various journals on community-based initiatives and participation, trust in governance networks, network management and boundary spanning, and performance of interactive governance.

Ben Farr-Wharton is an associate professor in management at the School of Business and Law, Edith Cowan University, Australia. His PhD explored the impact of social networks and business management skills on the labour outcomes of freelance workers within Australia's creative sector. Since 2013, Ben has been working with international and Australian colleagues to develop a more comprehensive understanding of the role of effective management on workplace outcomes, including factors such as employee performance, stress, safety, resilience, harassment and engagement.

John M. Kamensky is a senior fellow with the IBM Center for The Business of Government in Washington, DC. He was formerly deputy director of the National Partnership for Reinventing Government and worked at the Office of Management and Budget and the Government Accountability Office, both in the USA. He is a fellow of the National Academy of Public Administration, USA.

Robyn Keast is a professor in the School of Business and Tourism, Southern Cross University, Australia, who primarily studies networked arrangements and collaborative practices. She publishes extensively in public administration and public/social policy journals, co-edited *Network theory in the public sector* (Routledge, 2014), and co-authored *Social procurement and new public governance* (Routledge, 2016).

Rob Kivits is a senior lecturer in project management at Coventry University, UK. He holds a PhD in business management from Southern Cross University, Australia, in addition to an MSc in engineering and policy analysis from Delft University of Technology, the Netherlands. Rob applies this multi-disciplinary approach to his work and applied research, including large industry research projects across multiple arenas such as infrastructure, social services innovation, construction, mining, and the energy and telecommunications industries. He has published in international journals and is a member of an international research project team focused on collaborative service delivery models.

Erik-Hans Klijn is professor of Public Administration at the Department of Public Administration and Sociology, Erasmus University Rotterdam, the Netherlands. He has published in various journals on governance networks, complex decision-making and network management, and media attention and branding. Recent books include: *Branding in governance and public management* (Routledge, 2012, together with Jasper Eshuis), *Governance networks in the public sector* (Routledge, 2016, together with Joop Koppenjan) and *Innovations in city governments: Structures, networks and leadership* (Routledge, 2017, together with Jenny M. Lewis, Lykke Margot Ricard and Tamyko Ysa).

Christopher Koliba is a professor in the Community Development and Applied Economics Department at University of Vermont, USA, Co-Director of the Social Ecological Gaming and Simulation (SEGS) Lab and fellow at the Gund Institute on the Environment. His research interests include environmental governance, governance networks, community resilience, network performance and accountability, applied to water quality, food systems, energy systems, emergency and disaster response, and sustainable transportation systems. He is lead author of *Governance Networks in Public Administration and Public Policy, Second Edition* (Routledge) and published over seventy articles and book chapters in leading public administration and policy journals and books.

Aleksey Kolpakov is an assistant professor in the Department of Political Science at the University of Nevada, Reno. He holds a PhD in Public Affairs from the School of Public and Environmental Affairs at Indiana University, USA. He previously taught at Indiana University School of Public and Environmental Affairs, USA, and the Voinovich School of Leadership and Public Affairs at Ohio University, USA. His research focuses on collaborative governance and network management, applied to a wide variety of cases and settings, including the Case of Metro High School in Columbus, Ohio.

Robin H. Lemaire is an assistant professor in the Center for Public Administration and Policy in the School of Public and International Affairs at Virginia Tech, USA. She holds a PhD in public management from the School of Government and Public Policy at the University of Arizona, USA. Her areas of expertise are organization theory and the management of public and non-profit organizations. Within these, she has focused particularly on network analysis and on understanding the dynamics of inter-organizational networks. She has examined organizational networks formed to address various public issues, including child and youth health, tobacco cessation, family self-sufficiency and food access.

Scott Merrill is a research assistant professor in the Plant and Soil Science Department and Managing Director of the SEGS lab, University of Vermont, USA. He is a systems ecologist studying both natural and social-ecological systems. Projects include examining dynamics of change within pest-crop agroecosystems including aspects of climate change, examining ways to nudge human behaviour, and looking at motivating factors affecting water quality in the Lake Champlain watershed. He uses experimental gaming as a novel technique for collecting data to examine decision-making in social-ecological systems. His work aims to create applicable and predictive models to inform best management practices.

Sonia M. Ospina is a professor of public management and policy at the Robert F. Wagner Graduate School of Public Service, USA. She holds a PhD in sociology from the State University of New York, USA. An expert in qualitative research, she is interested in the participatory, inclusive and collaborative dynamics of democratic governance. Her most recent scholarly agenda focuses on the shift toward collective leadership, given the collaborative demands in organizational and societal levels of action. Following this agenda her publications include advancing relational leadership research and social innovation and democratic leadership.

Jörg Raab is an associate professor of policy and organization in the Department of Organization Studies, Tilburg, the Netherlands. He obtained his doctorate from the University of Konstanz, Germany, in 2000. He has done extensive research in the fields of organizations, inter- and intra-organizational relationships and networks as well as policy networks. He has published expansively, including in journals related to public administration and public management, such as *Public Management Review* and *International Public Management Journal*, among others. His current research focuses on the governance and effectiveness of networks.

Angel Saz-Carranza is the director of ESADE's Center for Global Economy and Geopolitics, and associate professor in the Department of Strategy and General Management (Universitat Ramon Llull). He earned a PhD from ESADE as a visiting scholar at Wagner School of Public Service (New York University). A beneficiary of La Caixa and Fulbright scholarships, he has managed several European Framework Program research grants. His work is published across numerous outlets, especially in the area of public administration.

Benedetta Trivellato is an assistant professor of management at the University of Milano-Bicocca, Italy. She holds a PhD in Information Society from the University of Milano-Bicocca. Her main research interests include innovation in the public sector, co-design of public services, design and management of public-private systems for services' provision, public leadership, social inno-vation and sustainability.

Ingmar van Meerkerk is an assistant professor in the Department of Public Administration and Sociology, Erasmus University Rotterdam, the Neth-erlands. He has published in various journals on boundary spanning, trust, citizen participation, democratic legitimacy of governance networks, per-formance and durability of interactive governance and community-based initiatives.

Siv Vangen is a professor of collaborative leadership, Director of the Centre for Voluntary Sector Leadership and Associate Dean for Research And Scholar-ship in the Faculty of Business and Law, at the Open University, UK. Her long-standing research agenda focuses on governing, leading and managing inter-organizational collaboration spanning public, non-profit and private organizations. Her empirical research has resulted in a body of practice-oriented theory and, in particular, the theory of collaborative advantage. She has published many research articles on collaboration and is co-author of *Managing to Collaborate: The Theory and Practice of Collaborative Advantage* (Routledge, 2005).

Joris Voets is an associate professor in the Department of Public Governance and Management, Faculty of Economics and Business Administration, Ghent University, Belgium. He obtained his doctorate in social sciences from KU Leuven, Belgium, in 2008, studying how intergovernmental relations are shaped and managed in multilevel arrangements in complex spatial proj-ects. His main research interests are (the management and performance of) networks and collaboration, and (the capacity for) local governance. He has co-authored several book chapters and papers in journals, including *Public Management Review*.

Asim Zia is a professor of public policy and computer science in the Depart-ment of Community Development and Applied Economics and in the Department of Computer Science at the University of Vermont, USA. His work advances computational policy analysis, governance network analy-sis, coupled natural and human systems and social ecological systems. His PhD in public policy from the Georgia Institute of Technology, USA, won the 2004–2005 best dissertation award by the Association for Public Policy Analysis and Management. He holds fellowships at the Gund Institute on the Environment, the Earth System Governance project and the Global Change Impact Studies Center.

1 A methodological perspective on network and collaboration research

Joris Voets, Christopher Koliba and Robyn Keast

Why a book on methods in network and collaboration research?

Networks and collaborations are now ubiquitous features of public governance systems. Around the world, local and national governments have developed policies and practices resulting in the formation of their own internally operated networks or have collaborated with other not-for-profit and sometimes for-profit bodies to create policy, governance and/or service delivery networks to work together to carry out some policy function. These networks can form through mandates, incentives or pressures to conform. There is every indication based on the literature, and especially from practice, that these collective forms of working together will remain a cornerstone of policy development and attendant service delivery. Given this current and ongoing reliance on networks and collaborative forms, and the significant efforts inherent to their formation and sustainability, there is mounting demand not just for enhanced understandings (an evidence base) of how to optimize their operation but also for evidence that they are delivering on promises and performance (Koliba 2014).

In his seminal article of 1997 Laurence O'Toole (1997) called for networks to be taken seriously in public administration. Since then a tremendous body of research, reports and literature on networks and other forms of interorganizational work has amassed (see for example, Isett et al. 2011; Popp et al. 2014; Provan, Fish and Sydow 2007; Provan and Lemaire 2012; Keast, Mandell and Agranoff 2014; Ferlie et al. 2011; Koliba et al. 2018). While acknowledging that this body of work has delivered important conceptual, theoretical and empirical contributions to the field, concerns persist that the methodological approaches to studying networks and collaboration have been underexamined (Berry et al. 2004; Milward and Provan 1998). More recently, drawn from both scholars (Kapucu, Hu and Khosa 2017; Grimmelikhuijsen, Tummers and Pandey 2017) and journal editorial boards (see for example, Perry 2012; Kelman 2015), additional voices have added to this argument that methodological advancements and improvement in rigour are needed to advance new knowledge, find causal relations, solutions to wicked problems, explanations for performance successes and failures, and new applications of network and collaborative design (Agranoff 2014: 203–204). Robinson (2006: 589), in a review of the ten years since O'Toole's petition, noted that researchers were clearly treating networks seriously, but called for methodological pluralism and innovation to pursue this future research agenda. This volume was written with this need in mind.

In discussing the rise of performance measurement within government operations, Beryl Radin observes that:

> If we want to operate within a complex and dynamic system, we have to know not only what its current status is but what its status will be or could be in the future, and we have to know how certain actions we take will influence the situation. For this, we need structural knowledge, knowledge of how the variables in the system are related and how they influence one another.
>
> (2006: 24)

Radin's (2006) point is worth revisiting in light of this volume. All of the methods found in this volume help to explore the relationship between the structures of inter-organizational networks and their functions. Therefore, there is a unit of analysis that is assumed here. There is also an important underlying consideration of how these networks and collaboratives are led and managed. In most instances, these methods are employed not only to describe but to evaluate, with evaluation aims being most directed to policy and practice.

Highlighting the value of using the network or other collective arrangements as the unit of analysis within the public management and administration field, Hans Bressers and Laurence O'Toole observe:

> An advantage of a network perspective is that it can be used to direct attention to the larger structures of interdependence. Instead of assuming that influence takes place only through direct and observable interactions, whether as personal relationships or among representatives of institutional interests, *a network approach – applied to portions of a policy process as varied as formulation and implementation – can investigate how the larger structure can have systematic effects on the behavior of individual actors as well as on the content of decisions, policy responses, and implementation efforts.* A network approach thus offers the chances to continue both interpersonal and structural explanations for policy-relevant events.
>
> (2005: 147, italics added)

Throughout the wide range of examples of quality research undertaken on networks found across this volume and the wider literature, it is very clear that the range of questions that can be answered through the application of any one of these methods and perhaps, as we note later in this chapter, combinations of methods (as in mixed-methods approaches) can shed light on one of four different clusters of questions framed by Zia, Koliba and Tian (2013):

1   Formation: how are networks formed? Who is included and who is excluded from these networks? What are the goals of these networks and how might they evolve over time?

2 Operation: how do networks operate? What type of activities are performed by networks? How do network actors behave? How do different institutional arrangements and socio-economic structures affect the operations of networks?

3 Performance and accountability: how do meta-governors manage the performance of networks? How could accountability flows be democratically anchored in networks?

4 Sustainability: how are effective networks sustained across spatial and temporal scales? What type of institutional arrangements could be facilitated by meta-governors to enable sustainability of effective and democratically-anchored networks?

The relationship between networks and collaborations is a close one. Studies have applied theories of collaboration to cohesively bring together different sectors, organizations and social groups (Crosby and Bryson 2010; Selsky and Parker 2005). Although there is no widely accepted theory of collaboration, a range of analytical frameworks exist (e.g. D'Amour et al. 2005; Huxham and Vangen 2005). However, the multitude of frameworks has resulted in a fragmented understanding of the collaborative process (Selsky and Parker 2005). John Bryson, Barbara Crosby and Melissa Middleton Stone (2006) identified the varied processes underpinning key components of collaboration, such as leadership, learning, and conflict management and trust. They define cross-sector collaboration as 'the linking or sharing of information, resources, activities, and capabilities by organizations in two or more sectors to achieve jointly an outcome that could not be achieved by organizations in one sector separately' (Bryson, Crosby and Stone 2006: 44). Yet Googins and Rochlin (2000) highlight how processes can be distinctly different for the collaboration of different types of groups, depending on the relationship between the groups and the values of each group.

Although applied collaboration theories have proven successful in facilitating cross-sectoral partnerships (Selsky and Parker 2005), the management of theory and its incorporation in existing practice is not always recognized in frameworks. As previously mentioned, the engagement of theory and practice is one of the core values for connecting practitioners and academic professionals to improve outcomes (Perkmann and Walsh 2008). Robyn Keast and Myrna Mandell (2014) have argued that collaborative ties may be understood as matters of degree. Several typologies for distinguishing differences between types of collaborative relationships have been posited (Gajda 2004; Frey et al. 2006; Keast and Mandell 2014).

Robert Agranoff and Michael McGuire have observed that 'Collaboration is a purposive relationship designed to solve a problem by creating or discovering a solution within a given set of constraints' (2003: 4). The importance of collaborative skills, collaborative processes and collaborative governance strategies for public administrators has been the subject of a great deal of literature, such as Robert Axelrod's application of game theory of cooperative behaviour (1980), Barbara Gray's articulation of collaborative processes (1989), Keast and Mandell's

(2014) distinctions between types of collaborations for social service delivery, the development of collaborative governance (Ansell and Gash 2008) and collaborative governance regimes (Emerson and Nabatchi 2015), even extending into the literature concerning collaborative public management (Bingham and O'Leary 2008).

We acknowledge that the range of questions that can and are being posed by researchers of networks and collaboratives are expansive, and this diversity is also reflected in the various chapters found in this volume. However, as social structures that exist to carry out explicit or implicit functions, these social structures possess lifecycles, exist in time and space, and cannot be divorced from their environments and larger contexts.

Therefore, it is our hope and expectation that this volume may be used by new and established researchers of networks and collaboratives and other multi-party arrangements to consider the relationship between methods and questions. As researchers of networks and collaboratives ourselves, the co-editors of this volume are firm believers in the adage that the questions you pose should drive your selection of methods. As scholars of public administration and public management, whose field has a long history of practitioner engagement, we believe it best to identify those questions that are of greatest concern to those actually managing within and across networks and collaboratives. This is an important point made by John M. Kamensky (Chapter 12) that is worth repeating.

The ubiquity of networks and collaboratives poses particular challenges and opportunities for those looking to study them. This edited collection of chapters by established and early career researchers sets out to address some of these concerns by exposing network/collaboration researchers to a more detailed, critical, yet structured, account of prominent research methods, as well as alert them to some less well-known alternatives. In so doing, this volume equips network/collaboration researchers with the means and innovations to push the boundaries of exploration and discovery.

What do we mean by methods in this book?

As the different authors and their chapters will show, we take an open and pluralist position regarding methods and methodologies. Such a diverse position fits the way network and collaboration research has developed over the years: it is not an exclusive domain of a single discipline, and insights rather combine different strands, theories and methods (e.g. Bogason and Zølner 2007; Klijn and Koppenjan 2015; Mandell 2014).

Rather than engaging in deep philosophical debates on research, network researchers are also pragmatists: depending on the type and nature of questions regarding networks and collaboration to be addressed, a requisite methodological mix should be adopted; you should create the methodologic mix that fits your purpose. Although John Gerring (2012) might think differently, we as editors indeed feel that 'we ought to regard (methodological) diversity as a mark of disciplinary maturity rather than as a mark of confusion and disarray' (6).

As long as researchers apply methods in a qualitative and transparent way, the knowledge gained is more important than adhering to the same methods other network and collaboration scholars might use – which does not mean there is no merit in doing so if you want to! For example, our philosophy is to do a social network analysis (SNA) if you want to as long as it fits your research question(s), but ensure you do it according to the standards of good SNA research (see Chapter 9 by Lemaire and Raab).

Gerring (2012) defines methods as 'a specific procedure for gathering and/or analysing data' and methodology as 'the tasks, strategies and criteria governing scientific inquiry, including all facets of the research enterprise' (6). Following his definitions, most chapters are focused on methods, but some chapters are closer to methodology. The chapter by Agranoff and Kolpakov (Chapter 2), for instance, is rather an all-encompassing research approach. In Chapter 5 on narrative inquiry by Dodge, Saz-Carranza and Ospina, the authors address this definitional issue, as they explain that narrative inquiry can be considered both method and methodology, with different theoretical traditions which also allow both 'light' and 'strong' applications by researchers. Chapter 7 by Siv Vangen on 'Research Oriented Action Research' (RO-AR) is also closer to methodology than a method in Gerring's terms. But again, rather than getting into the definitional debate about whether these chapters discuss a methodology or method, they are all relevant contributions and therefore considered 'methods' for the purpose of this book. It should be clear, however, that this book does not focus on methods as tools in the narrowest sense – that is, how to do interviews, how to analyse documents, and so forth. Rather, our authors raise critical questions, potentials, challenges and opportunities that exist around each approach. References are provided for those looking to gain stronger 'how to' support for using these approaches at the end of each chapter.

A final point here is that while these methods are mainly discussed in the context of doing research, many – if not all – of these methods can also be regarded as tools, for instance to evaluate networks and collaborations (Robinson et al. 2013). A proper SNA analysis, for instance, can indicate structural holes in the network that need to be filled to achieve better network outcomes, while Vangen's chapter shows an action-oriented strategy to consciously influence the collaborations and networks under study.

How the book is conceived and organized

We asked a very diverse group of authors to contribute to this volume. We not only mixed age, experience, gender and geographies but also different disciplinary backgrounds. This mix, in our view, not only represents quite well the different research traditions in network and collaboration research out there, but also fits in with the apparent rapprochement between these traditions with other colleagues and which we are actively trying to establish, for instance during joint panels at the annual conferences of the International Research Society of Public Management (IRSPM).

While we had the ambition to capture the whole range of methods used in network and collaboration research, this proves an ideal that is difficult to achieve. While we do have a broad mix of more traditional and more contemporary methods used in network and collaboration research, there is, for instance, no chapter on experiments as a method that seems to have gained popularity in public administration (Grimmelikhuijsen et al. 2017). We also expect that the digital revolution brings new methods to the table that include machine learning, artificial intelligence, and so forth. The chapter by Christopher Koliba, Asim Zia and Scott Merrill (Chapter 11) already points to these potential methodological innovations as well, but it is likely that this trend sparks several separate methodological paths warranting separate chapters (or even volumes) of their own.

This book is organized as follows. Following this introductory chapter, Robert Agranoff and Aleksey Kolpakov demonstrate in Chapter 2 how networks can be researched through a sequential explanatory design. Rather than discussing a single method like most chapters in this book, their chapter demonstrates an overall research design strategy. They discuss how grounded theory has been an essential building block for our current knowledge on networks and collaboration. After a qualitative analysis that helps to develop concepts and a theoretical framework, they turn to quantitative analysis to address their hypotheses. They show how different methods can be mixed sequentially and how important coding the data is. This iterative process has delivered significant results, for instance, how network design issues matter in their case study of the Metro School, a network involving sixteen school districts in central Ohio (Kolpakov, Agranoff and McGuire 2016). Their key lesson for all network and collaboration scholars out there is this:

> Years of experience, trial and error, and emerging conceptual coverage has led to the conclusion that a network analysis methodological approach involves a lot of hard and sustained work, a lot more than 'sending out a questionnaire' or 'talking to a few people'. The conceptual rewards, however, are considerable despite such investments.
>
> (Agranoff and Kolpakov, this volume, page 40)

Chapters 3 to 11 are focused more on single methods, although there is some variation in this respect as well. However, to ensure that there is sufficient consistency among these chapters, the following leading questions guided the authors. First, the method is introduced, specifying its origins, main features, relation to other methods and field of origin, and its suitability for studying networks and collaboration. A second dimension addressed is the relevance of the method: why is it relevant for researching collaboration and networks and/or for practitioners and what kinds of research questions, policy and administrative problems are best suited for this method? The third dimension focuses on the application of the method: how is the method applied in empirical research as well as by practitioners? The fourth guiding question relates to analysis: how are the data analysed, what tools are available, how are the data presented and what analytical challenges exist? A fifth element is the evaluation of the method by the authors: what is the added value and/or what are the strengths of the method and its application in researching networks and collaboration in particular? What are some of the main weaknesses, flaws, limitations? What are main 'lessons' for other researchers who might consider using the method, in terms of the method itself, the research design and the implementation? The final question discussed in the method chapters is the future of the method: what is the potential for this method in future research? How can the method be improved and to what network and collaboration research topics can/should it be applied? How and to what extent can/should this method be combined with others, particularly other methods highlighted in this book? For each method, suggestions for further reading are included: what are sources for more in-depth knowledge on this method (e.g. books, articles, websites, cases, conferences and scholars)? That final, practical point is important as well: we set out to make a state-of-the-art contribution in methods used in collaboration and network research and provide relevant key information following the questions and dimensions previously laid out in this chapter. We do not, however, try and capture each method in every detail – high-quality textbooks on most, if not all, of these single methods are available if you want to apply one or more methods in your research project.

In Chapter 3, Ming Cheng and Joris Voets discuss a foundational method for network and collaboration research, namely, the case method. Based on a limited systematic literature review, they show how the case study method has been used and developed over the years. They also organize the studies in the literature review along different lines that are also drawn from the case study method anthology. In doing so, they demonstrate that network and collaboration research covers all typical types and variations. In terms of underlying research questions and objectives, explanatory, interpretive and critical case studies are all found in the literature. The same goes for the intent of the design and the scale of the case study (intrinsic, instrumental or collective), and the extent to which single or multiple cases are studied taking a holistic or embedded unit of analysis: network and collaboration researchers do it all. They do see a trend that multiple case studies have become more numerous than single case studies in our field – but both are still present today. Cheng and Voets argue that the case study method is key for network and collaboration researchers for two main reasons: the method is very suitable for process tracing (discussed as a separate methodology by Robyn Keast in Chapter 8) and to explore complexity. However, they also point to two well-known challenges in using this method, namely the difficulty to delineate and reproduce a case in practice and the extent to which it leads to generalizable findings. Methodological rigour and moving from single to multiple case study designs can help to deal with these challenges. In terms of contributing to our body of knowledge, case studies included in the literature review have revealed important insights on the informal, dynamic and temporal dimensions of networks and collaboration. Next to arguing for more methodological rigour and more multiple case studies, they also see merit in more mixed-methods designs – see the second chapter by Agranoff and Kolpa-kov as one strategy for doing this. Their position is, however, clear: the case study method has not only delivered many significant results so far but will remain a key method for future collaboration and network research as well.

In Chapter 4, the focus shifts to another foundational method in the social sciences, namely, the survey approach. Based on a systematic literature review, Ingmar van Meerkerk, Jurian Edelenbos and Erik-Hans Klijn argue that this method has gained more ground in network and collaboration research in more recent times – notably from 2007 onwards. In this chapter they focus on sur-veys as the primary source for studying relationships between variables that are directly measured with the survey questionnaire and analysed with statisti-cal methods (excluding SNA, which is dealt with in Chapter 9 by Robin H. Lemaire and Jörg Raab). They show how the survey methodology is used nowadays to develop hypotheses and to refine and extend network theories, for example, on network management (Klijn, Steijn and Edelenbos 2010), although they also find that the decision to use this method is mostly missing in the reviewed articles. Acknowledging that the survey methodology allows one to generalize to a larger population, and advancements in statistical software like structural equation modelling (SEM) allow one to test more complex models, they argue that its use is likely to increase further. The unit of analysis, how-ever, is a key issue: the survey approach is easily applied to study attitudes and behaviours of individuals – like network management activities and styles – but is more challenging if the unit of analysis is the network as a whole. In that case, they argue, other data sources are preferably brought in. In reviewing the literature, the authors identify, discuss and illustrate three sets of factors and outcomes studied with this method. A first set focuses on the impact of mana-gerial behaviour on network performance and trust in the network. A second set studies 'specific relational characteristics between nodes of the network and their impact on performance or learning' (van Meerkerk, Edelenbos and Klijn, this volume, page 71). A third set focuses on structural characteristics of net-work actors, the network itself and the nature of issues dealt with as factors that affect the level of network activities, collaboration and performance. Two main limitations of the method are also discussed: the lack of detail in the data, not allowing one to take the full case-specific context into consideration, and the rather inflexible nature of the data collection instrument. In relation to the use of the method to study collaboration and networks, some particular issues are also raised, namely the challenge to measure outcomes and the issue of com-mon source bias. In terms of different survey designs, they distinguish two main alternatives: large *n*-design studies including many networks, and small *n*-designs focusing on a limited number of networks. They argue that the first strategy is used most in network and collaboration research, but that each strategy has advantages and disadvantages, and that scarcity of resources and access to respon-dents are part of the trade-off between both. In terms of data analysis, they show that a combination of presenting descriptive statistics, correlation analysis and linear regressions is quite popular, and that more advanced techniques are on the rise to test multiple relations of models – an argument also expressed by Dan Chamberlain and Ben Farr-Wharton in Chapter 13. To conclude, the authors foresee that the survey method will be used even more in the future (e.g. to do systematic comparative cross-country research and more longitudinal research), but also argue that more mixed-methods designs should be developed.

> In Chapter 5, Jennifer Dodge, Angel Saz-Carranza and Sonia M. Ospina delve into narrative inquiry as a research method in studying networks and collaboration. They warn that narrative inquiry can be considered more than 'just another method', as it encompasses a wide range of theoretical frameworks and methodological traditions that have evolved over time, but then focus on the narrative methodological applications to study networks. It is argued that narrative inquiry is used regularly to understand policy networks in general and in European public administration journals in particular. They point to unique insights derived from the use of this method in our field, notably its power to illuminate the subjectivity of network actors, the meanings actors hold about their experience or knowledge as network participants, and how networks can be shaped by powerful narratives or discourses that act as forces shaping what happens in networks and what they do in society.
>
> (Dodge, Saz-Carranza and Ospina, this volume, page 82)

The authors discuss the range of narrative traditions and the range of network forms (serendipitous networks, goal-directed networks and metaphorical networks) in the literature. They synthesize this information in twelve possible approaches to study networks empirically using narrative inquiry and focus on the five approaches that are actually used in the literature so far. These approaches are: (1) narrative as language to understand serendipitous networks and (2) narrative as language to understand goal-directed networks, (3) as metaphor to understand serendipitous networks and (4) as metaphor to understand serendipitous networks goal-directed networks, and (5) as a variable to understand metaphorical networks. For each approach, they demonstrate the main features, what insights can be attained, the limitations of each approach and what the future might bring. From this chapter it is clear that narrative inquiry is a promising method that, however, requires potential users to carefully consider which approach fits their research goals and ensure they know the rationales behind them. To do so, this chapter offers an original and broad framework to start from.

To continue on the path of discursive methods, Chapter 6 by Rob Kivits tackles Q methodology. Q methodology's key strength is that it:

> allows individual responses to be collated and correlated, so as to extract 'idealized' forms of discourse, latent within the data provided by individuals involved in the study . . . [and] helps to get to the bottom of what people really believe, rather than putting them into boxes. In doing so, the methodology neither tests its participants nor imposes a priori meanings.
>
> (Kivits, this volume, pages 107)

In doing so, it helps to reduce researcher bias and seems to fit the more grounded theory approach quite well. He illustrates that the method is not only relevant for network scholars, but that it can be a tool for practitioners as well. He discusses the example of a stakeholder analysis using Q methodology in the context of airport development to demonstrate how one general group of supporters should have been approached as four different groups of like-minded stakeholders with different motivations, requests, expectations and expected levels of interaction (Kivits and Charles 2015). Kivits also discusses the four stages to do a Q study: concourse establishment, concourse management, Q survey and statistical analysis (and how it differs from R methodology), demonstrating a set of steps that need to be followed rigorously to ensure a relevant outcome and how various software tools (like Leximancer) can help conduct each step. Despite some limitations – like relying on small numbers of people for data and not being able to identify how popular a frame of reference is – he considers it a promising tool that is useful in collaboration and network research. Like other authors in this volume, he also argues in favour of a multi-method strategy – in this case, combining discourse analysis and Q methodology.

In Chapter 7, Siv Vangen discusses 'Research Oriented Action Research' (RO-AR), which she defines as 'a phenomenological action research methodology developed by Colin Eden and Chris Huxham (1996, 2006)' (Vangen, this volume, page 126). In this sense, it is not simply a method and is closer to the type of contribution of Agranoff and Kolpakov in the second chapter. RO-AR is also strongly linked to a research program and the theory of collaborative advantage (Huxham and Vangen 2005), and is a particular form of action research. Being rooted in the context of inter-organizational collaboration, Vangen argues that RO-AR is particularly suitable for 'developing contextualized theory that relates closely to practice' (Vangen, this volume, page 128) in which the interventions of the researcher and the extent to which these actually meet collaborative or network needs, are a key feature of the methodology. Interestingly, this chapter shows the interrelations between theory, method and practice through practical transformation. In terms of theory building, it fits the grounded theory approach which Agranoff and Kolpakov discuss (Chapter 2) and the narrative analysis approach that Dodge et al. (Chapter 5) refer to as well. In this case, themes like goals, culture and leadership are developed from the bottom up and interventions to improve these themes in the cases under study are developed. Vangen illustrates the methodology using quite different cases, describing the process of an intervention and different steps taken to prepare and execute it. In doing so, potential links with other methods in this book become apparent – cognitively mapping members' values, beliefs and goals might be linked to the Q methodology as discussed by Kivits in Chapter 6. Vangen argues that RO-AR is a type of ethnography that relies primarily on naturally occurring data and uses interviews, focus groups and questionnaires, with a key principle to capture data as accurately as possible. In terms of conceptual development based on RO-AR, Vangen also defines five steps as part of an iterative cycle. Two main challenges that RO-AR faces are also discussed by Cheng and Voets in Chapter 3 on the case study method, namely, assuring rigour and validity. But as the foundational method of the theory of collaborative advantage, such issues can be overcome. Finally, in evaluating this methodology, she argues that it is resource- and time-consuming and therefore inappropriate for many research agendas. This key point fits our argument that methods should fit the overall research goal and questions.

Process tracing as another key method is discussed in Chapter 8. Robyn Keast unpacks this 'in-depth, systematic and theoretically driven interrogation of the chain of events involved in the implementation of interventions, programs or activities occurring within or across small-n cases for drawing descriptive and causal inference (Collier 2011: 824)' (Keast, this volume, page 142). This method might also be considered closer to an analytical strategy, since it shifts the focus from the causal effects between variables to mechanisms connecting causes and effects. In this respect, it has some resemblance with the QCA method discussed in Chapter 10. Social mechanisms are key in the study of social phenomena like networked and collaborative arrangements, which makes process tracing very fitting to study, for instance, collaborative leadership where three social mechanisms come into play (Keast and Mandell 2014). Three typical forms of process tracing are discussed by Keast: theory testing and theory building as two theory-centric forms, and the case-centric form. Each form entails a distinct approach as to how causal properties for different research settings or purposes are examined depending on the research questions and the ontological (theory) and epistemological (empirical) position of researchers – all three forms are used in collaboration and network research. Good process tracing requires four steps to be taken into consideration: (1) identifying and linking hypothesized mechanisms and components, (2) case selection, (3) collecting evidence, and (4) analysis and verification. Keast argues that it is a promising method for collaboration and network research for the following reasons: (1) demonstrated relevance for answering questions of impacts of decision-making, personal and collective agency; (2) allowing for more fine-grained case information that brings data closer to theory for more rigorous analysis and particularly for multiple causal pathways and emergent process developments at different levels of analysis; (3) flexibility in the use and integration of a variety of data types and sources and its ability to link to other methods; and (4) the analytical transparency as its 'demands for systematic breakdown of evidence and cross–checking of causal mechanisms can help tease out conceptual gaps and overlaps, allowing for more precise distinctions to be made between alternative theoretical schools' (Keast, this volume, page 152). There are, however, also limitations: a lack of definitional agreement on what mechanism are, its resource-intensive nature because of the extensive, longitudinal data required for process tracing and the subsequent data analysis, and the lack of systematic and transparent application. Despite these limitations, Keast argues that process tracing has the capacity to be a powerful tool for future network and collaborative research, but it should be clearly weighed against other methods and resources available before actually choosing it.

In Chapter 9, another foundational method of network and collaboration research is discussed, namely, SNA. Robin H. Lemaire and Jörg Raab, two proponents of the organizational sociology tradition in network research, unpack this method, which they define as a 'pivotal tool in the study and research of networks and collaboration because the distinguishing feature of network analysis is the focus on relationships between actors and the interdependencies these relationships create' (Lemaire and Raab, this volume, page 160). They discuss how SNA is rooted in mathematics and graph theory, and allows us to examine different units of analyses: individuals, individual organizations, partnerships, collectives of organizations, words (i.e. semantic network analysis) 'or any unit of analysis where the goal is to describe and analyse the structure of relationships between the units' (Lemaire and Raab, this volume, page 161). Lemaire and Raab focus in their chapter in particular on the use of the method to analyse inter-organizational networks in the public sector, and how the network can both be an independent (= network as a structure) or dependent variable (= network as a system). The use of this method requires a number of steps. In terms of data collection, this means: (1) bounding the network by defining the boundaries and nodes – a difficult challenge to determine who is in and who is not; (2) deciding on what relationship data need to be collected by specifying ties (content, strength, positive or negative); and (3) how to capture it exactly (typically through interviews and surveys, but also possible via observations and experiments or secondary data). These steps are discussed and illustrated in more detail by the authors, who also point to important ethical issues in data collection and reporting. An important issue is to be aware that the presentation of results could negatively impact organizations and individuals. Another point is a cost-benefit analysis: a proper SNA can put a heavy burden on respondents, so the value added needs to be clear and preferably not only relevant to the researcher but to the respondents as well. In terms of data analysis, different options are available but, typically, the data are put in a spreadsheet that is imported into various software programs (like UCINet or Visone) which then allow different analyses and visualizations. A major challenge, however, is the degree to which ties are confirmed or not, and how to deal with missing data, as this can fundamentally influence results of the analysis. They discuss descriptive static analysis as the most basic form (e.g. different centrality measures, density and centralization) at different levels, but also illustrate explanatory analysis that builds on statistical methods (like OLS regression, Quadratic Assignment Procedure (QAP) correlation, or Exponential Random Graph Models (ERGMs) or p$\star$ models) or more qualitative methods like QCA (see Chapter 10). In doing so, they demonstrate how this distinct method can also be actively linked to other methods discussed in this volume to allow for maximal results. Lemaire and Raab not only demonstrate how SNA is part of our methodological toolbox, but also show how it evolves into new directions by discussing dynamic analysis and its promise to help us learn more about the formation and development of networks. To conclude, on the one hand, the greatest added value of this method for our field is 'the systematic collection and analysis of the interdependent relationships between actors in a network' (Lemaire and Raab, this volume, page 182). On the other hand, however, the major challenge we face is 'to go beyond the mere description of the network metrics' (Lemaire and Raab, this volume, page 189). They are, however, convinced that the method will continue to develop, that it holds most promise at the network level as the unit of analysis in collaboration and network research, and that it has the potential to combine with other methods like QCA or narrative inquiry – a mixed-methods spirit both authors have demonstrated in their work as well in the recent past.

Denita Cepiku, Daniela Cristofoli and Benedetta Trivellato discuss Qualitative Comparative Analysis (QCA) in Chapter 10. This is a relatively new method in studying collaboration and networks but, as the authors argue, 'the configurational "spirit" can be found in many other public network works' (Cepiku, Cristofoli and Trivellato, this volume, pages 1–2). QCA is a method that particularly fits our field, because the specific context of networks often demands different factors (e.g. trust, leadership) in different combinations to achieve results. The configurational approach allows us, they continue to argue, to identify these different combinations of conditions and how they can lead to a similar outcome and thus help network managers to decide the 'right' directions in steering it. QCA fills a gap between the typical large *n*-methods like survey research and the small *n*-methods like case study research – QCA favours studies sizing between five and fifty cases. Like other methods, this method has a particular logic for theory building. Instead of building on variables and correlations, it is focused on sets and set-subset relationships. Crisp-set (csQCA) and fuzzy-set QCA (fsQCA) are the two main variants. Crisp-set requires coding conditions in a binary way (0 = not present, 1 = present), while fuzzy-set allows a score range between 0 and 1. Typically, QCA is a three-stage procedure: (1) case selection and description, (2) selection of conditions and scoring them and (3) analysing different causal paths. In the first stage the number of cases is linked to the number of conditions that can be included, and the number of conditions needs to be kept under control to avoid too much complexity in the analysis and the interpretation thereof. In the second stage the data are analysed through software in order to calibrate all conditions. This results in a so-called truth table that is to be analysed further following certain procedures to flesh out relevant configurations. Finally, these configurations should be interpreted via case-by-case interpretation, cross-case interpretation or 'limited historical' generalization. The authors illustrate this method using four examples, discussing each example in terms of research questions, data collection, data analyses and the relevant configurations found. One example is the study of fourteen Dutch spatial planning projects by Verweij et al. (2013) who 'used fsQCA to explore what combinations of three conditions – network complexity, network management and stakeholder involvement – are necessary or sufficient to achieve stakeholder satisfaction in governance networks' (Cepiku, Cristofoli and Trivellato, this volume, page 198). Like other chapter authors, Cepiku et al. are also optimistic about the potential and future use of this method in collaboration and network research, but also see potential in combining it with other methods like SNA. Theoretical questions to be studied in the future include network dynamics by tracking shifting configurations over time, across several levels of analysis (see also multilevel analysis arguments by Chamberlain and Ben Farr-Wharton in Chapter 13 or in Van Meerkerk et al. in Chapter 4) and studying the human–organizational interface.

Chapter 11 is the last single-method chapter in this volume. Christopher Koliba, Asim Zia and Scott Merrill discuss agent-based models (ABMs) and their use to study networks and collaboration. ABMs are computer models

> that allow autonomous agents, such as individuals, groups or organizational actors to act and interact with each other and their wider environments. As a result, networks of agents are simulated to create experiments to study the internal and external drivers of change and stability. . . . The ability to model agents as non-social actors (planned projects, built and natural infrastructure, etc.) as well, adds an additional capacity, allowing for models in which social actors engage with, and are shaped by, non-social objects.
>
> (Koliba, Zia and Merrill, this volume, page 210)

So ABMs allow for the generation of 'virtual' scenarios bridging the micro level of agent behaviour to macro outcomes at the systems level, and the particular strong point to add in non-social actors to the mix. According to the authors, such models can help us examine how such networks interact in dealing with particular governance designs, public policy analysis, public service delivery or common-pool resource management issues. These models connect agents (social actors, physical or natural objects, socially constructed objects of organized activities) with various parameters (resources, objectives) that can be toggled for simulation, and with agents that can interact with each other. The authors illustrate this using various examples, including the governance of water resources and the impact of equity and resource scarcity and flux on transportation project prioritization in intergovernmental settings. In discussing the method, the authors argue that the ABM method can be connected to other methods, most notably process tracing (Chapter 8) as a method to help in developing initial conceptual models. After all, defining model boundaries and parameters for ABMs requires some form of mapping the system, which can be done through other methods discussed in this volume. In doing so, ABMs not only draw on different data sources but also triangulate among them. The authors see ABMs as an interesting bridge across disciplines, 'with the modelling process and the model itself serving as a boundary object around which disciplinary frameworks combine' (Koliba, Zia and Merrill, this volume, page 223). While the authors are proponents of ABMs, they also point to major challenges, most notably perhaps which data on which agents and parameters need to be connected at what level to devise what kind of models? Other challenges include empirically validating ABMs, and how to model human decision-making in terms of the creative and thinking processes. Despite these challenges, the potential is substantial, and has been called for by eminent scholars like Elinor Ostrom – so who are we to argue with her?

Chapters 12 to 14 are of a more reflexive nature. We set out to get the views of a leading practitioner and of two early career researchers in the academic field about the methodologic side of network and collaboration research for practitioners and academics respectively. In Chapter 12, John M. Kamensky, a leading practitioner at the IBM Center for The Business of Government, who also co-edited (with Thomas J. Burlin) the book *Collaboration: using networks and partnerships* (2004), sheds light on network and collaboration methods. He discusses the straightforward question of what practitioners want to know about collaboration and networks and what that means in terms of methods. He contends that there is a bright future for collaborative networks in government, but also points to challenges for practitioners 'to better create the capacity to manage, sustain and evaluate the effectiveness of networks' (Kamensky, this volume, page 238) and that network and collaboration researchers can help to address these questions. In terms of relevant methods for practitioners in the future, he argues that social networking tools are promising. Real-time assessments with pulse surveys of networks or sentiment analysis of social media to understand changes in stakeholder perceptions, in his view, can support the development and assessment of networks. He also lays out some very clear and practical questions that leaders, managers and initiators of networks and collaboratives continue to ask about them.

In Chapter 13, Dan Chamberlain and Ben Farr-Wharton take on the daunting challenge to reflect on the future of methods in network and collaboration research as early career researchers coming from within different disciplines and research backgrounds in this field. They argue or 'predict' continued advances in statistical analysis that build on ERGMs and stochastic actor-oriented models (SAOMs). They also envisage more multilevel analysis to be carried out in the future (as do other chapters, for instance Chapter 8 on process tracing). This emphasis on levels relates to the key point of the network as the unit of analysis. While we typically focus on the network or collaboration as the unit of analysis and such focus in our research is important, it is also 'reductionist', as for instance actors (people and organizations) and their behaviour are not limited to membership of single networks, rather they are part of what Chamberlain and Farr-Wharton refer to as 'uber-networks'. ERGMs and SAOMs should not only allow us to include that multilevel reality into analyses, but also to 'radically advance predictive network modelling and network-optimization processes in practice' (Chamberlain and Farr-Wharton, this volume, page 246). Another promising path, they continue, is that of laboratory experiments. While not new, such experiments can help us to study more systematically how 'individual personalities influence perceptions of a network, networking behaviour, the dynamics of a network, and how network structures can affect individual perceptions, behaviours and relationships' (Chamberlain and Farr-Wharton, this volume, page 246). More interventions in networks are also likely to increase, linking network researchers and practitioners more strongly than ever. This idea clearly fits with Vangen's RO-AR to research inter-organizational collaboration within and across the public and non-profit sectors as developed in Chapter 7. We should not study collaboration and networks as innocent bystanders or external observers, but we are increasingly invited to actively shape, manage and evaluate collaboration and networks. In doing so, we both develop our insights theoretically and also (try to) help to achieve more effective network governance in practice. Moreover, Chamberlain and Farr-Wharton are firm believers in technological advancements to help the collaboration and network community move forward. On the one hand, big data analysis can help us to understand increasingly big and complex networks. On the other hand, better software tools for data collection and analysis are also being developed, for instance to carry out SNA. This also implies that we need to ensure that network and collaboration researchers have sufficient technological competencies and skills to understand and apply or even develop such improved methods – this is something to bear in mind in developing our methodological course schemes in bachelor's-, master's- and PhD-training schemes. Finally, they also point to the challenge of appropriation of network research. In a positive reading, the increased data and possibilities to analyse them can become strong tools for public organizations and governance to improve collaboration and network outcomes. The risk, however, is that such information is also misused by dark networks, by companies or by governments, for instance, to increasingly control society toward their desired aims. This point puts the ethical consideration for every researcher and practitioner on the table: what are the risks to be managed and ethical guidelines to be followed, to ensure that our work contributes to societal development, rather than the undermining of the latter?

In Chapter 14, we as editors draw some of the main themes and underlying currents generated from the rich chapters introduced herein. Major reflections developed in that chapter are: (1) the issue of bridging the qualitative-quantitative divide; (2) the call for and challenge of mixed methods; (3) the impact of increasing computational power; (4) the interaction between research and practice; (5) ethical considerations that become more even important, especially with the advent of advanced computing, big data and artificial intelligence; and, finally, (6) the importance of adaptation and reflexivity for all network and collaboration researchers – new, upcoming or established.

A bright future for network and collaboration researchers lies ahead, but it will require an open mind and continuous methodological learning, exploration, experimentation and dialogue to further our field. This volume aims to assist and guide students and scholars to study collaboration and networks empirically by demonstrating the core research methods for their investigation and evaluation. For each method, authors demonstrate its historical roots and developments to date, its main features, advantages and limitations and possible uses and illustrate it extensively with applications of network and collaboration research in the public and non-profit sector. The text showcases both methods developed by network researchers (e.g. SNA) and more common methods used in and adapted to network research (e.g. survey design).

So rather than trying to capture all technical details for each method available in separate textbooks, this volume presents a catalogue of compelling methods, discussing each method specifically in the context of collaborative arrangements and network structures.

As the public sector continues to rely on networks and collaborative practice to advance its policy and programmatic agenda, there is an ongoing imperative for scholars and practitioners to push ahead, learning more about these collective efforts – how to design, implement, govern, manage, and lead and use this information to optimize outcomes. In the book *Network theory in the public sector: building new theoretical frameworks* (edited by Keast, Mandell and Agranoff 2014), it was argued that, on its own, theory could only advance so far, and that new methods and combinations of methods were needed to push the boundaries of knowledge and practice. This edited volume has been developed to meet this methodological need – but in so doing it has also illuminated several accompanying new tasks and considerations for researchers and the procurers of research. This is a reminder to us all that working in and researching networks and collaborations is always a work in progress, and that our role therefore is both to rigorously apply our existing research modes and to champion new approaches that offer new opportunities.

Enjoy reading it!

References

Agranoff, R. 2014. "Bridging the theoretical gap and uncovering the missing holes." In *Network theory in the public sector: Building new theoretical frameworks*, edited by R. Keast, M. Mandell, and R. Agranoff, 193–209. New York: Routledge.

Agranoff, R. and M. McGuire. 2003. *Collaborative public management: New strategies for local governments*. Washington, DC: Georgetown University Press.

Ansell, C. and A. Gash. 2008. "Collaborative governance in theory and practice." *Journal of Public Administration Research and Theory* 18 (4): 543–571.

Axelrod, R. 1980. *The evolution of cooperation*. New York: Basic Books.

Berry, F., R. Brower, S. Choi, W. Goa, H. Jang, M. Kwon, and J. Word. 2004. "Three traditions in network research: What the public management research agenda can learn from other research communities." *Public Administration Review* 64 (5): 539–552.

Bingham, L.B. and R. O'Leary, eds. 2008. *Big ideas in collaborative public management*. Armonk, NY: M.E. Sharpe.

Bogason, P. and M. Zølner. 2007. "Conclusion." In *Methods in democratic network governance*, edited by P. Bogason and M. Zølner, 224–232. Houndmills: Palgrave.

Bryson, J.M., B. Crosby and M. Stone. 2006. "The design implications of cross-sector collaborations: Propositions from the literature." *Public Administration Review* 66 (6): 44–55.

Collier, D. 2011. "Understanding process tracing (the teacher)." *Political Science and Politics* 44 (4): 823–830.

Crosby, B.C. and J.M. Bryson. 2010. "Integrative leadership and the creation and maintenance of cross-sector collaborations." *The Leadership Quarterly* 21 (2): 211–230.

D'Amour, D., M. Ferrada-Videla, L. San Martin Rodriguez, and M. Beaulieu. 2005. "The conceptual basis for interprofessional collaboration: Core concepts and theoretical frameworks." *Journal of Interprofessional Care* 19 (suppl. 1): 116–131.

Eden, C. and C. Huxham. 2006. "Researching organizations using action research." In *Handbook of organization studies*, 2nd ed., edited by S. Clegg, C. Hardy, W. Nord, and T. Lawrence, 388–408. London: Sage Publications.

Emerson, K. and T. Nabatchi. 2015. *Collaborative governance regimes*. Washington, DC: Georgetown University Press.

Ferlie, E., L. Fitzgerald, G. McGivern, S. Dopson, and C. Bennett. 2011. "Public policy networks and 'wicked problems': A nascent solution?" *Public Administration* 89 (2): 307–324.

Frey, B.B., J.H. Lohmeier, S.W. Lee, and N. Tollefson. 2006. "Measuring collaboration among grant partners." *American Evaluation Association* 27 (3): 383–392.

Goldman, R. 1999. "The psychological impact of circumcision." *BJU International* 83: 93–102. doi: 10.1046/j.1464-410x.1999.0830s1093.x.

Gerring, J. 2012. *Social science methodology: A unified framework*, 2nd ed. Cambridge: Cambridge University Press.

Googins, B.K. and S.A. Rochlin. 2000. "Creating the partnership society: Understanding the rhetoric and reality of cross-sectoral partnerships." *Business and Society Review* 105 (1): 127–144.

Gray, B. 1989. *Collaborating: Finding common ground for multiparty problems*. San Francisco: Jossey-Bass.

Grimmelikhuijsen, S., S. Jilke, A.L. Olsen, and L. Tummers. 2017. "Behavioral public administration: Combining insights from public administration and psychology." *Public Administration Review* 77 (1): 45–56.

Grimmelikhuijsen, S., L. Tummers, and S.K. Pandey. 2017. "Promoting state-of-the-art methods in public management research." *International Public Management Journal* 20 (1): 7–13.

Huxham, C. and S. Vangen. 2005. *Managing to collaborate: The theory and practice of collaborative advantage*. London: Routledge.

Isett, K.R., I.A. Mergel, K. LeRoux, P.A. Mischen, and R.K. Rethemeyer. 2011. "Networks in public administration scholarship: Understanding where we are and where we need to go." *Journal of Public Administration Research and Theory* 21 (1): i157–i173.

Kamensky, J.M. and T.J. Burlin, eds. 2004. *Collaboration: Using networks and partnerships*. IBM Center for the Business of Government. New York: Rowman & Littlefield Publishers.

Kapucu, N., Q. Hu, and S. Khosa. 2017. "The state of network research in public administration." *Administration & Society* 49 (8): 1087–1120.

Keast, R. and M. Mandell. 2014. "A composite theory of leadership and management: Process catalyst and strategic leveraging: Deliberate action in collaborative networks." In *Network theory in the public sector: Building new theoretical frameworks*, edited by R. Keast, M. Mandell, and R. Agranoff, 31–50. Abingdon, UK: Routledge.

Keast, R., M. Mandell, and R. Agranoff, eds. 2014. *Network theory in the public sector: Building new theoretical frameworks*. New York: Routledge.

Kelman, S. 2015. "Letters from the editor." *International Public Management Journal* 18 (1): 1–2.

Kivits, R. and M.B. Charles. 2015. "Aviation planning policy in Australia: Identifying frames of reference to support public decision making." *Journal of Air Transport Management* 47: 102–111. http://doi.org/10.1016/j.jairtraman.2015.05.005.

Klijn, E.-H. and J. Koppenjan. 2015. *Governance networks in the public sector*. London: Routledge.

Klijn, E.H., A.J. Steijn, and J. Edelenbos. 2010. "The impact of network management strategies on the outcomes in governance networks." *Public Administration* 88 (4): 1063–1082.

Koliba, C. 2014. "Governance network performance: A complex adaptive systems approach." In *Network theory in the public sector: Building new theoretical frameworks*, edited by B. Agranoff, M. Mandell, and R. Keast, 84–102. New York: Routledge Press.

Koliba, C., J. Meek, A. Zia, and R. Mills. 2018. *Governance networks in public administration and public policy*, 2nd ed. New York: Routledge Press.

Kolpakov, A., R. Agranoff, and M. McGuire. 2016. "Understanding interoperability in collaborative network management: The case of Metro High." *Journal of Health Science* 4 (68): 318–332.

Mandell, M.P. 2014. "Introduction: Understanding theory." In *Network theory in the public sector: Building new theoretical frameworks*, edited by R. Keast, M. Mandell, and R. Agranoff, 3–14. New York: Routledge.

Milward, H.B. and K. Provan. 1998. "Measuring network structure." *Public Administration* 76 (2): 387–407.

O'Toole, L.J. 1997. "Treating networks seriously: Practical and research-based agendas in public administration." *Public Administration Review* 57 (1): 45–52.

Perkmann, M. and K. Walsh. 2008. "Engaging the scholar: Three types of academic consulting and their impact on universities and industry." *Research Policy* 37 (10): 1884–1891.

Perry, J.L. 2012. "How can we improve our science to generate more usable knowledge for public professionals?" *Public Administration Review* 72 (4): 479–482.

Popp, J., H.B. Milward, G. MacKean, A. Casebeer, and R. Lindstrom. 2014. *Collaborating across boundaries series inter-organizational networks: A review of the literature to inform practice*. Washington: IBM Center for the Business of Government. www.businessofgovernment. org/report/inter-organizational-networks-review-literature-inform-practice.

Provan, K.G., A. Fish, and J. Sydow. 2007. "Interorganizational networks at the network level: A review of the empirical literature on whole networks." *Journal of Management* 33 (3): 479–516.

Provan, K.G. and R.H. Lemaire. 2012. "Core concepts and key ideas for understanding public sector organizational networks: Using research to inform scholarship and practice." *Public Administration Review* 72 (5): 638–648.

Radin, B. 2006. *Challenging the performance movement: Accountability, complexity and democratic values*. Washington, DC: Georgetown University Press.

Robinson, S. 2006. "A decade of taking networks seriously." *Policy Studies Journal* 34 (5): 589–598.

Robinson, S.E., W.S. Eller, M. Gall, and B.J. Gerber. 2013. "The core and periphery of emergency management networks." *Public Management Review* 15 (3): 344–362.

Selsky, J.W. and B. Parker. 2005. "Cross-sector partnerships to address social issues: Challenges to theory and practice." *Journal of Management* 31 (6): 849–873.

Verweij, S., E.-H. Klijn, J. Edelenbos, and A. Van Buuren. 2013. "What makes governance networks work? A fuzzy set qualitative comparative analysis of 14 Dutch spatial planning projects." *Public Administration* 91: 1035–1055.

Zia, A., C. Koliba, and Y. Tian. 2013. "Governance network analysis: Experimental simulations of alternate institutional designs for intergovernmental project prioritization processes." In *COMPACT I: Public administration in complexity*, edited by L. Gerrits and P.K. Marks. Litchfield Park, AZ: Emergent Publications.

2 Researching networks through sequential explanatory design

Robert Agranoff and Aleksey Kolpakov

Introduction/overview

Network analysis is an emergent arena of inquiry that is slowly distinguishing itself from organization studies, providing a framework for asking questions and gathering data that focuses on intersectoral environments, the web of multiple, layered communication relationships among governments and non-governmental organizations (NGOs) (Hale 2011: 2). Our experiences in studying these entities point to the use of some form of mixed methods where the involved collaborators relate their shared experiences. Indeed, such a synergistic approach has taken advantage of the differences between qualitative and quantitative approaches (Creswell 2010: 59). Questions raised with regard to such issues as joint managerial approaches, organized structures, hybrid structural forms, network controls, use of open source technology and use of open source information are among the emergent challenges that call for new methodological tools to tap topical relevance (Agranoff 2014a: 203–204).

Examining boundary-crossing and network activity over the past several decades has brought home that the problems and questions that emerge point to some form of mixed-methods approach that can help capture their operational essence. In this regard, the mixed-methods approach seeks to integrate *prioritizing* and *sequencing* of preliminary data and follow-up contributions (Morgan 2014: 12–13). Furthermore, over the years it has evolved into what methodologists refer to as mixed-methods sequential explanatory design (Ivankova, Creswell and Stick 2006), normally with the quantitative phase offering a general understanding and the qualitative phase offering an opportunity to expand, refine and explain the statistical results. In practice, this sequence is sometimes reversed, depending on the questions investigated and depth of prior knowledge.

How do researchers 'tie down' the essential elements of networks in analysis given the myriad actors, organizations, differentiated missions and complex agendas, not to mention different kinds of network missions in the absence of hierarchical organization (Agranoff 2007)? Employing a mixed-methods approach, building on grounded theory qualitative and survey quantitative approaches, has been proven to work now for over two decades of exploration. Most recently, we have added to this broad analytic scope by adding new steps that include (1) program desk audits, (2) expert reactions and (3) focus groups. These mixed methods together resemble what are known as the previously named 'mixed methods sequential explanatory design' (Creswell 2010). This approach focuses on sequences that are connected and results that are integrated (Ivankova, Creswell and Stick 2006). This mixed approach has been utilized to address the most basic of network questions in organization and management. Most important, it has been able to allow us to uncover important differences between network organization and management and to identify and uncover critical production and process features that simple network surveys or published document analysis ordinarily would not (Voets, Van Dooren and DeRynck 2008).

This chapter is organized as follows. First, use of the grounded theory qualitative approach is identified, along with identification of the systematic analytical techniques and software employed. The quantitative survey approach and its uses are then explained, both for study general orientation and for in-depth analysis, followed by an explanation of how mapping or 'site mapping' in comparative case studies is undertaken to move network studies along. The final substantive section identifies our current five-phase sequential mixed-methods multiple network study that adds an audit first step and expert reaction, and later client focus groups, to the long-standing grounded theory and survey phases.

Grounded theory: cultivating multistage mixed methods

Despite the normal approach to sequential mixed methods, with quantitative phases in initial mapping, the connection with the qualitative phases begins here with a basic understanding of how the data are linked with pre-research conceptual understandings and mappings. This, to Maxwell (2004: 249), involves 'process theory . . . a different approach to explanation', that is, this creates an intersection between different ways of seeing knowing and interpreting – foundational elements of mixed method research (Maxwell 2010). Years of research in the field and reading reports indicated the importance of 'deep meanings' that could only be perceived through the understandings of those in the field and exploration of those meanings. Grounded networks, to Charmaz (2006), involve 'systematic, yet flexible guidelines for collecting and analysing qualitative data to construct theories grounded in the data themselves'. She maintains that, 'As grounded theorists, we study our early data and begin to separate, sort, and synthesize these data through qualitative coding. Coding means that we attach labels to segments of data that depend on what each segment is about' (2–3); it focuses on what is actually happening.

Grounded theory has suited an early public affairs attempt to make mixed-networks research that developed theories from research linked in practitioner-gathered data rather than by deduction through testing hypotheses from existing theories (Charmaz 2006, 2014). For its forerunners, Glazer and Strauss (1967), in practice grounded theory encompasses the blending of positivism and pragmatism through field research that includes overlapping collection of data, use of analytic codes and categories; constant comparisons, advancing theory development during each step; memo writing around categories, properties and relationships; sampling around theory construction, not for representativeness; and, literature reviews after developing the independent analysis (Charmaz 2006: 5–6). In effect, grounded theory is about how actors interpret reality, testing tentative ideas and conceptual structures against ongoing observations (Suddaby 2006: 636). Glaser and Strauss (1967) challenge the assumptions that qualitative research was atheoretical, impressionistic and unsystematic or that it is necessarily limited as a precursor to quantitative research. As A.M. Strauss (1995: 16) concludes, 'elaborating an extant theory involves multiple and ultimately systemic comparisons of various conditional dimensions as we look then for various associated interactions, processes, strategies and consequences'. In today's methodological parlance, grounded theory is used more generally to 'denote theoretical constructs derived from qualitative analysis of data' (Corbin and Strauss 2008: 1).

Application of grounded theory has been most useful in developing major network concepts. For example, in *Managing within networks* (Agranoff 2007: 3) a qualitative case study approach was instrumented through use of a discussion guide, where the same basic questions were asked, open-ended, of each network administrator/activist. Subsequent coding and memo writing led to the core finding that, among the fourteen networks studied, their 'action potential' varied, ranging from those limited to exchanging information to those making legally authorized policy decisions and resource allocations. Between these two types, so to speak, were networks that not only exchanged information but worked together to build partner capabilities, and still others that performed these functions and blueprinted mutual strategies that were ultimately decided upon and executed by the respective network agencies.

While some have advanced the idea that case studies are not useful for theory building or presumably for advancing practice (e.g. Adams and White 1994), our case research has been instrumental for theoretical analysis. Indeed, if organized and structured, case studies can overcome the 'common misconception that various research strategies should be arrayed hierarchically' and cases limited to exploratory phases (Yin 1984: 15).

In the fourteen networks studied, the 'grounded' case-based conceptual breakthrough on differentiated network types then led to a basic understanding of what networks actually do. Most important, few turned out to make policy or program decisions. Comparative cases in this way allow grounded theory-based cases for constructivist sensitivity, interpreting nuances of meaning and action, and 'becoming increasingly aware of the interactive and emergent nature of your data and analysis' (Charmaz 2006: 184; see also Corbin and Strauss 2008, Chapter 4).

Building theory: qualitative analysis

The illustrative network study to demonstrate the use of grounded theory building is based on our analysis of Metro School, a network involving sixteen school districts in central Ohio plus several research and higher education entities that focus on STEM (Science, Technology, Engineering and Mathematics) learning in a school and with the involvement of several research entities. The qualitative data analysis centred on the transcripts of the 'focused discussions' with twenty-eight key representatives of seventeen organizations involved in the network. The transcripts included information from responses to more than 400 total questions. As a means to answer the initial research question on change over time and further analyse the discussants' data, NVivo 9.0, a qualitative research software package, was used as an analytical and data sorting tool. The interview data involved coding responses in relation to the research questions and organizing the responses according to the research process outlined in Figure 2.1, based on the five-step process suggested by Carney (1990). First, a text was created based on the focused discussions with the twenty-eight key representatives of the seventeen organizations involved in the network. Second, different coding procedures prescribed by grounded theory were performed, resulting in the generation of codes and analytical notes. Third, themes and trends were identified by applying the theoretical or selective coding proposed by A.L. Strauss and Corbin (1998). Fourth, hypotheses were tested and text was reduced by analysing trends. The exploratory framework that finally emerged from the theoretical framework by employing the graphic features of modelling in NVivo were outlined. The coding procedures used in analysing the qualitative data of the focused discussions included a four-step process of coding: initial/primary/ open coding, focused coding, axial coding and theoretical coding (Charmaz 2006; Corbin and Strauss 2008).

First, the transcripts of the focused discussions or semi-structured discussions with the twenty-eight key representatives of seventeen organizations were downloaded to NVivo to construct the initial or primary coding. During the primary coding the data were examined with the following questions in mind (Charmaz 2006):

- 'What is this data a study of?' (Glazer 1978: 57; Glazer and Strauss 1967)
- What does the data suggest?
- Which theoretical category do the specific data represent (Glazer 1978).

Initial codes were created which were 'provisional, comparative and grounded in the data' (Charmaz 2006: 48). They were provisional, thus held to remain open to different analytical interpretations. In addition, they were open to enhance the fit between the data and the emerging theories explored to make continual sense of the data.

Among the most popular coding practices of grounded theory are word-by-word coding, line-by-line coding and incident-by-incident coding (Charmaz 2006). Of these, line-by-line coding was selected. Word-by-word coding was ruled out because archived data or internet data to identify particular images – that is, metaphors at the level of individual words – were not relevant. Incident-by-incident coding was also deemed inappropriate because the qualitative data collected by means of the focused discussions with network actors

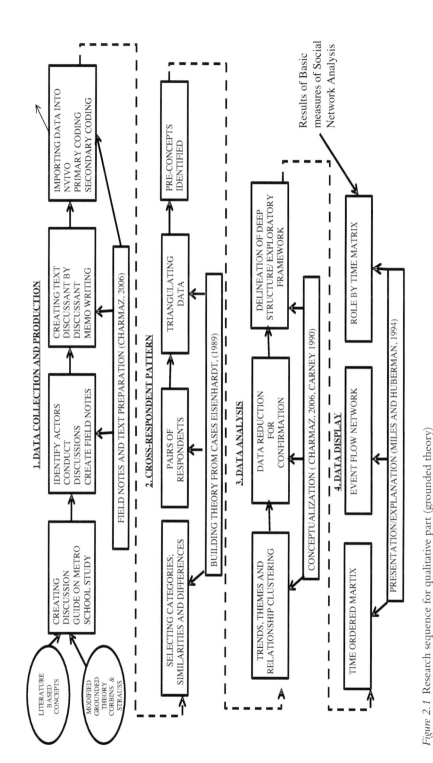

Figure 2.1 Research sequence for qualitative part (grounded theory)

Source: Kolpakov 2013, adapted from Agranoff, R. 2007

of the Metro High School project were not based on '[c]oncrete, behavioristic descriptions of people's mundane actions' (Charmaz 2006: 53). Taking into consideration the processes that are predominant for each stage in the evolution of public management networks, the following questions were also asked during the initial coding (Charmaz 2006: 51):

- What process(es) is at issue here? How can one define it?
- How does this process develop?
- How does the research participant(s) act while involved in this process?
- What do the research participants(s) profess to think and feel while involved in this process? What might their observed behaviour indicate?
- When, why and how do processes change?
- What are the consequences of the process?

Next, secondary coding included focused and axial coding (Charmaz 2006). *Focused coding* involves 'using the most significant and/or frequent earlier codes to sift through large amounts of data' and 'requires decisions about which initial codes make the most analytic sense to categorize your data incisively and completely' (57–58). Importantly, compared to the initial codes generated by word-by-word, line-by-line and incident-by incident approaches, focused coding tends to be more conceptual, specialized and directed (Glazer 1978).

During focused coding, codes emerge unexpectedly through concentrated and active engagement with the text. Instead of passively reading the text, the researcher can act upon the data so '[e]vents, interactions, and perspectives come into analytic purview that [the researcher] had not thought of before' (Charmaz 2006: 59). The focused codes are developed by comparing data to data, then subsequently refined by comparing the developed focused codes to other data in order to synthesize and explain the larger segments of data under study.

Axial coding is the critical process of transforming initial and focused codes into categories and subcategories that are related to each other by using a 'paradigm that involves conditions, context, action/interactional strategies and consequences' (A.L. Strauss and Corbin 1990: 96). Specifically, it 'relates categories to subcategories, specifies the properties and dimensions of a category, and reassembles the data [a researcher has] fractured during initial coding to give coherence to the emerging analysis' (Charmaz 2006: 60). For A.M. Strauss (1987), axial coding creates 'a dense texture of relationship around the "axis" of the category' (p. 64), which will lead to the development of main categories that can be used in the next step: theoretical coding. Axial coding is therefore intended for *sorting*, *synthesizing* and *organizing* large amounts of qualitative data with subsequently reorganizing them in new forms (Creswell 1998).

Axial coding allows one to regather the data and reassemble them as a whole. A.L. Strauss and Corbin (1998: 125) suggest using the questions 'when, why, who, how and with what consequences?' to establish the relational links between categories at the conceptual level. These questions helped explain the processes of development of the network over time in the case of Metro High School.

Almost every event in the history of Metro was analysed by using these questions. For example, the planning of Metro High School started from a regular breakfast meeting attended by executives from Battelle and Ohio State University (OSU) in the beginning of 2004, where a special math and science school was discussed. Each side was interested in particular features of some future school. Battelle was interested in advancing math and science education, perhaps creating a specialized high school, whereas OSU wanted to enhance the ability of its future students in the technical fields of science and engineering. This similarity of goals initiated the dialogues, which resulted in further collaboration among the future network champions and leaders.

The axial coding served by converting the text of the focused discussions into concepts that specify larger dimensions of the categories by linking them with subcategories. To ensure the scientific approach to the process of linking categories to subcategories, A.L. Strauss and Corbin (1998) suggest a particular organizing scheme to answer the questions of axial coding: conditions, actions/interactions and consequences. Conditions are understood as circumstances or situations that make individuals or groups behave in a particular way. For example, the following statement of one active network participant at the stage of planning reveals a situational factor regarding the formation of the Metro School: 'When I heard about the CES grant to state Metro I knocked on X's door "to get a post there".' In this sentence, the phrase 'the CES grant to start Metro' pointed in the direction of identifying that particular condition. Information about conditions was obtained by answering the why, where and how questions. Actions or interactions refer to the behavioural responses of respondents to a particular event, problem or issue. In the quoted sentence, hearing about 'the CES grant to start Metro' was the condition that resulted in the action of 'knocking on X's door to get a post there'. Information about actions or interactions was obtained by answering the by whom and how questions. Consequences refer to the outcomes of actions or interactions caused by the conditions: 'Consequences answer the questions about what happened as a result of those interactions or emotional responses' (Corbin and Strauss 2008: 89).

The final grounded theory step in coding is theoretical or selective coding, a coding made at the abstraction level. Theoretical coding is deeply rooted in initial, focused and axial coding, and is defined as a 'process of selecting the core category, systematically relating it to other categories, validating those relationships, and filling in categories that need further refinement and development' (A.L. Strauss and Corbin 1990: 116). Therefore, theoretical codes integrate the focused codes into a particular form and help the researcher tell a coherent story about the findings in a conceptual sense.

At the theoretical coding stage the researcher is also ready to do a case study write-up, which 'allows the unique patterns of each case to emerge before investigators push to generalize patterns across cases' (Eisenhardt 1989: 540). These cross-case patterns can be identified in different ways: (1) selecting particular categories or dimensions and searching for within–class similarities coupled with intergroup differences; (2) selecting pairs of cases and developing a list of differences and similarities for each pair; and (3) dividing data by sources and triangulating qualitative data with qualitative data, which is the case regarding the Metro study. Each respondent was treated as a separate case as cross-respondent analysis was conducted.

As the result of the iterative process of within-cases, along with the cross-case analysis, overall patterns, themes based on the coding process and relationships between variables became apparent. During this process, compared explanations while seeking patterns were considered, then established conclusions that were most congruent with the data were raised. This process was a rigorous and consistent mode of examining and comparing verbal data. Importantly, it should be noted that the NVivo analysis did not replace the coding process used, but rather pointed to quotes, comments and other types of notes that enabled development of conclusions that emerged from the interpretive coding.

In the next step, hypotheses or theoretical statements then begin to emerge that are supposed to fit existing data. Using replication logic, by treating multiple cases like experiments, one either confirms or disconfirms emerging hypotheses just as in traditional hypothesis testing research situations. The only difference is that disconfirmed hypotheses are not thrown away since they 'can often provide an opportunity to refine and extend the theory' (Eisenhardt 1989: 542).

To conclude, most important with regard to the Metro study were important political and operational issues that had to be taken into account. The initial design of Metro was to include only the most gifted and talented students from each of the sixteen districts. As the superintendents realized that this practice would reduce their overall school system performance indicators, they resisted with all force. As a result, a more 'random draw' of students was adopted. With regard to the network operation, important network management differences emerged between planning and operational phases. This allowed us to make important analytical distinctions, for example, with regard to resource allocations and programs. These key distinctions could only be understood through qualitative analysis. Grounded theory proved to round out understanding of the quantitative portion of the study.

Quantitative analysis through survey research

The network database normally begins with a closed-ended survey that provides a pre-case overview of the network scope and universe of participating entities. The respondents are always 'principals' who are involved in the network studied, normally public and NGO administrative officials, elected officials and key non-administrative leaders. The survey/quantitative portion of this chapter includes two network studies, a multi-city economic development study (Agranoff and McGuire 2004) and the Metro STEM study (Kolpakov, Agranoff and McGuire 2016). Theory building from case studies often serves as a bridge from rich qualitative evidence to mainstream deductive research: 'its emphasis on developing constructs, measures, and theoretical propositions makes inductive case research consistent with the emphasis on testable theory within mainstream deductive research' (Eisenhardt and Graebner 2007: 25).

The large-*n* study, *Collaborative public management: new strategies for local governments* is based on networked contacts and activities in cities in the United States (US) from the five states located in the East North Central (ENC) Census Bureau geographic division: Illinois, Indiana, Michigan, Ohio and Wisconsin. The supporting cases were drawn from a sample of localities in these states that responded to a nationwide mail survey sent out to 7,135 cities and 3,108 counties by the International City/County Management Association (ICMA). Questions addressed general economic development policies and practices. The questionnaire was sent to the chief administrative officer of all cities and counties with populations of 2,500 or more and to those cities and counties with populations under 2,500 that are recognized by ICMA as providing for an appointed position of professional management. Our study restricted the analysis to the responding cities in the five Midwest states: Indiana, Michigan, Ohio, Illinois and Wisconsin.

A second follow-along questionnaire by the authors addressing collaboration and economic development was designed and mailed to the chief administrative officers of the regional cities that responded to the ICMA economic development survey. All respondents from the 313 cities in the survey universe were aware that they were being surveyed again because of their response to the ICMA survey and that the results from both questionnaires would be linked and used to study collaboration and local economic development. The intent of this purposive sampling and multisurvey design was to capture the collaborative management actions of cities for which we had extensive local development data. Only five months separated the initial ICMA mailing and the mailing of the collaboration surveys, which contributed to the very high response rate of the second survey: 237 cities or seventy-six per cent of those responding to the initial survey. Subsequently, the six in-the-field case studies buttressed the rich survey data.

A portion of the survey instrument is reproduced in the additional material included at the end of this chapter. It stresses the leadership role and other connections that the literature on local economic development indicated as key. Most important, it measures *actions* and not opinions. Also, it presents matrices of activities and entities, federal and state contacts and their frequencies, modes of collaborative contact, policy and program instruments, combined program contexts and leverage devices and other program efforts. Finally, the survey asks city officials to identify collaborative barriers and obstacles to programming.

The survey data were reported in the final volume (Agranoff and McGuire 2004). The data allowed for elaboration and communication of different collaborative activities: types of horizontal and vertical collaborative activities (information seeking, adjustment seeking, policymaking and strategy-making, resources exchanges), types of linkages, network density and centrality, activity-based linkages, instruments of economic policy development (direct provision of services, subsidies, etc.) and many more variables that profiled collaborative activities. Among the most important set of findings and conclusions are those related to the concept that local jurisdictions did not always unquestionably comply or completely side step state and federal requirements or avoid higher-level grants and regulations but within intergovernmental contacts, along with NGOs, undertook many notably engaged 'ownsource' processes. With the help of the in-the-field-based qualitative discussions, we labelled these moves as 'juris-diction-based management', wherein cities and their local partners operate with locally developed economic development strategies and programs. This work proved to occupy around one-fifth of a city official's time, and involved a com-plex grid of activities that incorporated 'networking' and 'coalition-building' activities at the horizontal level as well as 'financing and regulatory activities with state and federal governments' (152). Moreover, the survey, buttressed by the six in-the-field case studies, elaborated and documented that collaboration is a complicated exercise (Bazeley 2010).

This quantitative focus returns to the Metro School study on network devel-opment and implementation. The data were gathered and determined by administering a two-page questionnaire employing a matrix of collaborator identity and key activities in the network. Each respondent was asked to identify up to sixteen individuals who were important in terms of involvement with Metro High School and to describe the types of network activities/engagement with which respondents were involved. The questionnaires were administered immediately after the qualitative one-and-a-half-hour discussions.

The original sample consisted of twenty-five focused-discussion participants who completed the social network questionnaires and an additional twenty-nine survey respondents, such as Metro High School administrators, teachers and other individuals involved in the operations of the Metro School. Since this study was a longitudinal case study, participant data were analysed at the different stages of network development. Therefore, the data of the additional twenty-nine survey respondents who completed the social network analy-sis (SNA) questionnaire but were not directly interviewed were omitted from the final sample to avoid response biases (Groves et al. 2004). To construct the social network data, the data from the twenty-eight focused discussions and the twenty-five SNA questionnaires completed by the discussants after the qualitative discussions were used to avoid response biases (Groves et al. 2004). Using a six-point Likert scale, ranging from 'Never' (0) to 'Daily' (5), respondents indicated the frequency with which they worked with the named individu-als on the following activities: providing information, receiving information, providing financial resource, receiving financial resources, joint planning, and involvement in project and policy negotiations.

For the quantitative data production process, the directed network of twenty-eight actors from the seventeen organizations involved in the Metro High School project at three developmental points were constructed: (1) the pre-project stage, (2) the planning stage and (3) the implementation stage. These three analytical phases of network development were constructed based on the results of coding the qualitative data and selected items from the survey. The pre-project stage is the stage before Metro High School was constructed and is represented by the relations defined as personal knowledge of someone involved with the Metro High School. This relationship was identified based on the survey question, 'How long have you known this person?' If the respondent indicated knowing a particular person for more than three years, the response was coded as '1', otherwise, the response was coded as '0'. The planning stage represents another key relationship – working with people at the planning stage – and includes various activities, such as initial meetings, curricula development, learning program development, finding and allocating resources, and so forth. The directed network at the planning stage was constructed based on the coding of the interview questions relevant to the development of the network, using the qualitative software package NVivo. The directed network during the implementation stage was constructed in a fashion similar to that of the directed network at the planning stage. However, the qualitative data for the construction of the implementation stage network were triangulated with the survey data because some respondents of the focused discussions did not fill out the SNA questionnaire or because their questionnaires contained incomplete information. The results of these triangulations indicated that the implementation network constructed based on the responses of respondents is very similar to the implementation matrix constructed based on the answers from the social analysis survey questionnaires. This validates the use of the focused discussion transcripts for constructing the directed network for the planning stage and this similarity of responses between the focused discussions and surveys serves as a reliability test. In addition, the research of Wright and Pescosolido (2002) suggests that we can rely on the interviews as a means for collecting longitudinal network data.

To test the static hypotheses of the structural theory of public management network development, the pre-planning, planning and implementation networks were analysed using exploratory and confirmatory SNA (Contractor, Wasserman and Faust 2006). A graphic representation of the exploratory and confirmatory SNA process in this proposed study can be found in Figure 2.2.

As part of the exploratory network analysis, commonly used measures of public management networks at the global level were computed and interpreted, such as centrality, density, reciprocation, transitivity and homophily (Wasserman and Faust 1994), using UCINET (Borgatti, Everett and Freeman 2002) to test some of the hypotheses regarding the development of public management networks over time.

In addition, the pre-project, planning and implementation networks were visualized using the network visualization software called NETDRAW, which is included as a part of the UCINET package. The visual representations allowed for differentiating between different subnetworks such as governance and management subnetworks as well as the different structures emerging in the networks over time. This tool can also provide a 'ballpark' estimation of homophily based on the individual characteristics of network actors. For example, the visualizations of the networks of Metro High School at the pre-project, planning and implementation stages showed the gender segregation among the

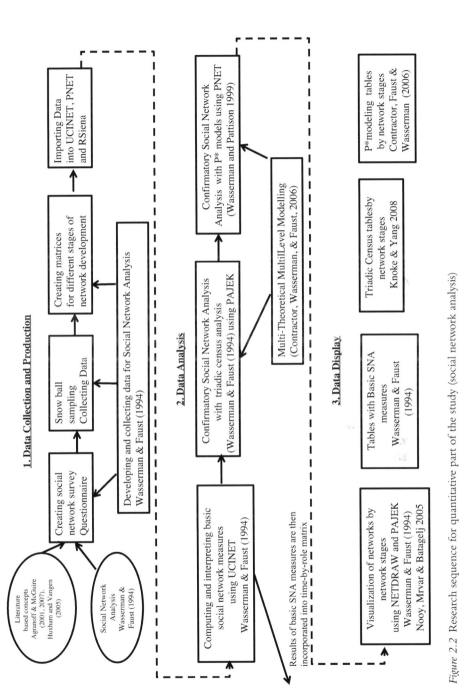

1. Data Collection and Production

Literature based concepts Agranoff & McGuire (2001, 2007). Huxham and Vangen (2005)

Social Network Analysis Wasserman & Faust (1994)

Creating social network survey Questionnaire

Snow ball sampling Collecting Data

Creating matrices for different stages of network development

Importing Data into UCINET, PNET and RSiena

Developing and collecting data for Social Network Analysis Wasserman & Faust (1994)

2. Data Analysis

Computing and interpreting basic social network measures using UCINET Wasserman & Faust (1994)

Confirmatory Social Network Analysis with triadic census analysis (Wasserman & Faust (1994) using PAJEK

Confirmatory Social Network Analysis with P* models using PNET (Wasserman and Pattison 1999)

Multi-Theoretical MultiLevel Modelling (Contractor, Wasserman, & Faust, 2006)

Results of basic SNA measures are then incorporated into time-by-role matrix

3. Data Display

Visualization of networks by network stages using NETDRAW and PAJEK Wasserman & Faust (1994) Nooy, Mrvar & Batagelj 2005

Tables with Basic SNA measures Wasserman & Faust (1994)

Triadic Census tablesby network stages Knoke & Yang 2008

P*modeling tables by network stages Contractor, Faust & Wasserman (2006)

Figure 2.2 Research sequence for quantitative part of the study (social network analysis)

Source: Kolpakov 2013

network participants without looking at the homophily indices. It showed that men tended to be central actors in the pre-project and planning stages.

Further analysis led to triadic network configurations, exponential random graph modelling, p★ models of network structure, various network configurations where concepts such as reciprocity, cyclic trends, transitive triads and out degrees and in degrees and, most important, homophily effects – that is, where network actors select one another based on similarity – are disclosed (Kolpakov 2013). In sum, utilizing the mixed method of coding qualitative (open coding) focused coding, axial coding and theoretical coding, plus quantitative survey responses, allowed for a sequential process orientation that focused on stages of network evolution or development. We consider these to be key findings derived from a quantitative and qualitative design.

Mapping in sequential mixed methods

In mixed methods it is normally necessary to find one or more efficient ways to visually represent the major analytical foci of a study, for both researcher conceptualization and to facilitate communication for potential readers and reviewers (Ivankova, Creswell and Stick 2006: 9). In multiple case studies this is sometimes referred to as site mapping. Employing grounded theory extends the research role through the writing stages, inasmuch as the discovery process extends into the writing and rewriting stages. As Charmaz (2006: 154) concludes, further insights and more creative ideas emerge as late as the writing stage, seeing clearer connections that are crucial phases in the analytic process, beyond mere reporting. Mapping out results then follows for demonstrating interactive conceptual relationships along with reporting of key results.

In addition to the sequenced methods diagrams presented, we illustrate the mapping component by looking at the two grounded-theory-based studies under demonstration and point to another. First, a verbal summary, an intergovernmental multi-state rural development project, sponsored by the federal government, but defined by the initial eight states and later twenty-one additional states engaged in this program, provides an overall picture of the actors that were engaged in the first four years of the program, from 1990 to 1994. It is reported in Radin et al. (1996: 201–202).

The mapping reported in this final rural study was essential to begin the analysis, as the research team found the predominance of projects in regulatory relief, databases, cooperative ventures, outreach activities and project demonstrations, resulted from new funding and changing policies. Overall, this mapping exercise by the research team brought to light many findings, for example how the rural councils steered clear of major state or federal efforts, particularly those with key interests in organized agriculture.

A second mapping exercise (see Table 2.1), a working document, involves the breakdown of one of the *Collaborative Public Management* case studies. It depicts the multiple transactions involved in Salem Indiana's effort to expand its industrial park. It was constructed entirely through the series of in–the–field

Table 2.1 Salem Indiana's industrial park expansion project

Project Component	Needed Action	Agreement/Approval					Funding Source/Obligation				
		Federal	State	City	Other Local	Private	Federal	State	City	Other Local	Private
1. Land Purchase	Find parcel			X	X	X	X	X	X	X	X
	Raise funds – US, EDA grant			X	X	X	X	X	X	X	X
	Rezoning			X							
	Contract – WEGP					X					X
2. Land Improvement/ Site Preparation	City appropriation			X	X				X	X	
	County ED Income Tax				X				X	X	
3. Building Construction	"Build Indiana" (Lottery fund) program		X					X			
	Fed-State, Small Cities Community Development Bloc Grant		X					X			
4. Business Attraction Packages	Tax Increment Financing		X	X	X				X	X	
	Indiana Industrial Bonds		X	X	X			X			
	8-year Tax Abatement (forgiveness)		X	X					X		
	Streamlined Permitting		X	X							
5. Water/Infrastructure Development	Increase water treatment capacity	X					X		X		X
	US Dept. of Agriculture Loan										
	US Housing and Urban Development Loan	X					X		X		X
	US EPA Loan	X					X		X		X
6. Human Resource Development	US Dept. of Labor-Workforce Development	X			X		X				
	Kentuckiana Community College				X					X	
7. Truck Bypass of City Center	Obtain Federal (60) and State (25) Privatization and Authorization; County (15) and city (5) "match"	X	X	X	X		X			X	

(Continued)

Table 2.1 (Continued)

Project Component	Needed Action	Agreement/Approval					Funding Source/Obligation				
		Federal	State	City	Other Local	Private	Federal	State	City	Other Local	Private
8. Park Operation	Extension of contract with Local Development Corporation			X	X	X			X	X	X
9. Business Attraction (future)	US Small Business Administration Loans with state and private venture capital match	X	X			X	X	X			X
10. Housing Development (middle income homes) (future)	US Dept. of Agriculture Home Loans	X			X		X				X
	US HUD – Senior Housing Construction (to free up existing homes)	X	X			X	X	X			X
	Indiana Housing Authority (Low income)		X			X	X	X			X
11. Computer and Technical Literacy (future)	Adult Education programs, US D of E Special Grant	X	X			X	X	X			X

Source: Compiled from field notes: Agranoff and McGuire (2004)

discussions and examination of documents, confirmed in part by analysing the survey response and by a follow-up telephone discussion with city officials and network partners.

It is relatively self-explanatory, in the sense that it identifies eleven distinct project components, identifies the requisite actions, the government and private interests involved and the funding sources and legal obligations. It demonstrates in a single chart the multiple jurisdictions and actors involved, as well as the disparate resource issues and the different actions needed in a collaborative project. The myriad contacts and connections needed in this one slice of administrative life is indicative of a highly networked challenge.

The third mapping exercise involves two maps (see Figures 2.3 and 2.4) related to the Metro School study. Figure 2.3 constitutes a research team *constructed* map of the Metro structure, including linkages to key learning centres, student experience sites, field placements, the sixteen school districts and many OSU connections and operations. This map was also created and field-tested after completion of the field investigations, facilitating many facets of the analysis. Figure 2.4 is an overview of the major actions and stages of the network's development. They were derived from multi-stage coding of respondents' recounting of the school's development, then organized by four management phases. In the larger study (McGuire and Agranoff 2014), each step was elaborated by the four network management behaviours elaborated in an earlier study: activation and mobilization, framing and synthesis (Agranoff and McGuire 2004). It allows for 'a detailed road map of how networks are managed from the perspective of the practitioner' (153). It was also confirmed that these proposed activities are all present, but in a less linear fashion than was originally understood; that there is no single network manager, but many; that a 'network culture' emerged based on negotiated and agreed principles; and, most importantly, that the work/contribution of each home organization is real, involved and significant.

This type of mapping gives the researcher a broad perspective on what the networks under study 'look like' from the participants' perspectives. Each component is grounded by an in-the-field-constructed quantitative and qualitative design, where the respondents' words and counted responses become the data.

New phases in sequential explanatory design

A research team that includes Agranoff, McGuire and Kolpakov is currently embarking on a sequential mixed-methods study that will add three small steps to our traditional survey and discussion-based field study approach. The recently initiated nationwide study investigates how the various US Medicaid Home and Community-Based Services (HCBS) waiver networks have emerged and operate in the fifty states. (Gettings 2011; Thompson 2012). These state-designed and supervised multi-organizational networks involve arrangements of state agencies, locally based public organizations (e.g. special districts and local governments), NGOs (for-profit and non-profit), and other health education and rehabilitative providers. It explores and explains the deep network structure and operations of

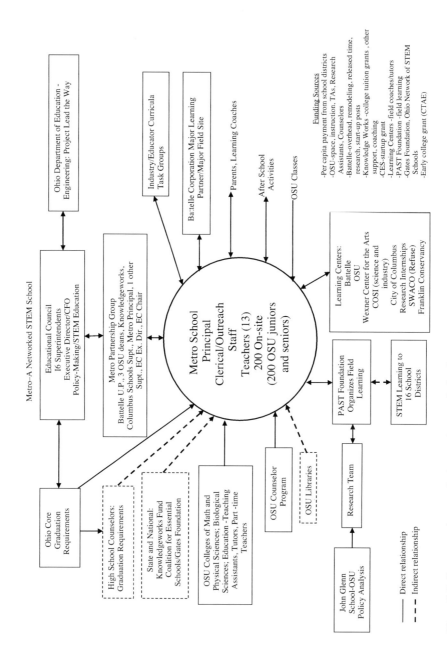

Figure 2.3 Constructed network chart and network development sequence

Source: Adapted from McGuire and Agranoff 2014. Reproduced by permission of Taylor and Francis Group, LLC, a division of Informa plc.

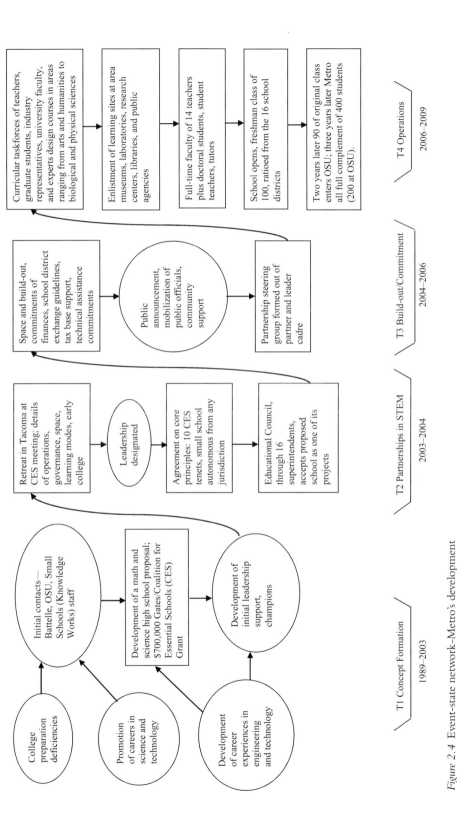

Figure 2.4 Event-state network-Metro's development

Source: Adapted from McGuire and Agranoff 2014. Reproduced by permission of Taylor and Francis Group, LLC, a division of Informa plc.

The figure presents the following stages:

T1 Concept Formation (1989–2003)
- College preparation deficiencies
- Promotion of careers in science and technology
- Development of career experiences in engineering and technology
- Initial contacts—Battelle, OSU, Small Schools (Knowledge Works) staff
- Development of a math and science high school proposal; $700,000 Gates/Coalition for Essential Schools (CES) Grant
- Development of initial leadership support, champions

T2 Partnerships in STEM (2003–2004)
- Retreat in Tacoma at CES meeting; details of operations, space, governance, learning modes, early college
- Leadership designated
- Agreement on core principles: 10 CES tenets, small school autonomous from any jurisdiction
- Educational Council, through 16 superintendents, accepts proposed school as one of its projects

T3 Build-out/Commitment (2004–2006)
- Space and build-out, commitments of finances, school district exchange guidelines, tax base support, technical assistance commitments
- Public announcement, mobilization of public officials, community support
- Partnership steering group formed out of partner and leader cadre

T4 Operations (2006–2009)
- Curricular taskforces of teachers, graduate students, industry representatives, university faculty, and experts design courses in areas ranging from arts and humanities to biological and physical sciences
- Enlistment of learning sites at area museums, laboratories, research centers, libraries, and public agencies
- Full-time faculty of 14 teachers plus doctoral students, student teachers, tutors
- School opens, freshman class of 100, ratioed from the 16 school districts
- Two years later 90 of original class enters OSU; three years later Metro all full complement of 400 students (200 at OSU).

intergovernmental management as they operate through federal and state legal and political channels. These operations involve externalization through NGOs linked to public agencies, and links to providers, families and clients.

This mixed-methods study focuses on the primary data gathered through Medicaid Waiver Plan 1915c for the intellectually/developmentally disabled (I/DD); that is, each state plan and approval reports a fifty-state email survey and case studies in the field. Also, at the selected case-study field level, discussion and responses to the email questionnaire will be clarified and explained in depth. The grounded theory in the field work will be followed by expert program reactors to the case study responses in a select number of states to ensure that what has been framed for trustworthiness, transferability and resonance (Pepper and Wildy 2009) are captured. The data collection also includes a series of focus groups employing discourse analysis with I/DD family members and with allied direct support providers in those same states (Onwuegbuzie et al. 2009). The focus groups will add considerable depth to the grounded-theory approach, offering a type of richness never previously undertaken, at least by this research team.

The flow chart in Figure 2.5 demonstrates the practice-theory-practice cycle being followed, through the sequential mixed-methods and policy feedback flow. As mentioned, this study incorporates the three new methodological steps. One, a desk audit of the fifty states, will allow for a systematic mapping of the terrain. It will look at all fifty state plans/applications and produce a set of aggregate statistics on services organization and interagency profiles, as well as summary mapping similar to those in Figures 2.2 to 2.4. It will offer a more detailed inventory of what all the states are doing, and how. The raw data set is primarily available from the US Centers for Medicare and Medicaid Services. The second study, to come after the field-based site visits, will enhance the case study preparation by having highly experienced external experts, one public and one non-public, react to the case material and present context- and problem-oriented verification of what is offered by administrators' responses in the field. Third, while in the field, a set of focus groups will be undertaken, involving client families and self-advocates, by another specialist who has direct experience with client families/caregivers and with key support service providers (e.g. schools and vocational rehabilitation). Focus group participants will be purposively selected based on issues raised in the field studies (Morgan 2014: 137). The focus groups will provide the most basic 'ground up' look at networks at the operating level (Pader 2006; Wagenaar 2011), and identify issues otherwise overlooked in other phases.

The study also looks for both types of facilitators and barriers to network structure and operations, plus analysis of extant inter-organizational dynamics within state networks, the contributions/products of taskforces and work groups, network structure and operations, procedures and agreement-making processes followed, capacity-building knowledge-development activities, sustainability plans, process analyses, continuous improvement activities and actions regarding system performance. Finally, the in-the-field study will explore in greater depth the key 'within-network' interactions (policy and management)

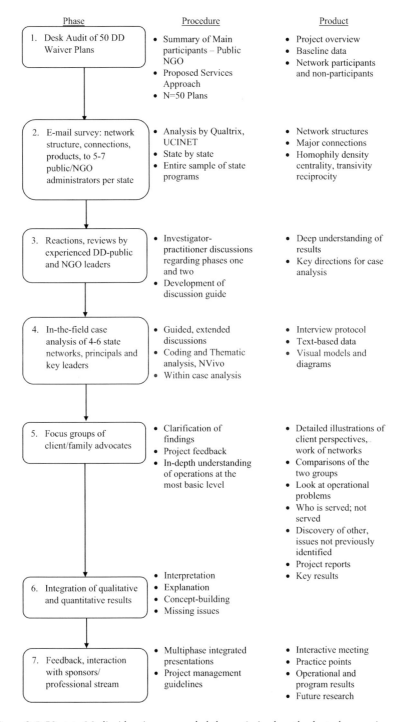

Phase	Procedure	Product
1. Desk Audit of 50 DD Waiver Plans	• Summary of Main participants – Public NGO • Proposed Services Approach • N=50 Plans	• Project overview • Baseline data • Network participants and non-participants
2. E-mail survey: network structure, connections, products, to 5-7 public/NGO administrators per state	• Analysis by Qualtrix, UCINET • State by state • Entire sample of state programs	• Network structures • Major connections • Homophily density centrality, transivity reciprocity
3. Reactions, reviews by experienced DD-public and NGO leaders	• Investigator-practitioner discussions regarding phases one and two • Development of discussion guide	• Deep understanding of results • Key directions for case analysis
4. In-the-field case analysis of 4-6 state networks, principals and key leaders	• Guided, extended discussions • Coding and Thematic analysis, NVivo • Within case analysis	• Interview protocol • Text-based data • Visual models and diagrams
5. Focus groups of client/family advocates	• Clarification of findings • Project feedback • In-depth understanding of operations at the most basic level	• Detailed illustrations of client perspectives, work of networks • Comparisons of the two groups • Look at operational problems • Who is served; not served • Discovery of other, issues not previously identified • Project reports • Key results
6. Integration of qualitative and quantitative results	• Interpretation • Explanation • Concept-building • Missing issues	
7. Feedback, interaction with sponsors/ professional stream	• Multiphase integrated presentations • Project management guidelines	• Interactive meeting • Practice points • Operational and program results • Future research

Figure 2.5 50-state Medicaid waiver, grounded theory/mixed methods study overview

Source: Adapted from Ivankova, Creswell and Stick 2006

with state and federal agencies, other state departments and with other primary actors (e.g. interest groups) in that state's HCBS network.

The sequential explanatory design aims to allow for a focused multinetworking management analysis (Agranoff 2013, 2014a, 2014b; Agranoff and McGuire 1999, 2004). It will provide practitioners who promote or operate in networks to learn how to extend human services programs outward beyond their organizations in order to serve clients by providing a broader understanding of how to proceed in the network era. In this sense, it will transform basic process research such that one proceeds practically to manage by network with others, which is an increasingly important skill for public administrators. For those who work in human services, it will provide a basic understanding of how to proceed in this complex world of programs, agencies and externalization of government programs. For scholars, the study breaks down and explains intergovernmental structures, operations and challenges, as policy and operational management become increasingly interoperable, ever-raising new program and administrative challenges, and changing the nature of administrative behaviour, as well as challenging how one applies the more traditional professions and specialties.

Conclusion

Years of experience, trial and error, and emerging conceptual coverage have led to the conclusion that a network analysis methodological approach involves a lot of hard and sustained work – a lot more than 'sending out a questionnaire' or 'talking to a few people'. The conceptual rewards, however, outweigh such investments.

A core analytical issue is that this approach drives home that local jurisdictions and home-grown networks forge their own situation-based packages, that government in the network era is not totally hollowing out but changing its role, that networks normally lack the legal standing or the power that governments do, or that most collaborative undertakings are mightily complicated and involve processes that, without the qualitative phases, would not necessarily have come out in surveys only (McGuire and Agranoff 2011). On the other hand, without the quantitative phase we would not know their frequency and significance in sifting through one or two voices to generalize to some larger whole. Most importantly, it is clear that these issues have always been tied to some understanding and solving by the sequential mixed-methods approach. As Morgan (2014: 230) concludes, 'applied research typically uses a much more flexible approach to joining the elements in the research design cycle'.

The approaches are predicated on a complex world where simple explanations do not fit well. Phenomena like networks and their role are the result of multiple forces coming together in complex and often unanticipated ways. Network analysis speaks out to uncovering multiple perspectives and analytic variations. Concepts nevertheless provide ways of talking about and arriving at shared understanding and experiences (Corbin and Strauss 2008: 6).

Networks and related collaborative approaches in emergent governance appear to add considerable value to our understanding by employing eclectic approaches like those identified in this chapter. In the complex and overlapping world of collaboration and networks both the verbal responses and instrumented variables prove to contribute to understanding this intractable arena of study.

Additional material

A sample of the survey instrument

The questions below refer to the intergovernmental activities carried out by your local government for economic development between the years 1992 and 1994.

1. Which of the following groups is the most active in promoting economic development in your community? *(Check only one)*

    ☐   a. Local government
    ☐   b. Publicly-owned development corporation
    ☐   c. A formal, incorporated or informal public/private partnership organization

    Does local government provide some funding?   YES ☐   NO ☐

    ☐   d. Chamber of Commerce

    Does local government provide some funding?   YES ☐   NO ☐

    ☐   e. Private business or foundation

    Does local government provide some funding?   YES ☐   NO ☐

2. Please indicate which of the persons listed below is primarily responsible for intergovernmental activities with respect to economic development (securing grants, applying for waivers, making agreements with counties, working with local groups, etc.)? *(Check only one)*

    ☐   a. City chief administrative officer
    ☐   b. City assistant administrative officer
    ☐   c. City development director
    ☐   d. City intergovernmental specialist
    ☐   e. City finance officer
    ☐   f. City budget analyst
    ☐   g. Development organization director
    ☐   h. Chamber of Commerce Director/President
    ☐   i. Other _____
    ☐   j. None designated

    If none designated, please indicate which official initiates discussions and negotiations of economic development issues with other governments by putting a corresponding letter from above in the space provided _____

3. What percentage of time does the individual in charge of development devote to intergovernmental activities? ___ %
4. Please rate the importance of each set of organizations listed below for your city's economic development policy activity. Only one organization should be checked in the first column, but you may check as many as needed for columns two and three.

External Government	Most Important (check one)	Important	Not important (as many as needed)
a. Federal government	☐	☐	☐
b. State government	☐	☐	☐
c. Substate agency (Reg. council/ planning agency/dev. District)	☐	☐	☐
d. County government	☐	☐	☐
e. Township government	☐	☐	☐
f. Special district	☐	☐	☐
g. Other city government	☐	☐	☐

Non-Governmental	Most Important (check one)	Important	Not Important (as many as needed)
a. Local development corporation	☐	☐	☐
b. Chamber of Commerce	☐	☐	☐
c. Enterprise zone	☐	☐	☐
d. Other public/private partnership	☐	☐	☐
e. Private developer	☐	☐	☐
f. Neighbourhood association/ citizen advisory board	☐	☐	☐
g. Financial institution	☐	☐	☐
h. Other _____	☐	☐	☐

Source: Internal document for Agranoff and McGuire (2004)

References

Adams, G.B. and J. D. White. 1994. "Dissertation research in public administration and cognate fields: An assessment of methods and quality." *Public Administration Review* 54 (6): 565–576.

Agranoff, R. 2007. *Managing within networks: Adding value to public organizations.* Washington, DC: Georgetown University Press.

Agranoff, R. 2013. "The transformation of public sector intellectual/developmental disabilities programming." *Public Administration Review* 73 (Sept/Oct): S127–S137.

Agranoff, R. 2014a. "Bridging the theoretical gap and uncovering missing holes." In *Network theory in the public sector*, edited by R. Keast, M. Mandell, and R. Agranoff. New York and London: Routledge.

Agranoff, R. 2014b. "Reconstructing bureaucracy for service innovation in the governance era." In *Public Innovation Through Collaboration and Design*, edited by Christopher Ansell and Jacob Torfing. London: Routledge.

Agranoff, R and M. McGuire. 1999. "Expanding intergovernmental management's hidden dimensions." *American Review of Public Administration* 29 (4): 352–369.

Agranoff, R. and M. McGuire. 2004. *Collaborative public management: New strategies for local governments*. Washington, DC: Georgetown University Press.

Bazeley, P. 2010. "Computer-assisted integration of mixed data sources and analyses." In *SAGE handbook of mixed methods in social and behavioral research*, 2nd ed., edited by A. Tashakkori and C. Teddlie, 431–468. Los Angeles: Sage Publications.

Borgatti, S.P., M.G. Everett, and L.C. Freeman. 2002. *UCINET for Windows: Software for social network analysis*. Harvard, MA: Analytic Technologies.

Carney, T.F. 1990. *Collaborative inquiry methodology*. Windsor and Ontario, Canada: University of Windsor, Division for Instructional Development.

Charmaz, K. 2006. *Constructing grounded theory*, 1st ed. Los Angeles: Sage Publications.

Charmaz, K. 2014. *Constructing grounded theory*, 2nd ed. Los Angeles: Sage Publications.

Contractor, M.S., S. Wasserman, and K. Faust. 2006. "Testing multitheoretical, multilevel, and the hypotheses about organizational networks: An analytic framework and empirical example." *Academy of Management Review* 31 (3): 681–703.

Corbin, J. and A.M. Strauss. 2008. *Basics of qualitative research: Techniques and procedures for developing grounded theory*. Los Angeles: Sage Publications.

Creswell, J.W. 1998. *Qualitative inquiry and research design*. Thousand Oaks, CA: Sage Publications.

Creswell, J.W. 2010. "Mapping the developing landscape of mixed methods research." In *SAGE handbook of mixed methods research*, 2nd ed., edited by A. Tashakkori and C. Teddlie. Los Angeles: Sage Publications.

Eisenhardt, K.M. 1989. "Building theories from case study research." *Academy of Management Review* 14: 532–550.

Eisenhardt, K.M. and M.E. Graebner. 2007. "Theory building from cases: Opportunities and challenges." *Academy of Management Journal* 50 (1): 25–32.

Gettings, R.M. 2011. *Forging a federal-state partnership: A history of federal developmental disabilities policy*. Washington: AAIDD/NASDDD.

Glazer, B. 1978. *Theoretical sensitivity*. Mill Valley CA: Sociology Press.

Glazer, B.G. and A.L. Strauss. 1967. *The discovery of grounded theory*. Chicago: Aldine.

Groves, R.M., F.J. Fowler, M.P. Couper, J.M. Lepkowski, E. Singer, and R. Tourangeau. 2004. *Survey methodology*. Hoboken, NJ: Wiley-Interscience.

Hale, K. 2011. *How information matters: Networks and public policy innovation*. Washington, DC: Georgetown University Press.

Ivankova, N., J.W. Creswell, and S. Stick. 2006. "Using mixed methods sequential explanatory design: From theory to practice." *Field Methods* 18 (1): 3–20.

Kolpakov, A. 2013. "Structural development of public management networks over time: Where process meets structure." PhD Dissertation, School of Public and Environmental Affairs, Indiana University, Bloomington.

Kolpakov, A., R. Agranoff, and M. McGuire. 2016. "Understanding interoperability in collaborative network management: The case of Metro High." *Journal of Health Science* 4 (68): 318–332.

McGuire, M. and R. Agranoff. 2011. The limitations of public management networks. *Public Administration* 89 (2): 265–284.

McGuire, M. and R. Agranoff. 2014. "Network management behaviors: Closing the theoretical gap." In *Network theory in the public sector*, edited by R. Keast, M. Mandell, and R. Agranoff. New York and London: Routledge.

Maxwell, J.A. 2004. "Using qualitative methods for pausal explanation." *Field Methods* 16 (3): 243–264.

Maxwell, J.A. 2010. "Using numbers in qualitative research." *Qualitative Inquiry* 16 (6): 425–482.

Morgan, D.L. 2014. *Integrating qualitative and quantitative methods: A pragmatic approach*. Los Angeles: Sage Publications.

Onwuegbuzie, A.J., W.B. Dickinson, N. Leech, and A.G. Zoran. 2009. "A qualitative framework for collecting and analyzing data in focus group research." *International Journal of Qualitative Methods* 8 (3): 1–21.

Pader, E. 2006. "Seeing with an ethnographic sensibility: Exploration beneath the surface of public policies." In *Interpretation and Method*, edited by Dvora Yanow and Peregrine Schwartz-Shea. Armonk, NY: M.E. Sharpe.

Pepper, C. and H. Wildy. 2009. "Using narratives as a research strategy." *Qualitative Research Journal* 912: 18–26.

Radin, B.A., R. Agranoff, A. O'M. Bowman, C.G. Buntz, J. Stevenhott, B.S. Romzek, and R.H. Wilson. 1996. *New governance for rural America: Creating intergovernmental partnerships*. Lawrence: University Press of Kansas.

Strauss, A. L. 1987. *Qualitative analysis for social scientists*. Cambridge: Cambridge University Press.

Strauss, A.M. 1995. "Notes and nature and development of general theories." *Qualitative Inquiry* 1 (1): 7–18.

Strauss, A.L. and J.M. Corbin. 1990. *Basic of qualitative research: Grounded theory procedures and techniques*. Newbury Park, CA: Sage Publications.

Strauss, A.L. and J.M. Corbin. 1998. *Basics of qualitative research: Grounded theory procedures and techniques*, 2nd ed. Thousand Oaks, CA: Sage Publications.

Suddaby, R. 2006. "What grounded theory is not." *Academy of Management Journal* 49 (4): 633–642.

Thompson, F.J. 2012. *Medicaid politics: Federalism, policy durability and health reform*. Washington, DC: Georgetown University Press.

Voets, J., W. Van Dooren, and F. DeRynck. 2008. "A framework for assessing the performance of policy networks." *Public Management Review* 10 (6): 773–790.

Wasserman, S. and K. Faust. 1994. *Social network analysis*. New York: Cambridge University Press.

Wagenaar, H. 2011. *Meaning in action: Interpretation and dialogue in policy analysis*. Armonk, NY: M.E. Sharpe.

Wright, E.R. and B.A. Pescosolido. 2002. "'Sorry, I forgot': The role of recall error in longitudinal personal network studies." In *Social networks and health*, edited by Judith A. Levy and Bernice A. Pescosolido, 113–129. Bingley, UK: Emerald Group Publishing Limited.

Yin, R.K. 1984. *Case study research: Design and methods*. Beverly Hills, CA: Sage Publications.

3 The case study in researching networks and collaborative arrangements

Ming Cheng and Joris Voets

Introduction

Introduced into public administration (PA) research more than six decades ago, the case study[1] approach is a foundational research method that has demonstrated its explanatory and explorative power regarding various PA and public management studies (McNabb 2010: 5). As this chapter demonstrates, this also holds true for the research on collaboration and networks. With their roots in some seminal organizational studies in sociology from the 1970s (Granovetter 1973, 1983; White, Boorman and Breiger 1976), concepts like network and collaboration have attracted increasing attention from scholars and practitioners for almost half a century (Heclo 1972; Olson 1971; Ostrom 1990; O'Toole 1997; Bogason and Zølner 2007; Thomson and Perry 2006). Focusing on network research as the specific domain, this chapter explores how the case study as a research method is still key for network scholars and practitioners, and what its main components are. While this chapter focuses on the case study method as used in network research in general, Agranoff and Kolpakov's chapter (Chapter 2) in this volume shows how the case study methodology can be an overall research approach. Cepiku, Cristofoli and Trivellato's chapter (Chapter 10) on Qualitative Comparative Analysis (QCA) then shows how the comparative case study method as a particular strand has been developed in recent years.

Approaching the case study in network research

Fundamentally, networks and other multi-party collaborative arrangements represent horizontal over vertical approaches to decision-making between interdependent actors based on a common vision or purpose, social exchange, mutuality and reciprocity (Powell 1990; Powell, Koput and Smith-Doerr 1996; Keast 2016). Case studies are therefore used frequently to investigate topics like network formation, configuration, structure, outcome and governance (Provan and Sebastian 1998; Hu et al. 2016), involving the strategies and interactions emerging within policy and governance networks (Klijn and Koppenjan 2016b; Voets 2014), as well as the democratic legitimacy generated through participation and deliberation in network arrangements (De Rynck and Voets 2006; Sørensen and Torfing 2009; Skelcher and Torfing 2010).

Although the case study method has been widely used as a distinctive form of empirical inquiry in network research, challenges concerning the limited rigour of the research design, sacrificing breadth for depth and an inability for theoretical generalization remain (Saz-Carranza, Salvador Iborra and Albareda 2016; Yin 2014: 47). Consequently, the role of the case study method in network research deserves a proper analysis. In recent review articles on network research the attention has largely focused on historical roots and current challenges (Isett et al. 2011), perceived schools of thought (Lecy, Mergel and Schmitz 2014) and social network analysis (SNA) (Kapucu, Hu and Khosa 2017). As yet, however, no particular stress has been placed on the case study method in network research. Therefore, the following questions are explored in this chapter: 'What is the case study, in terms of a methodology, concerned about?', 'Why is it relevant to study networks?', 'What are the insights and added value extracted from key case studies on networks?', 'What about the limitations of applying the case study method and how do we deal with them?' and 'What is the future of the case study method in network research?'

To answer these questions, we conducted a targeted and systematic review to inquire about relevant case studies on networks. In a recent review article on network research, thirty-nine journals were investigated and a list ranked by the number of network-related articles published in each journal was provided (Kapucu, Hu and Khosa 2017). Given that some of the aforementioned journals fall into the category of finance and accounting, management science and political science – showing the wide range of collaboration and network research studies – we limited our scope to the PA journal list, ranked by the journal impact factor in the Web of Science. After cross-referencing between the two sources and consulting with some network researchers, the following were selected as our targeted journals: *Public Administration Review*, *Public Administration*, *Journal of Public Administration Research and Theory* and *Public Management Review*. These four journals published the most network studies and showed significant influence within academia regarding public administration. While reviewing a more elaborate set of journals and including relevant books would certainly enrich and strengthen our analysis, this selection was considered sufficient for the purpose of this chapter and the limited resources available. Next, we searched those journals with *network* and *collaboration* as index terms in keywords and abstracts. Initially, 510 articles were collected. After excluding the ones using networks only as metaphors or adjunct terms, 288 articles were carried over to the next phase. In that next step, we delved into the methods section of each article and identified eighty-two articles in which a case study is at least a part of the research method. On the basis of these eighty-two case studies,[2] the rest of the chapter is structured into four parts. Firstly, features and variations of the case study as a research method and major strategies to select cases and collect data are briefly illustrated. Next, we turn to the relevance, strengths and limitations of the case study method in researching networks. The third section focuses on the observations from case studies in network research, highlighting the interpretive potential, expanding boundary, dynamic and contextual dimensions of networks. Finally, this chapter closes with some concluding remarks and future paths for developing the case study method in network research.

Basic concerns about the case study: features and variations

As one of the most traditional research methods, the case study enjoys great popularity in the PA field and shows its particular capacity to explore the issue of collective actions (Ostrom 1990). In this section we discuss some essential features and variations as well as major strategies to collect and analyse data that help to research networks and collaborative arrangements.

Common features of case studies

In decades of lasting academic endeavour, the controversies surrounding the definition and design of case studies abound. For instance, Yin (2014: 43) claims a case study should investigate a contemporary phenomenon within its real-world context. Woodside (2010: 2) insists that such a limitation is not necessary, especially when boundaries between the phenomenon and context are not clearly evident. Gerring (2006: 20) stresses that the case study is an intensive study of a single case aimed at shedding light on a larger class of cases. Although different scholars may stress different qualities of the case study, some common features can be identified through methodological discussions which are also manifested in network research.

Firstly, the case study functions as a bridge connecting theoretical propositions with empirical findings. Theory plays an essential role not only in clarifying the core concepts and framework prior to delving into cases, but in generalizing the lessons drawn from the case analysis (Yin 2014: 67–73). To be clear, following Yin (2014), theory and propositions essentially mean that you need to have some ideas up front about what you are expecting to find in order to ensure that you have some focus in your case study (17, 30). In a study applying the Anglo-governmentality perspective in a local network, the authors first developed a novel theoretical framework based on a literature review, which was then examined in two cases in the UK healthcare settings (Ferlie and McGivern 2014). Moreover, to reveal any relations between variables or factors effectively, data from multiple sources should be collected systematically. These data are descriptive, observational or even gathered from quantitative methods (Woodside 2010: 11; we elaborate further on the instruments to collect and analyse data in the next section). Last but not least, the case study is always used to propose an in-depth understanding about the actors, perceptions, behaviours and relations within network structures and collaborative arrangements; it acts as a robust reflection of the interactions between individuals and organizations within the unique context of each case. For instance, two case studies on network dynamics established some profound insights. On the one hand, a case study about the planning and decision-making of Mainport Rotterdam demonstrated that the difficulty in making joint inter-organizational policy decisions lies in the self-referential nature of network actors, rather than adhering to proposed network governance schemes (Teisman and Klijn 2002). On the other hand, O'Toole's (1996) study examined why and how the state revolving-loan funds scheme in the United States (US) was created, and that deregulation, decentralization and privatization would have consequences for both inter-organizational networks and programs in practice.

Major variations of the case study

Following these basic traits, variations of the case study emerge in the research on networks and collaborative arrangements. As demonstrated in Table 3.1, case studies can be classified into three groups based on different standards. Based on

Table 3.1 Major variations of the case study

Criteria for classification	*Variations*
Underlying research questions and objectives	• *Explanatory case study*: To develop a causal explanation of some social phenomenon, including building theories that may be used to explain a phenomenon
	• *Interpretive case study*: To go beyond simply describing or explaining a phenomenon and interpret what it means as well as what it is
	• *Critical case study*: To emancipate members of the society or group from some harmful condition or undesired circumstances, thereby eliminating the causes of alienation
Intent of the research design Scale of the case study	• *Intrinsic case study*: Researcher is interested in a certain case for some reason and wants to provide a better understanding of the subject case itself
	• *Instrumental case study*: Researcher wants to gain greater insight into a specific issue that often involves more than a single unit or organization
	• *Collective case study*: Several individual cases are studied together as a group because it is believed that they can contribute to greater understanding of a phenomenon, a population or some general organizational condition.
Number of primary cases as units examined in the study Number of embedded unit of analysis in each case	• *Holistic single case study*: With one complete unit of analysis, with no subunits analysed independently
	• *Embedded single case study*: Includes more than one participant unit of analysis to contribute to understanding of a single case
	• *Holistic multiple case study*: Includes more than one case but no subunits exist in each case
	• *Embedded multiple case study*: Involves multiple cases, each with multiple subunits included in the analysis.

Source: Adapted from McNabb 2010 and Yin 2014

the underlying research objectives, the first group includes explanatory, interpretive or critical case studies. Drawing on the intent of the research design and the scale of the case study, intrinsic, instrumental and collective case studies are specified as a second category (McNabb 2010: 41). Compared with the former two, the third group is based on a two-level case classification system on the basis of the scale and scope being the most common: the number of primary cases as units of analysis[3] examined in the study (scale) and the number of embedded units of analysis in each case (scope). There are then four types of case study, the holistic single case study, embedded single case study, holistic multiple case study and embedded multiple case study (McNabb 2010: 51; Yin 2014: 81). Notably, each of the four types has its own strengths, while some scholars believe that the strongest means of drawing inferences is to build a combination of within-case analysis and cross-case comparisons in a single study (George and Bennett 2005: 75). In network research a case study is often designed on account of the single-multiple/holistic-embedded distinction. Among the eighty-two case studies reviewed by us, thirty-nine of them are conducted with a single case, while forty-three studies are based on two or more cases. In particular, there are six case studies showing a mixed method with discourse analysis (e.g. Toke 2000), ethnographic analysis (e.g. Choi 2007), content analysis (Moynihan 2009), SNA (e.g. Robins, Bates and Pattison 2011; AbouAssi and Tschirhart 2018) and the grounded theory approach (e.g. Romzek, LeRoux and Blackmar 2012).

Designing case studies: general procedure and data collection

A second point is how to design and carry out the case study research. Numerous principles, schemes and processes to carry out a case study are demonstrated by scholars (see Gerring 2006; Woodside 2010). In general, five interlocking phases of a research design are especially important: framing the research questions, establishing theoretical propositions, defining key units of analysis, collecting the data from different sources and analysing the data for further interpretation (Yin 2014: 59; McNabb 2010: 65–77). Following these steps, cases are introduced as a bridge between theoretical propositions and empirical evidence to investigate the research question. On the one hand, despite the diverse strategies for choosing cases (see Gerring 2006: Chapter 5; Goertz and Mahoney 2012: Chapter 14), each case must be carefully and purposively selected to reproduce the relevant causal features of a larger universe (Gerring 2006: 88). With perceived representativeness and causal leverage, the case study can show its strong power in theory building or testing according to the logic of literal replication or theoretical replication (Yin 2014: 88).

On the other hand, different methods to collect the basic evidence of a case study are involved and widely elaborated in research designs. Yin (2014: 137) identified six commonly used sources of case study evidence: documentation, archival records, interviews, direct observation, participant observation and physical artefacts. In our review of studies on networks and collaborative arrangements, we found four main data collection methods: interviewing, observation, document analysis and analysis of archival records (McNabb 2010: 91). Interviews – typically with the network participants – are the most frequently used, as they help to uncover implicit ideas behind official statements by offering the personal interpretations concerning, for instance, the nature of the network as well as how and why actors were included or excluded (Hendriks 2008; Tomlinson 2010). Direct observation and analysis of documentary information finish second in the popularity poll. Especially when the access to key players in a case proves difficult or delicate, it is particularly important to collect enough documentary and archival evidence around the topic. As in a study on how network structures influence administrative corruption in Japan, to support the arguments with longitudinal data, Choi (2007) used and interpreted information obtained primarily from government documents, reports of international organizations, archival information from newspapers and magazines, and anecdotal evidence.

There is a trend, however, to mobilize multiple sources together, which is called the application of triangulation methods in the case study (Woodside 2010: 35). Using many different but complementary sources of evidence, triangulation in data collection is a major strength of the case study because every single source has its comparative advantages and weaknesses (Yin 2014: 153). For instance, with the information sorted from policy documents, media reports and twenty-seven in-depth interviews with a diverse range of network members from different backgrounds Hendriks (2008) revealed that the Dutch administration's attempt to steer energy networks and reform related less to its democratic goals than to its entrepreneurial and epistemic ones. The triangulation of data through interviews, focus groups and documentation was also included in the case study conducted by Keast et al. (2004) to inquire into the necessity of adjusting policies and management techniques and facilitating the positive attributes of networked arrangements.

Relevance of the case study in network research: Strengths and challenges

In deciding on the use of the case study method, scholars typically refer to the type of research question. According to Yin (2014: 9), the case study method is best suited to inquire into 'how' and 'why' questions, in a setting where no control on behavioural events is required or possible, and when the focus is on contemporary events. Researchers asking such questions are typically aiming to explain and test theories that involve causal and complex interactions that need to be traced over time, rather than counting mere frequencies or incidents (Yin 2014: 37). Studies investigating regulatory networks and interagency cooperation, for instance, show how the validity of a theory in a real-world setting is tested with the theory-based sampling (Lee 2010; Thomas 1997). George and Bennett (2005: 78) also argue that case studies are significantly valuable in testing hypotheses and particularly in developing certain theories by achieving high conceptual validity and addressing causal complexity. Some scholars argue that more explorative 'what' questions also fit with the case study method, although Yin (2014) argues that further refinement of a 'what' question might also lead to the choice of different methods (10). Depending on the way these questions are developed theoretically, case studies can both be explanatory as well as exploratory, investigating emerging hypotheses and propositions for further inquiry, which also helps to theory-build (Woodside 2010: 11; Yin 2014: 37). For instance, a single case study on the distinction between insider and outsider groups in networks contributes to conceptual and theoretical development about policy networks in an iterative theory-building process (Marsh et al. 2009). Saz-Carranza, Salvador Iborra and Albareda (2016), in turn, showed how a multiple case study can provide a more robust basis for theory building about governing inter-organizational goal-directed networks.

The significance of the 'how', 'why' and 'what' nature of research questions as a crucial driver for the application of the case study method is also supported by our review of eighty-two case studies on networks and collaborative arrangements in the public sector. Over half of these studies deal explicitly with 'how' and 'why' questions, such as how organizational context interacts with the implementation of networks (Currie, Grubnic and Hodges 2011) and why policy networks emerge and transform (Nunan 1999). Another twenty-five per cent of the studies focus on 'what' questions, probing into topics like commonalities among the structures of dark networks (Lauchs, Keast and Yousefpour 2011; Raab and Milward 2003) and the processes behind the facilitation that drive network performance (Giest 2015). Our review confirms the everlasting function of the case study as a research method to answer these types of questions. It could not only be used at early stages in theory building on network effectiveness, network management and collaborative governance (Agranoff and McGuire 2001; Ansell and Gash 2008; Provan and Milward 1995), but also in testing the validity of certain theoretical models and approaches more recently, for instance on network change and formation (see AbouAssi and Tschirhart 2018; Qvist 2017).

We now discuss two primary strengths of the case study method for network research in more detail.

Strengths in tracing processes and exploring complexity

The case study method fits well with the nature of the network concept, which evolved from a metaphor, an organizing concept and methodological terms, such as SNA, to an approach to understand collaborative forms of policy-making and service delivery (Provan and Kenis 2008; Isett et al. 2011). While perspectives may differ, network theorists more or less agree on two common characteristics of a network, namely: (1) the interdependency between a wide diversity of horizontally organized actors that (2) require complex interaction patterns and decision-making processes (Klijn and Koppenjan 2016a: 38; Sørensen and Torfing 2009: 9). The network concept therefore helps to describe the interactions between state and society, and the shadow structure of interests affecting policy through interconnections (Keast, Mandell and Agranoff 2014: 15–23), and helps to explore 'the relationship between the structural (patterns of relations) and processual (the art of networking) forms of networks' (Lewis 2011: 1228).

This nebulous nature of the network galaxy helps to explain why tracing processes and exploring complexities using case studies is so important. Since more details and techniques will be specified in the chapter on process tracing (see Chapter 8 in this volume by Keast), this chapter focuses generally on its utility in case studies. For instance, by examining service reform in the English National Health Service, researchers illustrate the establishment and consolidation of service reform within a network as well as the enactment of leadership in facilitating the process (Martin, Currie and Finn 2008). The work of Thomson and Perry (2006) also asserts the nonlinear and emergent nature of collaboration, calling for research into how parties interact over time. By analysing data covering nearly two decades, Saz-Carranza, Salvador Iborra and Albareda's (2016) comparative longitudinal case study of network administrative organizations (NAOs) depicts at length how the power dynamics of power bargaining affects NAOs' development in mandated networks. In a nutshell, what could be drawn from this evidence includes not only the indispensability of incorporating process tracing to make strong causal inferences (Goertz and Mahoney 2012: 103), but also the particular strength of the case study method in elucidating the cause-effect mechanisms which contain complex interactions between relevant factors.

Challenges in execution and generalization

Despite its obvious strengths as discussed in the previous section, the case study method also faces major challenges in terms of execution and generalization. The first challenge relates to the issues that occur when case study research is executed. Scholars must cope with all kinds of questions during the process, because 'goals are often difficult to measure, good data are difficult to obtain, side effects will probably occur but are difficult to trace' (Bogason and Zølner 2007: 6). This is further accompanied by the trouble in achieving controlled observations and deduction when collecting data and analysing cases (McNabb 2010: 43). In researching networks and collaborations unexpected variables can also come forth and interfere in the validity of causal inference. For instance, in drawing conclusions from three cases suggesting that wicked problems in environmental debate can be handled by enhancing and intensifying interactions between network actors, actor positions and institutional constraints are still hard to illustrate (Van Bueren, Klijn and Koppenjan 2003).

A second main challenge – and an evergreen for critics of the case study method – is the extent of generalizability that case study research can convey. While some might argue this to be an epistemological debate[4] – that is, is the case study method discussed from an interpretive or realist perspective? – it is clear that the often unique character of cases makes it virtually impossible for another researcher to replicate exactly the same study. The choice of exceptional cases based on replication logic also precludes a control group to contrast findings (Saz-Carranza and Ospina 2011). Consequently, especially for single case studies, the findings are unlikely to be extended to other networks and settings, despite how similar they are in scope or feature (McNabb 2010: 45). This may partially explain why some scholars regard the case study as 'an ambiguous designation covering a multitude of "inferential felonies"' (Gerring 2006: 6).

While we acknowledge the limitations of case study research, in terms of the objective of generalization, case studies should be treated as being generalizable to theoretical propositions rather than other cases (Lee 2010). In analytic generalization – as opposed to statistical generalization – lies the virtue of the case study (Yin 2014: 48). So, instead of providing statistical generalization based on structure and factor analysis, the case study is regarded as a better way to illustrate, understand and explain the processes and dynamics in networks and collaborative arrangements.

Dealing with challenges: methodological rigour and moving from single to multiple case study designs

As the execution of case study research is indeed a difficult task, more methodological rigour can strengthen your research. Being very transparent as a network researcher about the execution challenges faced and how they were solved helps to ensure the quality of the case study; that is, discussing the case selection criteria, delineating the cases exactly (e.g. which issues or actors were included or excluded and why), showing what questions interviewees were asked (e.g. the topic list), using a clear coding scheme (manually or supported by coding software like NVivo) and discussing the coding process and coding decisions in more detail, and so on, help to ensure that the findings can be put in the right perspective.

Next to more methodological rigour, scholars often call for more empirical research to further test the conclusive arguments or explorative models in different network patterns, policy areas, governance and political contexts (Ferlie and McGivern 2014; Hendriks 2008; Schout and Jordan 2005; Zheng, De Jong and Koppenjan 2010). Network researchers reporting case studies therefore often call for the use of other methods as well, such as those discussed in other chapters in this book. Improving the case study research design can also work. A multiple-case design with a comparative analysis based on two or more conflicting cases could offer more robust conclusions drawn from more than one context. The idea of more multiple, rather than single, case studies in network research and more mixed-methods strategies is not only promoted by network scholars (see Pedersen 2010; Saz-Carranza and Ospina 2011), but is also apparent in the PA network research published over the years.

As Figure 3.1 demonstrates, early network studies were typically single case studies (Milward and Provan 1998). But, over the years, network scholars have increasingly used comparative multiple-case designs (Saz-Carranza, Salvador

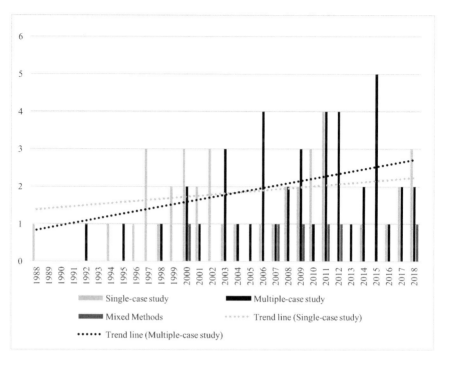

Figure 3.1 Evolution of major types of case studies in network and collaboration research

Iborra and Albareda 2016). Figure 3.1 depicts the evolutionary trend from 1988 to 2018 of the two major types of case studies in the eighty-two network studies we reviewed: thirty-nine single case studies and forty-three multiple case studies in total. The number of both types of studies published annually is demonstrated in the graph. The general trend of single case studies and multiple case studies is also shown, based on the linear trend analysis done in Microsoft Excel 2013. As the trend lines illustrate, the single case studies were relatively more dominant before 2004. However, the balance shifted mildly afterwards, showing that multiple case studies have become increasingly popular in recent years. Nevertheless, both types of case studies remain present in the literature to date. Within the eighty-two studies, six studies were conducted with a mixed-methods design, combining different methods 'to share the same research questions, to collect complementary data, and to conduct counterpart analyses' (Yin 2014: 97).[5] Four out of six were published in the last decade. In the case studying the processes of policy network formation (Toke 2000), for instance, discourse analysis was deployed to effectively explore the construction of cognitive structures, which was indispensable for completing the processes. In their study on predicting organizational behaviour in donor networks, AbouAssi and Tschirhart (2018) also combined case studies with a larger survey about the basic information on organizations' age, budget, staffing and programming, and integrated it to understand the organizational response to changing demands.

We might hypothesize that this (albeit modest) shift might be in part due to the overall increase in methodological maturity of the PA field in general, and in the network and collaboration field in particular. Another potential explanation might be that collaboration and network research is also maturing in terms of theory building. The accumulation of insights on network formation, network management and so on, might stimulate new research questions, with more theory testing and/or more complex case study research designs. At the same time, it is clear that: (1) case studies in general remain relevant in network and collaboration research and (2) single case studies are still part of the mix as well. For instance, with the single-case design, some researchers aim to interpret the fundamental elements in policy networks, such as what is the structural context and its relationship with network management and failure (Common and Acevedo 2006; Davis, West and Yardley 2011). Others explore some emergent network issues with a single case, including how to govern and manage cross-boundary collaborative networks with the use of information and communication technology (Chen and Lee 2018), as well as the institutional change within hierarchies, markets, networks and communities (Tenbensel 2018). On the other hand, multiple case studies in this field mostly provide further explanation and elaboration about the process and complexity of network governance. For instance, by examining mental health systems in several cities, Milward and Provan (2003) added both a time dimension and a qualitative richness to their earlier work on network management in the hollow state. With three network cases in Belgium, the US and Australia, Mandell and Keast (2008) also underlined the importance of different evaluation processes and tools in understanding the complexity of networked arrangements. The QCA chapter in this book (Chapter 10) shows how this idea of more comparative case study designs is put into practice in contemporary network research.

Insights from case studies on networks and collaborative arrangements: informal, dynamic and temporal dimensions explored

As this is a book on methodology, trying to capture all theoretical insights in the eighty-two studies falls outside the scope of this chapter. However, as Table 3.2 demonstrates, three major analytical dimensions of networks are explicitly explored thanks to the strength of the case study method. Firstly, observing the considerable presence of interactions operated beyond the formal structure and activities, more research has been investigating the informal dimension of networks (Isett et al. 2011). This has been identified as an emergent, but important, dimension for information sharing, capacity building, problem solving and service delivery (Provan and Kenis 2001). With a case study on incident command systems, network properties of crisis response have been proven to fundamentally affect the importance of trust in supplementing formal modes of control (Moynihan 2009).

Table 3.2 Three dimensions of insight from reviewed case studies

Dimensions	Findings
Informal	• Importance of trust in developing policy communities (Hindmoor 1998), supplementing formal modes of control (Moynihan 2009), building partnership input (Nolte and Boenigk 2011)
	• Informal accountability among individuals in networks of non-profit service providers (Romzek, LeRoux and Blackmar 2012)
	• Informal mechanisms that facilitate collaboration and service delivery (Romzek et al. 2014)
Dynamic	• Critical factors influencing the transformation of policy networks (Gains 2004; Nunan 1999)
	• The role 'policy image' and 'cleavage in the party system' played in network change (Pedersen 2010)
	• The dialectical approach explaining the processes of network transformation (Toke and Marsh 2003)
Temporal	• Long time span of the case helps to look at the issue of policy change and evolution, with different combinations of networks and agents interacting at different phases (Greenaway, Salter and Hart 2007)
	• Longer time frames are promising to evaluate the correlation between the perception of network structures and style of policy design (Keast et al. 2004)
	• The inception and development of a policy-mandated network are far from conflict free (Saz-Carranza, Alvador Iborra and Albareda 2016)

Also highlighting the importance of trust, other scholars claim that trust can not only help to develop policy communities (Hindmoor 1998), but is one of the most important partnership inputs in a disaster context (Nolte and Boenigk 2011). Furthermore, informal accountability and its relevant mechanisms have been studied using multiple cases to show the specific capacity in facilitating collaboration, joint production, coordination and integration of service delivery (Romzek, LeRoux and Blackmar 2012; Romzek et al. 2014).

A second insight from case studies concerns network dynamics. Rather than taking networks as stable entities and passive actors, case study researchers focus more on the dynamic dimension by tracing different processes where networks operate. This is supported by the studies on network change. Applying a dynamic approach to the analysis of policy-making processes, Nunan (1999) illustrated the reasons influencing the transformation of policy networks, including the power relations and conflicts between network actors, the role of government and the tight schedule exerted. From the perspective of both hardware and software issues, Gains (2004) claims the strategic selection and perceptions of network participants are powerful drivers of network change. Other explanations come from concepts such as 'policy image' and 'cleavage in the party system', with a comparative analysis based on two detailed case studies in Denmark (Pedersen 2010).

Finally, the relevance of the temporal dimension of networks shows clearly in some longitudinal studies (Currie, Grubnic and Hodges 2011). This argument also relates to the multi-party character of networks and collaborative arrangements, leading to increasingly complicated interactions between actors with diverse interest demands. For instance, to explore how power bargaining affects network development, a study on two regulatory networks in the European Union analysed longitudinally the evolution of governance forms of mandated networks (Saz-Carranza, Slavador Iborra and Albareda 2016), finding it to be a bargaining process involving network members' struggles and conflicts with NAOs. Also, a longer time frame and span can not only help analyse the issue of policy change and evolution involving interactions at different phases (Greenaway, Salter and Hart 2007), but can help investigate how policy-makers' understanding of network structures affects the style of policy design (Keast et al. 2004).

Conclusion: outlook of applying the case study

By discussing the common features, research design, data collection and related conditions of the case study in general, and its application in researching networks and collaborative arrangements in the public sector in particular, this chapter shows the strengths and potential limitations of the case study method, as well as some of the key insights drawn from relevant case studies. The case study method is clearly appropriate for the range of 'how', 'why' and 'what' questions that many network scholars dealt with yesterday, deal with today and are likely to deal with tomorrow. The case study method not only allows us to test theories by explaining, for instance, the process and complexity of networks and collaboration but also allows us to explore the emerging propositions regarding the informal, dynamic and temporal dimensions within.

However, despite such strengths, we need to deal with the challenges that case study designs face. Two main challenges are dealing with the critique that case study research lacks systematic procedures and that it cannot deliver unequivocal evidence that is generalizable. Yin (2014: 47) argues that four typical tests for social science methods in general (construct validity, internal validity, external validity and reliability) should also be addressed by case studies. Data triangulation using multiple sources of evidence, including semi-structured interviews with key network players, archival documents and reports, and even quantitative data derived from questionnaires, for instance, can improve construct validity (Keast et al. 2004; Poocharoen and Ting 2015; Van Bueren, Klijn and Koppenjan 2003). Triangulation of results and arranging meetings to discuss rival explanations with colleagues and interviewees can also help to increase internal validity of the results (Beach et al. 2012; Cristofoli, Macciò and Pedrazzi 2015). Reliability can be boosted by building and maintaining a database of the inquired cases, and carefully describing all steps and decisions taken in a case study protocol (Yin 2014: 45). In an era where research data management and data management plans are becoming increasingly important because of research ethics and methodological rigour, a proper case study database of the networks or network issues studied is simply a prerequisite (and a grant requirement). External validity can be improved by using replication logic in multiple case studies (Saz-Carranza, Salvador Iborra and Albareda 2016). When conducting qualitative research, such as a case study, a researcher often develops a finding for one or a small number of cases and it is natural to ask if the findings apply more generally (Goertz and Mahoney 2012: 96–97). As evidenced in previous sections of this chapter, case studies can depict an in-depth and processual image about the formation, functioning and development of network governance, meta-governance, democratic implications and effectiveness of networks (Lewis 2011). But we need to develop this further and ensure external validity to the extent possible. One path is for researchers who are linking the limitation of generalizing to a certain context or policy trait to locate the uniqueness in a system compared with other counterparts. Another path is based on the idea of analytical generalization discussed earlier, namely that small-*n* findings might stimulate a broader cross-case testing using a larger *n* (Lijphart 1971; see Chapter 10 in this volume on QCA as one promising way to move forward). A third path is to structurally engage in more mixed-methods research, linking the case study method with other methods. A limited number of network studies can provide inspiration, see for instance the combination with ethnographic analysis (Choi 2007), qualitative categorical analysis (Robins, Bates and Pattison 2011) and discourse analysis (Toke 2000). Some might even argue there is no alternative, as the combination between the case study method and other research methods can function as a better way to 'capture the multifaceted patterns of network interaction, which are mostly impossible to capture by using a single methodological tool' (Bogason and Zølner 2007: 20).

To conclude, we are convinced that the case study method is a foundational method that has been key to developing much of the contemporary knowledge on networks and collaborative arrangements. While the method – like every method – has its limitations, many current methodological developments either build and expand the case study method (e.g. QCA – see Chapter 10 in this volume), or allow the case study method to draw on a wider range of tools than 'old-school' interviewing, direct observations and document analysis (e.g. process tracing – see Chapter 8 in this volume). For many years to come, the case study as a method will remain a pillar for collaboration and network research but will be accompanied by and increasingly mixed with other methods in an ever-expanding catalogue.

Notes

1 To clarify the basic concepts in this chapter, the term 'case study' and 'case study method' are used to describe the research method. Accordingly, 'case studies', 'case research' and 'case study research' refer to the research conducted with the case study method.
2 They are partly demonstrated in the references and marked with an asterisk in particular.
3 The case is the unit of analysis, but defining and bounding the case (and thus the unit of analysis) is a difficult, two-fold challenge that case study researchers face (Yin 2014: 31). In network and collaboration research this challenge includes, for instance, the question of delineating the network. If the unit of analysis is a network, should the analysis then be limited to the formal members of the network, or are influential actors 'outside' the formal network but part of the actual, informal network, to be included? In a study on network management, the unit of analysis might be the formal network manager and their behaviour, competences and skills, but the unit of analysis might also be the relations between network members and

how each network member tries to influence them. See Chapter 2 in Yin's seminal book *Case Study Research: Design and Methods* (2014) for how to deal with this challenge.
4 See Yin 2014, McNabb 2010 or Gerring 2006 for more reflections about different perspectives in case study research.
5 In Figure 3.1, it might appear that 'mixed methods' are separate studies next to the single and multiple case studies. But this is not the case: 'mixed methods' in the graph are only a marker to demonstrate how many of the total single and multiple case studies published in a given year are also mixed method.

Further reading

To gain a comprehensive and detailed understanding of the evolution and content of the case study, please refer to the following monographs:

- Blatter, J. and M. Haverland. 2012. *Designing case studies: Explanatory approaches in small-n research.* Basingstoke: Palgrave Macmillan.
- George, A.L. and A. Bennett. 2005. *Case studies and theory development in the social sciences.* Cambridge: MIT Press.
- Gerring, J. 2006. *Case study research: Principles and practices.* Cambridge: Cambridge University Press.
- Goertz, G. and J. Mahoney. 2012. *A tale of two cultures: Qualitative and quantitative research in the social sciences.* Princeton: Princeton University Press.
- McNabb, D.E. 2010. *Case research in public management.* New York: M.E. Sharpe.
- Yin, R.K. 2014. *Case study research: Design and methods.* Thousand Oaks: Sage Publications.
- Woodside, A.G. 2010. *Case study research: Theory, methods and practice.* Bingley: Emerald Group Publishing.

To obtain a systematic and structured body of knowledge about how the case study method contributes to network research, please refer to the following studies:

- Bogason, P. and M. Zølner. 2007. *Methods in democratic network governance.* Basingstoke: Palgrave Macmillan.
- Keast, R., M. Mandell, and R. Agranoff. 2014. *Network theory in the public sector: Building new theoretical frameworks.* New York: Routledge.
- Klijn, E.H. and J. Koppenjan. 2016a. *Governance networks in the public sector.* New York: Routledge.

References

References marked with an asterisk were part of our review

AbouAssi, K. and M. Tschirhart. 2018. "Organizational response to changing demands: Predicting behavior in donor networks." *Public Administration Review* 78 (1): 126–136.★
Agranoff, R. and M. McGuire. 2001. "Big questions in public network management research." *Journal of Public Administration Research and Theory* 11 (3): 295–326.

Ansell, C. and A. Gash. 2008. "Collaborative governance in theory and practice." *Journal of Public Administration Research and Theory* 18 (4): 543–571.

Beach, S., R. Keast, and D. Pickernell. 2012. "Unpacking the connections between network and stakeholder management and their application to road infrastructure networks in Queensland." *Public Management Review* 14 (5): 609–629.★

Blatter, J. and M. Haverland. 2012. *Designing case studies: Explanatory approaches in small-N research.* Basingstoke: Palgrave Macmillan.

Bogason, P. and M. Zølner. 2007. *Methods in democratic network governance.* Basingstoke: Palgrave Macmillan.

Chen, Y.C. and J. Lee. 2018. "Collaborative data networks for public service: Governance, management, and performance." *Public Management Review* 20 (5): 672–690.★

Choi, J.W. 2007. "Governance structure and administrative corruption in Japan: An organizational network approach." *Public Administration Review* 67 (5): 930–942.★

Common, R. and B. Acevedo. 2006. "Governance and the management of networks in the public sector: Drugs policy in the United Kingdom and the case of cannabis reclassification." *Public Management Review* 8 (3): 395–414.★

Cristofoli, D., L. Macciò, and L. Pedrazzi. 2015. "Structure, mechanisms, and managers in successful networks." *Public Management Review* 17 (4): 489–516.★

Currie, G., S. Grubnic, and R. Hodges. 2011. "Leadership in public services networks: Antecedents, process and outcome." *Public Administration* 89 (2): 242–264.★

Davis, P., K. West, and L. Yardley. 2011. "Networks in open systems of governance: The case of an English local older persons' care system." *Public Management Review* 13 (5): 683–705.★

De Rynck, F. and J. Voets. 2006. "Democracy in area-based policy networks: The case of Ghent." *American Review of Public Administration* 36 (1): 58–78.

Ferlie, E. and G. McGivern. 2014. "Bringing Anglo-governmentality into public management scholarship: The case of evidence-based medicine in UK health care." *Journal of Public Administration Research and Theory* 24 (1): 59–83.★

Gains, F. 2004. "'Hardware, software or network connection?' Theorizing crisis in the UK Next Steps agencies?" *Public Administration* 82 (3): 547–566.★

George, A.L. and A. Bennett. 2005. *Case studies and theory development in the social sciences.* Cambridge: MIT Press.

Gerring, J. 2006. *Case study research: Principles and practices.* Cambridge: Cambridge University Press.

Giest, S. 2015. "Network capacity-building in high-tech sectors: Opening the black box of cluster facilitation policy." *Public Administration* 93 (2): 471–489.★

Goertz, G. and J. Mahoney. 2012. *A tale of two cultures: Qualitative and quantitative research in the social sciences.* Princeton: Princeton University Press.

Granovetter, M. 1973. "The strength of weak ties." *American Journal of Sociology* 78 (6): 1360–1380.

Granovetter, M. 1983. "The strength of weak ties: A network theory revisited." *Sociological Theory* 1 (1): 201–233.

Greenaway, J., B. Salter, and S. Hart. 2007. "How policy networks can damage democratic health: A case study in the government of governance." *Public Administration* 85 (3): 717–738.★

Hendriks, C.M. 2008. "On inclusion and network governance: The democratic disconnect of Dutch energy transitions." *Public Administration* 86 (4): 1009–1031.★

Heclo, H.H. 1972. "Review article: Policy analysis." *British Journal of Political Science* 2 (1): 83–108.

Hindmoor, A. 1998. "The importance of being trusted: Transaction costs and policy network theory." *Public Administration* 76 (1): 25–43.★

Hu, Q., S. Khosa, and N. Kapucu. 2016. "The intellectual structure of empirical network research in public administration." *Journal of Public Administration Research & Theory* 26 (4): 593–612.

Isett, K.R., I.A. Mergel, K. LeRoux, P.A. Mischen, and R.K. Rethemeyer. 2011. "Networks in public administration scholarship: Understanding where we are and where we need to go." *Journal of Public Administration Research and Theory* 21 (suppl. 1): i157–i173.

Kapucu, N., Q. Hu, and S. Khosa. 2017. "The state of network research in public administration." *Administration & Society* 49 (8): 1087–1120.

Keast, R. 2016. "Network governance." In *Handbook on theories of governance*, edited by C. Ansell and J. Torfing, 442–454. Cheltenham: Edward Elgar Publishing.

Keast, R., M.P. Mandell, K. Brown, and G. Woolcock. 2004. "Network structures: Working differently and changing expectations." *Public Administration Review* 64 (3): 363–371.★

Keast, R., M. Mandell, and R. Agranoff. 2014. *Network theory in the public sector: Building new theoretical frameworks.* New York: Routledge.

Klijn, E.H. and J. Koppenjan. 2016a. *Governance networks in the public sector.* New York: Routledge.

Klijn, E.H. and J. Koppenjan. 2016b. "The shift toward network governance: Drivers, characteristics and manifestations." In *Theory and practice of public sector reform*, edited by S. Van de Walle and S. Groeneveld, 158–177. London: Routledge.

Lauchs, M., R. Keast, and N. Yousefpour. 2011. "Corrupt police networks: Uncovering hidden relationship patterns, functions and roles." *Policing & Society* 21 (1): 110–127.

Lecy, J.D., I.A. Mergel, and H.P. Schmitz. 2014. "Networks in public administration: Current scholarship in review." *Public Management Review* 16 (5): 643–665.

Lee, E. 2010. "Information, interest intermediaries, and regulatory compliance." *Journal of Public Administration Research and Theory* 21 (1): 137–157.★

Lewis, J.M. 2011. "The future of network governance research: Strength in diversity and synthesis." *Public Administration* 89 (4): 1221–1234.

Lijphart, A. 1971. "Comparative politics and the comparative method." *American Political Science Review* 65 (3): 682–693.

Mandell, M.P. and R. Keast. 2008. "Evaluating the effectiveness of interorganizational relations through networks: Developing a framework for revised performance measures." *Public Management Review* 10 (6): 715–731.★

Marsh, D., D. Toke, C. Belfrage, D. Tepe, and S. McGough. 2009. "Policy networks and the distinction between insider and outsider groups: The case of the countryside alliance." *Public Administration* 87 (3): 621–638.★

Martin, G.P., G. Currie, and R. Finn. 2008. "Leadership, service reform, and public-service networks: The case of cancer-genetics pilots in the English NHS." *Journal of Public Administration Research and Theory* 19 (4): 769–794.★

McNabb, D.E. 2010. *Case research in public management.* New York: M.E. Sharpe.

Milward, H.B. and K.G. Provan. 1998. "Measuring network structure." *Public Administration* 76 (2): 387–407.

Milward, H.B. and K. Provan. 2003. "Managing the hollow state collaboration and contracting." *Public Management Review* 5 (1): 1–18.★

Moynihan, D.P. 2009. "The network governance of crisis response: Case studies of incident command systems." *Journal of Public Administration Research and Theory* 19 (4): 895–915.★

Nolte, I.M. and S. Boenigk. 2011. "Public: Nonprofit partnership performance in a disaster context: The case of Haiti." *Public Administration* 89 (4): 1385–1402.★

Nunan, F. 1999. "Policy network transformation: The implementation of the EC directive on packaging and packaging waste." *Public Administration* 77 (3): 621–638.★

Olson, M. 1971. *The logic of collective action: Public goods and the theory of groups.* Cambridge: Harvard University Press.

Ostrom, E. 1990. *Governing the commons: The evolution of institutions for collective action.* Cambridge: Cambridge University Press.

O'Toole, L.J. 1996. "Hollowing the infrastructure: Revolving loan programs and network dynamics in the American states." *Journal of Public Administration Research and Theory* 6 (2): 225–242.★

O'Toole, L.J. 1997. "Treating networks seriously: Practical and research-based agendas in public administration." *Public Administration Review* 57 (1): 45–52.

Pedersen, A.B. 2010. "The fight over Danish nature: Explaining policy network change and policy change." *Public Administration* 88 (2): 346–363.★

Poocharoen, O.O. and B. Ting. 2015. "Collaboration, co-production, networks: Convergence of theories." *Public Management Review* 17 (4): 587–614.★

Powell, W.W. 1990. "Neither market nor hierarchy: Network forms of organization." *Research in Organizational Behavior* 12: 295–336.

Powell, W.W., K.W. Koput, and L. Smith-Doerr. 1996. "Interorganizational collaboration and the locus of innovation: Networks of learning in biotechnology." *Administrative Science Quarterly* 41 (1): 116–145.

Provan, K.G. and P. Kenis. 2001. "Do networks really work? A framework for evaluating public sector organizational networks." *Public Administration Review* 61 (4): 414–423.

Provan, K.G. and P. Kenis. 2008. "Modes of network governance: Structure, management, and effectiveness." *Journal of Public Administration Research and Theory* 18 (2): 229–252.

Provan, K.G. and H.B. Milward. 1995. "A preliminary theory of interorganizational network effectiveness: A comparative study of four community mental health systems." *Administrative Science Quarterly* 40: 1–33.

Provan, K.G. and J.G. Sebastian. 1998. "Networks within networks: Service link overlap, organizational cliques, and network effectiveness." *The Academy of Management Journal* 41 (4): 453–463.

Qvist, M. 2017. "Meta-governance and network formation in collaborative spaces of uncertainty: The case of Swedish refugee integration policy." *Public Administration* 95 (2): 498–511.★

Raab, J. and H.B. Milward. 2003. "Dark networks as problems." *Journal of Public Administration Research and Theory* 13 (4): 413–439.★

Robins, G., L. Bates, and P. Pattison. 2011. "Network governance and environmental management: Conflict and cooperation." *Public Administration* 89 (4): 1293–1313.★

Romzek, B.S., K. LeRoux, and J.M. Blackmar. 2012. "A preliminary theory of informal accountability among network organizational actors." *Public Administration Review* 72 (3): 442–453.★

Romzek, B., K. LeRoux, J. Johnston, R.J. Kempf, and J.S. Piatak. 2014. "Informal accountability in multisector service delivery collaborations." *Journal of Public Administration Research and Theory* 24 (4): 813–842.★

Saz-Carranza, A. and S.M. Ospina. 2011. "The behavioral dimension of governing interorganizational goal-directed networks: Managing the unity: Diversity tension." *Journal of Public Administration Research and Theory* 21 (2): 327–365.★

Saz-Carranza, A., S. Salvador Iborra, and A. Albareda. 2016. "The power dynamics of mandated network administrative organizations." *Public Administration Review* 76 (3): 449–462.★

Schout, A. and A. Jordan. 2005. "Coordinated European governance: Self-organizing or centrally steered?" *Public Administration* 83 (1): 201–220.★

Skelcher, C. and J. Torfing. 2010. "Improving democratic governance through institutional design: Civic participation and democratic ownership in Europe." *Regulation & Governance* 4 (1): 71–91.

Sørensen, E. and J. Torfing. 2009. "Making governance networks effective and democratic through metagovernance." *Public Administration* 87 (2): 234–258.

Teisman, G.R. and E.H. Klijn. 2002. "Partnership arrangements: Governmental rhetoric or governance scheme?" *Public Administration Review* 62 (2): 197–205.★

Tenbensel, T. 2018. "Bridging complexity theory and hierarchies, markets, networks, communities: A 'population genetics' framework for understanding institutional change from within." *Public Management Review* 20 (7): 1032–1051.★

Thomas, C.W. 1997. "Public management as interagency cooperation: Testing epistemic community theory at the domestic level." *Journal of Public Administration Research and Theory* 7 (2): 221–246.★

Thomson, A.M. and J.L. Perry. 2006. "Collaboration processes: Inside the black box." *Public Administration Review* 66 (s1): 20–32.

Toke, D. 2000. "Policy network creation: The case of energy efficiency." *Public Administration* 78 (4): 835–854.★

Toke, D. and D. Marsh. 2003. "Policy networks and the GM crops issue: Assessing the utility of a dialectical model of policy networks." *Public Administration* 81 (2): 229–251.★

Tomlinson, I.J. 2010. "Acting discursively: The development of UK organic food and farming policy networks." *Public Administration* 88 (4): 1045–1062.★

Van Bueren, E.M., E.H. Klijn, and J.F. Koppenjan. 2003. "Dealing with wicked problems in networks: Analyzing an environmental debate from a network perspective." *Journal of Public Administration Research and Theory* 13 (2): 193–212.★

Voets, J. 2014. "Developing network management theory through management channels and roles." In *Network theory in the public sector: Building new theoretical frameworks*, edited by R. Keast, M.P. Mandell, and R. Agranoff, 118–136. New York: Routledge.

White, H.C., S.A. Boorman, and R.L. Breiger. 1976. "Social structure from multiple networks. I. Blockmodels of roles and positions." *American Journal of Sociology* 81 (4): 730–780.

Woodside, A.G. 2010. *Case study research: Theory, methods and practice*. Bingley: Emerald Group Publishing.

Yin, R.K. 2014. *Case study research: Design and methods*, 5th ed. Thousand Oaks: Sage Publications.

Zheng, H., M. De Jong, and J. Koppenjan. 2010. "Applying policy network theory to policy-making in China: The case of urban health insurance reform." *Public Administration* 88 (2): 398–417.★

4 Survey approach

Ingmar van Meerkerk, Jurian Edelenbos
and Erik-Hans Klijn

Introduction

In this chapter we reflect on the use of surveys as a method to study public sector or governance networks.[1] Surveys are a traditional method of data collection in social science research and can be used for different purposes. Although surveys can be used as a form of data collection in qualitative (comparative) analysis (e.g. in QCA), surveys are most often used in quantitative analysis, which is the focus in this chapter.

The survey approach has become quite popular among network scholars in the field of public administration in the last decade. This contrasts with the period before 2000 where there was limited attention to quantitative survey research on networks.[2] According to a recent review on quantitative methods used in the field of public administration (PA), quantitative methods are increasingly used in the study of governance networks (Groeneveld et al. 2015). Groeneveld et al.'s (2015) sample included 155 articles on governance networks published between 2001 and 2010, and almost half of this set used quantitative methods (45%). More specifically, since 2007 there has been a significant rise in the use of quantitative methods in this field of research. Of these quantitative-oriented articles, most use surveys as the primary source of data collection (Groeneveld et al. 2015: 75).

To narrow the scope and to make this chapter distinctive from the chapter on social network analysis (SNA) elsewhere in this book, we focus on surveys as the *primary* source for studying (relationships between) variables of interest. Variables of interest are directly measured with the survey questionnaire and analysed with (different forms of) statistical methods. We excluded SNA where surveys are also often used as a form of data collection, but where the analysis is focused on the structure of the network using network and graph techniques.

Approach

The objectives of this chapter are threefold. The first objective is to build understanding of the reasons why surveys are used in governance network studies. The second objective is to provide insights into key outcomes and focus points relative to the use of survey research to study governance networks. The third and final objective is to provide an overview regarding the pros and cons of survey research: what are its limitations, potentials and dilemmas in studying governance networks? To meet these objectives we conducted a limited, but systematic, review among quantitative governance network articles using surveys as the main source of data collection and the network as the main unit of analysis. We searched in the database Scopus for articles including the term 'survey' in the title, abstract or keyword within the field of governance networks. Next, we searched specifically in the *Journal of Public Administration Research and Theory* (JPART), as this is one of the top journals in PA and the leading journal when it comes to publishing quantitative articles on governance networks (Groeneveld et al. 2015).[3] In addition, we added a few articles mentioned by experts that were not yet in our set. As some authors are overrepresented through this search strategy, we limited the number of articles coming from the same (first) author to two.[4] This resulted in a selection of 22 articles, which we coded on several topics: focus of research, main variables of interest, design (unit of analysis and unit of observation), type of network studied, technique(s) used for analysis, limitations and strengths of study (mentioned by authors themselves and observed by reviewers).[5] Next to this review, we build on our own experience in using the survey approach on governance networks.

The structure of this chapter is as follows. We will first go deeper into the relevance of the survey approach: when is it useful to use quantitative survey methods to study governance networks? The second part goes deeper into the application and results of survey research on governance networks so far. We will answer the question: 'What kind of relationships are studied with this approach and what are the results?' In this part, we also reflect on our observations concerning the strengths and limitations of the survey approach. We will discuss several dilemmas in the design of survey research on governance networks. Lastly, we reflect on the future of the method: what are the next steps in the application of survey research for the study of governance networks?

Why use quantitative survey research to study governance networks?

The choice of a certain research method in general (and ideally) depends on the research problem at hand and the philosophical positions of researchers (Robson 2002; Haverland and Yanow 2012). Although there are certainly several examples to the contrary, a simple and general distinction is that quantitative methods are more often used for testing theory, while qualitative methods are used for developing theory. In that sense, the increasing use of quantitative methods in the field of governance network studies (since 2007) points at *the evolution of this research field* in which concepts and theories have been developed either by theoretical arguments and/or by case study research, and the field is in its 'next empirical stage' of testing and refining these theories. This shift is also pointed out by several overview articles on governance networks that have emerged in the last decade (see Isett et al. 2011; Klijn 2008). Network theory in PA commenced in the 1970s with the famous work of Scharpf et al. (see Scharpf 1978; Hanf and Scharpf 1978). However, it was only in the late 1990s and the first years of the 2000s that PA research on networks really got a boost (cf. Sørensen and Torfing 2007). In this first period, research mainly aimed at theory building and case study research. This resulted in a body of knowledge where theoretical assumptions and hypotheses were generated about several aspects of governance networks. Examples are the importance of network management strategies for achieving outcomes (Kickert et al. 1997; Agranoff and McGuire 1998), but also hypotheses about trust (Edelenbos and Klijn 2007), collaborative management (Ansell and Gash 2008), resource centralization (Provan and Milward 2001) and coordination form (Provan and Kenis 2008). Testing these assumptions with large data sets mostly occurred after 2005.

This is also reflected in our set of reviewed articles. Six (27%) of the twenty-two articles are from before 2005, and only two (9%) from before the year 2000. Hence, seventy-two per cent of the studies in our review were produced in the last twelve years, underlining the evolution in this field of research. Quantitative survey research is now increasingly used to test hypotheses derived from earlier theory development within the field (for example the work of Klijn, Steijn and Edelenbos (2010) on testing the impact of different network management strategies), but also to refine theories (e.g. Juenke's work on extending the model of Meier and O'Toole, see section 'Advantages of and arguments for using survey research') or to extend theories by making new connections with other bodies of literature (e.g. Van Meerkerk and Edelenbos (2017) on boundary spanning and servant leadership). A general and somewhat remarkable observation is that specific argumentation for why they used a survey as a specific method of data collection to study governance networks is not provided in the articles we reviewed.

Advantages of and arguments for using survey research

The big advantage of using a survey is that it provides a high level of general capability in representing a large population (e.g. Kelley et al. 2003). This makes it especially suitable for testing assumed relationships between theoretical concepts. Moreover, the increasing availability (and more easy use) of advanced statistical software makes it possible to test not only single relationships but more integral theoretical models. Structural equation modelling (SEM) is, for instance, an appropriate technique for testing more complex models (Nachtigall et al. 2003) and therefore is now also used in the study of governance networks; see for example, Korthagen and Klijn (2014) on the role of media logic and its effect on trust and performance of governance networks, and Van Meerkerk and Edelenbos (2017) on antecedents (executive support and facilitative management) of boundary-spanning behaviour and their (indirect and direct) effects on trust and performance. In the section on analysing techniques we go deeper into this topic.

Next, the unit of analysis is an important criterion for making a good choice concerning the research method. Quantitative survey research can be applied relatively easily for studying the attitudes and behaviour of individuals (Groeneveld et al. 2015). In this respect, it is not surprising that there is now considerable research on the use of specific network management activities and styles and their impact on collaboration in, and performance of, governance networks (e.g. Kelman et al. 2013; Klijn, Steijn and Edelenbos 2010; Meier and O'Toole 2001; Van Meerkerk, Edelenbos and Klijn 2015).

The survey approach becomes a bit more challenging when the network as a whole is the unit of analysis, though this is often an important aim of governance network scholars: to say something about the performance of the network or the level of trust within the network for example. Some scholars solve this puzzle by using another source of data for measuring the performance of the network, such as the level of (reduced) crime by a local governance network fighting crime (Kelman et al. 2013) or the district pass rate of students for measuring the performance of school districts (Meier and O'Toole 2001). In the section titled 'Measuring outcomes and the issue of common source bias' we further explore the topic of common source bias.

Questionnaires can also be used, assuming that individual perceptions about network performance or the level of trust are plausible indicators (e.g. Klijn, Edelenbos and Steijn 2010). This issue of how to measure variables at the network level remains an important discussion and dilemma within quantitative survey research on governance networks, as we will discuss further in section 'Design: amount of networks and respondents'.

Although qualitative research is well suited for studying multiplex relationships, generating a holistic analysis of governance networks, multilevel analysis can be an important next step for quantitative survey research to deal with different units of analysis. However, design dilemmas remain, as will be discussed later in the chapter.

A specific advantage of quantitative survey research is the systematic nature and use of statistical techniques, offering good opportunities for:

- developing, comparing and validating measurements
- testing theories and refining models.

This is not to say that qualitative research is not systematic. However, with the specific use of common measurement techniques and statistical data analysis, the measurement of certain theoretical constructs is far easier to replicate, interpret and compare. For example, the reliability and validity of questionnaire items for measuring certain constructs (e.g. network management, network performance, trust) can be statistically tested (assuming the theoretical foundation of the construct, the substantive validity, is sound). For example, Klijn, Edelenbos and Steijn (2010) developed a scale consisting of five items to measure 'trust' between actors in governance networks, building on items developed in the business management literature. This scale has been applied in different studies and to different networks and samples, and evaluated by different statistical analysis, thereby validating the measurement scale of this construct (e.g. Van Meerkerk and Edelenbos 2014).

Next, specific theoretical models can be tested and refined (e.g. by sharing data sets and/or using the same survey questionnaire). For example, Meier and O'Toole (2001) have developed a model that allows scholars to test for the impact of managers on a system and its outputs. Juenke (2005) has further developed this model, which includes the role of time, and tested it with the same data. His research looks separately at 'new' and 'established' managers in their respective networks, examining the impact of time in the system, showing that manager maturity and the quality of networking increases the impact of network management on outcomes (i.e. district pass rate), even though higher-quality managers with longer tenure 'work the network less'.

Besides the substantive arguments for using quantitative survey research in analysing governance networks, there are different practical advantages for using a survey. They are a low-cost way of data gathering (Kelley et al. 2003). Most of the effort lies in the careful design and testing of the survey and the analysis. Data gathering itself requires little effort (time and money), as in most cases a mail or online survey is used. This is a big difference compared to qualitative research, which often uses interviews. Another advantage is that the respondents all receive the same standardized questions (stimulus), eliminating the research-er's own biases and influence on the setting.

Disadvantages and pitfalls of survey research

Two general and often mentioned disadvantages of survey research are (e.g. Robson 2002; Kelley et al. 2003):

- lack of detail in the data and therefore also often a lack of case-specific context
- inflexible nature of the data collection instrument.

It is likely that the data gathered for each case (each network) will lack a certain level of detail and depth. Because of the requirement of standardization and limitations concerning the number of questions for receiving a reasonable response, the data gathered by survey research are not detailed. The standardization also has the consequence that there is no room for context-specific answers and adjusting questions specified to the contexts and circumstances in which the respondents work and act (sectors, jurisdictions, etc.). In the case of governance network studies, most studies (see next section) use the strategy of many networks and a very small sample for each network (often one respondent for each network; for example, the public manager, head of school or project manager). This provides little basis for going deeper into context-specific issues.

Surveys are fixed at the outset of the data collection process, and therefore cannot be changed during the data collection phase. This makes it a fixed design in which theoretical assumptions and research questions should be clear from the beginning (before designing and administrating the survey). This can be considered both an advantage and disadvantage of the approach, as it makes the data collection process very transparent and replicable but less flexible.

Surveys are a strong method to find correlations or even causal relations (when *longitudinal designs* or *survey experiments* are used). They are also suited to analyse network ties (and changes in network ties) and the network structure in general (see Lemaire and Raab's Chapter 9 in this volume on SNA). The rigour and large number make surveys suitable to test theoretical hypotheses on certain relations. Survey research is very suited to answer, for instance, the question as to whether the level of network management positively relates to performance (e.g. Meier and O'Toole 2003) or whether the level of trust positively relates to performance and network management strategies (e.g. Klijn, Edelenbos and Steijn 2010). Additional empirical research on how the mechanisms behind these relationships work can further explain these findings (next to theoretical assumptions), for example, by examining when actors learn more or feel less uncertainty in the network, how strategies affect this and/or when the level of trust between network actors is higher. Surveys are less suited to dig deeper into these questions for which qualitative research seems more suitable.

For more extensive discussions of the pros and cons of using a survey as a method of data gathering we refer the reader to general text books on research methods in the social sciences (e.g. Neuman 2002) or other overview articles (e.g. Lee, Benoit-Bryan and Johnson 2012) on survey research in PA. For survey questionnaire design issues, we refer the reader to general text books on survey research methods (e.g. Fowler 2013).

Application of survey research on networks: focus, outcomes and design (issues)

In this section we delve deeper into the results of our review of twenty-two quantitative survey articles on governance networks. Table 4.1 provides an overview of the focus of these studies, concerning the independent and dependent variables examined. It illustrates survey research on governance networks, its main focus and specific references. In this section we go deeper into the relationships central in the studies, how certain outcomes of networks (e.g. performance, collaboration) are studied, design issues (number of networks and respondents) and analysing techniques used.

The research covered by the articles includes many different types of networks. There is research on networks concerning policy- and decision-making in relation to watershed management (e.g. Lubell and Fulton 2008) and environmental projects (e.g. Klijn, Steijn and Edelenbos 2010), public service delivery networks on safety and fighting crime (e.g. Kelman et al. 2013), health care (e.g. Provan and Milward 1991) and education (e.g. Meier and O'Toole 2001).

As noted in the previous section, quantitative survey research is mostly used for testing specific hypotheses derived from theory. This was also the case in the set

Table 4.1 Focus of reviewed survey articles: factors and outcomes

Factors (independent variables)	Outcomes (dependent variables)	Authors
1. *Management and leadership* e.g. network management strategies, boundary-spanning activity	Performance, trust	Juenke (2005); Klijn, Steijn and Edelenbos (2010a); Meier and O'Toole (2001, 2003); O'Toole and Meier (2004); O'Leary, Choi and Gerard (2012); Van Meerkerk and Edelenbos (2014)
2. *Characteristics of network relationships* e.g. trust, collaboration, quality of interaction process	Performance, learning	Kelman et al. (2013); Klijn, Edelenbos and Steijn (2010b); Leach et al. (2013); Nohrstedt (2016); Van Meerkerk, Edelenbos and Klijn (2015); Ulibarri (2015)
3. *Structural characteristics of network, actors or issue* e.g. institutional-level norms, type of policy, location, resources, network size, service comprehensiveness	Network (management) activity, collaborative activity, performance	Agranoff and McGuire (1998); Gerlak and Heikkila (2011); Graddy and Chen (2006); Lubell and Fulton (2008); Percival (2009); Provan and Milward (1991); Shrestha (2013)

of articles we reviewed: all of them tested relationships between variables, mostly on the basis of specific hypotheses. In our review set only two articles didn't test hypotheses, but used the survey for different purposes: Airaksinen, Härkönen and Haveri (2014) for descriptive statistics and comparative group analysis (between countries) and O'Leary, Choi and Gerard (2012) for inductive analysis (using open-ended questionnaires) of managers' collaborative experiences. Table 4.1 presents the factors and outcomes studied in the articles. We have categorized the articles into three sets based on the factors studied, which we will discuss in the next subsection. For each set we illustrate how the survey method is used to examine particular relationships by elaborating specific examples.

Focus of survey research on governance networks

First, there is a set of articles focusing specifically on the impact of managerial behaviour (strategies, activities) on the performance of the network and/or the level of trust within the network. A substantial part of the articles come from the Americans, Meier and O'Toole, and from the Erasmus school on networks (research by Klijn, Edelenbos and Van Meerkerk). Meier and O'Toole (see Meier and O'Toole 2001, 2003) analyse network behaviour of superintendents in school districts. The strength of their approach is that they systematically collected data over several years (the survey is repeated every two years) and that they have more or less objective performance data (pass rate and scores of pupils on a universal test). They measure the number and frequency of contacts superintendents have with several actors in the network and relate these to performance and a wide range of other variables (like tenure of the network manager). Klijn, Steijn and Edelenbos (2010) take a different approach on a more or less similar question (analysing the impact of network management). They identified, based on network theory, a set of activities and asked the respondent to rate these activities for the project they are involved in (present-not present on a five-point scale). Then they analyse the relationship of these activities with the perception of the respondent about the performance of the network (perceived performance). Both approaches have their pros and cons (see also the section in this chapter titled 'Measuring outcomes and the issue of common source bias'). Measuring contact frequency is a more straightforward indicator compared to the approach of Klijn, Steijn and Edelenbos, but, on the other hand, it does not measure what is actually happening in these contacts. Interestingly, both research programs find strong and significant relations between network management and performance (and this is confirmed by other research; e.g. Akkerman and Torenvlied 2013).

Second, there is a set of articles focusing on specific relational characteristics between nodes of the network and their impact on performance or learning. This research focuses on the impact of collaboration (e.g. Kelman, Hong and Turbitt 2013), trust and/or the quality of the democratic governance process (procedural fairness, throughput legitimacy) (e.g. Leach et al. 2013; Van Meerkerk, Edelenbos and Klijn 2015) on the performance of the network or the learning process. For example, the study of Leach et al. (2013) on learning in governance networks focuses on the questions: 'To what extent are new knowledge and insights produced (who learns and what do actors learn?) in multi-actor collaborations?' and 'Under which circumstances do actors learn and how does learning occur?' To answer these questions survey research and semi-structured interviews were conducted. Leach et al. (2013) focused on marine aquaculture partnerships in different states in the United States; ten partnerships are included in their survey study. The number of respondents is 123. A partnership network is considered to comprise local, statewide or regional organizations that include the aquaculture industry, governmental agencies and nongovernmental organizations. An ordinary least squares (OLS) regression analysis is performed to find relationships between independent and dependent variables. The main focus is on characteristics of the relationship as independent variables, namely, partnership traits (e.g. diversity of partners, procedural fairness, scientific certainty and interpersonal trust). Next, individual traits of the learner (duration of participation, scientific and technical competence, consensus norm and demographics) are examined as independent variables. The dependent variable concerns learning, measured by knowledge acquisition (better understanding), and belief change (change in science belief and/or change in policy belief). With regression models Leach et al. (2013) indicate that new knowledge is correlated with traits of the partnership, including procedural fairness, trustworthiness of other participants, level of scientific certainty and diverse participation as well as with traits of the individual learner, including norms of consensus and scientific or technical competence. Contrary to expectations, knowledge acquisition is greater when the available science is uncertain and when stakeholders have lower technical competence.

The findings also challenge the idea that new information mainly reinforces existing beliefs. Instead, Leach et al. (2013) found that new knowledge acquired through the collaborative process primes participants to change their opinions on scientific or policy issues.

A third set of articles focuses on rather structural characteristics of the network (e.g. size, amount of resources, institutional-level norms), characteristics of the actors in the network (resources, experience) or the issue nature (complexity) as factors for affecting the level of network activity or collaboration, and in some cases also performance. For example, Provan and Milward (1991) examined the impact of institutional-level norms on network involvement of implementation networks concerning services for people with mental illness. In contrast to many other studies in our review, they examined one network, surveying multiple participating organizations ($N = 28$). They examined the comprehensiveness of services, the treatment philosophy (community support orientation), service emphasis and intensiveness of agency-client contact as independent variables and network involvement measured by distinct measures of service links and organizational links as the dependent variables. They found that the comprehensiveness of services, the extent to which the treatment philosophy is in line with dominant professional norms regarding involvement, and lesser intensiveness of agency -client contact positively affect network involvement. No relationship was found between service emphasis and network involvement.

After more than a decade of increasing quantitative research in the field of governance networks, knowledge on the effects of certain factors and network characteristics on various network outcomes (performance, legitimacy and learning) has improved considerably. For instance, the impact of the level of trust in the network, collaboration, network management and (competent) boundary spanners are found to be important for realizing good outcomes. Still, many puzzles and questions remain unsolved. For example, more (survey) research can be done to examine (the impact of) antecedents and contextual conditions of collaboration, boundary-spanning behaviour and network management, although some initial findings are emerging in this respect (e.g. Gerlak and Heikkila 2011; Van Meerkerk and Edelenbos 2017). Next, country-comparative survey research might further examine the relationship between governance traditions and culture and governance network characteristics and behaviour. For instance, differences in governance traditions and contextual circumstances might impact the effectiveness of certain management strategies. We will go deeper into further avenues of research in the conclusions of this chapter.

Measuring outcomes and the issue of common source bias

Across many of the studies we examined, some type of network performance was used as dependent variable, especially in the first two sets of articles in Table 4.1. Other outcomes studied are learning, collaborative activity in the network or, more basically, network involvement. These outcomes are measured in different ways, each way having its pros and cons. In general, there are two options here:

- measuring network outcomes by specific items in the survey
- measuring network outcomes by using another source of data other than the survey.

The advantage of the first option is that the researcher controls the measurement in the sense of using theoretically grounded constructs and developing specific items to measure these constructs. Examples include the studies of Klijn, Steijn and Edelenbos (2010) and Lubell and Fulton (2008). The disadvantage of this strategy is *the risk* of common method bias; in this case produced by a common source, therefore referred to as common source bias (CSB). In this case both independent and dependent variables are measured by the same instrument and at the same time (i.e. the same survey). CSB might result in inflated correlations between variables, resulting in biased findings. The issue of CSB and how to avoid it or to deal with this risk receives increasing attention in public management studies (Jakobsen and Jensen 2015; Meier and O'Toole 2013). George and Pandey (2017), reviewing the literature and the debate on common method bias in relation to survey research, argue that the issue of CSB should, however, not be exaggerated. They provide some clear arguments that claims on CSB in PA literature might be exaggerated and about why CSB might have become somewhat of an urban legend within PA. We agree with them that the issue of CSB in relation to surveys requires at least a nuanced and realistic perspective.

Despite this debate, it is clear that the risk of CSB should be reduced as far as possible when using a single survey for measuring both independent and dependent variables. There are several procedures that can help to prevent the issue of CSB, such as reducing item ambiguity by pretesting the survey, protecting respondent anonymity to reduce the risk of socially desirable responses and to avoid similar scale types (Podsakoff, MacKenzie and Podsakoff 2012). Furthermore, there are several statistical techniques that can be used to test for CSB (whether it is present). An often-used technique is the Harman one-factor test (Podsakoff and Mackenzie 2003), in which a factor analysis is conducted on all items which measure the core variables of the study. No single factor should account for most of the explained variance. However, this test is increasingly considered insufficient as it is unlikely that a single factor will fit the data. Moreover, there is no useful guideline as to what would be the acceptable percentage of explained variance of a single-factor model (Chang, Witteloostuijn and Eden 2010; Jakobsen and Jensen 2015). In addition, it is recommendable to use a so-called marker variable: correlating a variable that is theoretically unrelated to the variables of interest and for which its expected correlation with these substantive variables is zero (Lindell and Whitney 2001). For more extensive discussions on the pros and cons of procedures and techniques to avoid or to test for CSB, we refer the reader to Podsakoff, MacKenzie and Podsakoff (2012) and Jakobsen and Jensen (2015).

The clear advantage of the second strategy in measuring outcomes is that issues of common method bias are avoided a priori. Examples include the studies of Meier and O'Toole (2001, 2003) and Kelman, Hong and Turbitt (2013). The disadvantage of this strategy concerns issues of construct validity. For example, is network performance (as an often-used outcome, see Table 4.1) really measured by secondary data? Most research using this strategy uses archival data as some kind of proxy for measuring performance. For example, Meier and O'Toole (2001, 2003) use the school pass rate to measure the performance of school districts. The question then becomes what kind of performance measure is the district pass rate and what kind of performance dimension is measured: is it an organizational performance, network performance or rather an indicator of individual performance (such as the pupil)? Hence, risks of CSB are excluded, but questions of construct validity increase. Another example is the study of Kelman, Hong and Turbitt (2013), who use the reduction of crime rates to measure the performance of governance networks on crime fighting. This is a measure which is likely to be influenced by the whole network of participating actors. At the same time it is also a very specific focus on network performance, which might not match stakeholders' perceptions and definitions of performance in the governance network.

The clear advantage of the second strategy is the use of the 'hard nature' of the data, not influenced by perceptions of respondents. However, this does not directly mean that this data is objective. As George and Pandey (2017: 260) argue: 'archival data can be as flawed as, or even more than, self-reported data'; especially given that archival data is produced by other parties, which include risks that these data are influenced by other biases which can hardly be tested for. Moreover, archival data is far more difficult to replicate in other settings, whereas surveys are expected to, and typically do present a high standard of disclosure about the measurement procedures, instruments and so on, allowing other authors to replicate self-reported scales in different contexts and to identify how biases might creep in (George and Pandey 2017; Lee, Benoit-Bryan and Johnson 2012). These are important comments to consider when designing survey research and whether or not to include other data sources.

Design: amount of networks and respondents

Basically, there are two types of quantitative survey research on governance networks when considering the sample of networks and respondents used in the studies:

- Research that studies many networks. Most of these studies use one (or only a few) respondent for each network. Generally, a key node in the network is selected as the respondent, derived from the function and role of the respondent. This can, for example, be the chief administrative officer of a city (e.g. Agranoff and McGuire 1998), the leading project manager (e.g. Klijn, Steijn and Edelenbos 2010) or the superintendent of a school (Meier and O'Tool 2003), depending on the type of network.
- Research that studies one or a limited number of networks. These studies use many respondents for each network, mostly one respondent from each organization who is part of the network (e.g. Provan and Milward 1991).

Given scarce resources and possibilities to get respondents, this seems to be a quite clear trade-off in quantitative survey research on networks. The advantage of the first strategy is that many networks can be studied, providing many variations in the variables of interest, testing whether the assumed relationship holds in different networks and/or is influenced by specific characteristics of the network. The disadvantage is the low amount of data for each network represented by often only one respondent, which can pose challenges for the reliability and/or internal validity of the measurements. The advantage of the second strategy is more in-depth measurement of the variables of interest for a specific network (and certainly the patterns of contact within a network). However, in this case, it is difficult to generalize findings for the larger population of governance networks, posing challenges for the external validity of the findings.

Most of the articles (86%) in our review use the first strategy (many networks). In a slight departure from the norm, Leach et al. (2013) in their study on marine aquaculture partnerships used a somewhat mid-way design: surveying multiple participants of ten different partnerships, generating variation within and between networks.

Analysing techniques

In addition, most of the studies use a combination of presenting descriptive statistics, correlation analysis and linear regressions (OLS) for analysing the quantitative data (based on either the survey alone or in combination with other source data). Most of the studies test simple models and single relationships (direct effects of an independent on a dependent variable). This is partly the result of the technique used: ordinary linear regression analysis.[6]

Recently, more advanced techniques have been used to test multiple relations of a model, including indirect and direct effects, in the study of governance networks. For example, Korthagen and Klijn (2014), Van Meerkerk and Edelenbos (2014, 2017) and Van Meerkerk, Edelenbos and Klijn (2015) use SEM to test their theoretical models. This has several advantages compared to regression analysis (Byrne 2010). Firstly, SEM allow simultaneous analysis of all the variables in the model, instead of separately, and it enables measurement of direct, indirect and total effects (so called path analysis).[7] For instance, Van Meerkerk, Edelenbos and Klijn (2015) tested the effects of connective management on network performance and examined the mediating role of throughput legitimacy in this relationship. They indeed found a partly mediating role: connective management (positively) affects network performance, but for an important part through its effects on throughput legitimacy. This illustrates that the relationship between connective management and network performance is more complex, showing the impact of the democratic and deliberative quality of the decision-making process of governance networks in which the public manager can play an important role. Secondly, SEM has the capability to deal with latent variables by using separate factor loadings for the observed indicators (the survey items), thereby incorporating both unobserved constructs and observed indicators in the model. This is specifically useful in studies on governance networks in which latent constructs, such as 'trust' or 'network performance', are used. Thirdly, whereas traditional multivariate procedures are incapable of either assessing or correcting for measurement error, SEM provides explicit estimates of these error variance parameters, thereby improving the accuracy of the data analysis (Byrne 2010).

An important note is that SEM should be used to test causal models derived from theory-testing relationships that have a firm theoretical basis. Using existing data sets for such analysis runs the risk that the data and survey questions are not designed with the theoretical concepts in mind and thus either the operationalization of the concepts is not that strong, or the relations and variables are theoretically less interesting. Another warning is the temptation to (uncritically) increase the model fit based on the 'modification indices' function in which the SEM software suggests certain relationships, but which theoretically make little or no sense. We suggest looking to Nachtigall et al. (2003) for a good discussion on the pros and cons of using SEM. These possible mistakes related to data mining are, however, the 'usual suspects' in statistics.

Conclusions and suggestions for future survey studies on governance networks

In this chapter we have discussed advantages and disadvantages of the survey approach to the study of public governance networks. In general, there is a rise in quantitative survey research in studying governance networks. On the one hand, we argue this is caused by the evolution and maturity of the field; developed theories, largely based on case study research and theoretical conceptual work, are put to the test and extended and refined by survey research. On the other hand, this rise seems to be part of a general trend in the increasing use of quantitative methods in the discipline of PA (Groeneveld et al. 2015).

Survey research is especially suitable for testing assumed relationships between theoretical concepts. As we have discussed, there are already quite a large number of results, especially on the impact of network management and on the impact of various relational and network characteristics (like trust, collaboration, contacts between actors, tie types, etc.) on various outcomes, mainly some type of network performance. In general, survey research is especially useful and appropriate for studying individual behaviour, relationships and attitudes of network participants, relating this with network characteristics or outcomes (measured with the survey and/or another source of data).

One of the main dilemmas in applying survey research lies in choices concerning the number of networks studied, as there is (often) a trade-off between many networks, surveying one respondent for each network, versus a single or few networks, surveying many respondents for each network. Another key dilemma in the research design concerns the use of multiple data sources (avoiding risks of CSB) versus using the survey for measuring both dependent and independent variables (often offering better opportunities for more inclusive and refined operationalization of core concepts than using data not generated by the researcher). As discussed, each strategy has its pros and cons. In the ideal case we would suggest using both strategies, offering opportunities to contrast and control findings.

Based on our review and discussion, various avenues for future survey studies to advance the field can be pointed out. We discuss five suggestions.

First, the increasing availability (and more easy use) of advanced statistical software makes it possible to test not only single relationships, but more integral theoretical models. There is still a lot of room for development in this respect. By far, most of the studies we have reviewed and other studies in the field we know, still use ordinary regression analysis and do not test more integral theoretical models, although there are many opportunities to do so with current statistical methods, such as SEM. We discussed several examples in this respect.

Second, and related to the previous suggestion, we plea for the use of multi-level analysis. In our review of the literature we did not find studies in the field using this technique. This can offer opportunities to study relationships between variables across levels of analysis (network level, organizational level and/or individual level) and to deal with different units of analysis. This may also offer opportunities to deal with one of the design dilemmas discussed in this chapter: surveying multiple respondents for each network as well as studying multiple networks. Still, difficulties remain to generate such samples; however, when it comes to refined analysis of such multi-layered samples, multilevel analysis may offer good opportunities.

Third, with a few notable exceptions (e.g. the work by Meier and O'Toole), longitudinal research is still very scarce in quantitative survey research, as is the case for most large-*n* studies in PA (Groeneveld et al. 2015). Cross-sectional designs make it difficult to establish causality and to identify long-term effects. By conducting longitudinal panel studies the long-term evolution of networks can be studied. This offers opportunities to examine, for example, the use of different managerial strategies through time (and their effects) or the evolution of collaborations and the effects of specific interventions.

Fourth, systematic comparative cross–country survey research on networks is another avenue for future research. Differences in local conditions or governance traditions might moderate relationships between e.g. boundary-spanning activities, trust and performance. However, cross–country survey research on governance networks is a difficult and hard-to-realize design – one of the reasons we didn't come across many studies doing this type of research. One of the key difficulties pertains to the contextual differences between countries: the difficulty of comparing the same type of networks across (governance) cultures. Next, there are several practical difficulties, including administering the same questionnaire in different countries and in comparable samples. This would, in most cases, require intensive international collaboration, which require significant investments regarding time and costs. Concerning the selection of countries, it would be interesting and most beneficial to select countries deliberately on the basis of theoretical arguments; for example, comparing countries with different governance traditions and cultures.

Lastly, a mixed-methods approach combining quantitative with qualitative methods is also scarcely used but holds great promise. An exception in our review concerns the study of Shrestha (2013) on the impact of self-organizing network capital on the likelihood of funding success. He used a combination of surveys and interviews with all respondents included in the analysis. It is clear that this is a very time-consuming methodology but offers the advantage of combining statistical analysis on relatively large data sets, with insights from the qualitative data collection.

Notes

1 There are different terms in use for public sector networks. We use the term 'governance networks' as this is the broadest term which includes both service delivery networks and decision-making or collaborative networks. All have to do with governance processes, including public sector actors.
2 Of course, we have exceptions to that rule like the seminal study of Laumann and Knoke (1987) on policy domains.
3 Search terms used in Scopus: 'governance network', 'network governance', 'policy network', 'intergovernmental network' OR 'collaborative governance' AND 'survey' in the abstract, title or keyword. For the JPART search we used a more inclusive and time-intensive search: 'network' in the abstract, title or keyword AND 'survey' OR 'questionnaire' in the *full text*. The last search was conducted in November 2016.
4 In this respect, we refer to the first author. The selection includes more than two articles in which certain authors are participating, but the particular author is, in these cases, not the lead author.
5 The articles included in the review are given an asterisk in the reference list.
6 In deciding on which analysing techniques can be used or are appropriate, a general note is that there are some critical assumptions that must hold for linear regression to be used, including independent observations, a lack of multicollinearity and homoscedasticity of residuals, that must be satisfied to obtain valid results using this technique (Lee et al. 2012). For further discussion see, for instance, Lee et al. 2012.
7 As Nachtigall et al. (2003) explain: 'In contrast to ordinary regression analysis SEM considers several equations simultaneously. The same variable may represent a predictor (regressor) in one equation and a criterion (regressand) in another equation. Such a system of equations is called a model.'

References

References marked with an asterisk were part of our review
Agranoff, R. and M. McGuire. 1998. "Multinetwork management: Collaboration and the hollow state in local economic policy." *Journal of Public Administration Research and Theory* 8 (1): 67–91.★
Airaksinen, J., H. Härkönen, and A. Haveri. 2014. "Perceptions of legitimacy in Nordic regional development networks." *Public Organization Review* 14 (4): 457–476.★
Akkerman, A. and R. Torenvlied. 2013. "Public management and network specificity: Effects of colleges' ties with professional organizations on graduate's labor market success and satisfaction." *Public Management Review* 15: 522–540.
Ansell, C. and A. Gash. 2008. "Collaborative governance in theory and practice." *Journal of Public Administration Research and Theory* 18 (4): 543–571.
Byrne, B.M. 2010. *Structural equation modeling with AMOS: Basic concepts, applications, and programming.* New York: Routledge.

Chang, S. J., A.V. Witteloostuijn and L. Eden. 2010. "From the editors: Common method variance in international business research." *Journal of International Business Studies* 41: 178–184.

Edelenbos, J. and E.H. Klijn. 2007. "Trust in complex decision-making networks: A theoretical and empirical exploration." *Administration and Society* 39 (1): 25–50.

Edelenbos, J., B. Steijn, and E.H. Klijn. 2010. "Does democratic anchorage matter?" *American Review of Public Administration* 40 (1): 46–63.

Fowler Jr, F.J. 2013. *Survey research methods.* Thousand Oaks, CA: Sage Publications.

George, B. and S.K. Pandey. 2017. "We know the Yin: But where is the Yang? Toward a balanced approach on common source bias in public administration scholarship." *Review of Public Personnel Administration* 37 (2): 245–270.

Gerlak, A.K. and T. Heikkila. 2011. "Building a theory of learning in collaboratives: Evidence from the Everglades restoration program." *Journal of Public Administration Research and Theory.* doi: 10.1093/jopart/muq089.★

Graddy, E.A. and B. Chen. 2006. "Influences on the size and scope of networks for social service delivery." *Journal of Public Administration Research and Theory* 16 (4): 533–552.★

Groeneveld, S., L. Tummers, B. Bronkhorst, T. Ashikali, and S. Van Thiel. 2015. "Quantitative methods in public administration: Their use and development through time." *International Public Management Journal* 18 (1): 61–86.

Hanf, K.I. and F.W. Scharpf, eds. 1978. *Interorganizational policy making: Limits to coordination and central control.* London: Sage Publications.

Haverland, M. and D. Yanow. 2012. "A hitchhiker's guide to the public administration research universe: Surviving conversations on methodologies and methods." *Public Administration Review* 72 (3): 401–408.

Isett, K.R., I.A. Mergel, K. LeRoux, P.A. Mischen, and R.K. Rethemeyer. 2011. "Networks in public administration scholarship: Understanding where we are and where we need to go." *Journal of Public Administration Research and Theory* 21 (suppl. 1): i157–i173.

Jakobsen, M. and R. Jensen 2015. "Common method bias in public management studies." *International Public Management Journal* 18 (1): 3–30.

Juenke, E.G. 2005. "Management tenure and network time: How experience affects bureaucratic dynamics." *Journal of Public Administration Research and Theory* 15 (1): 113–131.★

Kelley, K., B. Clark, V. Brown, and J. Sitzia. 2003. "Good practice in the conduct and reporting of survey research." *International Journal for Quality in Health Care* 15 (3): 261–266.

Kelman, S., S. Hong, and I. Turbitt. 2013. "Are there managerial practices associated with the outcomes of an interagency service delivery collaboration? Evidence from British crime and disorder reduction partnerships." *Journal of Public Administration Research and Theory* 23 (3): 609–630.★

Kickert, W.J.M., E.H. Klijn, and J.F.M. Koppenjan, eds. 1997. *Managing complex networks: Strategies for the public sector.* London: Sage Publications.

Klijn, E.H. 2008. "Governance and governance networks in Europe: An assessment of 10 years of research on the theme." *Public Management Review* 10 (4): 505–525.

Klijn, E.H., A.J. Steijn, and J. Edelenbos. 2010. "The impact of network management strategies on the outcomes in governance networks." *Public Administration* 88 (4): 1063–1082.★

Klijn, E.H., J. Edelenbos, and A.J. Steijn. 2010. "Trust in governance networks; its impact and outcomes." *Administration and Society* 42 (2): 193–221.★

Korthagen, I. and E.H. Klijn. 2014. "The mediatization of network governance: The impact of commercialized news and mediatized politics on trust and perceived network performance." *Public Administration* 92 (4): 1054–1074.

Laumann, E. O. and D. Knoke. 1987. *The organizational state: Social choice in national policy domains.* Madison: University of Wisconsin Press.

Leach, W.D., C.M. Weible, S.R. Vince, S.N. Siddiki, and J.C. Calanni. 2013. "Fostering learning through collaboration: Knowledge acquisition and belief change in marine aquaculture partnerships." *Journal of Public Administration Research and Theory* 24 (3) 591–622.★

Lee, G., J. Benoit-Bryan, and T.P. Johnson. 2012. "Survey research in public administration: Assessing mainstream journals with a total survey error framework." *Public Administration Review* 72 (1): 87–97.

Lindell, M.K. and D.J. Whitney 2001. "Accounting for common method variance in cross-sectional designs." *Journal of Applied Psychology* 86 (1): 114–124.

Lubell, M. and Fulton, A. 2008. "Local policy networks and agricultural watershed management." *Journal of Public Administration Research and Theory* 18 (4): 673–696.★

Meier, K.J. and L.J. O'Toole. 2001. "Managerial strategies and behavior in networks: A model with evidence from US public education." *Journal of Public Administration Research and Theory* 11 (3): 271–294.★

Meier, K.J. and L.J. O'Toole. 2013. "Subjective organizational performance and measurement error: Common source bias and spurious relationships." *Journal of Public Administration Research and Theory* 23: 429–456.

Meier, K.J. and L.J. O'Toole. 2003. "Public management and educational performance: The impact of managerial networking." *Public Administration Review* 63 (6): 689–699.★

Nachtigall, C., U. Kroehne, F. Funke, and R. Steyer. 2003. "Pros and cons of structural equation modeling." *Methods Psychological Research Online* 8 (2): 1–22.

Neuman, L.W. 2002. *Social research methods: Qualitative and quantitative approaches*, 4th ed. Boston: Allyn and Bacon.

Nohrstedt, D. 2016. "Explaining mobilization and performance of collaborations in routine emergency management." *Administration & Society* 48 (2): 135–162.★

O'Leary, R., Y. Choi, and C.M. Gerard. 2012. "The skill set of the successful collaborator." *Public Administration Review* 72 (S1): 570–583.

O'Toole, L.J. and K.J. Meier. 2004. "Public management in intergovernmental networks: Matching structural networks and managerial networking." *Journal of Public Administration Research and Theory* 14 (4): 469–494.★

Percival, G.L. 2009. "Exploring the influence of local policy networks on the implementation of drug policy reform: The case of California's substance abuse and crime prevention act." *Journal of Public Administration Research and Theory* 19 (4): 795–815.★

Podsakoff, P.M., S.B. MacKenzie, and N.P. Podsakoff. 2012. "Sources of method bias in social science research and recommendations on how to control it." *Annual Review of Psychology* 63: 539–569.

Podsakoff, P.M. and S.B. MacKenzie. 2003. "Common method biases in behavioural research: A critical review of the literature and recommended remedies." *Journal of Applied Psychology* 88 (5): 879–903.

Provan, K.G. and P. Kenis. 2008. "Modes of network governance: Structure, management, and effectiveness." *Journal of Public Administration Research and Theory* 18 (2): 229–252.

Provan, K.G. and H.B. Milward. 2001. "Do networks really work? A framework for evaluating public-sector organizational networks." *Public Administration Review* 61 (4): 414–423.

Provan, K.G. and H.B. Milward. 1991. "Institutional-level norms and organizational involvement in a service-implementation network." *Journal of Public Administration Research and Theory* 1 (4): 391–418.★

Robson, C. 2002. *Real world research*, 2nd Ed. Malden: Blackwell Publishing.

Scharpf, F.W. 1978. "Interorganizational policy studies: Issues, concepts and perspectives." In *Interorganizational Policy Making: Limits to coordination and central control*, edited by K.I. Hanf and F.W. Scharpf, 345–370. London: Sage Publications.

Shrestha, M.K. 2013. "Self-organizing network capital and the success of collaborative public programs." *Journal of Public Administration Research and Theory* 23 (2): 307–329.★

Sørensen, E. and J. Torfing, eds. 2007. *Theories of democratic network governance.* London: Palgrave Macmillan.

Ulibarri, N. 2015. "Collaboration in federal hydropower licensing: Impacts on process, outputs, and outcomes." *Public Performance & Management Review* 38 (4): 578–606.★

Van Meerkerk, I. and J. Edelenbos. 2014. "The effects of boundary spanners on trust and performance of urban governance networks: Findings from survey research on urban development projects in the Netherlands." *Policy Sciences* 47 (1): 3–24.★

Van Meerkerk, I. and J. Edelenbos. 2017. "Facilitating conditions for boundary-spanning behaviour in urban governance networks." *Public Management Review* doi: 10.1080/14719037.2017.1302248.

Van Meerkerk, I., J. Edelenbos, and E.H. Klijn. 2015. "Connective management and governance network performance: The mediating role of throughput legitimacy. Findings from survey research on complex water projects in the Netherlands." *Environment and Planning C: Government and Policy* 33 (4): 746–764.★

5 Narrative inquiry in public network research

Jennifer Dodge, Angel Saz-Carranza and Sonia M. Ospina

Introduction

To what extent and how are scholars in public administration (PA) using narrative inquiry to study networks? To answer this question this chapter maps the range of theoretical and methodological approaches that integrate scholarship on narrative inquiry and networks. Our aim is to illustrate the unique contributions these approaches make to illuminate the dynamics of an increasingly networked and collaborative governance environment. Our literature review suggests that narrative inquiry is being used regularly to understand policy networks, especially in European PA journals. Narrative inquiry makes unique contributions to the study of networks, centring on its power to illuminate the subjectivity of network actors (their position in networks, how they understand it and how others understand them), the meanings actors hold about their experience or knowledge as network participants, and how networks can be shaped by powerful narratives or discourses that act as forces shaping what happens in networks and what they do in society. Despite these benefits, there are several promising applications that are largely unexplored and that have considerable potential to advance scholarship on networks and to address critical questions in the field.

Similar to other chapters in this volume, we focus on narrative *methodological* applications to study networks. But there is a level of complexity that must be considered from the start. This is because narrative inquiry encompasses a wide range of theoretical frameworks and methodological traditions that have evolved into a broad array of theory-method pairings. The literature on narrative inquiry is enormous and informed by many disciplines and fields, including linguistics and literary studies, the behavioural sciences like psychology, sociology and political science, and applied fields like management and PA, to name a few. There are thus many 'narratological' traditions that drive scholarship.

Our main contribution is to map these approaches and explore how narrative is being used in PA to understand networks, clarifying common assumptions of all approaches and distinctions in specific applications. We have made choices in developing this map. First, we have chosen to focus on the *narrative* traditions that feed into PA research most directly. We draw heavily from a series of articles published in *Public Administration Review* (PAR) in 2005 that articulate three distinct traditions of narrative and their core assumptions (Ospina and Dodge 2005a, 2005b; Dodge, Ospina and Foldy 2005), and update our perspective to encompass new developments.[1] Second, we draw heavily on theoretical assumptions about *networks* as used in the public management literature. As such, we build on the interrelated streams of research related to public management networks (Agranoff 2007), service delivery networks (Provan and Milward 2001), policy and governance networks (Kickert, Klijn and Koppenjan 1997) and social network analysis (SNA). We believe this approach will aid scholars in selecting from among the most promising narrative inquiry traditions for enriching PA's knowledge development about networks.

We start by offering an overview of, first, the range of narrative traditions and, second, the range of network forms in PA scholarship. We then propose a framework that crosses the categorizations to create a matrix of twelve *possible* approaches to study networks empirically using narrative inquiry. The heart of the chapter articulates the theoretical assumptions and methodological orientations underlying five approaches that are *actually used* in the field and provides an exemplar of each to make plain the types of insights they enable. We consider the implications of each approach, discussing contributions to the field, limitations and possible avenues of future research. We conclude by addressing the ways the narrative traditions we documented can advance scholarship on networks.

A framework to explore how narrative inquiry is used to study networks

Both narrative inquiry and network research encompass a variety of forms and influences. We review the broad range of approaches represented in both literatures and propose a framework for understanding networks in PA that builds on this diversity.

Multiple faces of narrative inquiry revisited

In an earlier series of articles (Ospina and Dodge 2005a, 2005b; Dodge, Ospina and Foldy 2005), we explored three basic traditions of narrative inquiry that draw on a range of epistemological and theoretical perspectives. Each one places different emphasis on one of three key theoretical assumptions common to all traditions. We showed how a scholar's theoretical emphasis greatly influences the choices they make when using narrative inquiry to understand the social world. The relative weight placed on these assumptions helps:

> translate narrative theory into specific methodological techniques for carrying out inquiry, with implications for different stages of research, from data collection to analysis and interpretation and even data presentation.

> Researchers make choices about how they translate these assumptions into
> a coherent research agenda based on their purposes and questions.
>
> (Dodge, Ospina and Foldy 2005: 291)

First, the *narrative as language* tradition assumes that narratives convey meanings, and the primary means to do so is language. Narrative scholars elicit stories to explore intentions, beliefs, values and emotions that are reflective of situated social realities, with an understanding that language represents an intersubjective reality; that is, a reality that is created through the interaction of individuals with their own subjectivities (understanding of themselves in a social world) (Riessman 2002). Second, the *narrative as knowledge* tradition assumes that human beings craft and tell stories both to create and to understand their experience (Bruner 2004), and these stories have formative value. Hence narratives carry practical knowledge gained by individuals through their experience. Third, the *narrative as metaphor* tradition assumes that individuals shape narratives for their own purposes but, at the same time, narratives become social forces that also shape individuals. They do so by giving meaning to the social worlds human beings inhabit, thus shaping their understanding of reality and who they think they are in that reality (Gergen 1985). Thus, some narratives become metaphors that point to deeper meanings about how the social order is constituted. For this chapter, and based on new developments in the field, we added a fourth category: *narrative as variable*. This tradition assumes that narrative elements exhibit regularities across time and place that can be measured quantitatively.

The heart of this chapter offers an overview of each of these narrative traditions and how they have been used to understand networks, providing exemplars from current applications in the PA literature. These approaches hold considerable promise to advance research and theory on networks in PA. To realize this promise, it is critical to distinguish among several types of networks that make up the current governing landscape.

A typology of the study of networks in public administration

The typology of networks presented here differentiates between serendipitous networks, goal-directed networks and metaphorical networks. This typology builds on several distinctions in the literature. Provan and Kenis (2008) and Kilduff and Tsai (2003) clarified the distinction between serendipitous and goal-directed networks. To this basic distinction, we add that networks can also be metaphorical. In metaphorical networks the nodes represent not relations among organizations or actors but rather representations of a shared characteristic. Our typology is similar to Keast, Mandell and Agranoff's (2013), but where they draw a distinction between public and business networks we distinguish between serendipitous and goal-directed networks.

First, serendipitous networks do not necessarily involve formalized, direct relations, but their 'members' are nonetheless co-implicated in mutually reinforcing (or even contradictory) actions within a particular policy domain. These networks are defined as patterns of social relations between interdependent actors and arise out of the sum of spontaneous dyadic relations among actors. These networks are neither consciously nor voluntarily created (although many of their dyadic relations may be). Serendipitous networks in the public sector involve actors related to a specific policy problem. In one example, Saz Carranza and Garcia (2012) analysed a serendipitous network of actors who contributed to the internationalization of a metropolitan region of Los Angeles. The network included universities, and actors from different governments, business associations, seaports and airports. This network was composed of nodes (actors) that interacted, but the network was not purposefully created and no one (except for the researcher) was conscious of the full network (see Figure 5.1).

Second, goal-directed networks are purposefully created to achieve a collective aim (Kilduff and Tsai 2003), and their connections are typically measured via the sum of dyadic communication patterns (importantly, goal-directed networks might emerge from a serendipitous network, for example when a latter network decides to assume network-level goals). For Provan and Kenis (2008) goal-directed networks are consciously created partnerships, alliances and joint ventures involving 'groups of three or more legally autonomous organizations that work together to achieve not only their own goals but also a collective goal' (231). Since collective action is often required for problem solving in the public and non-profit sectors (Agranoff and McGuire 2003), these networks are frequently the focus of PA research. Figure 5.2 illustrates an immigration coalition of the United States (US) East Coast. This goal-directed network is governed via a central broker and brings together different pro-immigration non-profits (for simplicity reasons, the figure illustrates a few of the members, not all of them). The network's goal is to collectively organize and execute advocacy campaigns in favour of immigrants, and membership to the network is formal and explicit.

Finally, Figure 5.3 illustrates the use of the network as an analytic metaphor to explore the conversation in Europe regarding energy policy. Nodes are key political actors (e.g. Canada, Japan or the EU energy Commissioner, Sefcovic) and policy issues (such as grid or biofuels), linked by relations of co-occurrence in the same tweets. The bolder the link, the greater co-occurrence. In this case, nodes do not 'talk' to each other as they do in serendipitous and goal-directed networks, nor do they interact in any other way, but are linked only according to being part of the same tweet. The links among nodes depict positive or negative co-occurrence, but not interaction. Thus, a node does not need to have interacted with another node but is linked to another node if they appear in the same tweet.

The three network forms are not always mutually exclusive. A goal-directed network necessarily involves dyadic interdependencies and interactions and may be part of a broader serendipitous network. The New York Immigration Coalition[2] (a goal-directed network), for instance, constitutes a piece of the American immigration serendipitous policy network.[3] Nonetheless, this network typology makes useful analytical distinctions to understand how narrative approaches can inform network research, as some approaches are used more often than others in researching certain types of networks.

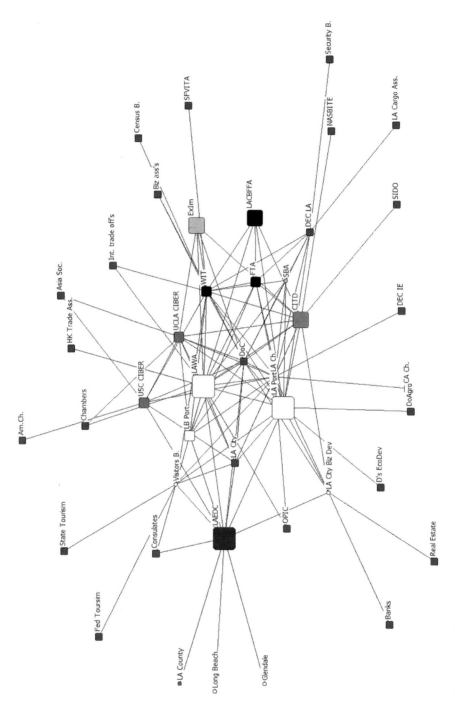

Figure 5.1 Policy networks as serendipitous networks

Source: The Los Angeles policy network of internationalization-supporting actors (Saz Carranza and Garcia 2012)

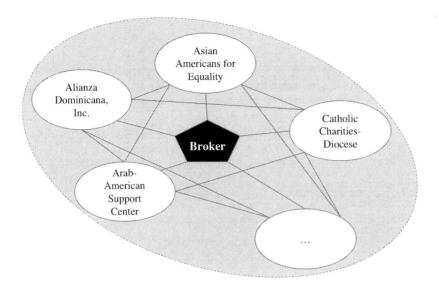

Figure 5.2 Goal-directed networks

Source: The National Immigration Coalition (Saz-Carranza and Ospina 2011)

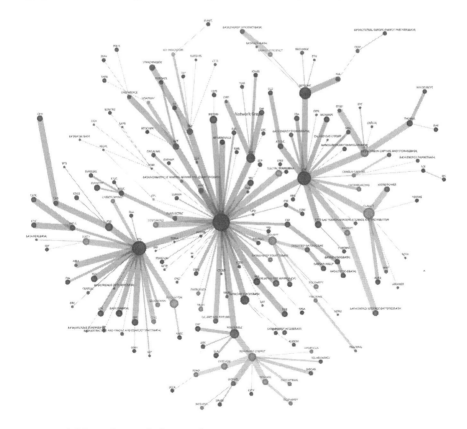

Figure 5.3 Network as analytic metaphor

Source: The issue-actor network of EU energy policy (Saz-Carranza, Unpublished, based on www.miniera.es)

A map of narrative inquiry approaches to study networks

Having presented an overview of the four traditions of narrative inquiry and the three forms of networks found in the PA literature, we now combine the typologies to create a matrix that categorizes twelve possible ways narrative inquiry can be used to build knowledge of networks. Furthermore, we populate this matrix with eighteen recent articles from PA journals that have applied narrative inquiry to study networks (see Table 5.1).[4] Our aim is to explicate how these narrative traditions have actually been used to study networks, and to explore underutilized applications.

In identifying and categorizing the articles, we observed that some studies explicitly pair narrative methodologies (narrative analysis) with narrative theory. Other studies make assumptions consistent with narrative theory but do not necessarily apply narrative methodologies or, conversely, use a narrative analysis methodology to answer their questions without making explicit connections to narrative theories. The choices reflected in the latter two alternatives (using narrative theory but not narrative methodology or vice versa) can yield excellent results to understand a particular dimension of networks, but represent a lighter application of narrative inquiry. We thus generally emphasize examples that offer what we call a 'strong' narrative approach (that uses both narrative theory and narrative methodology), while including references to 'light' approaches (that use one but not the other). More precisely, 'strong' forms of narrative inquiry tend to use an explicit narrative theory or methodology, focus on narratives as an object of study, and have some theoretical-methodological coherence rooted in a consistent epistemological position. 'Light' forms use narrative rhetorically, as a way of situating a study in a broader trend or 'narrative', more as a reference point to understand some other object of study. Finally, many used 'hybrid' methodologies or theories that integrate narrative inquiry with other theoretical or methodological approaches. In drawing these distinctions, we do not make a quality judgment, but reflect on the range of possible choices that are being made in the field about how to apply narrative inquiry, and to clarify the implications of the different approaches. Table 5.1 reflects these differences: we include the total number of articles in each category, and in parenthesis the number of articles that use narrative analysis in the strong sense.

It is worth noting that of the twelve cells in the matrix, only five were populated. This indicates that several possible approaches to narrative inquiry to study networks were not being used in this sample of articles in the study

Table 5.1 Using narrative inquiry to study networks

Narrative as Network	Language	Knowledge	Metaphor	Variable
Serendipitous network	3(2)		9(7)	
Goal-directed networks	2(1)		3(2)	
Metaphor				1(1)

period. Especially absent is the narrative as knowledge approach, but also the use of narrative to understand metaphorical networks, with the unsurprising exception that narrative as variable is being used to study metaphorical networks. These omissions might be due to our selection of journals. Other journals in the field might be more likely to include articles using narrative as knowledge or empirical articles about metaphorical networks. We will return to this point in the discussion.

Equipped with the conceptual framework already presented in this chapter, we explore how narrative inquiry is being used to study networks in the public management literature. Table 5.2 summarizes how we classified the eighteen papers, considering their primary methodology, methods of data collection and our characterization as strong or light. The reader will notice that researchers using the four narrative inquiry traditions may choose specific types of methodologies beyond the most obvious 'narrative analysis', depending on their theoretical assumptions. Likewise, some hybrid articles combine methodologies or data collection methods. The following sections describe the narrative traditions and how they were used to study networks in PA.

Using narrative as language to understand networks

The narrative as language tradition highlights the assumption that narrative is a medium of expression through which people convey meaning about their social realities (Dodge, Ospina and Foldy 2005). This highlights the social dimension of language as a means of making interaction coherent and even possible: 'According to this view, people create narratives to convey meaning about their experience with the world' (291). When a social group shares a common narrative – that is, when a narrative is empirically found to be common in the group – they share a common interpretation of their experience. Thus, the narrative as language tradition is useful for exploring people's experiences with some phenomenon of interest, such as organizational change (Feldman and Sköldberg 2002; Feldman et al. 2002) or the adoption of community policing (Davies and Thomas 2008). The idea is that 'narratives illuminate something about the constructed reality they reflect and about the experience and intentions of those engaged in it' (Dodge, Ospina and Foldy 2005: 291).

Instead of working deductively – starting with conceptual categories from theory and testing them empirically – researchers using this tradition begin inductively, treating participants' subjective experiences and meanings as valuable sources of information for theorizing about networks, what they mean and how they operate. Therefore, researchers will often conduct interviews among a range of actors who share a common experience; for example, of making moral decisions (Maynard-Moody and Musheno 2003). The interviewer prompts participants to narrate their experience; for example, by asking them to 'Tell me about a time when you . . .' The researcher will conduct a systematic comparative analysis of the diverse narratives of the same phenomenon from a range of people who have experienced it. The aim of the analysis is to distil 'the form,

Table 5.2 Articles by narrative tradition, methodology, data collection methods and strength of narrative inquiry (NI)

	Methodology										Data collection					NI
	Narrative Analysis	Discourse analysis	Decentered Interpretivism	Dramaturgy	Interview study (experience)	Ethnography	Q-Methodology	Case study	Content or thematic analysis	Semantic network analysis	Interviews	Focus groups	Documents	Observation	Questionnaire/ Quant. assess.	Strong/Light
Using narrative as language to understand serendipitous networks																
Hendricks (2009)		✓						✓			✓		✓	✓		Strong
Tomlinson (2010)		✓		✓				✓			✓	✓	✓			Strong
Keast et. al (2007)					✓				✓		✓	✓				Light
Using narrative as language to understand goal-directed networks																
Davies and Thomas (2003)	✓							✓			✓					Strong
Jacobs (2009)					✓			✓			✓	✓		✓		Light
Using narrative as metaphor to understand serendipitous networks																
Bang (2004)	✓	✓	✓					✓			✓	✓				Strong
Biebricher (2011)	✓	✓	✓					✓					✓			Strong
Gains (2009)	✓	✓	✓								✓					Strong
Goodwin and Grix (2011)	✓		✓					✓					✓			Strong
Needham (2009)	✓		✓						✓							Light
Mathur and Skelcher (2007)	✓				✓		✓				✓		✓		✓	Strong
Nohrstedt (2013)	✓	✓						✓					✓			Light
Fertlie and McGivern (2014)								✓			✓		✓	✓		Strong
Lejano and Leong (2012)	✓												✓			Strong

Using narrative as metaphor to understand goal-directed networks

Skelcher et al. (2005)	✓		✓	✓ ✓	Strong
Willems and Van Dooren (2016)	✓			✓ ✓	Strong
West (2005)	✓			✓	Light

Using narrative as variable to understand metaphorical networks

Choi and Lecy (2012)		✓ ✓		✓	Strong

content, and structure of the analysed stories, reflecting the qualitative orientation that looks for patterns of experience often across stories and sites' (Dodge,
Ospina and Foldy 2005: 291). The result is often an aggregated narrative that
conveys common stages or themes associated with some experience or set of
narratives conveying participants' subjective experience of the phenomena of
interest (although as the reader will see from the ensuing analysis, there are
considerable variations in our sample of articles, particularly those that integrate
narrative with other research traditions).

This narrative tradition has been used to study both serendipitous networks
and goal-directed networks in our sample of articles.

Understanding serendipitous networks

Using the 'narrative as language' tradition to study *serendipitous networks* focuses
on the ways participants give meaning to their experience operating within
stable patterns of spontaneous social relations organized around policy problems
(Klijn and Koppenjan 2000). The particular focus of analysis varies depending
on the research questions. For example, one could examine the experience of
coordination, cooperation or collaboration and what these terms mean to participants in practice (Keast, Brown and Mandell 2007), or the ways individual
actors 'enact' networks through their beliefs and actions (Tomlinson 2010). One
could also unpack the way sub-groups within the network use language to
not only interpret but also to define their experience in the network. Typically, sub-groups are not defined by their objective identity characteristics, but
by the narratives or discourses within which they make sense of, and define
the meaning of, their experience and identity. In either case, the emphasis is
on the subjective meaning participants in a network give to their experience,
rather than the relationships and interactions of network members per se (Klijn,
Edelenbos and Steijn 2010; O'Toole and Meier 2004).

Hendriks (2009) provides an exemplar. She examines democratic representation in a governance network in the Netherlands whose purpose was to steer
the country's transition away from fossil fuels toward more sustainable forms
of energy. Applying a combination of discourse analysis and dramaturgy, she
unpacks the meanings of 'representation' for participants, and how these meanings are enacted or 'performed' in the network. To tap into these experiences,
she used in-depth semi-structured interviews and other textual data. Unlike traditional qualitative coding that would identify key themes, her use of discourse
analysis and dramaturgy steered her analysis to examine the meaning of representation on two levels: (1) the way 'representation is staged and scripted' (694),
for example, through cues about who is to speak and when, the arrangement of
speakers and audience, and so on; and (2) the way representation is understood in
discourses (language). She finds that network governance evolved into a variety
of stages with unique scripts, participants and audiences, including a 'bottom-
up' innovation script that valorized the participation of experts in new energy
technologies. In other words, the operation of the networks – their discourses

and performances – were organized in such a way that supported or thwarted certain forms of representation and knowledge flows. She also found a variety of discourses to depict representation, including 'representation is problematic' and 'representation is about knowledge', among many others.

Future research using the 'narrative as language' tradition to study serendipitous networks could focus on the experience of network participants in relation to power. Important questions include 'How is power performed and enacted in practice?' and 'How do people experience power relations in the network?' This could complement structural and objective measures of power, such as centrality measures, structural holes or boundary spanners. One could also examine how networks are created through the language and actions of participants, particularly the meanings they attach to what they understand themselves to be doing. This approach could also produce knowledge regarding the subjective experiences of individuals within a network and their understanding of, for example, performance or an individual's ego network embedded in the serendipitous network.

Understanding goal-directed networks

Using the 'narrative as language' tradition to understand *goal-directed networks* also focuses on participants' experiences and the meaning they give to these experiences, but the experience of interest is collaborating across autonomous organizations in intentionally organized partnerships, alliances or ventures (Jacobs 2010). Commonly, the literature on goal-directed networks assumes some joint effort on the part of network participants to collectively define shared goals and to work toward those goals (Saz Carranza and Ospina 2011). Using narrative adds to the literature by exploring the *divergences* in participants' experiences of partnerships and the meanings they give to the goals (and other features) that define these arrangements. The approach assumes that partnerships are defined by broader narratives or discourses, such as 'New Public Management' (NPM), but rather than focus on the discourse or narrative as one might do in narrative as metaphor tradition (discussed under 'Using narrative as metaphor to understand networks') it emphasizes the agency of network participants to interpret those discourses from their own perspectives, and thus to transform them in local contexts. The divergences of interpretations and experiences within the network help explain the challenges of implementation that arise in goal-directed partnerships. As is common in the narrative as language tradition, this work draws on interview data to explore the subjective (and divergent) experiences and interpretations of participants in partnerships.

Drawing on discourse analysis, Davies and Thomas (2003), for instance, explore 'the attempts to "re-brand" the police, from "force" to "service"' under NPM in the United Kingdom (UK) police force, focusing particularly on 'the meanings that individuals bring to discourses of change and their own positioning within these meanings' (682). NPM emphasizes collaboration and partnership and introduces new policing identities into the police force that support these arrangements. These identities are also characterized by communicativeness, participative orientation and attunement to the service needs of the community. Davies and Thomas explore whether or not and how the police adopt these new identities or resist them in favour of traditional competitive and masculine identities of crime fighters. Drawing on interviews, Davies and Thomas unpack two contrasting subject positions (identities) available within the goal-directed networks in the NPM discourse in this case: (1) 'the professional-ethical policing subject' consistent with NPM, and (2) 'the competitive masculine subject' consistent with a traditional view of policing. While the professional-ethical cop identity emphasizes community partnerships (as a form of goal-directed network), cops resist it in favour of a traditional masculine identity that reinforces 'long hours culture' of the strong individual who 'devotes his or her life and identity to the organization' (696). In contrast, the professional-ethical identity offers 'women a positive and legitimate subject position' that 'maps onto the "emotional labour" of police work', but is also seen as 'antithetical to "real work"' in the traditional, masculine view of policing (696).

Future research using this tradition could focus on many different aspects of participants' experiences in goal directed networks. A promising avenue of research – also applicable to serendipitous networks – includes examining formal authority, and the experiences participants have of who holds authority and how authority is exerted. This is particularly important given the intrinsic autonomy of network members and the particularity of the concept of 'authority' in a network. In goal-directed networks, the authority relationship between members and the NAO (network administrative organization) is particularly interesting. One could also explore informal dynamics underlying goal-directed networks, which do not necessarily parallel formal network dynamics and structures. Scholars could examine, for example, informal mechanisms for collaboration through stories of participants' experiences, or how inter-organizational partners resist or adopt new identities associated with the creation of new service networks through government contracts or public-private partnerships. Questions would include 'How do participants adopt joint service goals or resist them in practice?' and 'How are government frameworks (re)interpreted and changed during implementation, and to what effect?'

Finally, the narrative as language tradition offers a valuable research strategy to explore effectiveness and performance. An objectivist-take, based on transaction cost economics, for instance, answers the question: 'When is a network the optimum structure vis-à-vis markets or hierarchies?' A narrative approach to goal-directed networks could complement this approach by unpacking when a network becomes too 'burdensome' to the point that 'inertia' trumps value creation (Huxham and Vangen 2000), or when normative motivations behind the creation of a goal-directed network override efficiency considerations. One might also investigate what performance and effectiveness 'mean' in a goal-directed network to expand our knowledge of performance management in practice.

Using narrative as knowledge to understand networks

In addition to *narrative as language, narrative as a way of knowing* is another broad tradition that can be applied to study networks. Like the narrative as language tradition, it assumes people convey something about experience through narratives, but its main emphasis is on the ways *people draw knowledge* from their lived experience (Dodge, Ospina and Foldy 2005; Koliba and Lathrop 2007). Narrative as knowledge draws 'attention to the learning embedded in stories about practice' (Dodge, Ospina and Foldy 2005: 292), since it assumes that narrative knowing – knowing from lived experience – can be applied to other contexts. The goals are to illuminate practitioners' tacit knowledge and share their 'theories in use'. The research product portrays, in narrative form, detailed knowledge that is derived from experience from which to draw broader lessons. One example is Steven Maynard-Moody and Michael Musheno's 2012 article about street-level bureaucrats and the normative judgements they make on a daily basis as they implement public policies.[5] While street-level bureaucrats are often unable to articulate the general principles they use to guide their normative judgments, the article shows how stories describing the practice of *making* these judgments offers the researcher 'rich evidence of the normative reasoning and context that shapes judgments and actions, thus revealing more than what 'they consciously know' (Maynard-Moody and Musheno's 2012: S21).

This tradition usually involves creating opportunities for practitioners to reflect on their own experience to build theory from practice. Researchers may interview network participants asking them to convey in narrative form their experiences negotiating goals in goal-directed networks; for example, to unearth 'know how' about cooperation not easily conveyed through surveys. Researchers may also facilitate focus groups of people in a common network or across networks. In this case, researchers may ask participants to narrate their experiences negotiating goals, but would look for propositions that apply *across* discrete networks. In other cases, narrative inquiry is integrated with action-oriented forms of inquiry such as action research, action learning or cooperative inquiry to create contexts where practitioners can narrate their experience to understand and improve their environment.

While promising, this tradition is not common in the PA literature,[6] so it was not surprising that it has not been used to study networks in our sample of articles. However, there are examples in the broader literature, such as Huxham and Vangen's (2000) iconic study of leadership in public and community inter-organizational collaborations. The study documents how leadership in collaborative networks happens. Drawing from action research interventions in UK partnerships (e.g. goal-directed networks), the authors created a data set that included texts reflecting participants' comments and actions, charts and plans, and descriptions of events in the life of a collaboration based on participation, documents, observations, field notes and interviews over time. Interactive cycles of analysis involved 'extensive discussions concerned with sense making, data massaging, and finding representations and links' as well as returning the insights to practitioners in workshops and other activities (Huxham and Vangen 2000: 1163).

Future research using narrative as knowledge could focus on exploring practitioners' tacit knowledge of how to facilitate collaboration and improve performance in policy networks or tacit knowledge sharing within the networks. Practice-grounded knowledge would help advance scholarship on networks and bridge the theory-practice divide in the field.

Using narrative as metaphor to understand networks

Unlike the *narrative as language* and *narrative as a way of knowing*, *narrative as metaphor* selects grand narratives or discourses in society as the focus of analysis. This tradition specifically differs from narrative as knowledge because of the scope of the researcher's approach to discourse. Narrative as metaphor connects embedded practices to grand theories at the macro level of analysis; that is, to hegemonic discourses and ideologies that help maintain the social order. In contrast, narrative as knowledge identifies specific know-how, theories-in-use and/or tacit knowledge as it is developed and manifested at the micro-level of organizational practice. Furthermore, this third tradition of narrative inquiry emphasizes the constitutive nature of narratives. The central idea is that the stories social actors tell take on a life of their own that then influence people's understanding of the world. Agreed upon interpretations of social life, influenced by historical contexts, are recreated over time through interactions, constituting 'grand narratives' or 'discourses' into which future generations are born, thus regulating social life. In research, narratives represent metaphors that capture deeper meanings about the social order.

The scholar privileging the *narrative as metaphor* tradition will look for invisible, often taken-for-granted, meanings weaved throughout institutional life, directing attention to alternative explanations and linking 'the immediate experience of social actors to broader institutions of meaning' (Dodge, Ospina and Foldy 2005: 293). Scholars begin by selecting a set of texts produced by particular institutions, a powerful individual or influential groups. Texts can include formal or informal written documents, such as policies, standard operating procedures, manifestos or cooperative agreements, but also verbal utterances, such as speeches, and even 'performances' and the arrangement of space (such as office cubicles that might reflect power differences). Methods of analysis involve critique and deconstruction of 'texts' (verbal, written or performed) to unpack their underlying assumptions and meanings. Analysis links the text (such as a policy) to its broader context (such as its historical period) and tacks back and forth analytically between meanings across the general and the particular, the hidden and the apparent, the abstract and the concrete. The result is often a document that makes hidden assumptions of a discourse explicit and that, if changed, could alter oppressive structures in society. Often scholars also analyse an alternative 'counter narrative' or 'counter discourse' in addition to a dominant one to show that the dominant perspective is not inevitable but can be changed.

By far, 'narrative as metaphor' is the most common and diverse tradition used in the PA literature, reflecting two broad research strategies: discourse analysis and hermeneutics (influenced by literary studies). While both methodologies have been used to explore networks in the PA literature, the discourse analysis strategy is much more common, especially in European PA journals, with eight articles in our sample. Perhaps this is because of the longer tradition and broader acceptance of discourse analysis in Europe compared to its rather fringe status in the US.

Understanding serendipitous networks

Applying the *narrative as metaphor* tradition to serendipitous *networks* means examining the ways grand narratives or discourses impose meaning in networks, as participants enact in those contexts internalized and broadly accepted messages from society. Unlike the *narrative as language* tradition, it assumes participants in the network have limited agency to interpret narratives from their own perspectives or to translate them for local contexts, as the network becomes a cultural context on its own. Instead, this tradition shows how narratives both open up specific possibilities for local action and constrain or omit other possibilities, ultimately shaping systems, programs and meanings in patterned ways. Rather than drawing on interviews, which are excellent for understanding the meanings individuals give to their experiences, the narrative as metaphor tradition uses texts and documents that typify the narrative in question (and may also supplement these with interviews). Many of the articles in our sample challenge the naïve egalitarian 'network governance' narrative, demonstrating that asymmetrical power relations remain the dominant feature of state-private relations (Goodwin and Grix 2011).

Because understanding serendipitous networks by way of the 'narrative as metaphor' tradition is the most popular PA use of narrative inquiry (see Table 5.2), the applications vary considerably. We identified four ways to understand serendipitous networks using this tradition: Bevir and Rhodes''decentered[7] approach', a hybrid that mixes the decentered approach with an objective analysis of institutional features guiding networks, Foucauldian discourse analysis and a hermeneutic approach. The first two are heavily influenced by institutional theory in political science and sociology.

First, the majority of the identified articles (Bang 2004; Biebricher 2011; Gains 2009; Goodwin and Grix 2011; Needham 2009) use Bevir and Rhodes' (2003, 2004, 2006) decentered approach to governance to explain serendipitous networks. The decentered approach aims to understand governance by focusing on the beliefs (or meanings) that inform the practices and actions of governing actors. Furthermore, these beliefs – about power and authority, for instance – are constituted by competing traditions, creating the likelihood that the meanings of governance in any context will be contested (Bevir and Rhodes 2010: vii).[8] In an exemplar of this approach, Biebricher (2011) examined the Faith-Based and Community Initiative (FBCI) in the US as an example of welfare-state restructuring toward more networked forms of governance. He examined how communitarian and public choice discourses have shaped the new governance arrangement. While the stated purpose of the FBCI was to increase the number of faith-based organizations delivering public services, it served instead to enhance 'a continuing retreat of the state from its redistributive functions with increased and at times repressive interventions into the lives of clients' (1001). By examining the traditions that informed this governing arrangement, Biebricher was able to trace how these interventions found 'their justification in a moralization of poverty [that] establish[ed] a causal nexus between virtuous behaviour and (lack of) prosperity' (1001). He also demonstrates the failure of the FBCI to implement network governance as the faith-based organizations resisted taking on the role of governmental service providers.[9]

Second, a variant or hybrid of the decentered approach tends to view narratives – or 'ideas' in their parlance – as one among other institutional factors that can explain policy or institutional change or stasis. These approaches explain networks through both subjective factors (ideas, culture, beliefs) and objective, institutional factors (structures). For instance, Mathur and Skelcher (2007) developed a framework for examining the 'democratic performance' of network forms of governance that includes three methodologies – criteria-based evaluation (from quality of democracy studies), narrative analysis and Q methodology. This approach assesses both the democratic 'hardware' and 'software' of network forms of governance using both objective measures and subjective meanings (see also Nohrstedt (2013), who applies the Advocacy Coalition Framework to the European volcano ashes crisis of 2010).

Third, Ferlie and McGivern (2014) apply an Anglo-Foucauldian 'governmentality' analysis to understand serendipitous networks as a complement to NPM and network governance explanations. Rather than operate through command and control or through contracts, Ferlie and McGivern show how governmentality structures 'the conduct of conduct . . . leading actors to think and act as those governing desire' (62). Control operates through the acceptance of 'dominant political rationalities and [their connection] to concrete technologies of governing' (62), such as the practices of evidence-based management. These 'technologies are more akin to "soft" organizational control systems (education and training, personal development and coaching)' (63), as they involve practitioners' internalization of 'external rules about how they should behave' (62), a phenomenon Foucault calls 'technologies of the self'. For this reason, 'Foucault offers an original perspective on indirect modes of government' so central to the practice of network governance. Ferlie and McGivern applied this approach to a 'managed network' of providers implementing evidence-based clinical guidelines created by the UK's National Health Service (NHS). Using textual analysis of archival data they illustrated how evidence-based governmentality provides specific rationalities, such as 'best international evidence' (which enables international elites to rise above clinical 'rank and file') and, building on interviews, showed how these rationalities are adopted in a specific Managed Sexual Health

Network not through command and control but through training, peer pressure and the comparison of local efforts against the international standards.[10]

Finally, Raul Lejano and Ching Leong (2012) used a hermeneutic analysis to study conflict between two policy networks over a wastewater recycling program in Los Angeles. They explained the paradoxical decision to shut down a project despite its demonstrated safety by exposing what they labelled 'a narrative of infeasibility'. The researchers conducted a structural-narrative analysis of a set of texts (news articles, magazines, technical bulletins and newsletters). Their analytical framework focused on the key structural features of competing narratives in the controversy in the form of antithetical elements in the text: purity and danger; open and closed information; expert and folk knowledge; and entrepreneurship and inertia. They used this framework to unpack 'the multiple and complex meanings particular to [this] policy situation' (Lejano and Leong 2012: 794), and to construct an initial narrative of the conflict that incorporated views of both policy networks. They then identified cues in the text about other meaningful aspects of the context that shed light on the main narrative, for example meaning policy actors evoked about a prior attempt to create a wastewater recycling program and reassessed the initial narrative in light of the analysis of context and other texts. This enabled them to produce a deeper understanding of the interpretations various participants gave to the conflict, and why the project was rejected.

Future research could explore how the grand narratives of network governance – for instance, as depicted in the texts of particular networks – shape serendipitous networks, creating new possibilities for governing, but also placing constraints on governing actors. Research questions might include 'How do competing grand narratives in serendipitous networks interact, and what effect does this have on what networks can and cannot produce for society?' (see for example, Metze and Dodge 2016), 'How do conflicting narratives affect serendipitous networks?', 'How do alternative narratives compete in serendipitous networks?', 'What consequences does such competition have for the serendipitous network and for society?' and 'Do serendipitous networks with uniformly shared narratives show low levels of conflict?' Another line of research drawing on the hybrid approach might explore the democratic potential or limitations of serendipitous networks. And a Foucauldian perspective might examine the governmentality of different forms of network governance: 'What are the technologies that manage the "conduct of conduct"?' and 'Who is empowered or disempowered through these technologies in the serendipitous network?'

The hermeneutic tradition, which is not often used in PA, holds promise for understanding the ways competing coalitions in a debate about public policy support or block socially beneficial programs and practices. It offers a powerful framework for unpacking underlying assumptions transmitted through particular narratives, for instance about the value of market-based versus bureaucratically directed forms of social action, and the ways conflicting meanings across coalitions come to structure debates and thus policy solutions.

Understanding goal-directed networks

Examining *goal-directed networks* from the 'narrative as metaphor' tradition also emphasizes the grand narratives or discourses in society but focuses on their underlying assumptions and meanings specifically about partnerships, ventures and alliances (versus spontaneous social relations). Scholars applying this tradition tend to take a critical view of the discourses, exposing their contradictions, tensions and pressures. Because scholars in this tradition assume that local actors have limited agency to interpret discourses from their own perspectives, they focus on how the actions of local actors are shaped by grand narratives in ways that constrain and open up their behaviour to produce dysfunctions, omissions and the like. As is common in the 'narrative as metaphor' tradition, data sources are most often composed of documents as texts rather than interviews. Scholars analyse these data to explicate the grand narratives of partnerships, delineating their major assumptions, emphases and omissions. They (sometimes) examine the local expression of discourses in networks, not as a means to understand how they are interpreted in local contexts but as a means to demonstrate the overall features of the discourse itself, and to provide evidence of its influence.

Three papers in our sample use narrative as metaphor to study goal-directed networks (Skelcher, Mathur and Smith 2005; Willems and Van Dooren 2016; West 2005). Each offers a hybrid that examines a combination of subjective and objective factors to explain partnerships, albeit within an overall social constructionist epistemology. Skelcher, Mathur and Smith (2005), for instance, studied partnerships through a comparative case study design that draws on interviews, a governance assessment, a questionnaire and various documents. Drawing on both institutional theory and interpretive policy analysis they examined the rules, norms and discourses that shape partnerships in these contexts. They found that the various institutional designs of partnerships – labelled 'club', 'agency' or 'polity' – 'reflect different settlements between [competing] discourses' of managerialism, consociationalism and participatory democracy that provide an overall set of rules for decision-making (573). They argue that network governance creates a tension between democratic guidance and effective service delivery, and each of the institutional designs for network governance provides 'a distinct solution to the democracy-delivery tension' (574).

Promising avenues of future research would include exploring the extent to which conflicting or diverse narratives present among members of the goal-directed networks affect its functioning. In other words, which narratives are more conducive to network functioning and when? When are contrasting co-existing narratives beneficial and when detrimental? One could also examine the kinds of discourses that shape goal-directed networks, unpack their assumptions about network behaviour and examine the implications of those narratives on the implementation of goal-directed networks. Some related questions include: 'Do narratives emphasize certain behaviours?' 'Do they make invisible certain kinds of work necessary to the operation of goal-directed networks?' 'Do they valorize certain actions while diminishing others?' and 'What are the consequences for creating social value, or upholding fairness and justice in the broader society?' The reader will note that some of these questions may also be helpful to better understand goal-directed networks by way of the narrative as knowledge tradition which, as indicated earlier, has been underused, despite its promise.

Using narrative as variable to understand metaphorical networks

The final tradition we identified to studying networks we label *narrative as variable*. This tradition assumes that the meaning of narrative elements are stable across time, space and context, and exhibit statistical regularities in their use and/ or dissemination that can be quantified. This tradition enables one to assess the relationship between key elements in a narrative, giving them relative weights within an overall framework.[11]

The narrative as variable tradition explores narrative theoretical concepts using quantitative or mixed qualitative-quantitative methodologies, especially quantitative network analysis, to map the relations between terms in a discourse. This tradition quantifies the distance in a text between meaningful elements in the discourse as a way to identify their importance and influence. It emphasizes the relational aspects of nodes (narrative elements in a discourse), and uses the term as a metaphor for conceptualizing and understanding social reality (Dowding 1995). Under this use of the network concept, nodes related to each other do not require a 'real' physical or virtual interaction, such as frequency of communication between organizations. The relations among nodes may merely represent nodes sharing some common characteristic, such as an opinion, origin, location or type. This use of the network concept is often accompanied by the use of SNA. Importantly, SNA can be used in studying the other two types of networks as well.

This tradition has been used to understand *network as an analytic metaphor*. For instance, Choi and Lecy (2012) have applied it to understand economic policy change in North Korea. Through a quantitative semantic network analysis, they were able to account 'for the association between concepts' in a discourse, capture 'the context of the discourse and allow for analysis of change over time' (595). They found that while change in North Korea seems to follow crises, 'the emergence of new policy topics occurs incrementally prior to change' suggesting that the 'foundations of economic reform in North Korea are yet weak and instable, and policy reform will continue to be vulnerable to the political influence of conservatives (589). Their approach is noteworthy for the tight fit between their theory of networks and their methodology.

The application of narrative as variable and SNA seems an obvious fit, as Choi and Lecy (2012) show. What is interesting here is that network analysis is not used to understand particular networks, but to conceptualize other phenomenon that may behave in ways similar to metaphoric networks. Mapping discourses and narratives through network analysis could be used to understand how grand narratives evolve and proliferate. This would represent another promising path through which to use narrative inquiry to illuminate network research. Rather than directly speaking to the question of how PA scholars are using narrative inquiry to study networks, it speaks to how network analysis can be used to study narratives.

Conclusion

This chapter set out to answer this question: 'To what extent and how are scholars in the PA field using narrative inquiry to study networks?' In general, we found a wide range of narrative and discursive approaches to understanding networks that have produced rich insights to advance scholarship on networks.

The most common approach to using narrative to study networks was the *narrative as metaphor* tradition. Scholars have drawn on myriad traditions within this broader category to study *serendipitous networks*, including Bevir and Rhodes' (2006) decentered approach, a hybrid that mixes this approach with quantitative analysis, and Foucauldian discourse analysis. Research in this category examines how grand narratives play out, opening up and shutting down possibilities for action in serendipitous networks. The *narrative as metaphor* tradition has also been used to study *goal-directed networks*, but only through hybrid forms that combine subjective and objective factors in an overall interpretive epistemology. These approaches demonstrate how a narrative that defines a network can have hidden purposes, unexpected omissions and can suppress positive impulses such as representation or democratic participation. It also challenges the often taken-for-granted assumption that network governance is good for society or that transition to it is inevitable, by showing how traditions and path dependencies can trump novel network narratives.

Scholars also make considerable use of the *narrative as language* approach to study both serendipitous networks and goal-directed networks. This approach illuminates the experiences of network actors and how they interpret their own actions in networks. It enables deep explorations of the experience of operating in goal-directed and serendipitous networks. It also highlights the social processes by which actors in networks resist top-down goal articulations, practice alternatives in the daily operations of networks and transform discourses in local contexts to meet their own purposes.

Despite these advancements, several promising opportunities for developing knowledge about networks using narrative inquiry are underutilized. The broader PA literature uses hermeneutics to study networks in the *narrative as metaphor* tradition (Lejano and Leong 2012; Borins 2011). Yet, this tradition has not been used to study networks in our sample of articles. Lejano and Leong's approach holds special promise for understanding the roots of conflict within serendipitous networks. Borins (2011) offers another approach that could aid in unpacking the features of deeply held cultural beliefs and values in society and how they shape understandings about the role of serendipitous networks and especially goal-directed networks. We also found no research article utilizing *narrative as knowing.* This tradition could be fruitfully applied to examine managerial work in goal-directed and serendipitous networks.

While narrative inquiry is more commonly found in European journals its use is still quite limited in PA research in general, despite its considerable potential to shed light on relevant questions in the field.

Acknowledgements

We would like to thank Seulki Lee for her excellent research assistance, especially for conducting literature searches, keeping track of our methodological process, and thoughtfully providing feedback on earlier drafts of this chapter.

Notes

1 To cover new material, and thus identify the current applications in the literature, we explored twenty-four articles published since 2005 reflecting new narrative research in PA. We searched for 'narrative' or 'discourse' in the top six PA journals in the ProQuest database from 2006 to 2016: *Journal of Public Administration Research and Theory, Public Administration Review, Governance, International Public Management Journal, Public Administration* and *Public Management Review.* Our initial search resulted in eighty-six articles. We excluded articles (1) about networks covered in the main section of the paper (eighteen), (2) that used 'narrative' or 'discourse' rhetorically rather than theoretically or methodologically (forty-one), and (3) a personal reflection and two prescriptive papers about the use of narrative analysis for exploring a theoretical framework (three). We grouped the remaining twenty-four articles into the three narrative approaches, and added a fourth approach, which we describe in the 'A map of narrative inquiry approaches to study networks' section of the chapter. The list of twenty-four articles is available upon request.
2 www.thenyic.org/
3 Moreover, while goal-directed networks can be analysed using different methodologies, they can also be analysed by applying the network concept metaphorically, such as linking nodes according to race, religion or educational background – in lieu of linking nodes in terms of physical, virtual, verbal or other interactions.
4 To populate this matrix we searched article abstracts in six public administration journals (*Journal of Public Administration Research and Theory, Public Administration Review, Governance, International Public Management Journal, Public Administration* and *Public Management Review*) from 1996 to 2016 for permutations of the keyword terms 'network', 'collaboration', 'partnership', 'coalition' or 'alliance' and 'narrative', 'discourse' or 'story'. The number of articles returned totalled twenty-eight. We eliminated ten articles because they used 'story' or 'discourse' sparsely or superficially, leaving eighteen articles for analysis. Based on a close reading of the final articles we positioned each study in the quadrants of the matrix.
5 As we described in earlier work (Dodge, Ospina and Foldy 2005), Maynard-Moody and Musheno's research spans the boundaries of our three approaches to narrative analysis.
6 The paucity of this approach in the PA literature might reflect researchers' tendency to label studies as 'action research' or its variants rather than narrative inquiry, even if the inquiry revolves around stories and narratives of experience. It might also reflect the difficulty of publishing action research in PA journals.
7 Please note, Bevir and Rhodes' original spelling of 'decentered approach' is used throughout this chapter.
8 While Bevir and Rhodes' approach might convincingly be situated within narrative as language – with its emphasis on the situated interpretations of governing actors – all

the articles in our sample tend to emphasize the constraining features of narratives and discourses on governing actors. They also tend to use documents as the source of data, although Bang (2004) uses interviews and Ferlie and McGivern (2014) use both documents and interviews.

9 In other examples, Bang (2004) examines the development of 'culture governance' in Denmark to show how network forms of governance require governing actors to discipline themselves into 'more communicative and cooperative modes' of engagement across old boundaries of public, private and voluntary sectors (159), while Needham (2009) explores the consumerist 'narrative' among members of the UK's criminal justice policy network to understand how the criminal justice system creates 'customers'. Gains (2009) explores how UK local officials interpret national reform narratives, including NPM. Goodwin and Grix (2011) critically explored the new governance form in practice in two cases in the UK – sports policy and education policy – contrasting it with 'governance narrative'. Using document analysis, they found that these fields exhibit elements of network governance but are also part of a state strategy that reduces the autonomy of decentralized agencies and creates their dependence on the centre.

10 Hajer and Wagenaar (2003) provide a highly influential Foucauldian approach to network governance.

11 Although we did not find any articles mentioning the Narrative Policy Framework in our sample, perhaps because it is more likely to appear in policy journals (e.g. Jones and McBeth 2010), we would include it within the narrative as variable approach. This approach departs from the interpretive variants of narrative inquiry by combining interpretive theoretical frameworks with positivist methodologies and methods. For a critique see Dodge 2015.

References

Agranoff, R. 2007. *Managing within networks: Adding value to public organizations.* Washington DC: Georgetown University Press.

Agranoff, R. and M. McGuire. 2003. "Inside the matrix: Integrating the paradigms of intergovernmental and network management." *International Journal of Public Administration* 26 (12): 1401–1422.

Bang, H.P. 2004. "Culture governance: Governing self-reflexive modernity." *Public Administration* 82 (1): 157–190.

Bevir, M. and R. Rhodes. 2003. *Interpreting British governance.* Abingdon, UK: Routledge.

Bevir, M. and R. Rhodes. 2004. "Interpretation as method, explanation and critique: A reply." *British Journal of Politics and International Relations* 6 (2): 156–161.

Bevir, M. and R.A. Rhodes. 2010. *The state as cultural practice.* Oxford: Oxford University Press.

Bevir, M. and R.A.W. Rhodes. 2006. "Interpretive approaches to British government and politics." *British Politics* 1 (1): 84–112.

Biebricher, T. 2011. "Faith-based initiatives and the challenges of governance." *Public Administration* 89 (3): 1001–1014.

Borins, S. 2011. *Governing fables: Learning from public sector narratives.* Charlotte, NC: Information Age Publishing, Inc.

Bruner, J. 2004. "Life as narrative." *Social Research* 71 (3): 691–710.

Choi, C. and J.D. Lecy. 2012. "A semantic network analysis of changes in North Korea's economic policy." *Governance* 25 (4): 589–616.

Davies, A. and R. Thomas. 2003. "Talking cop: Discourses of change and policing identities." *Public Administration* 81 (4): 681–699.

Davies, A. and R. Thomas. 2008. "Dixon of dock green got shot! Policing identity work and organizational change." *Public Administration* 86 (3): 627–642.

Dodge, J. 2015. "The deliberative potential of civil society organizations: Framing hydraulic fracturing in New York." *Policy Studies* 36 (3): 249–266.

Dodge, J., S.M. Ospina, and E.G. Foldy. 2005. "Integrating rigor and relevance in public administration scholarship: The contribution of narrative inquiry." *Public Administration Review* 65 (3): 286–300.

Dowding, K. 1995. "Model or metaphor? A critical review of the policy network approach." *Political Studies* 43 (1): 136–158.

Feldman, M. and K. Sköldberg. 2002. "Stories and the rhetoric of contrariety: Subtexts of organizing (change)." *Culture and Organization* 8 (4): 275–292.

Feldman, M., K. Sköldberg, R.N. Brown, and D. Horner. 2002. "Making sense of stories: A rhetorical approach to narrative analysis." Paper presented at the American Political Science Association Conference, December 8–11, Boston, MA.

Ferlie, E. and G. McGivern. 2014. "Bringing Anglo-governmentality into public management scholarship: The case of evidence-based medicine in UK Health Care." *Journal of Public Administration Research and Theory* 24 (1): 59–83.

Gains, F. 2009. "Narratives and dilemmas of local bureaucratic elites: Whitehall at the coal face?" *Public Administration* 87 (1): 50–64.

Gergen, K. J. 1985. "The social constructionist movement in modern psychology." *American Psychologist* 40 (3): 266.

Goodwin, M. and J. Grix. 2011. "Bringing structures back in: The 'governance' narrative, the 'decentred approach' and 'asymmetrical network governance' in the education and sport policy communities." *Public Administration* 89 (2): 537–556.

Hajer, M.A. and H. Wagenaar. 2003. "Introduction." In *Deliberative policy analysis: Understanding governance in the network society*, edited by M. Hajer and H. Wagenaar, 1–32. Cambridge: Cambridge University Press.

Hendriks, C.M. 2009. "The democratic soup: Mixed meanings of political representation in governance networks." *Governance* 22 (4): 689–715.

Huxham, C. and S. Vangen. 2000. "Leadership in the shaping and implementation of collaboration agendas: How things happen in a (not quite) joined-up world." *Academy of Management Journal* 43 (6): 1159–1175.

Jacobs, K. 2010. "The politics of partnerships: A study of police and housing collaboration to tackle anti-social behaviour on Australian public housing estates." *Public Administration* 88 (4): 928–942.

Jones, M.D. and M.K. McBeth. 2010. "A narrative policy framework: Clear enough to be wrong?" *Policy Studies Journal* 38 (2): 329–353.

Keast, R., K. Brown, and M. Mandell. 2007. "Getting the right mix: Unpacking integration meanings and strategies." *International Public Management Journal* 10 (1): 9–33.

Keast, R., M.P. Mandell, and R. Agranoff. 2013. *Network theory in the public sector: Building new theoretical frameworks*, Vol. 17. Abingdon, UK: Routledge.

Kickert, W.J.M., E.-H. Klijn, and J.F.M. Koppenjan. 1997. *Managing complex networks: Strategies for the public sector*. Thousand Oaks, CA: Sage Publications.

Kilduff, M. and W. Tsai. 2003. *Social networks and organizations*. London, GB: Sage Publications.

Klijn, E.-H., J. Edelenbos, and B. Steijn. 2010. "Trust in governance networks: Its impacts on outcomes." *Administration & Society* 42 (2): 193–221.

Klijn, E.-H. and J.F. Koppenjan. 2000. "Public management and policy networks: Foundations of a network approach to governance." *Public Management an International Journal of Research and Theory* 2 (2): 135–158.

Koliba, C. and J. Lathrop. 2007. "Inquiry as intervention: Employing action research to support an organization's capacity to learn." *Administration & Society* 39 (1): 51–76.

Lejano, R.P. and C. Leong. 2012. "A hermeneutic approach to explaining and understanding public controversies." *Journal of Public Administration Research and Theory* 22 (4): 793–814.

Mathur, N. and C. Skelcher. 2007. "Evaluating democratic performance: Methodologies for assessing the relationship between network governance and citizens." *Public Administration Review* 67 (2): 228–237.

Maynard-Moody, S.W. and M.C. Musheno. 2003. *Cops, teachers, counselors: Stories from the front lines of public service.* Ann Arbor: University of Michigan Press.

Maynard-Moody, S. and M. Musheno. 2012. "Social equities and inequities in practice: Street-level workers as agents and pragmatists." *Public Administration Review* 72 (SI): S16–S23.

Metze, T. and J. Dodge. 2016. "Dynamic discourse coalitions on hydro-fracking in Europe and the United States." *Environmental Communication*: 1–15. Online first: doi: http://dx.doi.org/10.1080/17524032.2015.1133437.

Needham, C. 2009. "Policing with a smile: Narratives of consumerism in new Labour's criminal justice policy." *Public Administration* 87 (1): 97–116.

Nohrstedt, D. 2013. "Advocacy coalitions in crisis resolution: Understanding policy dispute in the European Volcanic ash cloud crisis: Advocacy coalitions in crisis resolution." *Public Administration* 91 (4): 964–979.

Ospina, S.M. and J. Dodge. 2005a. "It's about time: Catching method up to meaning: The usefulness of narrative inquiry in public administration research." *Public Administration Review* 65 (2): 143–157.

Ospina, S.M. and J. Dodge. 2005b. "Narrative inquiry and the search for connectedness: Practitioners and academics developing public administration scholarship." *Public Administration Review* 65 (4): 409–423.

O'Toole, L.J. and K.J. Meier. 2004. "Public management in intergovernmental networks: Matching structural networks and managerial networking." *Journal of Public Administration Research and Theory* 14 (4): 469–494.

Provan, K.G. and P. Kenis. 2008. "Modes of network governance: Structure, management, and effectiveness." *Journal of Public Administration Research and Theory* 18 (2): 229–252.

Provan, K.G. and H.B. Milward. 2001. "Do networks really work? A framework for evaluating public-sector organizational networks." *Public Administration Review* 61 (4): 414–423.

Riessman, C.K. 2002. "Narrative analysis." In *The Qualitative researcher's companion*, edited by A. Michael Huberman and Matthew B. Miles, 217–270. Thousand Oaks, CA: Sage Publications.

Saz Carranza, A. and I. Garcia. 2012. *The support network for the economic internationalization of Los Angeles Metro.* Barcelona: ESADE, Center for Global Economy and Geopolitics (ESADEgeo).

Saz-Carranza, A. and S.M. Ospina. 2011. "The behavioral dimension of governing interorganizational goal-directed networks: Managing the unity-diversity tension." *Journal of Public Administration Research and Theory* 21 (2): 327–365.

Skelcher, C., N. Mathur, and M. Smith. 2005. "The public governance of collaborative spaces: Discourse, design and democracy." *Public Administration* 83 (3): 573–596.

Tomlinson, I.J. 2010. "Acting discursively: The development of UK organic food and farming policy networks." *Public Administration* 88 (4): 1045–1062.

West, K. 2005. "From bilateral to trilateral governance in local government contracting in France." *Public Administration* 83 (2): 473–492.

Willems, T. and W. Van Dooren. 2016. "(De)Politicization dynamics in public: Private partnerships (PPPs): Lessons from a comparison between UK and Flemish PPP policy." *Public Management Review* 18 (2): 199–220.

6 Q methodology

Rob Kivits

Introduction to Q methodology

Q methodology was invented by the psychologist William Stephenson in the 1930s, and most applications of Q methodology have been within the human behaviour field (Stephenson 1990). The purpose of Q methodology is to investigate the individual's own perspectives and opinions (Previte, Pini and Haslam-McKenzie 2007). It is considered a subjective science (Goldman 1999). The strength of Q methodology is that it allows individual responses to be collated and correlated, to extract 'idealized' forms of discourse, latent within the data provided by individuals involved in the study. Forms of discourse are complex and detailed and can be challenging for individuals to express in their own words when asked directly. To avoid leading the individual to an answer by placing words in their mouth, Q methodology allows the researcher to ask relevant 'side' questions, and through the responses unpack the dormant, underlying discourse that an individual adheres to. Due to the strength of the method, as well as its robustness proven over time, Q methodology has been increasingly used in other disciplines, such as political science, public policy, economics and environmental science. For example, through Q methodology, Dryzek (1993) proposes a four-fold categorization based upon the two dichotomies: Reformist-Radical and Prosaic-Imaginative. Dryzek extends his analysis to offer a range of sub-categories in his analysis of environmental discourses (see Table 6.1). While Dryzek's approach was not a full Q-methodology approach, it can be considered as one of the first steps toward fully utilizing the methodology.

The key to the Q approach is to consider the data in terms of the individual's entire pattern of responses – an 'internal pattern' – rather than looking for patterns among people. In effect, the respondents (and not the test) are the variables.

Q methodology is a rigorous research methodology that is congruent with the philosophical principles of person-centred approaches (Eden, Donaldson and Walker 2005), meaning that it helps to get to the bottom of what people really believe, rather than putting them into boxes. In doing so, the methodology neither tests its participants nor imposes a priori meanings. Participants are asked to decide what is meaningful and significant from their perspective. In general, most qualitative techniques assume that respondents have quite sophisticated

Table 6.1 Dryzek's classification of environmental discourses

	Reformist	Radical
Prosaic	Problem Solving	'Survivalism'
Imaginative	Sustainability	Green Radicalism

verbal skills to express their opinions. If respondents are not able to express their feelings or opinions clearly it is usually up to the researcher to interpret what the respondent meant. At this early stage of the research, where it is important to get the qualitative concepts right (to help set up potential future measurements for example), it is important to avoid researcher bias. Q methodology has been consistently demonstrated to take away much of the researcher bias at this important stage of the research (Barry and Proops 1999). This is because respondents use the statements from the Q sample rather than their own words to represent their opinions. With a large enough Q sample, if one allows for high variance in the sample, this technique has been proven to be very effective in representing respondents' opinions, as well as reducing researcher bias (Brown 1993).

This chapter addresses topics that will help to gain a clearer understanding of the method, its relevance and application, as well as how to evaluate and interpret outcomes in general.

Relevance of Q methodology

In addition to other methodologies discussed in this book, this chapter highlights the usefulness of Q methodology in researching networks and collaboration in the public sector. Q methodology is applied to unpack a stakeholder's frame of reference for viewing the world (de Bruijn and ten Heuvelhof 2000; van de Riet 2003; Ryan et al. 2006). A person's internal frame of reference, or policy frame, is unique and shaped over the years by personal experiences, education, culture and familial relationships (Butts 2008). Though unique for each person, a single person's policy frame on a certain topic can overlap to some degree with those of others. Within a community, multiple groups of people can exist that share similar policy frames (Gasper and Apthorpe 1996; Barry and Proops 1999). This overlapping part of the policy frames is henceforth referred to as the 'policy discourse' (Barry and Proops 1999; Kroesen and Broer 2009). A policy discourse describes the way in which a group of people looks at a topic and how they will consequently behave toward that topic; it also describes how they will interact with other people on that same topic (Skelcher, Mathur and Smith 2005; Kroesen and Broer 2009). In other words, by using Q methodology to unpack an individual's frames of reference and aggregating them (through factor analysis) into a policy discourse, it creates a unique vantage point from which to understand the expectations and motivations of participants of a network or collaboration. With the concept that 'knowing is half the battle', this information can provide particularly useful insight on how to facilitate and engage with stakeholders.

The policy discourses are highly context-specific and, when delved into and uncovered, they reveal different sub-groups – or stakeholder groups – within a group, such as a collaboration network. Stakeholder groups that do not share policy discourses are also more likely to use different vocabularies and jargon (van Eeten, Loucks and Roe 2002). This can result in stakeholders using a similar terminology, but attaching different meanings to it, thereby resulting in confusion, miscommunication and tensions between members – all leading to anti-collaborative behaviour. For example, even the word 'collaboration' can have myriad interpretations depending on a person's perspective. If it is simply assumed everyone understands it the same way there are likely to be misperceptions over actions in the future. Policy discourses also expose the underlying reasons for, or backgrounds to, stakeholders' objectives; that is to say, different stakeholders can have similar goals yet are driven by different motives. Conversely, stakeholders might share similar motives yet aim for different objectives. It follows that understanding these stakeholder groups in this way and classifying them accordingly can significantly enhance the effectiveness of engagement practices and, consequently, policy implementation (Gasper and Apthorpe 1996; McLaughlin 2005).

One particular area of application where this approach has been proven successful is the Airport Metropolis Research Project (2012). During this project it became evident that collaboration between a multitude of vastly different stakeholders had become obstructed by a lack of understanding between various parties. Some privatized airports considered their most important stakeholders to be private equity investors that had injected sufficient amounts into airports and therefore assumed that 'distanced' airport shareholders were more likely to prioritize economic-based objectives than those of alternative stakeholders such as local communities. However, regardless of the reasons – economic or otherwise – stakeholders were becoming more visible to airport managers. There was an emerging realization of the importance of sustaining a safe, profitable, environmentally sensitive and equitable airport business, understood as an evolving urban hub in its own right. Through an extensive stakeholder analysis using Q methodology, it became clear during the Airport Metropolis Research Project how certain important stakeholders, who were originally grouped as one (for example, 'the community'), should have been approached as four different groups of like-minded stakeholders, each with their own motivations, requests, expectations and expected level of interaction. Dealing with mindsets differing from an economical perspective to an ecological perspective, interspersed with different expectations on what 'collaboration' actually is, and who should be involved in a land-planning process, the outcome of this analysis proved to be an eye-opener for the problem-owners and made them realize their approach to their stakeholders needed to change.

The frames of reference component therefore allow nuanced, fine-grained and, often otherwise unavailable, insight into the real issues, rather than presenting stakeholders' interests. Within the specified context of the problem, in this instance a networking and collaboration context, those interests are likely to provide a certain degree of overlap among the stakeholders, thereby allowing for stakeholder grouping based on overlapping individual interests. Arguably, these interests are at an aggregated level (and not necessary a detailed one) and, for the application of engagement specifics, can matter a great deal. Simply having the initial grouping at hand, provided through the analysis, does not therefore mean that we also have an engagement tool ready. It is essential that through sequential steps that follow the analysis these stakeholders are further engaged to confirm any assumptions made through the analysis.

It can be difficult to forecast the actual outcome of a frame of reference analysis in advance; however, previous research, such as that carried out by Van Eeten (2001), and Kroesen and Broer (2009), shows that it is indeed possible, albeit within certain boundaries. First, assumptions will have to be made within the right context, without prejudice yet with prior knowledge of the context. Secondly, researchers will have to keep an open mind for when the outcomes do not meet the expectations to allow themselves to change their perspectives. When the context and boundaries of the research are confined to a narrow area, such as only perceptions on collaboration, a frame-of-reference analysis can produce sufficient detail within the given context to arrive at the level of analysis needed to group stakeholders by their interests. The methodology required and followed to arrive at this level of analysis is discussed in detail in this section.

The advantage of using frames of reference over traditional 'interest-based surveys' is that frames of reference unpack stakeholders' underlying, or unspoken, interests, rather than their outspoken interests. It is conceded that outspoken interests may appear more specific and detailed; however, they often obscure the underlying interests that are more essential to understand when devising stakeholder engagement strategies. To use an example from prior aviation-related research (Kivits and Charles 2015), an opponent to an airport might voice their desire to reduce the number of flights during the night. This would be the outspoken interest. The underlying interest, however, might be that this person has recently bought a small dog that is frightened by the loud noise of the aircraft flying over at night, and as a result soils the carpet. An alternative approach to this problem might be to facilitate noise-sensitivity training for the dog to remove the problem. The message is that by understanding the underlying interests better, targeted engagement can ensue, and mutually agreeable solutions can be found. In networking, when a facilitator understands the underlying reasons and interests for a participant to collaborate within the network, mutually rewarding goals are likely to be achieved more easily.

Although the proposed frame-of-reference analysis might not present specific detail regarding specific issues, it nevertheless provides a significant step forward with respect to additional understanding and potential differentiation. In an example of one of the frames of reference uncovered by Van Eeten (2001), the knowledge that one group of stakeholders believed that airplanes are a significant contributor to environmental pollution, yet at the same time believed that

technological advantages in the future could allow for mitigation of these problems, allowed Schiphol Airport Management to address these concerns more
specifically in its subsequent engagement strategies. It is therefore up to the
problem-owner to translate the more aggregated analysis of the frame of reference into specific tactical strategies.

In comparison, stakeholders' frames of reference are relatively static. While
research has shown how frames of reference can change over time (e.g. Kroesen
and Broer 2009), the scale is significantly larger compared to the rapid changes
in other factors. Changes in frames of reference take place gradually and over
decades (de Bruijn and ten Heuvelhof 2000; Butts 2008). This has its own
implications for stakeholder engagement practices, as one cannot be expected
to change one's view overnight.

Q-methodology application

It is essential to understand the way in which a group of people looks at a topic,
and how they will consequently behave toward that topic; this behaviour also
indicates how they will interact with other persons on that same topic (Skelcher,
Mathur and Smith 2005; Kroesen and Broer 2009). Therefore, Q methodology
has been used to capture these interactions, allowing for a much more narrative
breakdown of key viewpoints surrounding a particular topic.

In brief, Q methodology involves each participant in the sample (the P sample) sorting a series of 'statements' (a Q sample) representative of the breadth of
debate on an issue (the concourse) into a distribution of preference (a Q sort),
from which statistically significant factors are derived (Jeffares and Skelcher
2008). Participants can be approached in two ways to perform the sort. The
researcher can assist the participant in sorting the statements face to face, or the
sort can be done remotely using computer software.

There are four widely recognized stages to conducting a Q study (Jeffares
and Skelcher 2008; Dziopa and Ahern 2011): (1) concourse establishment, (2)
concourse management, (3) Q survey and (4) statistical analysis. The following
sections discuss in detail what is involved in each step.

Step 1 – concourse establishment

The first step is to establish the concourse. To do so, researchers can utilize document analysis or pre-surveys within each case, allowing for the possibility of
gaining a good understanding of the context early in the research. The various
stages of the *specific policy review* produce a large publicly available database of
context information on stakeholder perspectives on a particular issue. In addition, some issues also provide case studies that can be integrated into this step.
This therefore forms a second document set with detailed information on the
researcher's issue of interest.

It is to be expected that an analysis of available documents can identify
distinct and clear statements on the topic at hand, for example 'collaboration'.

These statements should be collected and coded for the compilation of the Q set.

Thematic text analysis can be used to investigate documents for key themes using, for example, Leximancer (Smith and Humphreys 2006) or NUDIST. Most qualitative analysis software enables the user to navigate the complexity of text in an automated fashion. The software identifies 'concepts', referred to here as 'themes', within the text – not merely keywords but focused clusters of related, defining terms, as they appear in the text, and not according to a predefined dictionary or thesaurus. The themes are presented in a compelling, interactive display so that users can clearly visualize and interrogate their interconnectedness and co-occurrence (which is as important as the themes themselves), right down to the original text that spawned the concepts. Leximancer, for example, embraces the complexity of language, thereby allowing the true meaning to emerge from the text itself, and without human bias (Smith and Humphreys 2006).

Identified themes should be compared with previous manually identified information for cross-comparison to ensure all possible information had been extracted from the available documents. The definition of themes after manually analysing the text, rather than before, ensures that the researcher approaches the text with a fresh and open mindset, able to identify alternative themes that might not be recognized by analytical programs. This is consistent with Peräkylä et al.'s (2008) advice that thematic coding is best approached informally when the analysis of text is complimentary to, but not pivotal in, the overall research design.

The concourse is constructed using statements from various sources to maximize the variance and depth of the concourse. Bracken and Fischel (2006) state that many different sources can be used for concourse development, including interview data, focus group data and analysis of academic, media, and other texts, or a combination of these. For example, Kivits and Charles (2015) studied the policy discourse in relation to airport expansion. In this case, ample interesting data were available. The airport expansion debate has been portrayed in-depth with the National Aviation Policy Paper (Australian Government 2009) development process, thereby resulting in numerous responses from government departments, industry stakeholders and community stakeholders. Australian media around airport expansion and statements from a first round of interviews have been added as a final step to create the concourse regarding Australian airport expansion. More than 5,000 submissions were put through qualitative concept analysis, and nine initial concourse areas of interest were identified, resulting in an initial set of 200+ statements (the Q set).

Step 2 – concourse management

The second step is reducing the entire concourse to a manageable series of statements. These statements should represent every aspect of the concourse and can therefore easily number in the hundreds. It is important to narrow down these statements for the Q sample. Numbers between thirty and one hundred are deemed manageable for participants (Barry and Proops 1999), though for obvious reasons a lesser amount of statements is easier to manage for a participant. It is important to ensure that the sample of statements remains representative of the diversity within the concourse (Jeffares and Skelcher 2008). Scholars use a range of methods to achieve this, including locating statements within a table where statements have different properties (Jeffares and Skelcher 2008).

For example, a concourse can be identified to span six key categories, on which multiple researchers involved reach consensus. A concourse represented by six different categories is well represented with a Q sample of five or six statements per category, resulting in a Q sample of thirty to thirty-six statements (Barry and Proops 1999). Six statements that are best representative of these key categories are selected through thorough examination, testing, critical review and repeating the process until a saturation point has been reached. One could, for example, use pilot studies and parties external to the research to help narrow the concourse.

Ideally, Q statements are short, stand-alone sentences, focused on a single topic, that are easy and quick to read and understand, and express an idea clearly and simply (Webler et al. 2009). These statements should always avoid double-barrelled statements, double-negatives or any other confusing language. To ensure that the Q sample used represents the entire concourse, strategic or stratified sampling should be used.

Step 3 – Q survey

The third step is transforming the reduced statement set of, for example, thirty-six statements into the actual survey. The final set of statements is called the Q sample. The sample population, the P sample, is asked to sort the Q sample into a Q sort (see Figure 6.1 for an example of a Q-sort grid used for thirty-four statements). The P sample should be a representative sample of a particular

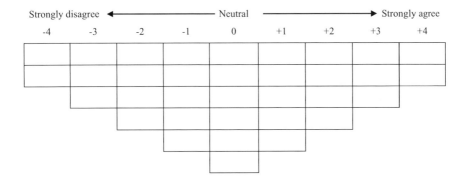

Figure 6.1 Example of a Q-sort grid for sorting the Q sample

demographic interest (for example, a sample could be all participants in a collaboration network under investigation).

The Q sort is undertaken by having respondents sort each statement in a grid, as presented in Figure 6.1. By using a grid the respondents are forced to select the statements with which they agree or disagree more in comparison with another statement. In this way, the patterns of subjective perspectives held within a group of respondents can be identified (Brown 1993).

In general, the erroneous assumption is often made that the forced, quasi-normal distribution is a supposed behavioural conclusion; that is, that persons, when left to their own devices, will naturally sort the statements in this way. Consequently, this could lead to the question '*Could it be that the participant, without the forced pattern, might have ranked the statements differently?*' This could occur and, in fact, probably will occur. Research over the decades, however, provides strong evidence that, given a suitably representative sample of stimuli (objects, pictures, odours, piano chords, weights, Q statements, etc.), persons judging the stimuli will tend to establish a hedonic midpoint that will produce balance (half above and half below the midpoint), and will distribute the stimuli in such a way as not to deviate significantly from a normal curve (McKeown and Thomas 1988; Brown 1993; Hogan 2008). In Q methodology, much of this depends on the quality and representativeness of the Q sample, which are achievements that the experimental design of Q samples helps to facilitate (Gallagher and Porock 2010).

Aside from these considerations, the most important point is that the forced distribution is not a behavioural assumption; rather, it is a formal model designed to assist with the Q sorting and provide conditions for revealing preferences. Left on their own, respondents are more likely to place all those statements with which they agree under the +5 and +4 options, thereby showing that they are in full agreement with those statements (as would happen with a survey based on R methodology[1]). Under the constraints of the forced distribution, the researcher can discover that there are two (or more) different kinds of people who 'agree'. Though similar statements might be selected for the +5 and +4, the difference in ranking that follows under the +3 and +2 columns will define the difference between these two groups that both 'agree'. Moreover, these differences are reliable, as could be determined by asking the same individuals to do the Q sort again a week later to see if the same factors emerge and are defined by the same individuals. Without the constraints of the forced distribution, such distinctions would be buried beneath the fact that all statements receive similar scores in a standard survey (Brown 1980; Thomas and Watson 2002).

Q sort can be performed manually or electronically. In either approach the sequence is the same. In larger Q-sample surveys it can be useful to use a two-staged approach, where participants are first asked to create three piles out of the statements: 'agree', 'disagree' and 'neutral' (cf. Brown 1993). Once these three piles have been created, the participant is then asked to look, for example, at the 'agree' pile, and select the one statement they agree with the most. This statement is placed on the furthest right-hand column of the Q grid. This is followed by doing the same for the 'disagree' pile. The statement the participant disagrees with the most is placed on the furthest left-hand column of the Q grid. The participant then goes back to the 'agree' pile, and now selects the next one they agree with the most, and so on and so forth. Only after the 'agree' and 'disagree' piles have been depleted will the participant address the 'neutral' pile. The Q grid in Figure 6.1 displays a 'forced' quasi-normal distribution, implying that participants need to decide which two statements they agree with most, which three statements they agree with second most and so forth (cf. Watts and Stenner 2005). When participants have placed all the statements in the responding boxes they are given the chance to change statements around before submitting the final result, or to have the final result recorded by the researcher. For electronic Q sort, researchers can use an open application, such as FlashQ or any other available software, to sort the Q statements.

Step 4 – statistical analysis

The final stage of the Q methodology is the statistical analysis, which enables the researcher to look at and interpret the sorts. The goal of this is to take the many viewpoints held by the individual participants and boil them down into a fewer number of frames of reference that represent sub-groups sharing common ideas, opinions and views. The statistical analytical tool used for this is factor analysis. This is the same mathematical process as used in common survey analysis, although the objective of applying factor analysis in Q methodology is different from standard statistical analysis or R methodology. One fundamental distinction is that of 'data reduction' versus 'understanding latent constructs'. In the former case, the research goal is to take a relatively large set of variables and reduce them to a smaller, more manageable number while retaining as much of the original variance as possible. In such uses, there is no attempt to interpret the resulting variables in terms of latent constructs, with the use being pragmatic and quantitative rather than theoretical and qualitative (Conway and Huffcutt 2003). By accounting for as much variance as possible the researcher can be confident that the findings relate to a significant part of the original target population.

Q methodology, however, is interested in making interpretations regarding constructs rather than purely reducing data. In Q methodology the *sample* and the *population* are different from those of R methodology. The *sample* refers to the set of statements, not the respondents. The emphasis is on the factor scores and the subjectivity involved. According to Brown (1980), these factors will reappear in essentially the same form, no matter what set of respondents provides the Q sort. As a result, the demand for a larger P sample diminishes.

A second difference between R methodology and Q methodology is that R methodology using cluster analysis might, at first sight, look like Q methodology, yet it does not develop the same understanding created by Q methodology (Stephenson 1990). In a Q study the variables are the Q sorts. If there are twenty Q sorts, created by twenty participants, there are twenty variables. A factor analysis attempts to bring this complexity down to a simpler picture, usually between two and five factors. It creates a new variable, a hypothetical Q sort, that represents what each person's frame of reference has in common with other people who share similar frames. Factor rotation enables the researcher to look for particular statement combinations in the sorts (Combes, Hardy and Buchan 2004). This typically produces one or more 'factors'. The researcher then interprets the cluster of statements within each factor to produce a statement of this discourse (Jeffares and Skelcher 2008). The process may include other states, including capturing qualitative information from respondents on the rationale for their Q-sort choices, or feeding the results back to respondents so that a richer understanding of the meanings identified can be gained (Brown 1980). It is then the task of the researcher to interpret the outcomes of the factor analysis, but not for best fit of variance for the population; rather, the factors must be interpreted and analysed to see whether additional factors introduce additional frames of reference (Hogan 2008). For instance, an additional factor may have low variance and add little to the overall explained variance of the set of factors, yet it might introduce a significantly different frame of reference not explained before.

The Q analysis: from Q data to frames of reference

The process of analysing the Q-sort data is assisted by using PQMethod, a program designed by Peter Schmolck that is available as freeware (Schmolck 2002). This software (latest update 2014) is easier to use for Q analysis than standard statistical software (such as SPSS), as it produces output that is specifically designed for Q research and is easy to interpret in a Q context. It is acknowledged here that the same analysis could have been performed using SPSS or other statistical packages, and a preliminary investigation has shown that near identical results are obtained, as supported by Hogan (2008) and Webler et al. (2007). That said, the ease of use of the program, supported by the specialization of the software, allows for significant time saving while analysing the data. PQMethod has been used extensively in earlier research, as evidenced by Block (1978), McKeown and Thomas (1988), Stainton-Rogers (1995), Brown (1996), Donner (2001) and Webler et al. (2009). This section details how the data are analysed using PQMethod. An extensive guide on how to use PQMethod is available at www.lrz.de/~schmolck/qmethod/pqmanual.htm and will not be treated in this chapter.

Data can be entered in two ways. The first is by following the data entry 'QENTER' option in the program. An entered Q sort of one respondent resembles the view displayed in Figure 6.1. As the entering of multiple Q sorts in PQMethod can take up a lot of time, it is easier to prepare a data file in Comma Separated Variable (CSV) format. CSV formatted files can be generated by, for example, Microsoft Excel.

Once the data are arranged appropriately for the PQMethod program, the next step is to run the factor analysis itself. PQMethod offers two factor analysis algorithms: (1) Centroid Factor Analysis (CFA) and (2) Principal Components Factor Analysis (PCA). PCA is the most common type of factor analysis, but CFA is popular among Q users who like to use the option to rotate factors by hand (Webler et al. 2007). Experiments for the data within this Q study prompted the conclusion that both PCA and CFA lead to the same conclusions and do not have any influence on the final outcome. This is common in most Q studies, with the preference for the researcher to rotate factors by hand or automatically seeming to be the main decision factor over whether to use CFA or PCA.

PQMethod offers two rotation methods: (1) manual rotation, and (2) a Varimax rotation. Varimax rotation is an automatic rotation of factors that minimizes the statistical variation in the data. Manual rotation is useful for testing particular hypotheses about how certain individuals' perspectives relate to each other. As this study does not involve testing a particular hypothesis on subjects' frames of reference, but rather takes an explorative approach to extract the existing frames of reference, the minimization of statistical variance is deemed more appropriate. As a result, a PCA in combination with a Varimax rotation is used.

From the outcome of the PCA, the analyst needs to determine how many factors will be analysed. There is no one objectively correct number of factors to use, and any number of factors will give insight into how people think about the issue at hand. Nevertheless, there are several rules of thumb that can be used to decide which number of factors provides the most useful results (Webler et al. 2009):

- *Simplicity*: All things being equal, fewer factors are better since it makes the viewpoints at issue easier to understand. Of course, simplicity should not be taken so far that important and interesting information about differences in people's views is lost.
- *Clarity*: The ideal factor solution is one in which each respondent loads highly on one, and only one, factor. Try to minimize the number of 'confounders' (people who load on multiple factors) and 'non-loaders' (people who do not load on any factor). If a few confounders persist, this indicates that those people have truly hybrid views. Furthermore, each factor should have at least two significant loadings (Webler et al. 2007). This means that at least two participants adhere to one factor with a significant loading (a loading at $p < 0.05$). The significance level of the factor loading is calculated by using: factor loading $> 1.96/([\text{n-statements}]^{0.5})$. For example, using thirty-six statements, the factor loading must be higher than 0.33.
- *Distinctness*: Lower correlations[2] between factors are better, as highly correlated factors are similar. Nevertheless, it is not necessarily bad to have high correlations if the factor is otherwise satisfactory. It may be that two factors agree on many issues but their points of disagreement are particularly important (e.g. if they disagree about a solution that is being proposed).
- *Stability*: When comparing the results of different numbers of factors certain groups of people tend to cluster together. This is an indicator that those

individuals really do think similarly. A good set of factors will preserve as many of these stable clusters as possible.

When the selection of the number of factors has been made, PQMethod creates an output file containing five important sections:

1   *Factor matrix with an X indicating a defining sort:* This is essentially the factor loadings table. It tells which respondents agreed with each factor and by how much.
2   *Correlations-between-factor scores:* These tell how similar the factors are statistically.
3   *Normalized factor scores for each factor:* These tables are essentially idealized Q sorts representing each factor. This table shows which statements are ranked higher and lower in a factor.
4   *Descending array of differences between factors:* These show which statements a given pair of factors ranked differently. They are ordered from the statements that the first factor ranked much higher to the ones that the second factor ranked much higher. These tables are useful to clarify the differences between two superficially similar factors.
5   *Distinguishing statements and consensus statements:* These tables list the statements that were ranked significantly differently between a given factor and all other factors and the statements that were not ranked differently by any factors.

Factor descriptions are based on the ranking of the statements extracted from the output file. The factors represent the different frames of reference that exist within the group of stakeholders. This process is a highly qualitative process and requires the analyst to be aware of the full context of the research. Since it is prone to research bias, the description of each factor is subjected to a rigorous iterative process where multiple researchers describe each frame of reference independently, after which the independent outcomes are compared, collated and re-examined by the researchers. Only after all researchers are satisfied with the outcome of each frame of reference are they considered for publication.

Evaluating Q methodology

Q methodology compared to standard survey methods

Q methodology makes use of statements – the Q sample – to gather the Q sort. The statements used in the Q sample are often different from survey statements, since survey statements must be completely unambiguous (Schonlau et al. 2009). Q statements can have some ambiguity. This is useful since it gives respondents more latitude to interpret the statements (Brown 1996; Hogan 2008). In a survey each question is meant to be interpreted independently of the other questions. In a Q study, however, respondents are asked to rank statements in the context of each other (McKeown and Thomas 1988). This is an important part of the Q-methodology process, as it sheds light on the relative importance of different aspects of a person's point of view and assists in achieving a more cohesive perspective. Third, the variables and the cases are reversed in surveys and Q studies (Thomas and Watson 2002). In a survey, the cases are people sampled from some population and the variables are the questions that are asked in the survey. In a Q study, the Q statements are the *sample* drawn from the *population* of statements that people are saying about the issue being studied. The variables thus are the Q sorts. In other words, surveys are good for examining the relationships among different ideas; for example, is 'trust in the airport manager' related to 'length of time living near an airport?' With Q methodology, however, researchers examine relationships between people; for example, 'Do stakeholders one, two and three have similar or different views on airport expansion?'

Participants actively configure their own subjective representation of a topic by modelling their viewpoint in the form of a Q sort. Meaning is not a categorical construct in Q methodology; rather, it is thoroughly contextual, discursive and social. It is formative, emergent and contingent, and an empirical abstraction which must be elaborated on and understood, rather than reduced (Hogan 2008). Q methodology is appropriate when the goal is to discover the existing perspectives about a general topic. Survey methods can also answer this question, but only by surveying hundreds of people. In contrast, a Q study only requires collecting data from one or two dozen people.

Strengths of Q methodology

Q methodology is useful as an evaluation tool, as a means of clarifying conflict among parties and to understand a situation better. Key strengths of Q methodology as an evaluation tool are that it (Hogan 2008):

- allows participants to define their own frame of reference;
- can be used when the number of people involved is small;
- clarifies areas of agreement, sometimes showing that there is more consensus among people than they realized;
- clarifies areas of disagreement by putting people's views in the larger context of their overall frame of reference;
- summarizes the many frame of references held by individuals into a few shared perspectives;
- allows participants to step back and think about the bigger picture and how all of their concerns fit together; and
- promotes understanding of others' frames of reference.

Limitations of Q methodology

Q methodology also has some minor drawbacks:

- A reliance on a small number of people for data can raise the chances that an important perspective is not identified.

- It cannot tell you how popular each frame of reference is. A Q study, for example, may show that there is one frame of reference among stakeholders that supports the airport's decisions at the site, while there are two frames of reference among the stakeholders that oppose the airport's decisions (each for different reasons). This does not equal the idea that one out of three of the stakeholders agrees and two out of three stakeholders disagree. For example, the first frame of reference might be shared by ninety per cent of the stakeholders and the other two each by five per cent of the stakeholders.

Future of the method and further reading

Today, Q methodology is being used in a wide range of applications. A recent search (March 2018) on journals available revealed over 600,000 results on the keyword 'Q methodology' for the past three years. Results varied across topics, such as 'tourism', 'stakeholder analysis', 'methodological discussion on Q', 'politics', 'nursing' and many others. To the author, this signifies that whilst Q methodology may not be the best-known research method, it has grown and expanded into many areas and has become more commonly accepted. A small discussion has been observed online, where the question was raised 'What is the difference between Q method and discourse analysis?' The essential difference can be described as perceiving Q methodology as oriented to subjectivity using a statistical model, whereas discourse analysis focuses on text products and processes by using linguistic analysis. Q methodology stresses individualism, while discourse analysis stresses communicative systems. Under a disciplinary regard, Q methodology would belong to clinical psychology, whereas discourse analysis could be argued to fit better with cultural sociology.

However, rather than comparing discourse analysis and Q methodology (which is still useful in understanding each method better), it is perhaps more interesting to observe the combination of discourse analysis with Q methodology. As discourse analysis can be performed using interview data (which are then used to generate statements for the Q sort, as described earlier in this chapter) and on any discussion done with participants during and after the Q sort. As such, Q methodology is a very important part of our analysis, focusing on accessing participants' 'attitudes' on specific topics, while discourse analysis has helped us to get there and helps in facilitating wider-ranging discussions. A different perception perhaps is to say that Q methodology's concept of concourse is more general than discourse, the latter being a special case of the former.

While a meta-analysis has not been performed, it is from (perhaps subjective) observation that most applications outside clinical psychology appear to follow this approach in one way or another. The following resources utilize Q as a method of discourse analysis:

- Addams, H. and J. Proops, eds. 2000. *Social discourse and environmental policy: An application of Q methodology*. Cheltenham, UK: Edward Elgar.

- de Graaf, G. 2005. "Veterinarians' discourses on animals and clients." *Journal of Agricultural and Environmental Ethics* 18: 557–578.
- Dryzek, J.S. 1990. *Discursive democracy: Politics, policy and science.* London: Cambridge University Press. (Chapter 9, "The measure of political man – and woman" 173–189.)
- Dryzek, J.S. 1994. "Australian discourses of democracy." *Australian Journal of Political Science* 29: 221–223.
- Dryzek, J. and L.T. Holmes. 2002. *Post-communist democratization: Political discourses across thirteen countries.* Cambridge, UK: Cambridge University Press.
- Kanra, B. and S.A. Ercan, 2012. "Negotiating difference in a Muslim society: A longitudinal study of Islamic and secular discourses in Turkey." *Digest of Middle East Studies* 21 (1): 69–88.
- Peng, Y. 1998. "Democracy and Chinese political discourses." *Modern China* 24: 408–444.
- Stainton-Rogers, W., ed. 1997–1998. "Using Q as a form of discourse analysis." *Operant Subjectivity* 21: entire issue.
- Stenner, P., ed. 2008–2009. "Special issue: Q and constructivism: Between discursive practice and subjective process." *Operant Subjectivity* 32: entire issue.
- Woolley, J.T. and M.V. McGinnis. 2000. "The conflicting discourses of restoration." *Society and Natural Resources* 13: 339–357.

Further notes on Q analysis and electronic resources

In this chapter the software PQMethod has been discussed; it is, as far as the author is aware, the most widely used program. One of the downsides is that it is a DOS-based program, which often causes nervousness for newcomers due to the old-school black screen and the requirement to step away from the mouse, but it is easy to navigate when you get going and it produces all of the output you need to interpret your Q sorts.

There is the newer (and also free) software available, called 'KenQ' that is receiving good reviews and has a more 'up-to-date' web-based navigation (https://shawnbanasick.github.io/ken-q-analysis/#section1).

For further resources, please visit any or all of the following.

Online material:

- Resources Q methodology website: www.qmethod.org
- Q methodology email discussion list: Send the command "subscribe Q-Method <your name>" (without quotations or brackets) to Listserv@listserv.kent.edu
- QMethod (computer freeware): https://qmethod.org/resources/software/
- PCQ (computer software): www.pcqsoft.com/
- Brown, S.R. 1996. "Workshop on Q methodology." [3 hours]. Available via streaming at the Q methodology website.

Journals:

- *Operant Subjectivity*, quarterly journal of the International Society for the Scientific Study of Subjectivity; contact Mark Popovich, ISSSS Treasurer: $30 ISSSS membership, journal included; $10 students.
- *Q-Methodology and Theory*, annual Korean-language journal of the Korean Society for the Scientific Study of Subjectivity.
- *Journal of Human Subjectivity*, semi-annual English-language journal published by the Korean Society for the Scientific Study of Subjectivity; produced and distributed by Communication Books, Seoul. $50/year.

Bibliographies:

- Brown, S.R. 1968. "Bibliography on Q technique and its methodology." *Perceptual and Motor Skills* 26: 587–613.
- Brown, S.R. 1977. "Q bibliographic update: A continuation of 'Bibliography on Q technique and its methodology." *Operant Subjectivity* 1: 17–26 (continued in subsequent issues).
- www.qmethod.org (searchable bibliography).
- For a further and very comprehensive overview of resources, please access:
- file:///Users/ac5611/Desktop/Q_Methodology_in_Assessment_and_Research.pdf

Notes

1 Regular factor analysis in which correlations between tests are analysed. Also called the R technique.
2 As a rule of thumb, correlations are considered to be weak below 0.4, moderate between 0.4 and 0.7, and strong above 0.7 (Tabachnick 2006). It is preferable that the correlation between the factors is below 0.4. For Q analysis, however, moderate correlations are acceptable when the composite reliability of each set of statements is high (Webler, Danielson and Tuler 2007).

References

Airport Metropolis Research Project. 2012. "Final report 2007–201." Prepared for ARC and Industry. www.networksandcollaborations.com.au/research_reports.html.

Australian Government. 2009. *National aviation policy white paper: Flight path to the future.* 978-1921095-96-2. Commonwealth of Australia.

Barry, J. and Proops, J. 1999. "Seeking sustainability discourses with Q methodology." *Ecological Economics* 28 (3): 337–345.

Block, J. 1978. *The Q-sort method in personality assessment and psychiatric research.* Springfield, IL: Charles C. Thomas.

Bracken, S.S. and J.E. Fischel. 2006. "Assessment of preschool classroom practices: Application of Q-sort methodology." *Early Childhood Research Quarterly* 21 (4): 417–430.

Brown, S.R. 1980. *Political subjectivity: Applications of Q methodology in political science.* New Haven, CT: Yale University Press.

Brown, S.R. 1993. "A primer on Q methodology." *Operant Subjectivity* 16 (3/4): 91–138.

Brown, S.R. 1996. "Q methodology and qualitative research." *Qualitative Health Research* 6 (4): 561–567.

Butts, C.T. 2008. "A relational event framework for social action." *Sociological Methodology* 38 (1): 155–200.

Combes, H., G. Hardy, and L. Buchan. 2004. "Using Q-methodology to involve people with intellectual disability in evaluating person-centred planning." *Journal of Applied Research in Intellectual Disabilities* 17 (3): 149–159.

Conway, J.M. and A.I. Huffcutt 2003. "A review and evaluation of exploratory factor analysis practices in organizational research." *Organizational Research Methods* 6 (2): 147–168.

De Bruijn, H. and E. ten Heuvelhof. 2000. *Networks and decision making*, 1st ed. Utrecht: Lemma.

Dziopa, F. and K. Ahern. 2011. "A systematic literature review of the applications of Q-technique and its methodology." *Methodology: European Journal of Research Methods for the Behavioral and Social Sciences* 7 (2): 39–55.

Donner, J.C. 2001. "Using Q-sorts in participatory processes: An introduction to the methodology." *Social Analysis: Selected Tools and Techniques* 36: 24–59.

Dryzek, J.S. and J. Berejikian. 1993. "Reconstructive democratic theory." *The American Political Science Review* 87 (1): 48–60.

Eden, S., A. Donaldson, and G. Walker. 2005. "Structuring subjectivities?" *Using Q methodology in human geography* 37 (4): 413–422.

Gallagher, K. and D. Porock. 2010. "The use of interviews in Q methodology: Card content analysis." *Nursing Research* 59 (4): 295–300. doi: 10.1097/NNR.0b013e3181e4ffff.

Gasper, D. and R. Apthorpe. 1996. "Introduction: Discourse analysis and policy discourse." *The European Journal of Development Research* 8 (1): 1–15.

Goldman, R. 1999. "The psychological impact of circumcision." *BJU International* 83: 93–102. doi: 10.1046/j.1464-410x.1999.0830s1093.x.

Hogan, A.L. 2008. "Users' metaphorical interaction with the internet." Doctor of Philosophy, University of Bath, Bath.

Jeffares, S. and C. Skelcher. 2008. "Democratic subjectivities in network governance: Using web-enabled Q-methodology with European public managers." Paper presented at the Annual Conference Group for Public Administration, Erasmus University, Rotterdam.

Kivits, R. and M.B. Charles. 2015. "Aviation planning policy in Australia: Identifying frames of reference to support public decision making." *Journal of Air Transport Management* 47: 102–111. http://doi.org/10.1016/j.jairtraman.2015.05.005.

Kroesen, M. and C. Broer. 2009. "Policy discourse, people's internal frames, and declared aircraft noise annoyance: An application of Q-methodology." *Journal of the Acoustical Society of America* 126 (1): 195–207.

McKeown, B. and D. Thomas. 1988. *Q methodology*. Newbury Park: Sage Publications.

McLaughlin, M.W. 2005. "Listening and learning from the field: Tales of policy implementation and situated practice." In *The roots of educational change*, edited by A. Lieberman, 58–72. Netherlands: Springer.

Peräkylä, A., C. Antaki, S. Vehviläinen and I. Leudar. 2008. *Conversation analysis and psychotherapy*, 1st ed. Cambridge: Cambridge University Press.

Previte, J., B. Pini, and F. Haslam-McKenzie. 2007. "Q methodology and rural research." *Sociologia Ruralis* 47: 135–147. doi: 10.1111/j.1467–9523.2007.00433.x.

Ryan, N., B. Head, R.L. Keast, and K.A. Brown. 2006. "Engaging indigenous communities: Towards a policy framework for indigenous community justice programs." *Social Policy & Administration* 40 (3): 304–321.

Schmolck, P. 2002. PQMethod (version 2.35). Available at http://schmolck.org/qmethod/index.htm (accessed 10/06/2019).

Schonlau, M., A. Van Soest, A. Kapteyn, and M. Couper. 2009. "Selection bias in web surveys and the use of propensity scores." *Sociological Methods & Research* 37 (3): 291–318.

Skelcher, C., N. Mathur, and M. Smith. 2005. "The public governance of collaborative spaces: Discourse, design and democracy." *Public Administration* 83 (3): 573–596.

Smith, A.E. and M.S. Humphreys. 2006. "Evaluation of unsupervised semantic mapping of natural language with Leximancer concept mapping." *Behavior Research Methods* 38 (2): 262–279.

Stainton-Rogers, R. 1995. "Q methodology." In *Rethinking methods in psychology*, edited by J.A. Smith, R. Harré, and L. Van Langenhofe, 178–192. Thousand Oakes, CA: Sage Publications.

Stephenson, W. 1990. "Fifty years of exclusionary psychometrics." *Operant Subjectivity* 13: 105–120.

Tabachnick, L.S.F. 2006. *Using multivariate statistics*, 5th ed. Boston: Allyn & Bacon.

Thomas, D.M. and R.T. Watson. 2002. "Q-sorting and MIS research: A primer." *Communications of the Association for Information Systems* 8: 141–156.

Van de Riet, O.A.W.T. 2003. *Policy analysis in multi-actor policy settings: Navigating between negotiated nonsense and superfluous knowledge*, 1st ed. Delft: Eburon Publishers.

Van Eeten, M.J.G. 2001. "Recasting intractable policy issues: The wider implications of the Netherlands civil aviation controversy." *Journal of Policy Analysis and Management* 20 (3): 391–414.

Van Eeten, M.J.G., D. Loucks and E. Roe. 2002. "Bringing actors together around large-scale water systems: Participatory modeling and other innovations." *Knowledge, Technology, and Policy* 14 (4): 94–108.

Watts, S. and Stenner, P. 2005. "Doing Q methodology: Theory, method and interpretation." *Qualitative Research in Psychology* 2 (1): 67–91.

Webler, T., S. Danielson, and S. Tuler. 2007. *Guidance on the use of Q method for evaluation of public involvement programs at contaminated sites*, 41. Greenfield, MA: Social and Environmental Research Institute.

Webler, T., S. Danielson, and S. Tuler. 2009. *Using Q method to reveal social perspectives in environment research*. Greenfield, MA: Social and Environmental Research Institute.

7 Researching inter-organizational collaboration using RO-AR

Siv Vangen

Introduction

This chapter focuses on the application of Research Oriented Action Research (RO-AR) to research inter-organizational collaboration within and across the public and non-profit sectors. RO-AR is a phenomenological action research methodology developed by Colin Eden and Chris Huxham (1996, 2006) which they and others have used to study aspects of management and organizations generally and inter-organizational collaboration specifically; the latter being the focus here. To that end, this chapter draws on a program of empirical research into governing, leading and managing collaborations that has been ongoing since 1989, and which has relied primarily on RO-AR. As a program of research, it is concerned with the development of conceptual knowledge that can inform practice and which has accumulated into the still evolving theory of collaborative advantage (TCA) (Huxham and Vangen 2005; Vangen and Huxham 2014). The aim in this chapter is to provide a brief introduction to RO-AR and to explore its applicability to research on collaboration.

Action research, of which RO-AR is a particular type, was pioneered in the United States in the 1940s, most notably by Kurt Lewin (1946). Lewin argued that research for social practice needs to be concerned with 'the study of general laws . . . and the diagnosis of specific situations' (36). He pointed to, among other things, the need to design methods for recording ill-structured data and to focus on the relationship between perception and action through taking an interpretist approach to research. In a similar vein, action research aimed at understanding organizations and organizational change began at the Tavistock Institute in the United Kingdom (UK) in 1947. With the aim of conducting research and developing knowledge, the Tavistock Institute developed new participatory approaches to organization change and development. In the years that have followed, a number of related approaches have emerged including *action science* (Argyris, Putnam and Smith 1985), *action inquiry* (Torbert 1976), *action learning* (Mwaluko and Ryan 2000; Revans 1982), *appreciative inquiry* (Cooperrider and Srivastva 1987; Cooperrider, Whitney and Starvos 2008) and *participatory action research* (Argyris and Schon 1991; Whyte 1991). Given the growth in popularity of these kinds of research methods, the literature is unsurprisingly both large and somewhat confusing. Nevertheless, and notwithstanding inherent differences, these methods all involve learning from interventions in organizations with the purpose of bringing about change and advancing knowledge. A distinguishing feature between them is the relative emphasis on *change* (or practical transformation) and the development of more *general knowledge* (i.e. theory). The *primary purpose* of the systematic engagement with action in praxis may be the immediate development of an individual, an organization or a community (e.g. via appreciative inquiry or action learning) or it may be to inform the development of theory on the aspect of management or organizations that is being researched, as is the case with RO-AR. The validity of RO-AR, however, rests fundamentally on the intervention being useful in practice. This close relationship with practice enhances the potential of a theory ultimately developed to inform other contexts. Eden and Huxham (2006: 388) distinguish RO-AR from other action research approaches, specifically, from the following:

- organizational intervention projects that do not satisfy characteristics of *rigorous research*;
- research within an organization that does not satisfy characteristics of *action orientation*; and
- forms of action research that do not have research output as their primary *rasion d'etre*.

The aim of this chapter is to highlight key features of RO-AR and to show how it may be used to produce good research on collaboration. In what follows, we look at the relevance of RO-AR to research on collaboration, and provide an account of the application of the method in developing the theory of collaborative advantage, along with an overview of issues pertaining to data capture and analysis. The chapter also offers a brief evaluation of the method and some thoughts on rigour and relevance for researchers who may wish to apply the methods in future research on collaboration.

The relevance of the method

Over the last three decades, organization and management theory has increasingly covered a range of new topics and organizational forms, including inter-organizational collaboration and networks (Buchanan and Bryman 2007; Cunliffe 2011). These developments have resulted in new ways of researching and theorizing the complexity of organizational life (Cunliffe 2011; Jarzabkowski et al. 2013) alongside considerable methodological inventiveness (Buchanan and Bryman 2007), a renewed interest in the application of phenomenological research (Gill 2014), the use of grounded theory (O'Reilly, Paper and Marx 2012) and increasing popularity of some qualitative research designs, including action research (Aguinis et al. 2009; Huxham and Vangen 2003). In terms of the relevance of RO-AR for researching collaboration and developing contextualized theory to inform practice, the characteristic of the context of collaboration and the ability of the method to capture that context are clearly important factors.

With regards to context, public organizations, along with their non-profit and private sector partners, typically collaborate to address 'wicked' and 'relentless' problems (Rittel and Webber 1973; Weber and Khademian 2008) that sit in the inter-organizational domain (Trist 1983) beyond individual organizations' capabilities to tackle them effectively on their own (Vangen and Huxham 2014). Collaborative arrangements typically aspire for organizations to combine their resources – including their experiences, expertise, assets, cultures and values – in ways that allow them to achieve something that none of them could achieve on their own; they aim to create synergies and collaborative advantage (Gray 1989; Lasker, Weiss and Miller 2001; Huxham and Vangen 2005; Quick and Feldman 2014; Bryson, Crosby and Stone 2015). Fundamentally, that creation of synergy and advantage requires collaborative arrangements that simultaneously protect and integrate the partners' uniquely different resources that are brought to bear on their joint purpose (Vangen 2017a). Thus, collaborative partners typically deliver services and remits within traditional, vertical, command-and-control relationships, while they simultaneously participate in collaborative relationships that support the delivery of their joint goals (Huxham and Vangen 2005; Ospina and Foldy 2015; Ospina and Saz-Carranza 2010; Quick and Feldman 2014; Vangen and Huxham 2012). Collaborative contexts as such typically comprise a combination of both autonomous organizational hierarchies and collaborative governance structures. Moreover, such contexts are highly dynamic as they are subject to changing public policies and varying stakeholder engagement and preferences (Huxham and Vangen 2000; Cropper and Palmer 2008; Thomson and Perry 2006; Quick and Feldman 2014). For these reasons, a collaborative context is typically a complex web of overlapping, dynamic, hierarchies and systems that comprise competing designs and processes, all of which are necessary to deliver collaborative advantage. They are, in other words, inherently paradoxical in nature and characterized by contradictions and tensions (Vangen 2017a).

The context of collaboration clearly has implications for the extent to which methods are appropriate for empirical research and contextualized theory development. Certainly, researchers have argued that mainstream theories cannot capture adequately the complexity of collaborative contexts and have begun increasingly to use alternative methods and multi-paradigm approaches (Clarke-Hill, Li and Davies 2003; Das and Teng 2000; Gibbs 2009; Ospina and Saz-Carranza 2010; Zeng and Chen 2003). RO-AR sits within the phenomenological and interpretive paradigms (Kuhn 1970) and is a type of ethnography inasmuch as it relies primarily on naturally occurring data (Galibert 2004; Golden-Biddle and Locke 1993). The method itself does not demand a particular ideological perspective; rather, as it relies on an action-oriented intervention that is useful in practice, it requires the acceptance of the management ideologies of those being researched. The research is designed around a *practice-oriented agenda* rather than a research-focused ontological or ideological position. As far as the research aims are concerned, an important assumption is that individuals' perceptions of reality are reflected in their actions and hence that data collected about their actions better reflect their 'theory in use' rather than their 'espoused theories' (Argyris 1977). This then enhances the relevance of the method when the aim is (as is the case for the TCA) to develop contextualized practice-oriented theory. Ideological perspectives about, for example, the empowerment and participation of particular stakeholder groups are important in some types of action research, but in RO–AR these are only important as far as they are relevant to the practice-oriented agenda. This position is akin to a practice ontology which requires 'a tolerance for complexity and ambiguity' and engagement with organizational life through 'observing and working with practitioners' (Feldman and Orlikovski 2011). RO–AR, alongside other forms of qualitative research that engage with practice, is particularly appropriate for developing contextualized theory that relates closely to practice (Eden and Huxham 2006; Huxham and Hibbert 2011; Pettigrew 1997).

Method application

In essence, the RO–AR method entails interpretive theorizing from data gathered during organizational interventions on matters that are of genuine concern to the organizational participants and over which they need to act (Eden and Huxham 2006; Huxham and Vangen 2003). When RO–AR is used for research on collaboration, it involves learning from interventions in collaborative contexts, with the dual purpose to bring about a practical transformation and develop conceptual knowledge. The researcher's intervention is thus a key part of the research design (Gill and Johnson 1997). The intention of a planned intervention is to learn from organizational participants' actions as well as having a direct influence on their future actions with regards to the subject of the research. Importantly, the research outputs that can ultimately be gained from the intervention constitute the researcher's reasons for getting involved. The validity of the method, however, rests on the intervention itself being driven by a genuine need in a practice context. As can be gleaned from the examples that follow, interventions are therefore often initiated by a practitioner rather than a researcher (see also Rapoport 1970).

The research program that gradually emerged into the (still evolving) TCA has included interventions in a large number and variety of collaborative contexts. It has involved a large number of participants, including directors of collaborations, partnership managers, managers in public, private and non-profit organizations involved in collaborations, and representatives of specific stakeholder groups across the UK and (to a limited extent) elsewhere. The collaborative contexts have ranged from simple dyads to complex international networks and have spanned public policy, including health, area development and regeneration, children services, education, social welfare, the environment and many more. I and my colleagues have been involved as researchers acting in a variety of capacities, including supporting individuals seeking to develop particular collaborations and inter-organizational governance forums, designing and facilitating collaborative seminars, workshops and leadership development events, contributions to practice seminars and conferences, direct participation in collaborations both as participants and as initiators and leaders, and con- tributing to policy development. One key focus in this program is to explore why collaboration often leads to inertia, rather than advantage, and what this means in terms of how practitioners involved might act to increase their effec- tiveness. Other specific foci have been the nature of governance structure and leadership that can most effectively bring about positive outcomes in collab- orative contexts. The aimed-for output has been, and continues to be, theory that can inform governing, leading and managing collaboration in practice. A key concern therefore is always to design a research process that can facilitate a link between theory and practice. This aim is consistent with Whyte (1991: 8), who stated that 'it is important, both for the advancement of science and for the improvement of human welfare, to devise strategies in which research and action are closely linked'.

A founding block in the TCA research program has been the development of 'themes in collaboration' (Vangen 1992, 1998) – these are 'in vivo' labels (Glaser 1992; Strauss and Corbin 1998) given to a broad grouping of issues raised repeatedly by practitioners as causing anxiety and rewards. These theme labels are portrayed in Figure 7.1. Consistent with the aim to develop better contextualized, practice-oriented theory, the themes guide the development of the TCA (Vangen and Huxham 2010, 2014). An ongoing research aim therefore is to develop a deeper understanding of the challenges related to each theme, including the relationships between them, and to conceptualize this in ways that can develop theory on collaboration *and* inform practice. The three examples to be outlined in the following paragraphs illustrate how RO-AR was used to develop three such themes relating to goals, culture and governance (leadership).

As RO-AR projects have this dual purpose of practical transformation and theoretical development, it follows that each intervention is not designed around

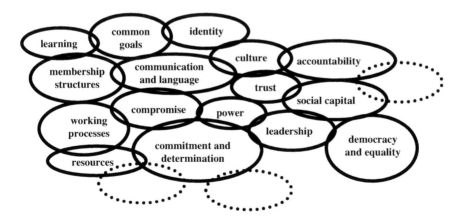

Figure 7.1 Collaboration themes

a specific research question but is guided by a need in practice. The theory, including the conceptualizations pertaining to the various themes, is developed incrementally from a range of interventions that vary from long-term ones, lasting for several years, to short, one-off events. For illustrative purposes, three different types of interventions are outlined briefly in the following paragraphs.

The first example involved an alliance of approximately 100 public and non-profit organizations working on different aspects of poverty alleviation in Scotland. At the time of our involvement, the alliance had a newly formed working group comprising eight public agencies and non-profit organizations committed to working jointly on children and poverty. My colleagues and I were asked by the director to design an intervention that would help the group form, and the members to commence their joint work. It was agreed that we would facilitate a series of workshops that would help the members identify key issues and agree on a direction for their joint work. In preparation for the workshops, and to help ensure that the members' diverse areas of expertise and experience were represented adequately, it was agreed that I would interview each member twice about their views of what the collaboration should aspire to achieve.

In this particular intervention I captured the interviews using 'cognitive mapping', which was shared with and elaborated upon in the second interview. These maps were then entered into the Decision Explorer software and organized into a 'group map', which effectively included all members' expressed values, beliefs and goals relating to the collaboration's activities. This aggregated model formed the basis for discussion in a series of four workshops (facilitated by a colleague), during which participants were involved in clarifying, negotiating and reviewing the goals identified by the analysis in the light of past experience and considering and agreeing future actions. The model was amended during workshops as understandings were clarified and new ideas emerged. For the participants, the intervention ended after the fourth workshop, when it was felt that sufficient agreement on key issues and goals for the joint work had been reached. In terms of the research, though this initial work yielded a preliminary conceptual framework on goals in collaborative context, the goals theme was developed over a number of years and drawing on data gathered via a number of subsequent interventions in different collaborative contexts. A comprehensive framework on the goals was eventually published some seventeen years later. The framework and a detailed outline of the research approach including the cognitive mapping can be found in Vangen and Huxham (2012).

Thankfully, not all conceptual development from RO-AR takes that long! As is usual with RO-AR, however, most of the 'collaboration themes' have been developed incrementally from data gathered from a number of interventions spanning a number of years. The second example, which has thus far informed the development of the cultural diversity theme is, however, an exception because the specific opportunity yielded exceptionally rich empirical data. The conceptualizations of that theme developed from an intervention in one large UK-based organization that collaborates with many other organizations across the world. The intervention took place following a request from a senior manager about help with addressing challenges experienced by the individuals who manage these various collaborations on behalf of the organization. Following agreement with the participants, the intervention entailed a series of four in-house development events which focused on exploring ways of understanding and managing key challenges pertaining to the collaborations that they managed. Thirty-five managers participated in these events.

The first three events all began with a brief introduction to relevant TCA themes (divergent goals, power and trust, and structural ambiguity respectively) followed by facilitated activities in which the participants explored a theme in relation to their own experiences. While the participants managed a range of different partnerships, they all had a level of shared understanding gained from working in the same organization. It was therefore appropriate to design activities that enabled individuals to share and make sense of the challenges that they were experiencing. Each event closed with a plenary discussion encouraging further reflection and consolidation of learning (for them and me) facilitated (I believe) by my understanding of collaboration gained over several years. In terms of data capture, each activity involved them writing on post-its and flip-charts and I took notes during and immediately after each event. I also produced a brief report following each event.

The fourth event was different. It became increasingly clear that cultural diversity was a key theme for the organization participants. And at that time, in my judgement, there was no extant conceptual model on managing cultural diversity that could inform adequately the design of a 'theory into practice' activity similar to those of the first three events. In preparation for this event, therefore, we agreed that I would interview individuals about their experiences of culture in the collaborations that they manage. I used an open-ended, unstructured format which adhered to the principle that initial temporary suppression of pre-understanding would allow for new and alternative ways of understanding a phenomenon, which in turn can facilitate the extension of theory (Gummesson 1991). It thus allowed me to incorporate participants' views of what cultural diversity is and what role it plays in the collaborations that they manage. During the interviews, which lasted between sixty and ninety minutes, individuals talked freely about their current experiences at a time when it was necessary for them to take action rather than purely reflect on events of the past. This resulted in a large amount of reliable, detailed and subtle data – including examples of practices they use to address issues associated with cultural diversity. Apart from the significantly larger number of participants, the process of recording and organizing the interview data was similar to that used with the poverty alliance example as outlined earlier. Data analysis identified key challenges relating to the management of cultural diversity and these then informed the design of the activities explored and elaborated upon with the participants during the fourth development event. The theoretical conceptualizations that emerged later from this intervention can be found in Vangen and Winchester (2014) and Vangen (2017a, 2017b).

During the course of developing the TCA we also used RO-AR alongside other forms of qualitative research. This third example is from a funded project where the stated research aim was to explore the governance of partnerships. Following an introduction from the Chief Executive of a voluntary organization with whom we had an established relationship, we began to work with the Head of the City Council's Regeneration Team who was leading the implementation of a new neighbourhood regeneration strategy for the City Council. The strategy was to be implemented collaboratively with a number of public and non-profit organizations. The project involved many action research elements, including my colleagues and I acting as 'a sounding board' to the Head of the Regeneration Team (who consequently significantly changed her approach to the implementation of the strategy) and us actively facilitating workshops for collaboration participants. Yet, for a variety of reasons, the project also entailed standard qualitative data collection methods such as semi-structured interviews, participation in and observation of workshops, observation of meetings, obtaining documentation, informal conversations, emails as well as meetings with key individuals. In many ways, the design that emerged offered the best of both worlds: the ability to capture data about key individuals' actions *and* the convenience of 'standard' data capture for research purposes. The outputs from the governance project can be found in Vangen, Hayes and Cornforth (2015) and Cornforth, Hayes and Vangen (2015).

The three examples outlined in the previous paragraphs were all quite different in terms of the interventions, data gathering and analysis, and this of course is typical of action research as it is designed around a practice agenda. Yet, from the perspective of research, they also had in common the aim to ultimately produce practice-oriented theory about collaboration. Fundamentally, they all met the RO-AR requirements of rigorous research, action orientation and research output as the primary *rasion d'etre*. More detailed descriptions of the methods used in these three examples can also be found in the articles where they were published.

Data capture and analysis

The issues of data capture and analysis have already been alluded to in the previous section. In RO-AR, as highlighted in the examples, the data capture and analysis are integral parts of the intervention. Data collection and analyses are undertaken concurrently, in a developmental fashion, which informs the intervention and promotes the emergence of theory grounded in empirical data (Eisenhardt 1989; Marshall and Rossman 1989). The data so gathered are typically qualitative in nature, with the analyses undertaken being qualitative, inductive and developmental (Burell and Morgan 1979; Cassell and Symon 1994; Gill and Johnson 1997).

While RO-AR, as a type of ethnography, relies primarily on naturally occurring data, it can also include interviews, focus groups and questionnaires where this is a natural part of the intervention. What sets this data collection apart is the aim to uncover issues of relevance to the specific intervention, rather than a specific research question. While interviews, for example, can take different formats, they do not generally include participants responding retrospectively to a set of questions derived from extant research. So, the data collected is 'naturally occurring' to the extent that the focus is on issues that will need to be acted upon rather than events of the past.

As with any empirical research, deliberate and systematic data collection is essential, whether it be data collected naturally as part of the intervention (e.g. notes made on flipchart at a meeting) or data collected in parallel to the intervention but for research purposes only (e.g. reflective notes made by the researcher). Importantly, the specific intervention role undertaken by the researcher will affect what data are available for collection, and the history, context and politics of the intervention will be important to the interpretation of that data. Throughout the many interventions that have formed part of the TCA program, the expressed experiences, views, action-centred dilemmas, and actual actions of participants have been recorded as research data in a variety of ways:

- *by participants:* flipcharts, notes, post-its and (occasionally) anonymous but formally collected feedback on interventions
- *by researchers:* detailed and reflective notes during or immediately following events, memos, meetings and conversations, diaries and interview data capture (including digital recording, notes and cognitive maps)
- *by participants and researchers:* records of interactive facilitated activities during an intervention (e.g. Decision Explorer group maps or 'cluster' analysis) and email exchanges
- *of participants and researchers:* video and tape recordings of interventions.

The main principle adhered to has always been to capture data as accurately as possible. It has included taking very detailed notes on participants' views and responses, conversations between them and with us, including views expressed and decisions made, any implications that the intervention is having in practice (negative as well as positive and who is affected), our impressions of what participants appear engaged by, how they react to different suggestions including theoretical frameworks and so on). Data have also been collected via video and digital recordings, albeit not as standalone devices. When appropriate, we have given individuals the opportunity to verify the data that we have collected, and we have on occasion given them the opportunity to feedback anonymously. The latter was particularly important when we used a form of Participatory action research (PAR) alongside RO-AR; PAR involves practitioners in the research design which changes the relationship between the researcher and the researched as well as the interest in and *ownership* of the data (Huxham and Vangen 2003). Over the years, the various interventions have yielded a vast amount of data on many different aspects of collaboration. Typically, as has been illustrated in the examples given earlier, theoretical insight has emerged incrementally from interpretive analysis of the data following individual and sequential interventions.

In the phenomenological paradigm, the development of theory results from a process of inductive analysis of empirically collected data (see for example, Bryman and Bell 2015; Easterby-Smith, Thorpe and Lowe 1991). RO-AR lends itself to the development of 'emergent theory' (Eisenhardt 1989), which has some similarities with 'grounded theory' (Glaser and Strauss 1967; Strauss and Corbin 1998). Eden and Huxham (2006) particularly stress the theory and practice cycle:

> RO-AR is concerned with a system of emergent theoretical conceptualizations, in which theoretical constructs develop from a synthesis of that which emerges from the data and that which emerges from the use in practice of the body of theoretical constructs which informed the intervention and research intent.
>
> (396)

In TCA there is a specific focus on the development of theory that is meaningful for use in practice. Ultimately, this yields conceptualizations that capture the complexities of organizational life through the 'highlighting of issues, contradictions, tensions and dilemmas', rather than through generating synthetic explanatory variables (Langley 1999).

Theorizing practice-oriented research in ways that meet the dual requirement of practice and the development of a field of knowledge is not straightforward (Pettigrew 1997; Eden and Huxham 2006). Data analysis and subsequent development of theoretical constructs will not proceed in a linear, neat fashion, but more likely the process will be cyclical, creative, messy, fascinating, time-consuming and at times perhaps even frustrating and ambiguous. As the output is not intended to be 'context bound' (Greenwood and Levin 1998: 75), research findings need to be presented in language that is not situation specific. This requirement is similar to generating outputs from case studies in a manner that allows them to become theoretical vehicles for the examination of other cases (Yin 2003). Using a reflexive approach when interpreting the data can also aid understanding of how the emergent conceptualizations can both be representative of the situation in which they were generated and be applicable in others (Alvesson and Sköldberg 2000). Deriving useful conceptualizations is inevitably an iterative process that entails experimenting with different possible ways of writing concepts (Eden and Huxham 2006; Huxham and Hibbert 2011).

Given the aim and nature of the analysis as outlined in this section, and illustrated in Figure 7.2, it follows that there cannot be a predefined method or a single 'best practice' approach to analysis.

For the purpose of research (on collaboration) rather than practice, analysis usually involves a number of steps, which are repeated until a specific conceptualization has been completed, including:

1   a close examination of data collected for research purposes from one or more interventions to identify items that are relevant to a specific theme (e.g. trust, leadership or identity) and which can then be included in the analysis;

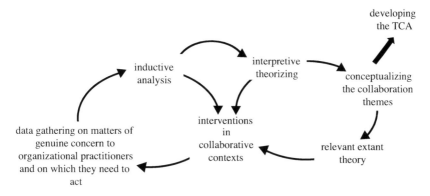

Figure 7.2 Inductive RO-AR analysis in developing the TCA

2   a review, including a process of triangulation, of the selected data items to look for emerging themes, patterns and categories;
3   a sense-making process to ascertain if a conceptual framework can be developed;
4   an iterative process of writing and data analysis to develop conceptual constructs and frameworks (this has on occasion spanned years); and
5   a review of literature to inform sense-making and conceptual development.

With respect to step two, it is worth noting that the revisiting of different data sources within the cyclical process illustrated in Figure 7.2 offers powerful means of triangulating the data (Eden and Huxham 2006). A traditional definition of triangulation involves the act of bringing more than one source of data to bear on a single point (Marshall and Rossman 1989). In RO-AR, data from different sources can be used to corroborate, elaborate or illuminate the research in question. Within RO-AR, triangulation can make use of the data collected through any of the listed steps. Importantly, the data are not expected to triangulate upon a single point per se but, rather, the lack of triangulation should be used as a dialectical device for generating new concepts (Eden and Huxham 2006).

With respect to step five, in the TCA, literature has informed both the development of the conceptual framework (for an outline of the 'leadership theme' theory development see, for example, Huxham 2003) and the process of developing practice-oriented theory (see for example my article on using the paradox lens for this purpose; Vangen 2017a). Given the large volume of variously captured data, and the iterative, inter-related analytical process outlined earlier in this section, any software that can allow the amount and variety of data flexibly will aid the inductive analysis process. In developing the TCA we have primarily used Decision Explorer developed by Eden and Ackermann (1998). Where we have used NVivo it has tended to be for data storage rather than analysis per se. In general, any tool that encourages creativity rather than rigidity in analysis is likely to be more useful. Readers who would like more detail about specific analysis can also refer to articles where TCA has been developed gradually over the last two decades.

A brief evaluation of the method

It has been argued in this chapter that inter-organizational collaboration is a complex phenomenon and that RO-AR is a method that is appropriate for empirical research and theory development. In particular, it has been argued that the close connection between practice and research that is necessary in RO-AR render the method particularly appropriate for developing contextualized practice-oriented theory. This is a specific aim pursued in the development of the TCA, which has been drawn on for examples throughout this chapter.

As a variety of phenomenological research, RO-AR undoubtedly establishes a close connection between the researcher and the organizational participants. As such, it undoubtedly has the potential to provide a rich, contextual insight that cannot be gained easily in other ways. Yet, interventions in organizations require a high level of trust between the researcher and the practice participants; there is a risk associated with any intervention in any organizational context, including a risk that the intervention can result in negative rather than positive implications in practice. There is also a risk that the intervention will not yield useful data as far as advancing the research agenda is concerned. In RO-AR, therefore, the researcher will inevitably take a leap of faith. In terms of the content of the 'naturally occurring' data, the researcher will usually have to rely on interventions in multiple organizational contexts. In comparison, a case study approach (Yin 2003) can provide the researcher with greater control over the data collected and a better sense at the outset of whether the case study will surface data of relevance to a specific research question. However, as the data captured in RO-AR are 'naturally occurring', they can provide the kinds of insight that can yield better contextualized theoretical data in the context of collaboration.

RO-AR (like inter-organizational collaboration itself) is resource- and time-consuming and not a panacea for research in the collaboration context; it would be inappropriate for many research agendas. It is not likely to be favourable when other methods can adequately capture the research aims. This is likely to be the case, for example, when a researcher wishes to pursue a narrowly focused research question or test out the applicability of a specific theory in the context of collaboration. It does, however, offer particular opportunities for better contextualized practice theory development compared to other methods. Each intervention can provide rich data about what people do and say, and what theoretical frameworks and concepts are used and found useful, when organization participants are faced with a genuine need to take action. RO-AR therefore has the potential to provide new and unexpected insights that are important for theoretical developments (Whetton 1989).

Issues of rigour and relevance in future applications

The main validity concern facing RO–AR is the dilemma of rigour and relevance (Argyris and Schon 1991; Gill and Johnson 1997; Rapoport 1970). Interventions in organizations will necessarily be one-off and so it would not be possible to demonstrate rigour via repeatability. In terms of relevance, the phenomenological argument is that explanations of naturally occurring phenomena are relatively worthless unless they are grounded in observation and experience (Gill and Johnson 1997). The validity of RO–AR rests on relevance as it is concerned with the investigation of 'contemporary, naturally occurring activities' (Yin 2003). As with any qualitative research design, it will be important to demonstrate that it was planned and executed in a methodologically rigorous manner (Cassell and Symon 1994). In RO–AR it is unlikely to be possible to define in detail every single step of the research. Yet, it will be important to provide enough detail for the research to be assessed according to whether it was likely to provide a thorough, precise and accurate understanding of the phenomenon researched (Marshall and Rossman 1989).

In terms of the validity of the emergent theory, the arguments about relevance and rigour are closely related. Whether or not theory generated from RO–AR is relevant depends largely on whether the views, experiences and actions of organization participants – on issues that were of genuine importance in practice – are accurately captured and accounted for in the development of the theory. It may be argued that the variety of data that can be captured via RO–AR, including the participants' ability to comment on that data, can help ensure that their views are accurately captured. Whether or not participants' views are reflected in the development of the research relates to the way in which the data are analysed. The validity of the emerging theory thus relates to the methodological soundness and rigour by which the data are captured and analysed. Scientific rigour may be argued from the point of view that RO–AR encourages the researcher to undertake a rigorous process of checking interpretation of meaning with the practitioners and, in that respect, the standard of accuracy of emerging theories may be enhanced (Whyte 1991). That process of rethinking both theory and practice strengthen both and thus helps to ensure the validity of the theory (Eden and Huxham 2006; Gill and Johnson 1997; Whyte 1991).

Glaser and Strauss (1967) propose two criteria for evaluating the quality of a theory. They suggest that the theory should be sufficiently analytic to enable some generalization to take place, but at the same time it should be possible for people to relate the theory to their own experiences, thus sensitizing their own perceptions. The generalization measure of usefulness and validity relates to the transferability of the theory (Lincoln and Guba 1986). The burden of demonstrating the applicability of one set of findings rests more with the investigator, who would make that transfer, rather than with the original investigator (Lincoln and Guba 1986). For the RO–AR researcher, an important aim therefore is to allow the reader to judge the relevance of their generalization to assess whether or not it is applicable to other contexts (Glaser and Strauss 1967; Marshall and Rossman 1989).

Further reading

Eden, C. and C. Huxham. 2006. "Researching organizations using action research." In *Handbook of organization studies*, 2nd ed., edited by S. Clegg, C. Hardy, W. Nord, and T. Lawrence, 388–408. London: Sage Publications.
Huxham, C. 2003. "Action research as a methodology for theory development." *Policy and Politics* 31 (2): 239–248.
Huxham, C. 2003. "Theorizing collaboration practice." *Public Management Review* 5 (3): 401–423.
Huxham, C. and P. Hibbert. 2011. "Use matters . . . and matters of use: Building theory for reflective practice." *Public Management Review* 13 (2): 273–291.
Huxham, C. and S. Vangen. 2003. "Researching organizational practice through action research: Case studies and design choices." *Organizational Research Methods* 6 (3): 383–403.
Reason, P. and H. Bradbury. 2001. *Handbook of action research: Participative inquiry and practice.* London: Sage Publications.
Vangen, S. 2017. "Developing practice-oriented theory on collaboration: A paradox lens." *Public Administration Review* 77 (2): 263–272.

References

Aguinis, H., C.A. Pierce, F.A. Bosco, and I.A. Muslin. 2009. "First decade of organizational research methods: Trends in design, measurement, and data-analysis topics." *Organizational Research Methods* 12 (1): 69–112.
Argyris, A. 1977. "Double look learning in organizations." *Harvard Business Review* September–October: 115–125.
Argyris, C., R. Putnam, and D.M. Smith. 1985. *Action science.* San Francisco: Jossey-Bass.
Argyris, C. and D. Schon. 1991. "Participatory action research and action science compared: A commentary." In *Participatory action research*, edited by W. Whyte, 85–97. London: Sage Publications.
Alvesson, M. and K. Sköldberg. 2000. *Reflexive methodology: New vistas for qualitative research.* London: Sage Publications.
Bryson, J.M., B.C. Crosby, and M.M. Stone. 2015. "Designing and implementing cross-sector collaborations: Needed and challenging." *Public Administration Review* 75 (5): 647–663.
Buchanan, D.A. and A. Bryman. 2007. "Contextualising methods choice in organizational research." *Organizational Research Methods* 10 (3): 483–501.
Burell, G. and G. Morgan. 1979. *Sociological paradigms and organisational analysis.* London: Heinemann.
Bryman, A. and E. Bell. 2015. *Business research methods*, 4th Ed. Oxford: Oxford University Press.
Cassell, C. and G. Symon. Eds. 1994. *Qualitative methods in organizational research: A practical guide.* London: Sage Publications.
Clarke-Hill, C., H. Li, and B. Davies. 2003. "The paradox of co-operation and competition in strategic alliances: Towards a multi-paradigm approach." *Management Research News* 26 (1): 1–20.
Cooperrider, D.L. and S. Srivastva. 1987. "Appreciative inquiry in organizational life." In *Research in organizational change and development*, Vol. 1, edited by R.W. Woodman and W.A. Pasmore, 129–169. Stamford, CT: JAI Press.

Cooperrider, D.L., D.W. Whitney, and J.M. Starvos. 2008. *Appreciative inquiry handbook: For leaders of change,* 2nd ed. Brunswick: Crown Custom Publishing, Inc.

Cornforth, C., J.P. Hayes, and S. Vangen. 2015. "Understanding changes in the governance of public: Nonprofit collaborations: Collaborative windows, collaborative entrepreneurs and internal tensions." *Nonprofit and Voluntary Sector Quarterly* 44 (4): 775–795.

Cropper, S. and I. Palmer. 2008. "Change, dynamics, and temporality in inter-organizational relationships." In *The Oxford handbook of inter-organizational relations,* edited by S. Cropper, M. Ebers, C. Huxham, and P.R. Smith. Oxford: Oxford University Press.

Cunliffe, A. 2011. "Crafting qualitative research: Morgan and Smircich 30 years on." *Organizational Research Methods* 14 (4): 647–673.

Das, T.K. and B.S. Teng. 2000. "Instabilities of strategic alliances: An internal tensions perspective." *Organization Science* 11 (1): 77–101.

Easterby-Smith, M., R. Thorpe, and A. Lowe. 1991. *Management research: An introduction.* London: Sage Publications.

Eden, C. and F. Ackermann. 1998. *Making strategy: The journey of strategic management.* London: Sage Publications.

Eden, C. and C. Huxham. 1996. "Action research for management research." *British Journal of Management* 7 (1): 75–86.

Eden, C. and C. Huxham. 2006. "Researching organizations using action research." In *Handbook of organization studies,* 2nd Ed., edited by S. Clegg, C. Hardy, W. Nord, and T. Lawrence, 388–408. London: Sage Publications.

Eisenhardt, K.M. 1989. "Building theories from case study research." *Academy of Management Review* 14: 532–550.

Feldman, M.S. and W.J. Orlikovski. 2011. "Theorizing practice and practicing theory." *Organization Science* 22 (5): 1240–1253.

Galibert, C. 2004. "Some preliminary notes on actor-observer anthropology." *International Social Science Journal* 56: 455–466.

Gibbs, J. 2009. "Dialectics in a global software team: Negotiating tensions across time, space and culture." *Human Relations* 62 (6): 905–935.

Golden-Biddle, K. and K. Locke. 1993. "Appealing work: An investigation of how ethnographic texts convince." *Organization Science* 4: 595–616.

Gill, M. 2014. "The possibilities of phenomenology for organizational research." *Organizational Research Methods* 17 (2): 118–137.

Gill, J. and P. Johnson. 1997. *Research methods for managers,* 2nd ed. London: Paul Chapman Publishing Ltd.

Glaser, B.G. 1992. *Basics of grounded theory.* Mill Valley CA: Sociology Press.

Glaser, B. and A. Strauss. 1967. *The discovery of grounded theory: Strategies for qualitative research.* New York: Aldine de Gruyter.

Gray, B. 1989. *Collaborating: Finding common ground for multiparty problems.* San Francisco: Jossey-Bass.

Greenwood, D.J. and M. Levin. 1998. "Action research, science, and the co-optation of social research." *Studies in Cultures, Organizations and Societies* 4 (2): 237–261.

Gummesson, E. 1991. *Qualitative methods in management research,* Revised ed. Newbury Park: Sage Publications.

Huxham, C. 2003. "Action research as a methodology for theory development." *Policy and Politics* 31 (2): 239–248.

Huxham, C. and P. Hibbert. 2011. "Use matters . . . and matters of use: Building theory for reflective practice." *Public Management Review* 13 (2): 273–291.

Huxham, C. and S. Vangen. 2000. "Ambiguity, complexity and dynamics in the membership of collaboration." *Human Relations* 53: 771–806.

Huxham, C. and S. Vangen. 2003. "Researching organizational practice through action research: Case studies and design choices." *Organizational Research Methods* 6 (3): 383–403.

Huxham, C. and S. Vangen. 2005. *Managing to collaborate: The theory and practice of collaborative advantage.* London: Routledge.

Jarzabkowski, P., M. Smets, R. Bednarek, G. Burke, and P. Spee. 2013. "Institutional ambidexterity: Leveraging institutional complexity in practice." *Research in the Sociology of Organizations* 39: 37–61.

Kuhn, T. 1970. *The structure of scientific revolutions*, 2nd ed. Chicago: The University of Chicago Press.

Langley, A. 1999. "Strategies for theorizing from process data." *Academy of Management Review* 24: 691–710.

Lasker, R.D., E.S. Weiss, and R. Miller. 2001. "Partnership synergy: A practical framework for studying and strengthening the collaborative advantage." *The Millbank Quarterly* 79: 179–205.

Lewin, K. 1946. "Action research and minority problems." *Journal of Social Issues* 2: 34–46.

Lincoln, Y. and G. Guba. 1986. *Naturalistic inquiry.* London: Sage Publications.

Marshall, S. and G.B. Rossman. 1989. *Designing qualitative research.* London: Sage Publications.

Mwaluko, G.S. and T.B. Ryan. 2000. "The systemic nature of action learning programmes." *Systems Research and Behavioral Science* 17: 393–401.

O'Reilly, K., D. Paper, and S. Marx. 2012. "Demystifying grounded theory for business research." *Organizational Research Methods* 15 (2): 247–262.

Ospina, S.M. and A. Saz-Carranza. 2010. "Paradox and collaboration in network management." *Administration and Society* 42 (4): 404–440.

Ospina, S.M. and E.G. Foldy. 2015. "Enacting collective leadership in a shared-power world." In *Handbook of public administration*, 3rd ed., edited by J. Perry and R.K. Christensen. San-Francisco: Jossey-Bass.

Pettigrew, A. 1997. "The double hurdles for management research." In *Advancements in organizational behaviour: Essays in honour of Derek Pugh*, edited by T. Clarke. Aldershot: Ashgate.

Quick, K.S. and M.S. Feldman. 2014. "Boundaries as junctures: Collaborative boundary work for building efficient resilience." *Journal of Public Administration Research and Theory* 24: 673–695.

Rapoport, R. 1970. "Three dilemmas in action research." *Human Relations* 23 (6): 499–513.

Revans, R.W. 1982. *The origins of growth of action learning.* Bickley, Kent: Chartwell-Bratt.

Rittel, H. and M. Webber. 1973. "Dilemmas in a general theory of planning." *Policy Sciences* 4: 155–169.

Strauss, A. and J. Corbin. 1998. *Basics of qualitative research*, 2nd ed. London: Sage Publications.

Torbert, W.R. 1976. *Creating a community of inquiry: Conflict, collaboration, transformation.* New York: Wiley.

Thomson, A.M. and J.L. Perry. 2006. "Collaboration processes: Inside the black box." *Public Administration Review* 66 (S1): 20–32.

Trist, E. 1983. "Referent organizations and the development of inter-organizational domains." *Human Relations* 36 (3): 269–284.

Vangen, S. 1992. "Local community groups combating poverty: Focusing on collaboration." MSc Dissertation, University of Strathclyde, Glasgow.

Vangen, S. 1998. "Transferring insight on collaboration to practice." PhD Dissertation, University of Strathclyde, Glasgow.

Vangen, S. 2017a. "Developing practice-oriented theory on collaboration: A paradox lens." *Public Administration Review* 77 (2): 263–272.

Vangen, S. 2017b. "Nurturing culturally diverse collaborations: A focus on communication and shared understanding." *Public Management Review* 19 (3): 305–325. http://dx.doi.org. libezproxy.open.ac.uk/10.1080/14719037.2016.1209234.

Vangen, S. and C. Huxham. 2010. "Introducing the theory of collaborative advantage." In *The new public governance? Critical perspectives and future directions*, edited by S. Osborne, 163–164. London: Routledge.

Vangen, S. and C. Huxham. 2012. "The tangled web: Unraveling the principle of common goals in collaborations." *Journal of Public Administration Research and Theory* 22: 731–760.

Vangen, S. and C. Huxham. 2014. "Building and using the theory of collaborative advantage." In *Network theory in the public sector: Building new theoretical frameworks*, edited by R. Keast, M. Mandell and R. Agranoff, 51–67. New York: Taylor and Francis.

Vangen, S., J.P. Hayes, and C. Cornforth. 2015. "Governing cross-sector inter-organizational collaborations." *Public Management Review* 17 (9): 1237–1260.

Vangen, S. and N. Winchester. 2014. "Managing cultural diversity in collaborations: A focus on management tensions." *Public Management Review* 16 (5): 686–707.

Weber, E.P. and A.M. Khademian. 2008. "Wicked problems, knowledge challenges, and collaborative capacity builders in network setting." *Public Administration Review* 68 (2): 334–349.

Whetton, D. 1989. "What constitutes a theoretical contribution?" *Academy of Management Review* 14 (4): 490–495.

Whyte, W., ed. 1991. *Participatory action research*. London: Sage Publications.

Yin, R. 2003. *Case study research: Design and methods*, 3rd ed. Thousand Oaks, CA: Sage Publications.

Zeng, M. and X.P. Chen. 2003. "Achieving cooperation in multiparty alliances: A social dilemma approach to partnership management." *Academy of Management Review* 28 (4): 587–605.

8 Process tracing

Robyn Keast

Introducing process tracing

Process tracing involves an in-depth, systematic and theoretically driven interrogation of the chain of events involved in the implementation of interventions, programs or activities occurring within or across small *n* cases for drawing descriptive and causal inference (Collier 2011: 824). Researchers using process tracing generally look to understand how, over time, X produces a series of actions and conditions that interact with each other (or do not) to produce Y. In this way, process tracing goes beyond identifying a correlation between elements to discovering the underlying causes (George and Bennett 2005) providing, as Collier (2011: 823) submits, the 'inferential leverage often missing in qualitative research'.

Originating in cognitive psychology to examine micro-aspects of individual decision-making (using narrative-based analysis; for an overview see Falleti 2016), process-tracing techniques were subsequently extended to flesh out what were considered to be the narrow, theoretical explanations of social events (Todd and Benbasat 1987; Falleti 2016). As more advanced procedures were added, including the specification of mechanisms (Kittel and Kuehn 2013), process tracing was re-focused on outlining and 'testing' hypotheses, informing how, why and under what conditions one event leads to another.

Having briefly introduced process tracing, its origins and research foci, the remainder of this chapter provides a more detailed description of the approach, including identifying its key features and forms, and its relevance as a methodological/analytical tool for examining public sector networks and collaborations, both of which emphasize process as a core operating element (Gray 1989; Thompson and Perry 2006). Public sector examples are used to demonstrate this relevance. Key challenges and best practice strategies are also discussed, along with available resources to guide implementation. The chapter concludes with a reflection on the promise, pitfalls and future potential of process tracing within this context.

Process tracing: features and relevance

Claims that process tracing can 'contribute decisively both to describing social phenomena and to evaluating causal claims' in complex arenas (Collier 2011: 823) have raised process tracing's salience as a research methodology, leading to its application across a range of fields, for example, political science (Collier 2011; Kay and Baker 2015), international development (Barnett and Munslow 2014; Checkel 2006, 2008), manufacturing (Hunt 1996) and organizational studies (Hernes 2014). Such disciplinary diversity has generated a proliferation of forms and approaches. The result, as Surel (cited in Trampusch and Palier 2016: 438) asserts, is a 'methodological stretching', ranging from descriptive and/or historical approaches to outlining component parts and their connections, to the use of quantitative or mixed methods and a priori theoretic approaches designed to isolate causal aspects and confirm the hypothesized change or rule out potentially competing causal explanations (Hall 2006; Mahoney 2012; Kincaid 2012).

As this discussion indicates, process tracing shifts the research emphasis from the causal effects themselves – that is, the expected value of the change in outcome – to the mechanisms connecting the cause with the effect. Several authors note that this shift in emphasis represents the main difference between process tracing and statistical analysis (Mayntz 2004; Gerring 2007, 2008; Falleti 2016).

Mechanisms

Mechanisms are core to process tracing, with social mechanisms deemed the most appropriate for the study of social phenomenon (Hedström 2005: 24; Little 2013), such as networked and collaborative arrangements. Little's (2014) catalogue isolates several social mechanisms relevant to networks and collaborations, including norms, reciprocity and relationships. Put simply, a social mechanism refers to a sequence of social events or process steps, defined as 'parts', actioned by actors (people, organizations or other entities) that, under certain conditions (known or unknown), deliver a change in human social relations or outcomes (Elster 1998; Gross 2009). Mechanisms can focus on the spatial, temporal and functional organization of the parts leading to an outcome (Glennan 2008: 422).

Social mechanisms are conceived less in singular (micro) or static terms, but rather as a set of meshed parts, held together by an overarching, theoretically induced theme (George and McKeown 1985: 35). This feature allows for an elevation to a macro-level analysis and can account for the equifinality/multifinality or multiple paths toward similar ends, which are central features of social life (George and Bennett 2005; Trampusch and Palier 2016).

Beach and Pedersen (2013) break social mechanisms into two component parts that are individually necessary components or phases of the theorized mechanism: (1) entities (objects, actors or institutions engaging in the activity), and (2) actions and activities that produce change (for example, relationship building, communicating). Stimulus can be said to link mechanisms at different temporal stages via influence on these two component parts. An overarching theoretical proposition or hypothesis informs the social mechanism and shapes the nature of the actions or activities. Figure 8.1 illustrates how these mechanisms and component parts fit together.

Parallels can be drawn between this two-part understanding of a social mechanism and Keast and Mandell's (2014) collaborative network framework. Their collaboration leadership framework comprises three theorized mechanism

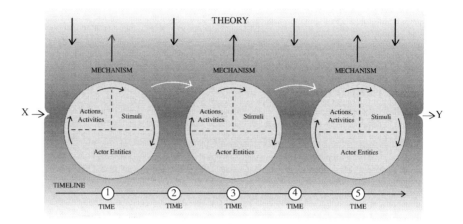

Figure 8.1 Mechanism flows

component parts that fit onto the two-component framework, once again driven by stimulus: (1) the identification of a shared issue (entities A); (2) the application of social tools/relational infrastructures (actions and activities A) and (3) deliberate managerial action (actions and activities B). In part one, a common issue or crisis leads to agreement on the need for a different way of working, where various new project members come together, via a facilitated process or person, to reach shared agreement on a problem and willingness to work together. In part two, the entities are the process catalysts, that is, the actors responsible for creating a conducive network environment, which occurs through actions and events (workshops, social interactions and the creation of a shared language) and which leads to stronger network connections that are subsequently actioned in part three by network managers (strategic leveragers), who use deliberate network management activities, including mobilization and brokering strategies, to deliver collective outcomes.

The operationalization of mechanisms can be further illustrated with the Hunger and Nutrition Commitment Index (HANCI) project, which assessed the impact of HANCI interventions on reframing debates and solutions at both the political and technical levels (te Lintelo et al. 2016). Program personnel developed a theory of change, positing how the HANCI intervention was likely to influence policy outcomes, and this was used to identify the causal mechanisms. The sequencing of components is illustrated in Figure 8.2, where X represents the start point –the establishment of the project – and Y, the outcome. In between are the three 'mechanism parts' and/or sets of effort stimulating change, implemented by relevant actors. For example, part one relies on 'IDS' producers using communication strategies and targeted partnership activities to promote the use of HANCI, while in part two non-elite policy personnel draw on HANCI evidence to shape policy messages to influence programmatic and

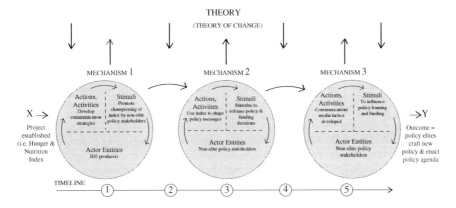

Figure 8.2 A causal mechanism explaining network effects

Source: Adapted from te Lintelo 2016

funding decisions. Finally, in part three, policy personnel use media and communication tactics to enhance the understanding and commitment of policy elites to act on findings.

As the illustration suggests, process tracing drills into the minuscular of social phenomena, 'the nuts and bolts, cogs and wheels' (Elster 1989: 3), to explain outcomes including, as highlighted in the figure, the behaviours, thinking and perceptions that shape decision-making as well as the presence of information and other factors that stimulate actions (George and McKeown 1985; Bates et al. 1998: 111; Waldner 2012: 64–65).

Two ontological approaches guide the study of mechanisms: deterministic and probabilistic (Bennett and Checkel 2015: 10–11; Kay and Baker 2015; Trampusch and Palier 2016). A deterministic approach narrows in on the link between X and Y, positing that a specific mechanism will always produce a specific outcome (Mayntz 2004: 245), while probabilistic perspectives argue that, in complex systems of dynamic interacting parts, it can't be presumed that the same mechanism will always result in the same outcome or vice versa (Glennan 1996; Falleti and Lynch 2009: 1147). The researcher's ontological and epistemological stances, combined with the questions to be answered, affect the type of process tracing to be applied (George and Bennett 2005; Beach and Pedersen 2013), including whether an inductive or deductive approach is required (Trampusch and Palier 2016).

Process-tracing forms

Case- and theory-centric forms

Despite the numerous definitions and applications of process tracing (see Trampusch and Palier 2016), there is consensus of three main forms: theory testing and theory building (both theory-centric) and case-centric. Each offers distinct approaches to the examination of causal properties for different research settings or purposes, depending on the questions to be answered and the ontological (theory) and epistemological (empirical) stances adopted by researchers (George and Bennett 2005; Beach and Pedersen 2013; Trampusch and Palier 2016).

Case-centric studies are most relevant for explaining the occurrence of a specific set of events in relation to the outcome (Kay and Baker 2015: 6), as well as why this might have happened within a designated time and place – especially when the case or cases present as complex, multi-factorial and context-specific, and therefore are not easily generalizable (Hall 2006; Beach and Pedersen 2013). They follow an inductive approach in which narratives shape the explanations ideally without influence of a priori assumptions or theory. However, the case narrative must go beyond just describing events to generate a detailed exposition of the 'causal web' connecting actions and outcomes (Reyker and Beach 2017: 261; Hall 2006).

Although not explicitly defined as such, Innes and Booher (2010) applied a form of case-centric process tracing to 'link the choices made in process design to the outcomes' of six collaborative examples (85). Drawing widely from participant narratives, they concluded that deliberately designed and implemented collaborative processes result in more extensive and longer-term outcomes. Process mapping, as a variant of process tracing, is also implemented by public administration scholars but, rather than looking for traces of processual evidence, this approach unpacks network processes by sequentially analysing the actions of actors, their 'games' and the networks formed (Koppenjan and Klijn 2004). The work of Stevens and colleagues is emblematic of this approach in examining the role of collaboration in meta-governance arrangements (Stevens and Verhoest 2016) as well as the identification of causal links between collaboration management and innovation (Stevens 2017; Stevens and Agger 2017). Typically, case-centric forms of process tracing are undertaken without reference to mechanisms (Hall 2006), or treat mechanisms in an abstract manner, which Beach (2017) categorizes as 'lite' or 'minimalist' process tracing.

Alongside the case-centric modes are the two theory-centric approaches: theory building and theory testing. *Theory-building* process tracing also uses an inductive approach to isolate and unpack events leading to an outcome and create new hypotheses. It is employed where there is:

1   evidence of an existing correlation between x and y, but little knowledge or understanding of the link between cause (*X*) and outcome (*Y*);
2   when an outcome (*Y*) is known but there is uncertainty about what causes it (*X*) (Beach and Pedersen 2013: 17; Centre for Development Impact 2015: 2).

Theory-building process tracing is evidenced in Kristianssen and Olsson's (2016) study, which analysed shadowing and elite interviews to scrutinize the processes involved in establishing a Swedish Municipal Service Centre. From this analysis, a detailed timeline and narrative was constructed allowing the process to 'speak for itself' (36), highlighting the following key steps: a dual emphasis on service and efficiency, and high-level institutional support.

By way of contrast, *theory-testing* process tracing follows a deductive approach designed to test existing theories and determine whether the hypothesized causal mechanism exists and functions as expected. It starts with the assumption that both the cause (X) and the outcome (Y) are known and postulates a theory about how Y and X are related. Following Beach and Pedersen (2013), theory-testing process tracing is employed when:

1   there are existing deductions concerning a causal mechanism linking X and Y in a case;
2   deductions from existing theorization concerning a mechanism can easily be made (Centre for Development Impact 2015: 2).

In this mode, attention is directed to collecting and building an uninterrupted evidence chain to test pre-established theoretical claims or hypotheses.

Theory-testing process tracing is evidenced in Ulibarri and Scott's (2016) study of the effects of collaboration process on hydro-power licencing, which set out four hypotheses on collaboration processes (H1: high collaboration processes exhibit greater network density, H2: high collaboration processes exhibit lesser tendency to have empty ties, H3: higher collaboration processes exhibit stronger tendency for reciprocal ties, and H4: high collaboration processes will exhibit lower triad closure) and tested these using social network analysis (SNA) based on participant observation and meeting data. The analysis showed that the duration of hydro-power relicensing was not associated with the level of collaboration, highlighting instead regulatory and facility characteristics as efficiency drivers. The Bangladesh Secondary Education (Asian Development Bank 2015) and HANCI (te Lintelo et al. 2016) studies also provide comprehensive accounts of theory-guided process tracing, showing the development and testing of hypotheses and mechanisms related to their respective reform processes.

Despite the outward separation of inductive and deductive approaches to process tracing described in this section, in practice it often combines both (Bennett and Checkel 2015; Beach 2017). For example, inductive approaches can help to reconceptualize findings that challenge initial deductively developed hypotheses (see Asian Development Bank 2015) or be implemented as a precursor to deductive testing to ensure that theoretical mechanisms have been adequately elaborated, while deductive means could be applied for deeper interrogation or confirmation of initial inductive findings, as with the Kristianssen and Olsson (2016) example.

Relevance of method to public sector networks and collaborative arrangements

The confluence of several factors contributes to process tracing's relevance as an analytical approach and tool to study public sector networks and collaborations.

First, is the well-established, and growing, appreciation of the essential role of process, defined as a systematic and unfolding series of choices, decisions, actions, activities, events and practices in guiding network and collaborative behaviour and outcomes (Gray 1989; Thompson and Perry 2006; Innes and Booher 2010; Keast and Mandell 2014). Since relationships are the connective tissue for networks and collaborations, process factors necessarily have a relational or socially focused orientation; for example, shared goals, trust, consensus and decision-making (Gray 1989; Koppenjan and Klijn 2004).

As awareness of attending to process grows, policy-makers, network managers and practitioners are seeking deeper insights as well as more concrete, nuanced knowledge of the processes needed to craft networks and collaborative policies, programs and practices that are more effective and sustainable, as well as to improve their management. Varda, Shoup and Miller (2012) note that public sector network research is increasingly 'link[ing] outcomes to such factors as how the network is structured, and the processes managed'. While clearly 'getting the process right' is essential to successful collective working, over-zealous attention to process issues at the expense of other features, such as appropriate management and leadership, exposes these initiatives to the risk of 'collaborative inertia' (Hibbert and Huxham 2005: 59) or network failure – concerns identified in the Bangladesh policy reform study noted previously.

Closely related to enhanced processual design and implementation is the mounting pressure to demonstrate that funds and effort invested in establishing and working in networks and collaborative arrangements are making a difference to public well-being or producing added public value (Rogers et al. 2015; Scheirer 2005). The growing demand for information on the performance of these arrangements, as well as insights on how to sustain collective effort and outcomes, is generating renewed interest in research and evaluation approaches that not only answers questions about performance but are also capable of delivering refined insights into how the results emerge (Schmitt and Beach 2015).

Finally, as highlighted earlier in the chapter, networks and collaborations exhibit complex, dynamic and iterative properties that can generate numerous alternative routes and processes, including tipping points and feedback loops, to reach similar goals (Bennett and Elman 2006; Starke 2013). Process tracing accommodates such equifinality, as it

> Consider(s) the alternative paths through which the outcome could have occurred and offers the possibility of mapping out one or more potential causal paths.
>
> (George and Bennett 2005, 206–207)

The organic way in which networks and collaborations often unfold, coupled with the prospect of alternative paths to similar outcomes confounds the ability of standard statistical tools to track processes or directly link action to outcomes

(Thompson and Perry 2006; Varda et al. 2012; Rocco and Thurston 2014). This issue has opened the door to approaches such as process tracing (and qualitative comparative analysis [QCA] discussed in Cepiku, Cristofoli and Trivellato's Chapter 10 in this volume) that place greater emphasis on understanding complex relationships, irregularities, temporality and iterativeness (Kay and Baker 2015). Furthermore, as Falleti (2016) notes, process tracing can be applied at different levels of analysis, thus allowing for micro, meso or macro examinations of process, and can be coupled with other research approaches to deliver more comprehensive insights (Kay and Baker 2015; Beach 2017). As such, process tracing adds to the methodological diversification and transparency increasingly called for within public sector research.

Conducting process tracing

The following outlines the main steps for theory-testing process tracing, since this is the more expansive form, with variations for other forms noted where relevant. The steps are not prescriptive, but act as a guide since process tracing itself is often unfolding and therefore fluid in its implementation (Beach and Pedersen 2013).

Step 1: identifying and linking hypothesized mechanisms and components

1   Form the hypothesized mechanism into an unbroken causal chain of action (which can include feedback loops; Gerring 2008) by elaborating each mechanism component part to identify which entities (described as nouns, such as people, organizations) are expected to conduct which actions (described as verbs, for example relationship building, influencing) at each specified time, and how these are linked these together into a seamless pattern of interaction.
2   Operationalize the mechanism by specifying the expected observable evidence for each mechanism and the links between component parts; that is, what evidence would confirm that each part of the mechanism/s happened or did not happen, and what evidence would show that a previous component part of the mechanism happened because of the previous mechanism/s (Collier 2011: 825).
3   Feasible measurement proxies can be considered that support or fail the hypothesis as well as identify plausible alternative theories (Hall 2006; Kay and Baker 2015).

Process maps (see Figures 8.1 and 8.2) or charts (see Voorberg, Bekkers and Tummers 2014; te Lintelo et al. 2016) may be used to illustrate how the causal elements and their relationships link together, as well as to identify the expected traces of evidence. Gerring (2007: 181) stresses such diagrams must precisely and explicitly articulate the argumentation and expected evidence to provide a conceptual and empirical value-add, as well as contribute any theoretical refinement (Bennett 2016).

Step 2: case selection

For studies seeking to probe causal validity, cases should be selected that

- represent the mechanism under examination based on theoretical expectations (Schimmelfennig 2015); Voorberg et al. (2014) provide a case selection rationale for a theory-testing study of co-creation, which centred on the detailed interrogation of the dependent variable 'successful public-co-creation' (6);
- sufficiently demonstrate that X and Y are present and contain appropriate information; and/or
- ideally are supplemented by detailed case knowledge, acquired through, for example, an initial qualitative mapping of the processes, or take a more systematic form such as QCA (Beach and Rohlfing 2015).

These case-selection principles are not necessary for explanatory/case-centric process-tracing forms as they are focused on describing the conditions of a nominated case of interest.

Step 3: collecting evidence

Collecting evidence should involve the following actions:

1   Data are collected over the multiple stages of the process for each mechanism part, as well as to capture broader contextual effects (Bates et al. 1998; George and Bennett 2005).
2   Data may be sourced from: (1) primary sources: such as observations, interviews, focus groups; and/or (2) secondary sources: including archives, documents (strategic plans, reports, meeting minutes) as well as grey literature (policy documents, internal reports, cabinet documents).
3   The reliability of each data source is assessed to identify potential biases and limitations.
4   Multiple data sources are employed to cross-check, verify accuracy and triangulate evidence.

Notionally, theory-building process tracing commences at this step, although inductive assumptions are rarely immune from prior experience, theorization or hypotheses.

Step 4: analysis and verification

1   Data evidence collected on each mechanism part is assessed against expected benchmarks to verify that it is present and functioning as proposed. This may occur initially through a thorough qualitative account of how the process has unfolded over time, including at a minimum a detailed articulation of the relevant actors, their actions and stimuli, as well as how individual

or multiple actors' aggregate actions combined to produce the collective outcome (Hedstôm and Swedberg 1998).

2 Qualitative analysis is undertaken using descriptive analytical tools, such as thematic analysis or computerized analytical forms, including, for example, NVivo for text and/or multimedia data, and Leximancer for natural language and text analysis; quantitative analytical forms, such as QCA, use statistical measures to more deeply dissect and make sense of the process components (Kay and Baker 2015). Multi-methods approaches are increasingly utilized, for example, Ulibarri (2015a, 2015b) combined quantitative analysis from a large survey sample with analysis of qualitative material (documentation and interviews) to confirm the presence of key collaboration criteria and extended this in Ulibarri and Scott (2016) to include SNA.

3 Depending on the preliminary findings, review and refine the theory and mechanisms or check for alternative explanations.

4 Four tests have been developed to further assess whether the evidence attained provides empirical support for the postulated theory, and is necessary and/ or sufficient explanation for the cause of the effect: straw in the wind, hoop test, smoking gun and doubly-decisive/definitive (Van Evera 1997):

- *Straw-in-the-wind*: lends support to an explanation without definitively ruling it in or out.
- *Hoop test*: failed when a case examination shows the presence of a necessary causal condition when the outcome of interest is not present. Common hoop conditions are more persuasive than uncommon ones.
- *Smoking gun:* passed when a case examination shows the presence of a sufficient causal condition. Uncommon smoking gun conditions are more persuasive than common ones.
- *Doubly-definitive:* passed when a case examination shows that a condition is both necessary and shows sufficient support for the condition.

See Collier (2011) and Centre for Development Impact (2015) for extended explanations and applications.

Once the process is complete, the researcher should be able to assert a degree of confidence in each part of the hypothesized mechanism, based on the evidence collected and the tests applied. The HANCI and Bangladesh reform studies both provide expansive accounts of the application of these tests and of theory-testing process tracing more generally, covering the selection of tests and the analysis undertaken in arriving at decisions. Voorberg et al.'s (2014) theory-testing examination of co-creation and the suite of work by Ulibarri (2015a, 2015b, 2017; Ulibarri, Cain and Ajami 2017) using case centric and theory testing are good examples to follow.

Evaluating process tracing: benefits and limitations

Although only recently adopted as a research tool for public administration, as demonstrated in this chapter (see also Willems and Van Dooren

2012; Yang 2012; Charbonneau et al. 2017), there is growing use of process tracing more generally within the sector as well as specifically for examining networked and collaborative arrangements. An increasing number of these studies have demonstrated its relevance for answering questions of impacts of decision-making, personal and collective agency as well as the nature and sequencing of process variables. Indeed, its value in uncovering new insights into collective processes has been explicitly noted (see Ulibarri 2015b; Stevens and Verhoest 2015).

The generation through process tracing of fine-grained case information brings data closer to theory for more rigorous analysis (Beach and Pedersen 2013; Kay and Baker 2015), enabling several public-sector research objectives to be met, spanning identifying and systematically describing social occurrences, evaluating explanatory hypotheses, discovering new theories and detailing insights into causal mechanisms. Tansey (2007) summarizes the process-tracing value-add, noting that it generates and assesses foundational data, using inductive and deductive means, to enhance efforts in theory development, theory testing and case description. Gerring (2007, 2008) adds that the distinctive procedures of process tracing can be extended to support or supplement other case study methods, such as comparative case studies and large-*n* designs. It can also deal with multiple causal pathways and account for emergent process developments as well as function at different levels of analysis (Kay and Baker 2015) – all features pertinent to the study of networks and collaboration.

Another benefit of process tracing is its flexibility in the use and integration of a variety of data types and sources (e.g. survey, archives, interviews), and the growing application of complementary methodologies that can extend insights and enhance the rigour of findings as well as provide greater transparency within and across research modes (Moravcsik 2014). For instance, the rich narrative created to identify interaction patterns can also use analytical tools, such as discourse analysis and QCA (Blackman, Wistow and Byrne 2013), agent-based modelling (Checkel 2013) and SNA (for more on SNA as a mechanism-based approach for network causality see Dorien 2001).

Finally, the demands for systematic breakdown of evidence and cross-checking of causal mechanisms can help tease out conceptual gaps and overlaps, allowing for more precise distinctions to be made between alternative theoretical schools (Checkel 2005). For example, findings from the HANCI study challenged long-standing views on the indicator standards that influence reforms and highlighted the stronger effect of local context on outcomes (te Lintelo et al. 2016). Analytical transparency is also argued to contribute more broadly to the advancement of methodological rigour (Moravcsik 2014; Kay and Baker 2015).

At the same time, limitations are apparent, most notably the lack of definitional agreement on mechanisms, with Mahoney (2001) identifying twenty-four versions and with more recent additions by Shaffer (2014), and arguments as to if and how mechanisms differ from related concepts, such as intervening variables (Falleti 2016). It has been suggested this definitional confusion can be overcome by creating a commonly accepted understanding of the term.

The extensive, longitudinal data required for process tracing makes it more resource-intensive, and therefore potentially costlier, than orthodox case study approaches, with results weakened by data gaps (George and Bennett 2005; Beach 2017) or tests that have not been correctly matched to the research purpose (Collier 2011: 4). Data analysis is also time-consuming, as it requires deep engagement in the details of the case process, elsewhere described as 'soaking and poking' (Bennett and Checkel 2015), to build the 'uninterrupted causal path' needed for causal/inferential strength (George and Bennett 2005: 222). Likewise, it is easy to become overwhelmed by the potentially vast quantity of data generated, leading to infinite loops of analysis, or overlook external, contextualizing events and conditions that may have contributing effects. And, as Berends (nd, slide 4) notes, there is limited agreement as to the sequencing and integration of data and narratives to optimally present findings and verify inferences, leading to inconsistent reporting styles.

The lack of systematic and transparent application, especially the explicit depiction of how the mechanisms brought about outcomes, is argued to undermine confidence in results (Punton and Welle 2015). Similarly, Beach (2017) points to quality concerns related to 'lite' process-tracing forms (described earlier), due to their minimalist treatment of mechanisms and therefore the superficial evidence trails applied. Related to this, Checkel (2005) and others (Hall 2006; Mayntz 2016; Kay and Baker 2015; Falleti 2016) warn against the often-limited transparency in identifying underpinning ontological and epistemological positions in process-tracing research. These authors stress the need for a clear articulation and linkage of researchers' underpinning assumptions, as this directly affects both the process-tracing variant to be applied and whether an inductive or deductive approach is required (Trampusch and Palier 2016). As process tracing evolves and increasingly incorporates multi-methods, a stronger appreciation of the differences in these approaches will be necessary in addition to transparency in process-tracing research design, implementation, analysis and reporting (Moravcsik 2014). Finally, the detailed narrative involved in reporting process tracing may narrow publishing options, as many public management journals have stringent word limits (Gerring and Cojuaru 2016; Schimmelfennig 2015) and, likely, for this reason there are few good published examples of process tracing (Punton and Welle 2015).

The future of process tracing

As demands for improved understandings of the role of processes in networks and collaborations increase, process tracing as a research methodology/approach is likely to become more pertinent, either as a stand-alone tool or to supplement other methodological and analytical forms. George and Bennett (2005) have long argued process tracing should be included in every researcher's methodology repertoire. Process tracing's value has been enhanced by several advancements that move beyond its prior philosophical concerns to emphasize its practical implementation (Hays 2016; Kay and Baker 2015), including teaching tools (Collier 2011), the development of efficiency principles (Waldner 2015) and quality strategies and check lists (Beach and Pedersen 2013).

As relatively late adopters of process tracing (Charbonneau et al. 2017), public management researchers can also leverage more recent conceptual and technical advancements, such as the use of Bayesian logic to increase confidence in the conclusiveness of theorized causal mechanisms (Schmitt and Beach 2015; Befani and Mayne 2014), with the latter suggesting a combination of process tracing with contribution analysis. Several scholars (Collier 2011; Kay and Baker 2015) further predict that counterfactual reasoning (positing of alternative possible causal processes, counter to actual causes) will be an important future focus for process-tracing research development, arguing that the exploration of outlier explanations may offer useful unexpected insights (Levy 2008). Also promising is the rise of online forums and other digital publication venues better able to accommodate the longer narrative reporting of process tracing or capable of including supplementary materials, such as documentary evidence, as attachments (Gerring and Cojuaru 2016), although at present these are not always eligible for citation.

To conclude, process tracing has the capacity to be a powerful tool for the future of network and collaborative research. In the end though, it is worth remembering that, while it appears deceptively simple, process tracing is complicated, sometimes chaotic, often capricious, and demands rigorous and meticulous application and extensive resources.

Further reading

- Special issues on this topic include the *New Political Economy* (Vol. 21 No. 5) www.tandfonline.com/toc/cnpe20/21/5?nav=tocList) and the *Academy of Management Journal* (Vol. 1, No. 56).
- An array of methodological training courses, summer schools, workshops and symposia are available. The Academy of Management regularly sponsors professional learning and development workshops on process methods at its annual conference. Similarly, the European Consortium for Political Research Winter School held a week-long training program on Advanced Process Tracing Methods (see https://ecpr.eu/Events/PanelDetails.aspx?PanelID=4532&EventID=103).
- Training sessions have also been offered by the Consortium for Qualitative Research Methods (CQRM), sponsored by the Maxwell School of Public Administration, Syracuse University (www.maxwell.syr.edu/moynihan/cqrm/Short_Courses_at_APSA).
- Practical support is available through dedicated websites and forums, such as the ASPA: Qualitative Transparency Deliberations website (http://processresearchmethods.org/process-research-literature/), as well as the teaching tools provided though the Centre for Development Impact. Finally, Collier (2011) provides an excellent and concise description of four process-tracing tests and how they can be applied in practice.

References

Asian Development Bank (Independent Evaluation). 2015. "Policy reform in Bangladesh's secondary education (1993–2013) causal process tracing and examining the Asian Development Bank's contribution." Topic Paper: 15. www.adb.org/sites/default/files/evaluation-document/177777/files/topical-ban-sec-educ.pdf.

Bates, R., A. Avner-Greif, M. Levi, J-L. Rosenthal, and B. Weingast. 1998. *Analytic narratives.* Princeton, NJ: Princeton University Press.

Barnett, C. and T. Munslow. 2014. "Process tracing: The potential and pitfalls for impact evaluation in international development." Summary of Workshop 7 May 2014, Institute of Development Studies in December 2014, Brighton, United Kingdom. https://www.academia.edu/26070995/Process_Tracing_The_Potential_and_Pitfalls_for_Impact_Evaluation_in_International_Development.

Beach, D. 2017. "Process-tracing methods in social sciences." *Qualitative Political Methodology* doi: 10.1093/acrefore/9780190228637.013.176.

Beach, D. and R. Pedersen. 2013. *Process-tracing methods: Foundations and guidelines.* Ann Arbor, MI: University of Michigan Press.

Beach, D. and I. Rohlfing. 2015. "Integrating cross-case analyses and process tracing in set-theoretic research: Strategies and parameters of debate." *Sociological Methods and Research* 47 (1): 3–36.

Befani, B. and J. Mayne. 2014. "Process tracing and contribution analysis: A combined approach generative causal inference." *Institute Development Studies Bulletin* 45 (6): 17–36.

Bennett, A. 2016. "Do new accounts of causal mechanisms offer practical advice for process tracing?" *Qualitative and MultiMethod Research: Newsletter of the American Political Science Association's QMMR Section* 14: 1–2.

Bennett, A. and J. Checkel. 2015. "Process tracing: From philosophy to best practices." In *Process tracing: From metaphor to analytic tool*, edited by A. Bennett and J. Checkel, 3–8. Cambridge: Cambridge University Press.

Bennett, A. and C. Elman. 2006. "Qualitative research: Recent developments in case study methods." *Annual Review of Political Science* 9: 455–476.

Berends, H. (nd). "Composing qualitative process research." PowerPoint. Kin2 Research, VU Amsterdam. http://processresearchmethods.org/wp-content/uploads/2016/08/Berends-ComposingQualitativeProcessResearch.pdf.

Blackman, T., J. Wistow, and D. Byrne. 2013. "Applying Qualitative Comparative Analysis to understand complex policy problems." *Evaluation* 19 (2): 126–140.

Centre for Development Impact. 2015. "Applying process tracing in five steps." Practice Paper Annex 10 (April). www.ids.ac.uk/cdi.

Charbonneau, E., A. Hendersen, B. Ladouceur, and P. Pichet. 2017. "Process tracing in public administration: The implications of practitioner insights for methods of inquiry." *International Journal of Public Administration* 40 (5): 434–442.

Checkel, J. 2005. "It's the process stupid! process tracing in the study of European and international politics." Centre for European Studies Working Paper #26. University of Oslo (October). www.arena.uio.no.

Checkel, J. 2006. "Tracing causal mechanisms." *International Studies Review* 8 (2): 2–370.

Checkel, J. 2008. "Process tracing." In *Qualitative methods in international relations: A pluralist guide*, edited by A. Klotz and D. Prakash, 114–129. New York: Palgrave Macmillan.

Checkel, J. 2013. "Socialization and organized political violence: Theoretical tools and challenges." Simons Papers in Security and Development, No. 28/2013. School for International Studies, Simon Fraser University, Vancouver, November 2013.

Collier, D. 2011. "Understanding process tracing (the teacher)." *Political Science and Politics* 44 (4): 823–830.

Dorien, P. 2001. "Causality in social network analysis." *Sociological Methods and Research* 30 (1): 81–114.

Elster, J. 1989. *Nuts and bolts for social sciences.* Cambridge: Cambridge University Press.

Elster, J. 1998. "A plea for mechanisms." In *Social mechanisms,* edited by P. Hedström and R. Swedberg, 45–73. Cambridge, UK: Cambridge University Press.

Falleti, T. 2016. "Process tracing of extensive and intensive processes." *New Political Economy* 21 (5): 455–462.

Falleti, T. and J. Lynch. 2009. "Context and causal mechanisms in political analysis." *Comparative Political Studies* 42 (9): 1143–1166.

Gerring, J. 2007. *Case study research: Principles and practices.* New York: Cambridge University Press.

Gerring, J. 2008. "Review article: The mechanistic worldview: Thinking inside the box." *British Journal of Political Science* 38 (1): 161–179.

Gerring, J. and C. Cojuaru. 2016. "Arbitrary word limits to scholarly speech: Why (short) word limits should be abolished." *Qualitative and Multimethod Research* Spring/Fall: 2–12.

Glennan, S. 1996. "Mechanisms and the nature of causation." *Erkenntnis* 44: 49–71.

Glennan. S. 2008. "Mechanisms." In *The Routledge companion to the philosophy of science,* edited by S. Psillos and M. Curd. London: Routledge.

Gray, B. 1989. *Collaborating: Finding common ground for multiparty problems.* San Francisco, USA: Jossey-Bass.

George, A. and T. McKeown. 1985. "Case studies and theories of organizational decision making." *Advances in Information Processing in Organizations* 2: 21–58.

George, A. and A. Bennett. 2005. *Case studies and theory development in the social sciences.* Cambridge, MA: MIT Press.

Gross, N. 2009. "A pragmatist theory of social mechanisms." *American Sociological Review* 74 (3): 358–379.

Hall, P. 2006. "Systematic process analysis: When and how to use it." *European Management Review* 3: 24–31.

Hays, C. 2016. "Process tracing: A laudable aim or high tariff methodology." *New Political Economy* 21 (5): 500–505.

Hedstôm, P. 2005. *Dissecting the social: On the principles of analytical sociology.* Cambridge: Cambridge University Press.

Hedström, P. and R. Swedberg, eds. 1998. *Social mechanisms: An analytical approach to social theory.* Cambridge UK: Cambridge University Press.

Hernes, T. 2014. *A process theory of organization.* Oxford University Press: Oxford, UK.

Hibbert, P. and C. Huxham. 2005. "A little about the mystery: Process learning as collaboration evolves." *European Management Journal* 2: 59–69.

Hunt, V. 1996. *Process mapping.* New York, USA: John Wiley & Sons Inc.

Innes, J. and D. Booher. 2010. *Planning with complexity: An introduction to collaborative rationality for public policy.* Abingdon, UK: Routledge.

Kay, A. and P. Baker. 2015. "What can causal process tracing offer to policy studies? A review of the literature." *Policy Studies Journal* 43 (1): 1–17.

Keast, R. and M. Mandell. 2014. "A composite theory of leadership and management: Process catalyst and strategic leveraging: Deliberate action in collaborative networks." In *Network theory in the public sector: Building new theoretical frameworks,* R. Keast, M. Mandell, and R. Agranoff, 31–50. Abingdon, UK: Routledge.

Kittel, B. and D. Kuehn. 2013. "Introduction: Reassessing the methodology of process tracing." *European Political Science* 12: 1–9.

Koppenjan, J. and E. Klijn. 2004. *Managing uncertainties in networks.* London: Routledge.

Kincaid, H. 2012. "Mechanisms, causal modelling and the limitations of traditional multiple regression." In *Oxford handbook of philosophy of social sciences*, edited by H. Kincaid, 46–64. New York: Oxford University Press.

Kristianssen, A. and J. Olsson. 2016. "A municipal service center: For what and for whom? Understanding the political nature of a public administration reform process." *Scandinavian Journal of Public Administration* 20 (3): 33–54.

Levy, J. 2008. "Counterfactuals and case studies." In *The Oxford Handbook Of Political Methodology*, edited by J.M. Box-Steffensmeier, H.E. Brady, and D. Collier, 627–644. Oxford: Oxford University Press.

Little, D. 2013. "Social mechanisms and scientific realism: Discussion of 'mechanistic explanation in social contexts'." *Social Epistemology Review and Reply Collective* 1 (3): 1–5. http://wp.me/p1Bfg0-9i.

Little, D. 2014. "A catalogue of social mechanisms." https://understandingsociety.blogspot.co.nz/2014/06/a-catalogue-of-social-mechanisms.html.

Mahoney, J. 2001. "Beyond correlational analysis: Recent innovations in theory and method." *Sociological Forum* 16 (3): 682–693.

Mahoney, J. 2012. "The logic of process tracing in the social sciences." *Sociological Methods and Research* 41 (4): 570–597.

Mayntz, R. 2004. "Mechanisms in the analysis of social macro-phenomena." *Philosophy of Social Sciences* 34 (2): 237–259.

Mayntz, R. 2016. "Process tracing, abstraction, and varieties of cognitive interest." *New Political Economy* 21 (5): 484–488.

Moravcsik, A. 2014. "Transparency: The revolution in qualitative research." *Political Science* January: 48–53. www.princeton.edu/~amoravcs/library/transparency.pdf.

Punton, M. and K. Welle. 2015. "Straws-in-the wind, hoops and smoking guns: What can process tracing offer to impact evaluation?" Centre for Development Impact Practice Paper Number 10, April 2015. file:///C:/Users/PC%20User/Downloads/CDIPracticePaper_10.pdf.

Reyker, Y. and D. Beach. 2017. "Process-tracing as a tool to analyse discretion." In *The principal agent model and European union politics*, edited by T. Delreux and J. Adriaensen, 255–281. Cham, Switzerland: Palgrave Studies in Union Politics, Palgrave Macmillan.

Rocco, P. and C. Thurston. 2014. "From metaphors to measures: Observable indicators of gradual institutional change." *Journal of Public Policy* 34 (91): 35–62.

Rogers, P., A. Hawkins, B. McDonald, A. MacFarlan, and C. Milne. 2015. "Choosing appropriate designs and methods for impact evaluation (November)." Report prepared for the Office of the Chief Scientist, Department of Industry, Innovation and Finance. Canberra, Australia.

Scheirer, M. 2005. "Is sustainability possible? A review and commentary on empirical studies of program sustainability." *American Journal of Sustainability* 26 (3): 320–347.

Schimmelfennig, F. 2015. "Efficient process tracing: Analyzing the causal mechanisms of European integration." In *Process tracing in the social sciences: From metaphor to analytical tool*, edited by A. Bennett, and J. Checkel. Cambridge: Cambridge University Press.

Schmitt, J. and D. Beach. 2015. "The contribution of process tracing to theory-based evaluations of complex aid instruments." *Evaluation* 21 (4): 429–447.

Shaffer, P. 2014. "Two concepts of causation: Implications for poverty." *Development and Change* 46 (1): 148–166.

158   *Robyn Keast*

Starke, P. 2013. "Qualitative methods for the study of policy diffusion: Challenges and available solutions." *Policy Studies Journal* 41 (4): 561–582.

Stevens, V. 2017. "How to manage collaborative policy innovation networks? Practical lessons from a Flemish coastal protection initiative." *Journal of Public Administration and Governance* 7 (4): 94–116.

Stevens, V. and A. Agger. 2017. "Managing collaborative innovation networks: Practical lessons from a Belgian spatial planning initiative." *Journal of Public Administration and Governance* 7 (3): 154–173.

Stevens, V. and K. Verhoest. 2015. "Theorising on the metagovernance of collaborative policy innovations." ICPP Conference, Milan.

Stevens, V. and K. Verhoest. 2016. "How to metagovern collaborative networks for the promotion of policy innovations in a dualistic federal system?" *The Innovation Journal: The Public Sector Innovation Journal* 21 (2): 1–26.

te Lintelo, D. 2016. From index to impact? "Process tracing the policy impact of the Hunger and Nutrition Commitment Index (HANCI)." Presentation, 10 November 2016. www.slideshare.net/NatalieStewart18/presentation-process-tracing-hanci-ids-nov2016.

te Lintelo, D., T. Munslow, R. Lakshman, and K. Pittore. 2016. *Assessing the policy impact of 'indicators': A process-tracing study of Hunger and Nutrition Commitment Index (HANCI).* Brighton, England: Institute of Development Studies.

Tansey, O. 2007. "Process tracing and elite interviewing: A case for non-probability." *Sampling Political Science and Politics* 40 (4): 765–772. www.nuffield.ox.ac.uk/politics/papers/2006/tansey.pdf.

Thompson, A.M. and J. Perry. 2006. "Collaboration processes: Inside the black box." *Public Administration Review* 66 (6): 20–31.

Todd, P. and I. Benbasat. 1987. "Process tracing methods in decision support systems: Exploring the black box." *MIT Quarterly* 11 (4): 493–512.

Trampusch, C. and B. Palier. 2016. "Between X and Y: How process tracing contributes to opening the black box of causality." *New Political Economy* 21 (5): 437–454.

Ulibarri, N. 2015a. "Collaboration in federal hydropower licensing: Impacts on process, outputs, and outcomes." *Public Performance and Management Review* 38 (4): 578–606.

Ulibarri, N. 2015b. "Tracing process to performance of collaborative governance: A comparative case study of federal hydropower licensing." *Policy Studies Journal* 43 (2): 283–308.

Ulibarri, N. 2017. "Does collaboration affect the duration of environmental permitting processes?" *Journal of Environmental Planning and Management* 61 (4): 617–634.

Ulibarri, N., B.E. Cain, and N.K. Ajami. 2017. "A framework for building efficient environmental permitting processes." *Sustainability* 9 (2): 180.

Ulibarri, N. and T. Scott. 2016. "Linking network structure to collaborative governance." *Journal of Public Administration Research and Theory* 27 (1): 163–181.

Van Evera, S. 1997. *Guide to methods of political science.* Ithaca, NY: Cornell University Press.

Varda, D., J. Shoup, and S. Miller. 2012. "A systematic review of the collaboration and network research in public affairs literature: Implications for public health research and practice." *American Journal of Public Health* 102 (3): 554–571.

Voorberg, W., V. Bekkers, and L. Tummers. 2014. "The key to successful co-creation: An explanation of causal processing." Paper presented at European Group for Public Administration Conference, Speyer, Germany, 10–12 September.

Waldner, D. 2012. "Process tracing and causal mechanisms." In *Oxford handbook of philosophy of social sciences*, edited by H. Kincaid, 65–84. New York: Oxford University Press.

Waldner, D. 2015. "What makes process tracing good? Causal mechanisms, causal inference, and the completeness standard in comparative politics." In *Process tracing: From metaphor to analytical tool*, edited by A. Bennett and J. Checkel, 126–152. Cambridge University Press.

Willems, T. and W. Van Dooren. 2012. "Coming to terms with accountability." *Public Management Review* 14 (7): 1011–1036.

Yang, K. 2012. "Further understanding accountability in public organizations: Actionable knowledge and the structure: Agency duality." *Administration & Society* 44 (3), 255–284.

9 Social and dynamic network analysis

Robin H. Lemaire and Jörg Raab

Introduction

In this chapter we discuss the use of social and dynamic network analysis for researching networks and collaboration in the public sector. Network analysis is an analytical toolbox and method that is strongly linked with the study of networks and collaboration. It has become a pivotal tool in the study and research of networks and collaboration because the distinguishing feature of network analysis is the focus on relationships between actors and the interdependencies these relationships create. Given the prevalence of networks and collaboration in contemporary research and practice in public management, it may be taken for granted that relationships often influence political or administrative actions. When network analysis first emerged, however, it was in contrast to the focus on attributes of individuals and organizations that dominated the research on organizations. What network theory and analysis brought to light is how the action of individuals and organizations often has as much to do with other individuals and organizations as it does with individual and/or organizational attributes, and how actors are embedded in a web of relationships that enable and constrain their actions (Granovetter 1985).

The theoretical origins of network theory are mostly rooted in sociology and anthropology and one can trace these origins back to classic works on social structure. The methodological origins of the method, though, are mathematics and especially graph theory. The field usually attributes the earliest foundations of social network analysis (SNA) to Moreno (1934) and his development of the sociogram, which is a graphic representation of social links (i.e. the network plots one will often see produced by network analysis). Early applications of network analysis in public sector research include those by Laumann and Pappi (1973), who used network analysis to examine community influence, and Padgett and Ansell (1993) who utilized the method to explain political control and the birth of the Renaissance state in Florence. Since then, network analysis has been applied to the study of emergent as well as consciously created networks, whether those are networks for the provision of services in the public sector or policy networks.

Relevance of method

Network analysis offers a number of contributions to the study of the public sector. The unit of analysis can be individuals, individual organizations, partnerships, collectives of organizations, words (i.e. semantic network analysis) or any unit of analysis where the goal is to describe and analyse the structure of relationships between the units. As scholars have noted (e.g. Isett et al. 2011), the idea of networks is often used as a metaphor to capture the social context in which many actions are often embedded. The use of network analysis, though, is typically employed to find the patterns of structures and the implications of those structures. The structures can be intra-organizational networks (e.g. Siciliano 2017), the structures managers create through networking (e.g. Ryu and Johansen 2017) or the systematic description of social and political systems (Laumann and Knoke 1987). In the case of the latter, the systems being examined could be political systems, international state systems, governance systems or service delivery systems. Thus, the value of network analysis in the study of networks and collaborative arrangements is broad, with its application to different levels of analysis and to the many different lenses from which to examine social structure.

Because we cannot cover in this brief review the many uses of network analysis, and because other reviews of the use of network analysis exist (see Hu, Khosa and Kapucu 2016), we focus on the systematic description of social, political and administrative systems, such as the inter-organizational networks depicted in the public sector which has been the core of our own research. Often the premise behind collaboration and networks in the public sector is for organizations to work together, whether that means public agencies working together or cross-sector collaboration. Network analysis can be, and is, used to study partnerships or contracts between two organizations or even the context these arrangements are embedded in (e.g. Carboni 2017). However, we will mostly focus on the formally created structures involving multiple organizations that we have primarily studied and discuss our observations from using network analysis to advance our understanding of these structures. Network analysis maps out the relationships that exist between organizations, with 'relationships' defined based on the type of connection important to the system (i.e. information sharing, giving or receiving advice, shared resources, coordinated services, etc.). It is especially relevant for the study of formally created structures because it can be used to shed light not only on the relationships that exist and the attributes of those relationships, but also the relationships that may be expected but are absent.[1]

Shedding light on the overall structure of these systems based on the dyadic inter-organizational relationships can be important for practice, especially if the network analysis is linked to outcomes, like performance outcomes of organizations and/or the systems as a whole. In practice, people tend to assume networks exist, but they often lack an awareness of the broader landscape of other organizations and the connections, visible or concealed, among others in the field. Lack of awareness can impact the ability of managers to strategically situate their organization and lead to missed opportunities to develop valuable partnerships, or failure to recognize where power in the system may rest – which in turn impacts the structure of the system overall. Even if organizations are aware of one another, oftentimes, critical information is not being shared with one another. Without even basic organizational information (who the organization serves, the services provided, etc.) being shared across agencies, the greater collaborative opportunities that we often tout in the literature will be limited. Even when relationships between organizations do exist and lead to collaboration, these relationships are typically reliant on people, rather than being institutionalized, and people come and go. Examining the structure of relationships can provide additional insights that can be used to diagnose or evaluate and inform interventions or efforts to increase awareness, sharing of information, and the development and institutionalization of collaborative relationships.

In addition, network analysis also offers ways to operationalize concepts classically linked to the public sector, like power, influence, control and reputation. It offers an approach for systematically collecting data on the relationships that form the basis of these concepts. This tool thus makes it possible to empirically assess these concepts, not on the basis of more or less biased insiders or experts, but independently on the basis of the underlying relationships (see for example the seminal work on the Organizational State by Laumann and Knoke 1987).

Applying the method

Network analysis has been increasingly applied in the study of public sector networks and collaboration since the application by Provan and Milward (1995), though it has gained momentum since 2005 (Hu, Khosa and Kapucu 2016). Provan and Milward used network analysis in their study of four mental health networks, specifically in their operationalization of network integration, which were measures of network density and centralization (see the following paragraphs for discussion of these measures). These measures were calculated using the reported inter-agency relationships based on referrals sent, referrals received, case coordination, joint programs and service contracts.

Since the study by Provan and Milward (1995), multiple threads of the application of network analysis have developed (again, see Hu, Khosa and Kapucu 2016). The application of network analysis to the study of formally created social and political network systems can either be through examining the network as an independent variable(s) or as a dependent variable. To understand the difference between applying network analysis to the study of a dependent versus an independent variable, it is important to separate out the network as a system and the network as a structure. For instance, Provan and Milward (1995) studied the network structure as an independent variable, but the dependent variable was the network system's performance. They employed network analysis to operationalize one of the independent variables, level of centralized integration, but the dependent variable was stakeholder perceptions of performance (i.e. the ability to meet stakeholders' expectations with mental health services).

A more recent example of network structure as an independent variable is the work of Raab, Mannak and Cambré (2015), who performed network analysis on a subset of the networks in their study and then subsequently built proxies for centralization and density to achieve a larger *n* to explain the outcomes of crime-prevention networks. In a first round, ten networks were subjected to in-depth analysis through document reviews, interviews, observations and a survey among network participants. In a second round, semi-structured interviews were conducted with the network managers of twenty-nine cases. Proxy measures of centralization for the second round were validated with the quantitative centrality scores collected in the first round of data collection. Proxies that were used to qualify the structure as centralized/not centralized were the presence of roles such as chairpersons or process managers who coordinated different case and information flows between partners and organizations. Whether the network was centralized or not centralized was in turn used to explain, along with other conditions, the performance of the network systems. Performance is not the only outcome explained by factors operationalized by the use of network analytic concepts. Hu, Khosa and Kapucu (2016) catalogue the literature using SNA into the various outcomes of network governance, formation and configurations, in addition to performance.

Examples where network analysis has been used for the dependent variable is when the structure of the network itself is the outcome of interest. Scheinert et al. (2015) compared the various subnetwork structures of a watershed governance network and found two groupings, one based on information sharing, technical assistance and project collaboration, and the other on reporting and financial resource sharing. Lemaire et al. (2017) analysed the changes in the density and centralization of a tobacco-cessation network over time to highlight the centralizing force of the network administrative organization on the overall structure. Employing Exponential Random Graph Modelling (ERGM), Henry, Lubell and McCoy (2010) studied how social capital and beliefs influence the structure of policy systems, finding that policy coalitions are knit together by policy brokers promoting relationships between other actors. Utilizing network analysis to learn about network structure typically necessitates networks to compare. One can compare the different types of ties within one system, as did Koliba et al. (2017) or Raab (2002); one system/network over time as with Lemaire et al.'s (2017) article; multiple systems, as with the comparison of regions in Henry et al.'s (2010) study; or policy fields in different countries, as in Knoke's (1996) study.

Data collection

Bounding the network

The first step in collecting data on networks is bounding the network. One of the advantages of networks is their fluidity and flexibility (Powell 1990), and determining who is in the network is typically a difficult task and one that can be a delicate issue, even in the case of formally organized networks. Though there may be a stable core set of organizations involved in the network, others may come and go (Provan and Lemaire 2012). However, for the purposes of studying a network, it has to be decided which actors comprise the network. Just as any study must decide what the population or sample is, researchers have to identify boundaries to place around the network for the purpose of studying it, but these boundaries are typically artificial. Even if a network has formal membership there may be many organizations that are important stakeholders, or involved in network activities, or important to the goal of the network, but that are not formal members. Researchers, though, are usually working within time and resource constraints and cannot necessarily include every organization that is connected to the network in some way, and so a strategy for deciding who to include and not include for the purposes of the study is necessary. Developing this strategy can be a delicate issue because the boundaries set by the study may not match with how all members conceive the network and it can also skew the results of the study, as discussed in the next paragraphs.

There are different strategies researchers can take for establishing the boundary, with realist, nominalist and relational being the most common (Laumann, Marsden and Prensky 1989; Knoke and Yang 2008). Using the realist strategy, the researcher adopts the perception of the network actors, usually a key actor or actors, and which entities they feel are relevant to the network. For the nominalist approach, the researcher determines a vision for establishing membership, which may be certain attributes, formal membership, attendance at events, and so on. The relational approach consists of the researcher relying on the network actors themselves to ascertain network membership. Most commonly, researchers combine different strategies for establishing the boundary.

Whichever strategy is used, what is important is to be mindful of how the boundary strategy influences the findings. Actors at the periphery of the network may be more central to a network bounded in a different manner, especially since networks are nested within networks (Rethemeyer and Hatmaker 2007). For instance, Figure 9.1a presents a network plot for a family self-sufficiency network initiative. Because family self-sufficiency is a broad goal involving many services and sectors, including all relevant actors was beyond the capacity of the study. The shapes[2] in the plot indicate the service sector, and one could easily remark that the organizations shaped as diamonds (income/employment) are not central to the network. However, one should also note how few diamonds there are – to the frustration of those in that service sector. If more income/employment organizations and/or businesses in the area had been included in the study the organizations shaped as diamonds might well have been more central to that broader network, due to more ties among each other, as well as possibly playing key bridging roles connecting employers with the agencies in other service sectors – like zooming out a photograph to see the fuller picture. Another example is the network in Figure 9.1b, which is a child education and development network in close geographical proximity to the family self-sufficiency network. The highlighted organizations in each plot are the same programs providing services important to both initiatives, but because their focus is primarily education it is not surprising that they are central in the child education and development network in Figure 9.1b and at the periphery of the one in Figure 9.1a. These two examples demonstrate how descriptions of networks based on network analysis need to be interpreted in the context of how the network was bounded.

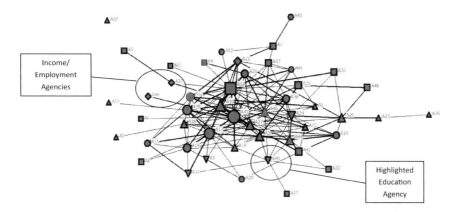

Figure 9.1a Network plots depicting issues in bounding the network: family self-sufficiency network

Shapes indicate the service sector of the organization, size indicates degree centrality, thick borders indicate respondents, lines indicate confirmed information sharing relationships and thickness of line indicates the intensity of the information sharing.

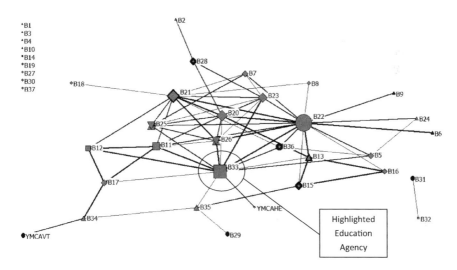

Figure 9.1b Network plots depicting issues in bounding the network: child education and development network

Shapes indicate the geographical region of the organization, size indicates degree centrality, thick borders indicate respondents, lines indicate confirmed information sharing relationships and thickness of line indicates the intensity of the information sharing.

A related step to bounding the network is deciding what a node is. Nodes are the entities connected by relationships, and what is considered a node depends on the nature of the network and the research interest. Nodes can be individuals and often individuals are the respondents. Nodes can also be words, events, or anything that aligns with the intent of the research.[3] In the plots presented in Figures 9.1a and 9.1b, the nodes are organizations and are represented by the shapes, and the lines connecting shapes indicate the existing relationships. When determining what a node is, it is important to recognize that the unit of observation is not necessarily the same as the unit of analysis. For instance, individuals can respond on behalf of themselves, the programs in which they work, or the organizations for which they work. In the study of organizational networks, as with the study of organizations in general, organizations cannot respond (or be observed) for themselves and researchers are often reliant on individuals to represent organizations. There are of course challenges to relying on individuals to represent organizations; individuals may not have complete knowledge and their perspectives may not be representative of other organizational members. To minimize these challenges, often multiple individuals may be selected for each organization, but then the researcher may face problems with aggregating contradictory responses about an organization's relationships. There is no easy solution to these issues since these issues are not necessarily unique to the study of organizational networks as they have plagued organizational research in general for decades (Klein, Dansereau and Hall 1994).

Type of relationship(s)

Once the question of boundary and nodes has been determined, it must also be decided what relationship data will be collected. Tie content is very important. As social beings, humans maintain many different types of relationships, and the same is true of organizations. There are many possible types of ties, most of which can be broadly categorized as expression of affect, influence, exchange of information, or exchange of goods or services (Tichy, Tushman and Fombrun 1979). These various ties may or may not overlap. For instance, organizations may train with one another, as in the case of emergency response training. Though they train with one another, this does not ensure that they will also share information with each other or refer clients to one another. The set of organizations an organization co-trains with may be a different set of organizations to which they refer clients. Therefore, a researcher cannot collect data on ties between nodes without specifying the type of relationship. Examples of types of ties commonly examined in the research on networks and collaboration in the public sector are information exchange, client referral, service coordination, shared resources, alliances, and so on.

Specifying tie content is also essential because the structure of networks will likely vary by the type of relationship (Mandell and Keast 2008). For instance, an

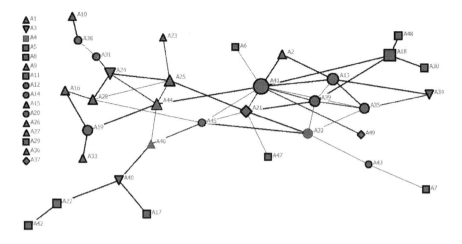

Figure 9.2 Network plot demonstrating tie structure of family self-sufficiency network

Shapes indicate the service sector of the organization, size indicates degree centrality, thick borders indicate respondents, lines indicate confirmed resource sharing relationships and thickness of line indicates the intensity of the resource sharing.

information-sharing network may look very different from a referral network and this may especially be true when comparing networks involving tangible or intangible resources. Huang and Provan (2006) found variation in the structure of tangible versus intangible ties in their examination of a mental health network. Figure 9.2 depicts the same family self-sufficiency network as in Figure 9.1, but the tie represented in Figure 9.1 is information sharing whereas the one presented in Figure 9.2 is based on shared resources. A comparison of the two plots demonstrates how the network structure is dependent on the type of tie being examined.

It is the case that many organizations will maintain multiple types of ties with one another, which is what is referred to as multiplex ties. Multiplex ties are ones based on multiple tie contents (for example sharing information, coordinating services and sharing resources) and are typically considered more robust, because even if one activity stops then the relationship still exists. The assumption behind many collaborative arrangements is that organizations are connected in multiple ways; thus, network researchers often collect data on several types of relationships to compare and contrast tie structure, as in Figures 9.1a and 9.2, but also to examine the multiplex relationships.

To make the analysis of tie structure and multiplex relationships meaningful, determining which types of tie are of interest to the research and network context is necessary and then it must be decided how best to capture that data. Some tie content may be easy to capture with objective data, as with

attendance at meetings; other ties can only be captured based on perceptions,[4] like whom one considers a friend. What the researcher may also want
to consider is the flow of various types of tie. Some content flows are zero
sum, as with resource exchanges, but others are not. Some content can only
flow along one path at a time, like tangible goods, whereas others can flow
along multiple paths at the same time, like information (for a discussion of
flow see Borgatti 2005). In addition, content determines whether the tie is
directed – that is, has a direction from the sender to the receiver like forward-
ing information or sending versus receiving referrals – or whether the ties are
undirected – that is, resources can flow in both directions, as in the case of the
reciprocal exchange of information.

Content is not the only facet to consider, as strength of the tie is oftentimes
important to consider because there is value to both weak and strong ties
(Granovetter 1973; Uzzi 1997). Though there may be value to both strong
and weak ties, it may be important to the research question and analysis not
to treat those ties equally. Provan et al. (2012) found that organizations in a
tobacco-cessation network with strong ties to researchers were the ones aware
of the most evidence-based practices. There are many ways to operationalize
the strength of tie; one can gauge the intensity of the tie, the frequency of the
tie, or the quality of the tie. Another way to conceptualize tie strength is as
multiplexity, but the difference between multiplexity and the other ways of
operationalizing strength is that multiplexity can be constructed from data on
ties (i.e. both information sharing and resource sharing ties), whereas the other
concepts are an attribute of the tie itself. Whether to use intensity, frequency,
quality or multiplexity should be based on the intent of the research and which
dimension of strength is relevant to the research question. Lemaire and Provan
(2017) examine the dyadic attributes that predict the extent to which organizations in a child and youth health network are working with one another
by examining both the degree of collaboration, measured by multiplexity, as
well as the quality of the relationship, measured by a Likert scale. Also to
note, regarding strength of tie, without strength, relationships are dichotomous
(0=no tie, 1=tie), but with strength the data are typically ordinal, as with the
use of a Likert scale by Lemaire and Provan. The researcher needs to consider
the difference between working with dichotomous and ordinal data when
choosing how to aggregate ties and which measures and analytical tools are
appropriate.

Another important tie attribute to consider is whether the relationship is
positive or negative. Labianca and Brass (2006) note the tendency for researchers
to emphasize positive ties and argue for the need to balance the 'social ledger'
by also examining negative ties. Labianca and Brass define positive ties as those
that are beneficial and negative as those that are liabilities. Examining negative
relationships in the study of networks and collaboration in the public sector
may be especially important, since the field recognizes that organizations are
often in networks with their competitors (Bunger 2013). One could consider

how competition or conflict as a negative tie influences the likelihood of collaboration – a positive tie. Along similar lines, one could examine how distrust is different from the absence of trust, and examining which organizations distrust which other organizations may be essential in understanding network structures and the lack of stability or even collapse of networks. One reason for the over-emphasis of positive ties and the underemphasis of negative ties in research is because collecting data on negative ties can be more difficult due to the often more sensitive nature of negative ties (Labianca and Brass 2006). A researcher may have greater ethical issues to consider when collecting and reporting data on negative ties.

Data source

In addition to determining what data to collect, how to collect the data is another matter. In principle, the full arsenal of data collection methods in the social sciences is available for collecting relational data as the basis for a network analysis. Data can be collected from primary or secondary sources. Primary data sources typically include surveys and interviews, but observation and experiments are possibilities as well. Observation and experiments have been valuable methods of collecting quantitative relational data in other disciplines (see for example observations in anthropology by Bernard (2011) or the classic study in organizational ethnography by Roethlisberger and Dickson ([1939] 2003), for experiments see studies in exchange theory by Cook et al. (1983)). However, we are not aware of its use yet for the study of networks and collaboration in the public sector. Secondary data are often extracted from documents and records that contain information about the relationships of actors, such as transcripts from Commissions of Inquiry (Lauchs, Keast and Yousefpour 2011), large data sets (first-year student data), health records, and so on.

Survey/interviews

When collecting primary data, most often the relational data are collected via questionnaires or interviews. The organizational network systems that are typically studied in the policy, governance and collaborative network literature usually involve many organizations. Collecting the relational data between all these organizations via observation requires a great deal of time and burden on researchers, so questionnaires and interviews offer a relatively easy way of systematically collecting the data on relationships. When examining the structure of a network system, a high response rate is imperative to gain valid results, since an analysis of the overall structure can be biased with many missing responses. Therefore, many researchers rely on interviews, in person or by phone, and questionnaires are filled out together with the respondents. Since network questions can be burdensome and, thus, response rates can be low, scheduling an interview offers a window of time in which most respondents are willing to provide responses to the demanding questions which can boost response rates. In addition, interviewing people creates a direct contact between the interviewer and the respondent and provides the opportunity for respondents to ask any questions they have. This direct contact often helps to overcome the concerns respondents have regarding conveying information about their organization's relationships openly, or the frustrations they may have in trying to respond to question styles which may be new to them. An effective and efficient strategy is also to agree with network members to attend network meetings and distribute questionnaires at the end of a meeting to complete on the spot. Another strategy that has been successful for Lemaire and colleagues is to invite respondents to several in-person sessions where the research project is presented and then respondents are invited to complete the survey, preferably on a computer provided. These sessions offer the same benefits as interviews, but with the added benefit of requiring less time on the part of the researcher; however, this strategy is only feasible when respondents are in geographical proximity to one another. Data can also be collected via electronic questionnaires, for example Survey-Monkey or other online survey platforms, but an additional conversion routine is needed to transform the data into a matrix format needed for the analysis.

Two basic approaches exist for collecting network data via survey or interview. The researcher can either construct a roster beforehand – that is, a complete list of all actors in the network – and then ask respondents to provide information on the ties (specifying certain types) the respondent has with the actors listed on the roster. Alternatively, a name-generator approach can be used in which the researcher defines a type of tie and asks the respondents to provide actors' names (see Wasserman and Faust 1994: 45–48).

The roster method involves a matrix in which the names of the actors are typically listed in rows and the different type of ties in the columns. Often, researchers also give respondents the chance to nominate additional actors to include at the end of the roster, providing an additional check for the boundary specification. Researchers should provide in the introduction to the roster a definition for each type of tie as thoroughly as possible, as well as examples if possible, to minimize the extent to which respondents interpret tie content differently. Respondents can also be asked for the strength of each tie by indicating a value for the tie; that is, responses will range from 0 (no tie) to the number value indicating the highest strength. Again, researchers should clearly specify and define strength in the questionnaire. For example, respondents can be asked for the frequency of an interaction (once a day, once a week, once a month) or intensity of the relationship (a scale of importance of the tie to the organization's work). Researchers should be aware that each cell is essentially one question, and the larger the roster and the more types of ties, the greater the number of questions. For example, a network of thirty actors and two types of ties constitutes fifty-eight (two lots of twenty-nine) questions. The use of online survey tools, with the various display/skip/carry forward/if then logic options, can help reduce the burden on respondents. Even still, researchers should consider how taxing and difficult it can be for respondents to be presented with long rosters and should make every effort to present the roster in a way that is less overwhelming for the respondent. For instance, rather than an alphabetical list, the roster could be organized by grouping sets of actors into categories that are meaningful, for instance by service sector in the case of service delivery networks (e.g. health, education, etc.). For an example of a roster template see Provan et al. (2005).

In contrast, name-generator approaches can be less overwhelming for respondents. However, while respondents do not have to grapple with long lists of actors, respondents may find it more difficult to have to generate names rather than select them from a list. Another disadvantage of the name-generator method is that respondents may more easily forget to list certain actors without the help of a list. Typically, a cap is placed on the number of actors a respondent is asked to name, and researchers should consult the considerable literature on the name-generator approach to understand the advantages and limitations of the various options (see Borgatti, Everett and Johnson 2013). Especially in the case of studying social and political network systems, a name-generator approach may not provide a full picture of the network's overall structure. Oftentimes, though, a combination of a roster and name generator is used; the roster is used to capture the structure of the network and name-generators are used to gather more information, such as who actors perceive as influential or admirable.

Secondary data

Unlike in other disciplines, we are not aware of databases or data sets readily available for researchers studying public sector networks. There are instances, though, of scholars using existing data sets collected for other purposes and analysing the data using network methods, as Marcum, Bevc and Butts (2012) did with their study of disaster-response networks. The use of secondary data typically involves culling network data from existing sources and there are numerous sources that offer rich opportunities to cull relational data. Especially in the twentieth century, public administration produced an enormous amount of documents in the form of letters, memos, minutes, records etc. containing information about the interaction between actors in the public sector. As archives become more accessible and digitized, opportunities to use these resources to extract relational data will be abundant. Though relational data was not presented in the paper, the recent article by Jensen (2016) provides an example of the historical network research opportunities archives present. Data collection of this nature can be cumbersome; however, as letter recognition and computer-aided coding further improve, there might be interesting possibilities to utilize archives. The twenty-first century is also producing archives full of relational data, though of a different nature since these records are mostly based on electronic exchange and social media. There are numerous examples from other disciplines of data being extracted from these sources, but the case has yet to be made for using these data sources to examine public sector networks, since the data openly available often have low validity to capture inter-organizational structures or a researcher has to gain access to confidential email traffic which is extremely rare.

Ethical issues in data collection and reporting

When collecting relational data, the raw data cannot be anonymized because it is necessary to know the sender and the receiver of a tie. This need presents ethical challenges less likely to occur with other approaches to data collection. Respondents often want assurance that the data will not be published, especially regarding sensitive data like trust and relationship quality. Some respondents might also object to publishing a sociogram where the relationships of each actor, and therefore the original responses to the questions, are visible. Researchers need to pay special attention to ethical issues when data are collected on the personal relationships of individuals (for ethical guidelines researchers should follow see Borgatti and Molina 2005), but what we want to emphasize, however, is that consideration should be given to ethics even when the data are aggregated to the organizational level. When the nodes in visual representation are labelled, the potential is there for conclusions to be drawn about the organizations. For instance, node A26 is an isolate in Figure 9.1a, meaning that this organization did not have any confirmed information sharing ties with any other organization in the network. If labelled, an organization like A26 could be penalized by funders for not collaborating with others, or the image of organizations could be negatively impacted because of their position in the network. On the other hand, plots like those presented in the figures can be meaningless to the network without organization labels. Therefore, researchers should consider how the presentation of the results could negatively impact organizations and consider what information should be provided and what information should be masked.

In addition, as with any study, respondents should always have the possibility to entirely withdraw from the data collection without sanctions but, in the case of relational data, this possibility should also be possible not only as direct respondents but also as third parties; that is, information of others about relationships with those individuals also has to be excluded from the analysis (Borgatti and Molina 2005). Even though there are different potential impacts and ethical issues dependent on the type of nodes, individuals, type of ties and the way in which results are communicated, researchers should be very attentive and transparent toward the respondents and clearly communicate in an accompanying statement who will have access to the data and how the data will be analysed, and the results communicated.

Another ethical issue we regard as important is the dilemma of the use of the research in consideration of the response burden. As discussed in the previous section, collecting network data using respondent surveys can incur a heavy response burden and network researchers need to consider what they are asking of respondents (e.g. time) in return for what benefit. Rather than collecting data purely for research purposes, even if that research has practical implications, researchers should make the effort to incorporate a benefit to the respondents – even if that benefit is something as simple as the researcher presenting back the results.

Analysis

The most common method to store and organize network data is in a spread-sheet, which can then be imported into most software programs. Most network analytic programs have options to import data through one of the formats supported by Excel or other spreadsheet programs. Network data can be organized as adjacency matrices or as nodelists or as edgelists. Figures 9.3a, 9.3b, and 9.3c depict the same network ties but organized in the three different formats. Adjacency matrices are the most common form, where actors are listed in the rows

Actors	1	2	3	4	5	6
1	**0**	0	0	1	0	1
2	0	**0**	1	1	1	1
3	0	1	**0**	0	0	1
4	1	1	0	**0**	1	0
5	0	1	0	1	**0**	0
6	1	1	1	0	0	**0**

Figure 9.3a Various options for storing and organizing network data: binary adjacency matrix

1 4 6 (actor 1 has ties with 4 & 6)
2 3 4 5 6
3 2 6
4 1 2 5
5 2 4
6 1 2 3

Figure 9.3b Various options for storing and organizing network data: binary nodelist

1 4 (a tie between actors 1 and 4)
1 6
2 3
2 4
2 5
2 6
3 2
3 6
4 1
4 2
4 5
5 2
5 4

Figure 9.3c Various options for storing and organizing network data: binary edgelist

Actors	1	2	3	4	5	6
1	**0**	0	0	3	0	1
2	0	**0**	2	1	1	3
3	0	3	**0**	0	0	1
4	2	1	0	**0**	3	0
5	0	1	0	3	**0**	0
6	2	1	3	0	0	**0**

Figure 9.3d Various options for storing and organizing network data: valued tie adjacency matrix

and columns and an entry of '1' in a cell indicates that there is a relationship from the actor listed in the row to the actor listed in the column. An entry of '0' indicates the absence of a relationship. In lieu of binary numbers, values can be used instead to indicate the strength of a tie as depicted with Figure 9.3d. The diagonal of a matrix, the bold numbers in Figures 9.3a and 9.3b, indicates self-reflexive ties which are usually forced to equal zero unless the researcher is also interested in those self-ties. For very large networks with a low percentage of existing ties – that is, a big matrix with mostly empty cells – it is recommended to use a node list or edgelist format (also called dl format). The different formats and the precise notation are explained in the UCINet help function or in Borgatti, Everett and Johnson (2013: 63–70). Network data in dl format can also be imported into the major network analytic programs, and many programs, like UCINet, can transform data from one format to another. Visualization programs like 'Visone' or 'Gephi' even offer the possibility to draw the network on the basis of the data respondents have provided in the form of a sociogram and then convert the graph into an adjacency or affiliation matrix.

One consideration to note when preparing network data for analysis is the question of what to do with unconfirmed ties. For many types of ties, preserving the direction of the tie is important, for instance when one is looking to understand how advice seeking and advice giving are undertaken. However, ties with reciprocal natures, like information sharing, where the idea is that information flows both ways, the expectation is that both actors will recognize the tie. Often the information provided by respondents about the (non-)existence of a tie will contradict the information provided by other respondents. Reasons for this can be that respondents overstate their own relations, have an incorrect memory, differences in interpreting the content of a relationship or multiple respondents from the same organizations make different statements about their organizations' ties. However, incorrect data are different from inconsistent data and should be treated differently. If ties are reciprocal in nature, researchers may opt to confirm ties to increase the reliability of the data. Confirming ties means taking into account the information provided by both actors of a tie (for a discussion on how to treat unconfirmed ties see Hennig et al. 2012: 93–97).

Results in network analysis can be highly sensitive to missing data. Despite some research, for example Borgatti, Carley and Krackhardt's (2006) research on the robustness of centrality measures, there is still no generally accepted protocol on how to deal with measurement error and missing data. The negative impact on results is estimated to be especially large if the error is systematic; that is, all actors of a certain type do not respond, or the network is relatively sparse. In that case the omission of a tie can have a very large impact on global centrality measures, but otherwise measures have been found to be robust to missing data (Costenbader and Valente 2003). Therefore, the analysis of the (global) structure of a network is especially sensitive to missing data (Kossinets 2006); thus, when examining the structure of a network system in the public sector, the general rule of thumb is that an eighty percent response rate is the acceptable level. In any case, researchers should examine how missing data might influence the results. One way to do this is by comparing the results based on the exclusion of non-respondents, with the partial inclusion of non-respondents based on the data provided by other respondents (i.e. the ties other actors reported to the non-respondent).

Descriptive static analysis

The most basic analysis encompasses a description of the structure of the network and the prominence of actors in that structure. The analysis can then refer to one point or period in time for which the data were collected or across several periods or points in time (longitudinal analysis). At the node level, what will typically be examined is how important an actor in a network is. The most frequently used measure in this regard is centrality. There are numerous centrality measures with the most basic being degree centrality (the total number of ties), whereas other measures incorporate different facets of structural prominences into the measure. Some examples of three other measures include closeness centrality (degree of nearness or farness to all other actors in the network), betweenness centrality (degree to which an actor provides short paths connecting other actors in the network) and eigenvector centrality (degree to which an actor is connected to other central actors). Centrality measures are typically highly correlated with one another (Valente et al. 2008), but researchers should use the centrality measure that best aligns with their research question and the construct they are operationalizing (for details on the different centrality measures see Wasserman and Faust 1994). Simple degree centrality is a good indicator of position within the network structure, whereas closeness might be used to indicate the degree to which an organization is structurally embedded and has direct access to the other actors in the network. Betweenness centrality is often used to highlight actors that function as brokers, while eigenvector centrality may be most appropriate for operationalizing power. Researchers should also be aware that different types of ties require different centrality measures to come to a valid interpretation (Borgatti 2005). Betweenness centrality, for example, is most appropriate for ties with a flow of material or immaterial resources, like information or money. Prominence measures, like eigenvector centrality, in combination with specific types of ties, like advice or resources, can also serve as a good operationalization of influence and power in a social system. Table 9.1 provides examples of types of ties and different centrality measures.

Table 9.1 Illustrative types of ties, network measures and their interpretation in network studies

Type of tie	Measure	Interpretation
Information exchange Relations are pipes that enable the flow of information With which other organizations does your organization regularly exchange information [with regard to . . . point of interest of research, goals of the network, activity of the organizations]? Ties are undirected	Degree Centrality	Node level. Indicates the number of direct information exchange relations with other organizations in the network (local centrality measure). The higher the number, the higher the amount of information that is exchanged directly with other actors. A high degree of centrality can signal the danger of information overload.
	(Flow) Betweenness Centrality	Node level. Indicates how often an organization is on the shortest path between any two other organizations in the network (betweenness). Flow betweenness takes all paths into account and weighs them in the calculation (the longer, the less weight). The higher the betweenness centrality, the greater the chance for an actor of controlling the flow of information within a network or being a bottleneck. Sometimes also used as operationalization for brokerage position.
	Closeness Centrality	Node level. Average number of steps an organization in a network needs to reach any other organization in a network. The higher the closeness centrality the less steps are in between the focal organization and any other organization; that is, direct and indirect access to information.
	Clique, n- clique, clan, n-clan, k-plex	Subnetwork level. Indicates sub-groups in a network. Represents zones of denser communication compared to other parts of a network. Overlapping cliques are a form of integration that can be a substitute for overall integration through density.
	Density	Network level. Percentage of existing ties. Indicates the level of connectedness of organizations in a network. A high density in information exchange indicates a high amount of information exchange between organizations with a lot of redundant ties, which allows for many paths through which information can be disseminated.

Centralization	Network level. Calculated by node level centrality; various centrality measures can be used. Indicates to what extent the network is reliant on one or a few central organizations to provide the paths for information to flow. Highly centralized information sharing can be inefficient because of bottlenecks, but it can also allow for the information flow to be controlled, which might allow for efficient coordination or ensuring the accuracy/ reliability of the information being exchanged.
Degree Centrality	Node level. High degree centrality can signal direct access to resources.
Shared Resources Relations are pipes along which resources flow, but tangible resources unlike with information. With which other organizations does your organization share resources ([funding, sponsorship of events, materials, shared staff or volunteers, space, technology, etc.) with regard to . . . (point of interest of research, goals of the network, activity of the organizations)]? Ties are undirected.	
(Flow) Betweenness Centrality	Node level. High betweenness centrality can indicate important resource brokers.
Eigenvector Centrality	High level indicates an organization sharing resources with those that are themselves sharing resources with many others; that is, having very good access to the overall resource pool in the network.
Clique, n-clique, clan, n-clan	Subnetwork level. Group of organizations that share resources mainly with each other.
Density	Network level. High density indicates that the organizations are broadly sharing resources with one another.
Centralization	Network level. Indicates that most of the sharing of resources is concentrated around a few key organizations (i.e. primary funder who shares resources with many other organizations). High centralization indicates concentration of resource flows in a network.

(Continued)

Table 9.1 (Continued)

Type of tie	Measure	Interpretation
Advice Relations indicate who seeks out whom for advice. Which other organization does your organization turn to for advice [with regard to . . . (point of interest of research, goals of the network, activity of the organizations) to better achieve its mission? Ties are directed.	Degree Centrality (indegree and outdegree)	Node level. Since tie is directed, difference between indegree (incoming ties) and outdegree (outgoing ties). Outdegree centrality is the number of other organizations from which the focal organization seeks advice (note that a capped name generator approach will limit the value of outdegree centrality). Indegree indicates the number of times the focal organization was selected by other organizations. A high indegree indicates a popular source for advice whereas a high outdegree indicates organizations seeking out many other organizations for advice.
	Eigenvector Centrality, Status	Node level. Measure is calculated on the basis of the number of incoming ties and the centrality of the sender; that is, how much the sender is sought out by others. Organizations with a high eigenvector centrality/status are consulted by important other organizations in the network which signals a high reputation and influence.
	Clique, n-clique, clan, n-clan, k-plex	Subnetwork level. Group of organizations that mutually advice each other more often than other organizations in the network.
	Density	Network level. High density indicates that the organizations broadly seek out advice from each other.
	Centralization	Network level. A high centralization based on eigenvector centrality indicates that many important organizations turn to the most central organization for advice. This in turn signals a strong concentration of influence in the network.

At the subnetwork level, several concepts are available to identify groups of actors that more closely interact with each other than with the rest of the network. Cliques are one such type of group, which usually has a strict definition indicating that every actor in the group is connected to every other actor. However, tools exist to relax the strict definition and researchers can use n–cliques (n indicates the maximum path length connecting members), n–clans or k–plex (k indicates the acceptable number of lines that can be absent) to identify these sub-groups. These tools can be used to identify coalitions or subcommunities in the network.

At the network level, researchers may want to examine the level of cohesion/ integration of the network or how centralized it is. The most common measures at this level are density and centralization. Density indicates the number of ties that exist out of the number of ties possible, and centralization indicates the degree to which the network is structured around one or a few most-central actors. As with actor centrality, there are numerous ways to calculate centraliza- tion, but the selection of the appropriate measure should be determined by the research question and the type of tie (see Table 9.1). Both density and central- ization are percentages, with 100% indicating all ties present for density and full reliance on one central actor for centralization (imagine hub and spoke or a star structure). There are no ideal ranges for evaluating density and centralization, and high levels of density and centralization are not necessarily more effective than lower levels. Rather, what should be considered is what is appropriate for tie content, a less-dense and highly centralized information-sharing network provides a very different flow from a highly dense less-centralized one; the net- work context, high centralization, may be effective for crime prevention (Raab et al. 2015) but not for disaster response (Marcum et al. 2012); or the questions driving the analysis, like how resilient the structure would be to changes to the system and a highly centralized network could fragment if the central node leaves the network (Lemaire et al. 2017).

Density and centralization are the most basic and common network-level measures, but there are other ways to describe the structure of the network. For instance, integration has been measured on the basis of the degree of overlap- ping cliques (see Provan and Sebastian 1998), and other measures can indicate the degree of fragmentation of the network. Multiplexity is another concept proposed as being important to network structure (Provan and Milward 2001). Examining the extent of multiplexity in the overall network provides a way of assessing how robust the structure is and whether it will be vulnerable to shocks that may impact certain ties (Koliba et al. 2017).

Explanatory analysis

Next to basic descriptive analysis, network analysis can also be used in explanatory analysis; Koliba et al. (2017) found embeddedness in the information-sharing relationships to be correlated with values of a food systems network. Which tools are appropriate for the analysis depends on whether the network data are being used as the dependent variable or the independent variable. If the network data are being used to generate independent variables, then it is possible to include these variables in an ordinary least squares (OLS) regression. For example, one can explain the relative impact of an actor's network position on their/its influence in a decision-making process.

When the network data are the basis of the dependent variable, standard linear regression is oftentimes not suitable. If the goal of the analysis is at the tie level; that is, to explain the likelihood of ties between actors – then other methods besides OLS regression need to be used. Since observations are not independent of each other – that is, the existence of a tie between A and B might influence the existence of a tie between A and C, and due to problems of autocorrelation, linear regression is not appropriate. Two options are available for this type of analysis. One option is Quadratic Assignment Procedure (QAP) correlation or QAP regression. QAP functions similarly to OLS regression but includes a second step which compares the results of the correlation or regression with the results from random networks simulated from the network data being analysed. QAP correlation can be used to compare networks of similar sizes or compare different types of ties for the same network. Scheinert et al. (2015) used QAP to analyse the structural variation of the various subnetwork structures of a watershed governance network, whereas its use by Kapucu and Hu (2016) was to analyse the relationships among emergency management networks and examine the predictive power of a pre-established network arrangement. QAP regression can be used to explain how dyadic attributes (like homophily) explain the strength of a tie. Lemaire and Provan (2017) used QAP regression for their examination of the dyadic attributes that predict which organizations in a child and youth health network had multiplex and high-quality relationships. Like with OLS, QAP regression cannot be used to examine the existence or non-existence of a tie (i.e. binary outcome).

To analyse the latter, Exponential Random Graph Models (ERGMs) or p★ models can be used. In addition, what QAP does not do is consider the various network effects that influence the presence or absences of ties. If the goal is to identify micro configurations and explain the underlying processes of networks from a structural perspective, ERGMs are the best option. Berardo and Lubell (2016) used ERGM and found contextual variables like strength of formal institutions and capacity of individual policy outcomes to influence the shape of complex governance systems. ERGMs are based on maximum likelihood estimation and can take into account the effects of transitivity, reciprocity, and so on (for a detailed introduction to these models see Robins 2011).

At the network level, the small number of whole networks that can realistically be investigated within one research project limits the options for meaningful systematic comparison. Here, Qualitative Comparative Analysis (QCA) offers a useful solution to deal with small and medium *n* studies (see the contribution by Cepiku and Cristofoli in this volume and Raab, Lemaire and Provan 2013). As a set-theoretic approach based on the analysis of necessary and sufficient conditions, QCA is well suited to the comparative analysis of multiple networks, including conditions based on network analytic measures, because it does not have the same assumptions of linear regression and allows for multilevel analysis.

In addition, QCA is a configurational approach and the use of a configurational approach is valuable to parsing out the inherent complexity of networks in the public sector. QCA was used by Raab, Mannak and Cambré (2015) in their study of the conditions associated with effective crime-prevention networks, and Lemaire (forthcoming) used QCA to examine goal congruency and the various tie portfolios of network members in a child and youth health network.

Dynamic analysis

Recently, in the field of social networks more and more research has been conducted on the dynamic nature of networks. Though few examples currently exist of the primary data collection of longitudinal network research on networks in the public sector (one exception being the study of Smoking Cessation Quitlines, see Mercken et al. 2015), more and more longitudinal studies are in the works (for example research currently being conducted by Lemaire and colleagues). Numerous examples also exist of dynamic analysis of networks studied via extraction from secondary data (see Marcum, Bevc and Butts 2012; Ingold and Fischer 2014). The emphasis with dynamic analysis lies on sociometric explanations for network change and evolution, and we view this area as potentially valuable to learn more about the formation and development of networks. Currently, the prevailing option available for longitudinal analysis is actor-based simulation models, specifically the program SIENA (Snijders, van de Bunt and Steglich 2010), which is also available as a package in R. In order to conduct dynamic or longitudinal network analysis, researchers must have data on the network for at least two points in time. Collecting data across time periods can be especially challenging for inter-organizational networks in the public sector, since organizations might drop out of the network in between data points, individual representatives may change due to turnover, or they may have to be excluded from the analysis due to non-response. Mercken et al. (2015) offer an example of the utilization of Siena to examine the dynamics of a public sector network over time and the effect on the implementation of best practices, as well as provide insights on the challenges that may arise from working with longitudinal network data.

Visualization

The visualization of networks has been a prominent feature of network analysis since its earliest empirical applications in the 1930s. With the advent of personal computers and visualization software since the 1990s, visualization can now easily be used for data entry, data exploration and the communication of results. It is especially of value in more applied settings, where network graphs can be used to communicate results to practitioners more intuitively than is the case with network metrics (see Brandes et al. 1999; Raab 2002). Visualizations provide network members the opportunity to see the structure of the network and to evaluate how it compares with what they expect or want, and then to develop interventions on how to strengthen the network. In scholarship, visualizations are helpful to visually depict structural elements of networks relevant to the implications of the research, but care should be taken in doing so. Network visualizations do not necessarily show anything on their own and many plots, especially dense ones, are indecipherable to the reader. There are numerous computer programs available for visualization. Examples include: Netdraw (included in the UCINet package, see the 'Future of the method' and 'Further reading' sections in this chapter for more information), which is user friendly and offers numerous options for making plots visually appealing; Visone, which is especially suited to depict the prominence of actors in networks; Pajek for larger networks; and SoNIA or ORA for dynamic visualization.

Evaluating the method

The greatest added value of SNA for researching networks and collaboration in public management is the systematic collection and analysis of the interdependent relationships between actors in a network. In that way, we can gain insight in the structural characteristics of a network in a valid and reliable way either at one point in time or across time. Social network concepts make it possible to operationalize and analyse central theoretical concepts in the study of networks, organizations and collaboration in the public sector, like integration (density and centralization, overlapping cliques), coordination (density and centralization), cooperation, hierarchy (eigenvector), actor roles (blockmodels), power and influence (betweenness or eigenvector centrality) or even the legitimacy (indegree) of actors. In the past, before the development of the network analytical toolbox, researchers had to use these theoretical concepts mostly on the basis of anecdotal evidence rather than on the basis of rigorous operationalization and data collection. Most effectively, network analysis in public management has been used in the systematic description of whole networks and the formation of independent structural variables to explain the effectiveness of networks and point to areas of strengthening.

Even though the network analytic toolbox has matured and been validated in the last few years, the major challenge remains, at least in its application in public management, to go beyond the mere description of the network metrics – that is, 'actor A is the most central one' or network X is more centralized than network Y – and come to a deeper understanding about the meaning and theoretical implications of the results. From our perspective, key to a solid network analysis is for the analysis to match the research question, the unit of analysis, the theoretical concepts, the types of tie, the appropriate network metrics and the research context.

Future of the method

Social network analytical methods are by now widely recognized, validated and well documented. Also, the available computer programs are often freeware (Visone, Pajek, Siena, ERGMs) or relatively cheap (UCINet, Net-draw) and run reliably. Therefore, from a methodological and technical point of view, the method can now be used relatively easily by researchers. With regard to longitudinal network analysis and hypothesis testing, the method is still advancing and we should see more and more studies of networks in the public sector that use these advanced techniques. However, we strongly believe that the biggest gains will not simply be in the utilization of advanced methods, but in linking the use of advanced network analytical methods to build or test theory and in finding ways to make data collection more efficient and reliable. Since public management is strongly interested in the collective effects of networks and collaboration, the main unit of analysis will likely be at the network level. The goal therefore should be to conduct studies of multiple network systems that are based on a larger number of networks in order to have more variation, be able to include more independent variables in the analysis and generally gain more confidence in the generalizability of the results. Another option is to move toward more efforts to streamline methods and instruments across research projects to compile databases of comparable networks as a joint effort in the field. Alternatively, we could invest in data collection from documents or through experiments/serious gaming with public managers, which would allow us to more efficiently and effectively collect (longitudinal) network data on a larger amount of networks (Van den Oord et al. 2017). These approaches would allow researchers to move from description to explanation. In this endeavour, we see great potential in combining SNA with qualitative research methods, as discussed in the four chapters on narrative analysis in this volume, and QCA (see Cepiku and Cristofoli in this volume). Such an approach not only helps in dealing with a small and medium number of cases but would also contribute to a configurational understanding of network functioning and outcomes (Raab, Lemaire and Provan 2013).

Further reading

Books on social network analytic methods

- Robins, G. 2015. *Doing social network research: Network-based research design for social scientists.* Thousand Oaks, CA: Sage Publications.
- Hennig, M., U. Brandes, J. Pfeffer, and I. Mergel. 2013. *Studying social networks: A guide to empirical research.* Frankfurt/New York: Campus Verlag.
- Wassermann, S. and K. Faust. 2003. *Social network analysis: Methods and applications*, Vol. 8. Cambridge: Cambridge University Press.
- Scott, J. 2013. *Social network analysis: A handbook*, 3rd ed. Thousand Oaks, CA: Sage Publications.
- Hanneman, R.A. and M. Riddle 2005. *Introduction to social network methods.* Riverside, CA: University of California, Riverside (published in digital form at http://faculty.ucr.edu/~hanneman/).

Conference

- Sunbelt Network Conference. "Usually in the spring." Next to general methods sessions also sessions on Policy Networks, Administrative Networks and Dark Networks (see the website of the International Network for Network Analysis: www.insna.org/).

Articles

- Lecy, J.D., I.A. Mergel, and H.P. Schmitz. 2014. "Networks in public administration: Current scholarship in review." *Public Management Review* 16 (5): 643–665.
- Varda, D., J.A. Shoup, and S. Miller. 2012. "A systematic review of collaboration and network research in the public affairs literature: Implications for public health practice and research." *American Journal of Public Health* 102 (3): 564–571.

Tools

A wide variety of software tools are available for conducting network analysis. Electronic survey platforms easily adaptable for collecting network data:

- Qualtrics (www.qualtrics.com)
- SurveyMonkey (www.surveymonkey.com/)

Inserting relational data by hand:

- Office Excel, UciNet (https://sites.google.com/site/ucinetsoftware/home
- Visone (www.visone.info), Gephi (https://gephi.org/)

Analysing data

- UciNet, Visone, Pajek (http://mrvar.fdv.uni–lj.si/pajek/), Netdraw, R, Gephi
- UCINet provides descriptive analysis tools as well as data transformation and hypothesis testing. Visone, Netdraw and Pajek provide descriptive analysis tools with visualization. Visone has an interface with Siena.
- ERGMs, Siena (www.stats.ox.ac.uk/~snijders/siena/), also available in R, can be used for hypothesis testing and longitudinal network analysis.

Dynamic analysis

- ORA: www.casos.cs.cmu.edu/projects/ora/download.php
- SoNIA: https://web.stanford.edu/group/sonia/

Notes

1 Oftentimes, more can be learned from the absent relationships than from focusing on which relationships do exist. For instance, many scholars and practitioners argue that the failures in preventing the 9/11 attack in the United States had a great deal to do with the lack of information sharing between several of the agencies involved in homeland security. The absence of information sharing relationships in that case is an example of the value of examining missing ties in addition to existing ties. The presence/absence of relationships is different from examining positive versus negative ties, which can be thought of as 'good' ties versus 'bad' ties.

2 The names of the organizations have been masked with generic coding (A1, A2, etc . . .) for this discussion, but typically they would be labelled. However, see the discussion further down on ethics for consideration of the issues involved with labelling.

3 It is also important to remember the nestedness of networks and that, in actuality, networks are multimodal, meaning there are multiple sets of nodes possible (i.e. board interlocks and how individuals are connected via board membership or citation analysis and how scholars are connected through being cited in the same publication). Due to space restrictions, and since most of the research on networks in the public sector examines a single mode and the ties they have with each other (i.e. organization – organization), we will keep our discussion to single-mode analysis, but multimodal analysis has been used to study public sector networks, such as the embeddedness of contracts in larger networked systems of exchange (Carboni 2015) or the clustering of different stakeholders around the words used to frame issues (Lim et al. 2016).

4 When collecting data from individuals based on their perceptions or recollections, it is best to provide a definition for each type of tie as well as examples if possible.

References

Bernard, H.R. 2011. *Research methods in anthropology: Qualitative and quantitative approaches.* Lanham, MD: Rowman Altamira.

Berardo, R. and M. Lubell. 2016. "Understanding what shapes a polycentric governance system." *Public Administration Review* 76 (5): 738–751.

Borgatti, S.P. 2005. "Centrality and network flow." *Social Networks* 27 (1): 55–71.

Borgatti, S.P., K.M. Carley, and D. Krackhardt. 2006. "On the robustness of centrality measures under conditions of imperfect data." *Social Networks* 28 (2): 124–136.

Borgatti, S.P., M.G. Everett, and J.C. Johnson. 2013. *Analyzing social networks.* Thousand Oaks, CA: Sage Publications.

Borgatti, S.P. and J.L. Molina. 2005. "Toward ethical guidelines for network research in organizations." *Social Networks* 27 (2): 107–117.

Brandes, U., P. Kenis, J. Raab, V. Schneider, and D. Wagner. 1999. "Explorations into the visualization of policy networks." *Journal of Theoretical Politics* 11 (1): 75–106.

Bunger, A.C. 2013. "Administrative coordination in nonprofit human service delivery networks: The role of competition and trust." *Nonprofit and Voluntary Sector Quarterly* 42 (6): 1155–1175.

Carboni, J.L. 2015. "Measuring risks of organizational failure in contract exchange structures." *Complexity, Governance & Networks* 2 (1): 45–64.

Carboni, J.L. 2017. "Ex post contract market structure: Implications for performance over time." *The American Review of Public Administration* 47 (5): 588–598.

Cook, K.S., R.M. Emerson, M.R. Gillmore, and T. Yamagishi. 1983. "The distribution of power in exchange networks: Theory and experimental results." *American Journal of Sociology* 89 (2): 275–305.

Costenbader, E. and T.W. Valente. 2003. "The stability of centrality measures when networks are sampled." *Social Networks* 25 (4): 283–307.

Granovetter, M. 1985. "Economic action and social structure: The problem of embeddedness." *American Journal of Sociology* 91 (3): 481–510.

Granovetter, M.S. 1973. "The strength of weak ties." *American Journal of Sociology* 78 (6): 1360–1380.

Hennig, M., U. Brandes, J. Pfeffer, and I. Mergel. 2012. *Studying social networks: A guide to empirical research*. Frankfurt/New York: Campus Verlag.

Henry, A.D., M. Lubell, and M. McCoy. 2010. "Belief systems and social capital as drivers of policy network structure: The case of California regional planning." *Journal of Public Administration Research and Theor* 21 (3): 419–444.

Hu, Q., S. Khosa, and N. Kapucu. 2016. "The intellectual structure of empirical network research in public administration." *Journal of Public Administration Research and Theory* 26 (4): 593–612.

Huang, K. and K.G. Provan 2006. "Resource tangibility and patterns of interaction in a publicly funded health and human services network." *Journal of Public Administration Research and Theory* 17 (3): 435–454.

Ingold, K. and M. Fischer. 2014. "Drivers of collaboration to mitigate climate change: An illustration of Swiss climate policy over 15 years." *Global Environmental Change* 24: 88–98.

Isett, K.R., I.A. Mergel, K. LeRoux, P.A. Mischen, and R.K. Rethemeyer. 2011. "Networks in public administration scholarship: Understanding where we are and where we need to go." *Journal of Public Administration Research and Theory* 21 (suppl. 1): i157–i173.

Jensen, L.S. 2016. "The twentieth-century administrative state and networked governance." *Journal of Public Administration Research and Theory* 27 (3): 468–484.

Kapucu, N. and Q. Hu. 2016. "Understanding multiplexity of collaborative emergency management networks." *The American Review of Public Administration* 46 (4): 399–417.

Klein, K.J., F. Dansereau, and R.J. Hall. 1994. "Levels issues in theory development, data collection, and analysis." *Academy of Management Review* 19 (2): 195–229.

Knoke, D. and S. Yang. 2008. *Social network analysis*, Vol. 154. Thousand Oaks, CA: Sage Publications.

Knoke, D. 1996. *Comparing policy networks: Labor politics in the US, Germany, and Japan*. Cambridge: Cambridge University Press.

Koliba, C., S. Wiltshire, S. Scheinert, D. Turner, A. Zia, and E. Campbell. 2017. "The critical role of information sharing to the value proposition of a food systems network." *Public Management Review* 19 (3): 284–304.

Kossinets, G. 2006. "Effects of missing data in social networks." *Social Networks* 28 (3): 247–268.

Labianca, G. and D. J. Brass. 2006. "Exploring the social ledger: Negative relationships and negative asymmetry in social networks in organizations." *Academy of Management Review* 31 (3): 596–614.

Lauchs, M., R. Keast, and N. Yousefpour. 2011. "Corrupt police networks: Uncovering hidden relationship patterns, functions and roles." *Policing and Society: An International Journal of Research and Policy* 21 (1): 110–127.

Laumann, E.O. and D. Knoke. 1987. *The organizational state: Social choice in national policy domains*. Madison: University of Wisconsin Press.

Laumann, E.O., P.V. Marsden, and D. Prensky. 1989. "The boundary specification problem in network analysis." *Research Methods in Social Network Analysis* 61: 87.

Laumann, E.O. and F.U. Pappi. 1973. "New directions in the study of community elites." *American Sociological Review* 212–230.

Lemaire, R.H. (forthcoming). "What is our purpose here? Network relationships and goal congruence in a goal-directed network." *American Review of Public Administration.*

Lemaire, R.H. and K.G. Provan. 2017. "Managing collaborative effort: How Simmelian ties advance public sector networks." *American Review of Public Administration* https://doi.org/10.1177/0275074017700722.

Lemaire, R.H., K.G. Provan, L. Mercken, and S.J. Leischow. 2017. "Shaping the evolution of the information flow: The centralizing mechanisms in the evolution of the North American tobacco quitline consortium." *International Public Management Journal* 1–22.

Lim, S., F.S. Berry, and K.H. Lee. 2016. "Stakeholders in the same bed with different dreams: Semantic network analysis of issue interpretation in risk policy related to Mad Cow disease." *Journal of Public Administration Research and Theory* 26 (1): 79–93.

Mandell, M.P. and R. Keast. 2008. "Evaluating the effectiveness of interorganizational relations through networks: Developing a framework for revised performance measures." *Public Management Review* 10 (6): 715–731.

Marcum, C.S., C.A. Bevc, and C.T. Butts. 2012. "Mechanisms of control in emergent interorganizational networks." *Policy Studies Journal* 40 (3): 516–546.

Mercken, L., J.E. Saul, R.H. Lemaire, T.W. Valente, and S.J. Leischow. 2015. "Coevolution of information sharing and implementation of evidence-based practices among North American tobacco cessation quitlines." *American Journal of Public Health* 105 (9): 1814–1822.

Moreno, J.L. 1934. *Who shall survive? A new approach to the problem of human interrelations.* Washington, DC: Nervous and Mental Disease Publishing Co.

Padgett, J.F. and C.K. Ansell. 1993. "Robust action and the rise of the Medici. 1400–1434." *American Journal of Sociology* 98 (6): 1259–1319.

Powell, W.W. 1990. "Neither market nor hierarchy: Network forms of organization." *Research in Organizational Behavior* 12: 295–336.

Provan, K.G., J.E. Beagles, L. Mercken, and S.J. Leischow. 2012. "Awareness of evidence-based practices by organizations in a publicly funded smoking cessation network." *Journal of Public Administration Research and Theory* 23 (1): 133–153.

Provan, K.G. and R.H. Lemaire. 2012. "Core concepts and key ideas for understanding public sector organizational networks: Using research to inform scholarship and practice." *Public Administration Review* 72 (5): 638–648.

Provan, K.G. and H.B. Milward. 1995. "A preliminary theory of interorganizational network effectiveness: A comparative study of four community mental health systems." *Administrative Science Quarterly* 40 (1): 1–33.

Provan, K.G. and H.B. Milward. 2001. "Do networks really work? A framework for evaluating public-sector organizational networks." *Public Administration Review* 61 (4): 414.

Provan, K.G. and J.G. Sebastian. 1998. "Networks within networks: Service link overlap, organizational cliques, and network effectiveness." *Academy of Management Journal* 41 (4): 453–463.

Provan, K.G., M.A. Veazie, L.K. Staten, and N.I. Teufel-Shone. 2005. "The use of network analysis to strengthen community partnerships." *Public Administration Review* 65 (5): 603–613.

Raab, J. 2002. "Where do policy networks come from?" *Journal of Public Administration Research and Theory* 12 (4): 581–622.

Raab, J., R.S. Mannak, and B. Cambré. 2015. "Combining structure, governance, and context: A configurational approach to network effectiveness." *Journal of Public Administration Research and Theory* 25 (2): 479–511.

Raab, J., R.H. Lemaire, and K.G. Provan. 2013. "Chapter 10: The configurational approach in organizational network research." In *Configurational theory and methods in organizational research*, edited by P.C. Fiss, B. Cambre, and A. Marx, 225–253. Bingley, UK: Emerald Group Publishing Limited.

Rethemeyer, R.K. and D.M. Hatmaker. 2007. "Network management reconsidered: An inquiry into management of network structures in public sector service provision." *Journal of Public Administration Research and Theory* 18 (4): 617–646.

Robins, G. 2011. "Exponential random graph models for social networks." In *Handbook of Social Network Analysis*, edited by J. Scott and P.J. Carrington. Thousand Oaks, CA: Sage Publications.

Roethlisberger, F.J. and W.J. Dickson. (1939) 2003. *Management and the Worker*, Vol. 5. London, UK: Psychology Press.

Ryu, S. and M.S. Johansen. 2017. "Collaborative networking, environmental shocks, and organizational performance: Evidence from hurricane Rita." *International Public Management Journal* 20 (2): 206–225.

Tichy, N.M., M.L. Tushman, and C. Fombrun. 1979. "Social network analysis for organizations." *Academy of Management Review* 4 (4): 507–519.

Scheinert, S., C. Koliba, S. Hurley, S. Coleman, and A. Zia. 2015. "The shape of watershed governance: Locating the boundaries of multiplex networks." *Complexity, Governance & Networks* 2 (1): 65–82.

Siciliano, M.D. 2017. "Ignoring the experts: Networks and organizational learning in the public sector." *Journal of Public Administration Research and Theory* 27 (1): 104–119.

Snijders, T.A.B., G.G. van de Bunt, and C.E.G. Steglich. 2010. "Introduction to stochastic actor-based models for network dynamics." *Social Networks* 32: 44–60.

Uzzi, B. 1997. "Social structure and competition in interfirm networks: The paradox of embeddedness." *Administrative Science Quarterly* 42 (1): 35–67.

Valente, T.W., K. Coronges, C. Lakon, and E. Costenbader. 2008. "How correlated are network centrality measures?" *Connections (Toronto, Ont.)* 28 (1): 16.

Van den Oord, S., F. Bertels, J. Geurts, R. Lenstra, P. Kenis, and B. Cambré. 2017. "Development of a network game for coordination of service delivery to people with a chronic illness." *International Journal of Care Coordination*. doi: 10.1177/2053434517733842.

Wasserman, S. and K. Faust. 1994. *Social network analysis: Methods and applications*, Vol. 8. Cambridge: Cambridge University Press.

10 Qualitative comparative analysis in public network research

Denita Cepiku, Daniela Cristofoli
and Benedetta Trivellato

Introduction

The configurational approach and Qualitative Comparative Analysis (QCA) are relatively new approaches and methods in public network research. Having long been a focus of attention for organizational scholars, a 'configuration' may be defined as 'any multidimensional constellation of conceptually distinct characteristics that commonly occur together' (Meyer, Tsui and Hinings 1993: 1175).

Actually, the core idea of the configurational approach that organizations should be considered as constellations of interconnected factors to be studied from a systemic and holistic perspective (Fiss 2011; Fiss, Marx and Cambré 2013) was already present in one of the most famous works in public network research. Provan and Milward (1995), in fact, identified the network's context as a necessary condition that, in combination with some characteristics of the network's structure, leads to network success. As Raab, Lemaire and Provan (2013) highlight, these arguments were configurational in nature but, due to the methodological development at the time, they were treated as linear relationships. The configurational 'spirit' can be found in many other public network works (see for example Keast and Mandell 2013), even if addressed differently from a methodological point of view. It was only with the development, first, of QCA as a research method (Ragin 1987, 2008; Fiss 2007, 2009), and then with its extension to the public network field, that the configurational approach started to characterize public network research.

Verweij et al. (2013) were the first to publish a study that was configurational in nature. They focused on fourteen governance networks and explored how the combination of three conditions (namely network complexity, network management and stakeholder involvement) can equally lead to stakeholder satisfaction. Moving from Provan and Milward's (1995) study, Raab, Mannak and Cambré (2015) focused on thirty-nine crime-prevention networks in the Netherlands. They explored how network context (in terms of resource munificence and stability) combines with network integration and network governance modes to achieve good performances. Starting again from Provan and Milward's (1995) model, Wang (2016) focused on twenty-two neighbourhood governance networks in Beijing, in search for the determinants of network effectiveness. He investigated which combinations of network integration, resource munificence, network stability and neighbourhood socioeconomic status (SES) can equally lead to good performance. On the basis of the assumption that 'one size does not fit all', in 2016 Cristofoli and Markovic focused on twelve networks for homecare assistance in Switzerland, and explored which combinations of network context, structure, mechanisms and management equally lead to good performances.

It is true that the configurational approach and the subsequent application of QCA (Ragin 1987, 2008; Fiss 2007, 2009) in public network research is still in its infancy. Nevertheless, scholars are increasingly convinced that their development can help further advance our knowledge of public networks. For instance, Raab, Lemaire and Provan (2013) identified three reasons to use a configurational approach and QCA in public network research.

Firstly, they argue that networks are 'clusters of interconnected structures and practices' (Raab, Lemaire and Provan 2013: 227), and their outcomes are often the result of the combination of all these factors. Secondly, networks are nested entities, and their outcomes often depend on factors across multiple levels. Thirdly, networks are not separated from the context in which they operate, and their functioning and outcomes are often influenced by their socio-political-economic and institutional environment. The configurational approach allows exploration of the combined effect of all those factors. 'Rather than trying to simplify networks, the configurational approach embraces in fact their complexity' (Raab et al. 2013: 246). It allows us to investigate networks 'from a systemic and holistic view', and to explain network functioning and outcomes in terms of multiple configurations of factors, and not as the result of individual and independent variables.

Moreover, public networks in different circumstances often need different factors to function and succeed. The configurational approach allows the identification of the multiple combinations of conditions that can lead to the same outcome. This is very important for managers and practitioners, because one unique pathway to network success often does not exist, and network managers must be able to identify alternatives.

Lastly, the sample size in public network research is often limited by the difficulty in collecting data about whole networks. The study of a whole network requires, in fact, the collection of data from all partner organizations, and this limits the sample size. The configurational approach and QCA extend the analysis from a small to a medium sample size.

In the following we will first go back to the origin of the configurational approach and of the QCA method and present their characteristics. Then, we will show how to implement a public network study on the basis of the QCA method; this will be followed by a review of the main public network studies currently using QCA as a research method. The concluding part of the chapter provides some insights about the value-added of the QCA method for network research and its potential in future research.

The configurational approach and QCA

The idea that organizations should be conceived as constellations of inter-connected factors and can be better understood from a holistic and systemic perspective is one of the core concepts in organization studies. However, it is also one of the least-developed concepts (Fiss, Marx and Cambré 2013). This is mainly due to a lack of methodological tools that enable working with combinations of interconnected factors jointly leading to expected outcomes (Fiss 2007).

It was with the development of the QCA as a research method (Ragin 1987, 2000, 2008) that researchers were provided with a new set of tools, consisting of a set-theoretic approach and Boolean algebra, to explore how multiple combinations of factors (or configurations of conditions, in QCA parlance) can produce the expected outcome.

The origin of QCA can be traced back to the tradition of comparative case-based sociology. It is, however, with the work of Charles Ragin (1987, 2000, 2008) that it was systematized and transformed into a coherent approach. Ragin was firmly convinced that social phenomena tend to occur together with other social phenomena, and that assuming the isolated effects of individual variables does not make sense. He firmly believed that the ceteris paribus principle, typical of variable-oriented studies, cannot help to understand the world. On the other hand, he also believed that deep knowledge of individual cases, typical of qualitative analysis, is not helpful whenever generalizations cannot be derived. As a result, there was the need of an approach that keeps context-sensitivity, while identifying regularities (to rephrase Rihoux and Ragin 2009).

Within this framework, Ragin developed QCA as a middle way between the case-oriented and the variable-oriented approaches, able to incorporate the advantages of both research traditions and to fill the methodological gap between very small and very large-n studies. QCA combines, in fact, both the principles of analytical induction, typical of case-study research, with an attempt to observe patterns across cases, typical of variable-oriented research. Normally, QCA is used in research designs comparing five to fifty cases (small and intermediate n-size). In this range, there are often too many cases for researchers to keep all the case knowledge 'in their heads,' but too few cases for most conventional statistical techniques.

In what follows, we will summarize the main features of QCA as a method based on a set-theoretic vision of the world. In the next paragraph, we will show the process of QCA implementation on the basis of the principles of Boolean algebra.

According to the principles of a set-theoretic understanding of the world, QCA relies on sets and set – subset relationships and not on variables and correlations (Ragin 2000, 2008; Fiss 2007). The attributes of single cases are not conceived as variables but as set-relationships. In this perspective, cases are assigned as a member in a set (the process of assigning cases in a set is labelled 'calibration'), and the effect of each individual causal condition is measured as set membership. On top of it, relationships among conditions are not explored in terms of correlations among variables *ceteris paribus*, but as set – subset relationships, thus assuming interconnection among conditions as the rule rather than the exception. For instance, in order to explain which configurations lead to high network performance, QCA examines members of the set of 'high-performing' networks and then identifies the combinations of network characteristics associated with the outcome of interest (high performance).

As a consequence, causality is not simply based on one-to-one relationships among isolated variables. There are no single mono-causal explanations for outcomes:

> What makes a certain feature . . . causally relevant in one setting and not in another is the fact that its causal significance is altered by the presence of other features (that is, its effect is altered by context). Similarly, apparently different features can have the same effect depending on which other features they are associated with. . . . This is a primary justification for examining cases as wholes and for trying to decipher how different causal factors fit together.
>
> (Ragin 1987: 49)

Causality is based on the principles of *complex causation* and *equifinality*. Causal complexity refers to the fact that certain outcomes are often the result of combinations of conditions: conditions operate in combination rather than independently (*conjunctional causations*). Equifinality means that different paths of conjunctional causations of conditions can lead to the same outcome (Ragin 1987) (*multiple conjunctural causation*). Causality is also asymmetric (*asymmetric causation*): the set of conditions leading to a positive outcome may be different from the set of conditions leading to the absence of it.

Last but not least, the shift to set – subset relationships allows researchers to explore *necessity and sufficiency* in causal relationships. Normally, in correlation analysis variables are assumed to be at the same time necessary and sufficient. However, a condition may be necessary for the occurrence of the outcome, but at the same time its presence does not ensure the achievement of the outcome (it is not sufficient). The set-theoretic approach allows to shed light on the following: conditions are necessary in those situations where each time the outcome is present, the condition is also present; conditions are sufficient in those situations where each time the condition is present, the outcome is also present.

Three specific techniques can be subsumed under the heading of QCA: QCA using conventional crisp-set (csQCA), multi-value QCA (mvQCA), and fuzzy-set QCA (fsQCA) (Rihoux and Ragin 2009). csQCA requires binary data, and cases are encoded as dummy variables (1 = for membership in a set and 0 = for absence in a set). fsQCA allows the scaling of membership scores, and thus allows partial membership in a set (Ragin 2000). These membership scores range from 0 (full non-membership) to 1 (full membership). The crossover point 0.5 is the point of maximum ambiguity. mvQCA allows multi-value conditions, or better it allows to take into account whether and which category of a condition is present; however, it is the least used of the three techniques. Thus, in the following we will focus on csQCA and fsQCA.

The implementation of QCA

This section presents the main operations involved in QCA.[1] The formalized steps of the process, based on the logic of Boolean algebra and implemented by a set of computer programs,[2] aim to identify the configurations of conditions leading to the outcome. The researcher must first produce a data table, where each case displays a specific combination of conditions and an outcome. The software then produces a truth table, which displays the data as a list of configurations, where each configuration is a given combination of some conditions and an outcome. A specific configuration may correspond to several observed cases. The subsequent step of the analysis involves Boolean minimization; this implies reducing the long Boolean expression, which consists of the long description of the truth table, to the shortest possible expression. More specifically, the QCA software uses Boolean algebra to implement a mode of logical comparison through which each case is represented as a combination of causal and outcome conditions. The aim is to reduce the unique configurations of conditions observed throughout the cases to the minimum combinations of conditions which are necessary for the outcome to occur (Kitchener et al. 2002). The result of such a Boolean minimization is a so-called 'minimal formula' – corresponding to the list of the configurations – which unveils the regularities in the data. It is then up to the researcher to interpret this minimal formula, possibly in terms of causality.

The QCA procedure can be divided into three main phases (Rihoux and Lobe 2009). The first phase involves case selection and description, and is followed by a second phase where conditions are selected and expressed in numerical scores (calibration) and where all the steps to obtain the minimal formulas are performed (this is the analytic, computer-aided part of QCA). In the third phase, the different causal paths obtained through the minimal formulas are interpreted. The main components of this process are then described.

Case selection and data collection

The selection of cases for QCA usually relies on purposive sampling. As QCA looks at commonalities across the same outcome in cases, researchers often begin with the outcome of interest they wish to study to identify the population of cases of theoretical interest (Greckhamer, Misangyi and Fiss 2013). In other instances, the researcher selects cases that show some common background features, and that display some variation of some aspects, where the latter will be the conditions and outcome in the model (Rihoux and Lobe 2009). Moreover, this purposeful sampling may be iterative and guided by the original research question and the relevant theory, justifying the inclusion of each case on theoretical grounds (Rihoux and Ragin 2009). Small-*n* studies typically involve between twelve and fifty cases, while large-*n* QCA studies will involve more than fifty and even thousands of cases (Greckhamer et al. 2008). The researcher's relationship to the cases – and their knowledge of each case – will inevitably be different between small-*n* and large-*n* QCA studies (Greckhamer, Misangyi and Fiss 2013). As with *n* conditions, there are 2n possible combinations where the number of cases to be selected depends on the number of conditions involved in the theoretical model. The generally accepted rule of thumb is as follows: four to five conditions require twelve to fifteen cases, five to six require fifteen to thirty-five cases, and seven to eight conditions require more than fifty cases.

Case knowledge is required to a certain extent for case selection, as well as to ensure the availability of data on all the variables that are relevant to the research question. This knowledge can be acquired through different data collection strategies and methodologies. Different methods apply for different levels of cases; at the macro and meso levels for instance, multiple sources of data can be used, including existing case studies, official statistical data, textual data from various types of documents, archival data, surveys, and so forth. Expert interviews also allow to gain further knowledge from an actor's perspective. At the micro level, qualitative methods usually become more relevant, and include participant observation, in-depth interviews, direct observation, testimonials, narratives and focus groups (Rihoux and Lobe 2009).

Model specification and selection of conditions

The way conditions are selected is related to the purpose of QCA within the study. If the aim is theory testing, then theory points at the key factors, though case knowledge should be relied upon to decide whether the theory can indeed be applied to the case under scrutiny. If, conversely, QCA is mostly used for exploratory purposes or for theory building, then cases play a central role (Rihoux and Lobe 2009).

The number of causal conditions included in the causal model by the researcher plays a critical role, especially in small-*n* settings (Marx 2010; Rihoux and Ragin 2009); that is, those with ten to fifty cases (Greckhamer, Misangyi and Fiss 2013). With a higher number of conditions, the number of logically possible configurations of conditions will increase, and each case will tend to become its own unique configuration, which makes it difficult for QCA to find any commonality across cases in explaining the outcome as well as to rule out ill-specified theoretical models (Greckhamer, Misangyi and Fiss 2013). Moreover, the difficulty of interpreting the findings also increases with the number of conditions, because of an increase of both the number of configurations that may be sufficient (and/or necessary) for the occurrence of an outcome and of the complexity of the configurations themselves. As a result, seven to eight (or fewer) conditions are usually appropriate, whereas the results of an analysis involving more than eight to ten conditions are likely to be intractable (Ragin 2008).

Analysis of necessary and sufficient conditions: in search for the multiple configurations leading to the outcome

The subsequent phase is the computer-aided part, which relies on Tosmana and/or fsQCA as commonly used software. In csQCA set memberships are evaluated in a dichotomous manner: cases are thus classified as either 'fully in' (1) or 'fully out' (0) of the sets based on theoretical or empirical knowledge. The setting of the threshold should rely on informed judgment, theory and/or be case-driven. In fsQCA, the operation that corresponds to this dichotomization is called 'calibration'. In a way, a fuzzy set can be seen as a continuous variable that has been purposefully calibrated to indicate degree of membership in a set. The calibration is achieved by relying on theoretical and substantive knowledge, so as to define the three qualitative breakpoints: full membership (1), full non-membership (0) and the crossover point where there is maximum ambiguity (0.5). In addition to this three-value set, more fine-grained fuzzy sets can also be used by the researcher (see Table 10.1), which are useful especially when sub-stantial information about the cases is available but the nature of the evidence is not identical across cases (Ragin 2009). Calibrating all conditions as well as the outcome produces the fuzzy-set data matrix. Specific software is then used to transform the assigned membership scores into dichotomized values.

Once data are displayed in a dichotomized way, a truth table is constructed to display them.

Before performing the core QCA operation it is often useful to examine the truth table to solve the so-called 'contradictory configurations', which occur when cases in the same configuration show different outcomes. Among the strategies that are available to solve these contradictions (Ragin 2008; Rihoux and Ragin 2009) are the addition, removal or replacement of one or more of the theoretically important causal conditions in the model, or the re-examination of the ways in which sets (including the outcome set) are operationalized and cali-brated. Another strategy involves gaining deeper knowledge of each of the cases to identify aspects that would help to resolve the occurring contradictions. A

Table 10.1 Crisp versus fuzzy sets

Crisp set	Three-value fuzzy set	Four-value fuzzy set	'Continuous' fuzzy set
1 = fully in	1 = fully in	1 = fully in	1 = fully in
0 = fully out	0.5 = neither fully in nor fully out	0.67 = more in than out	Degree of membership is more in than out:
	0 = fully out	0.33 = more out than in	$1 > x_i > 0.5$
		0 = fully out	0.5 = crossover
			Degree of membership is more out than in:
			$0.5 > x_i > 0$
			0 = fully out

Source: Adapted from Rihoux and Ragin (2009)

final approach involves reliance on a frequency criterion: if only one in twenty cases is contradictory (e.g. nineteen cases have the outcome of high performance and one has the outcome of not high performance), one could make the judgment that this does not constitute a theoretically significant contradiction but may more reasonably be assumed to involve factors such as coding error or randomness (Greckhamer, Misangyi and Fiss 2013). As it will be better explained later, the generally accepted threshold is 0.8 (Ragin 2008).

Another important step involves exploring – through the analysis of necessary conditions – whether any of the conditions can be regarded as necessary for causing the outcome. This is done by examining whether a single condition is always present or absent in all cases where the outcome is present (Fiss 2007; Ragin 2006). A condition is regarded as necessary if the consistency score exceeds the threshold of 0.9 (Schneider et al. 2010), where consistency measures the degree to which the cases align to the particular rule: the more cases that fail to meet this rule for necessary conditions, the lower will be the consistency score (Ragin 2006).

The core phase that follows is the analysis of sufficient conditions through the Boolean minimization, or the search for the multiple configurations of conditions leading to the outcomes. A key step here relates to deciding whether or not to take into account the 'logical remainders' (i.e. logically possible combinations of conditions for which no empirical cases exist) that enable the researcher to obtain a more parsimonious minimal formula. If one chooses the radical strategy of allowing the software to exploit *all* useful logical remainders (so as to obtain the most parsimonious minimal formula possible), no particular 'return to the cases' is required. If one opts for the 'intermediate solution' – that is, a minimal formula derived with the aid of only those logical remainders that are consistent with the researcher's theoretical and substantive knowledge – one must go back to the cases and decide which logical remainders will be used by the software (Rihoux and Lobe 2009).

The subsequent step involves reducing the truth table to meaningful configurations. Based on their frequency of empirical instances, some configurations will be classified as relevant and others as irrelevant. This implies that the researcher needs to select a *frequency* threshold; that is, the minimum number of cases that must be observed for each configuration for it to be considered relevant for purposes of causal analysis of necessity and sufficiency. The appropriate number will depend on the aim of the research. In the case of small-*n* studies, it is common to specify a minimum frequency of one or two cases; for large-*n* studies, this number could be significantly higher. Greckhamer, Misangyi and Fiss (2013) suggest that, when setting their minimum frequency thresholds, large-*n* researchers strike a balance between the inclusion of at least eighty per cent of the overall cases and a relatively high number of cases per configuration.

A *consistency* cut off also needs to be defined for coding the outcome as present or absent. Consistency describes the proportion of cases belonging to any particular configuration: while it is desirable to have consistency as close to 1 as possible, (near) perfect consistency is more likely to be obtained in small-*n* studies (Ragin 2006). Regardless of the sample size, Ragin (2008) has suggested a minimum consistency of 0.80. Whereas most studies tend to apply this rule, a specific consistency cut off can also be set by the researcher based on the characteristics of the data, especially in the case of small-*n* studies where this effort may not be particularly work-intensive. An example of this approach is provided by Verweij et al. (2013), as described in the next section.

Through a series of paired comparisons between configurations that only differ in one respect – in the presence/absence of one condition, while all of the others are identical – we can derive a simpler equation or minimal formula for the conditions leading to the outcome.

The minimization procedure presents three formulas or solutions to each truth table analysis: (1) a 'complex' solution that avoids using any counterfactual cases (rows without cases, or logical remainders); (2) a 'parsimonious' solution, which permits the use of any remainder that will yield simpler (or fewer) recipes; and (3) an 'intermediate solution', which uses only the remainders that survive counterfactual analysis based on theoretical and substantive knowledge (which is input by the user).

The solution or minimal formula is expressed as combinations of conditions in the language of the Boolean algebra. The use of upper-case letters denotes the presence of a condition, whereas the use of lower-case letters denotes its absence.[3] The logical operator 'and' is indicated by the * sign, and 'or' by the + sign). The notation => denotes the logical *implication* operator.

The solution can be assessed on the basis of certain parameters. First, the *solution coverage* expresses the explanatory power of the solution; that is, how much of the outcome is covered by all configurations (Rihoux and Ragin 2009). Two additional measures allow determining the fit of each configuration: consistency and coverage. *Consistency* displays the proportion of cases consistent with the outcome; that is, the number of cases that exhibit a given configuration of attributes as well as the outcome, divided by the number of cases that exhibit the same configuration of attributes but do not exhibit the outcome (Fiss 2011).

Coverage assesses the proportion of instances of the outcome that exhibit a certain causal combination or path (Fiss 2007). A solution or path is informative when its consistency is above 0.75–0.80, and its raw coverage is between 0.25 and 0.65, although small variations are also acceptable (Urueña and Hidalgo 2016).

Interpretation

The last step of the process involves interpreting the solution, which can be done in three main ways. The *case-by-case interpretation* involves re-examining individual case narratives using the core conditions indicated by the solution. This can be done, for instance, by translating the conditions in the solution into a causal narrative whose validity can be tested with key informants and stakeholders whenever possible. With *cross-case interpretation*, the researcher tries to identify similarities or contrasts across case narratives, building on the terms of the solution; typically, those cases that are clustered in connection with a given term are examined in parallel. The researcher is then able to make sense of multiple-case narratives; that is, to identify common narratives across several cases. The last approach – *'limited historical' generalization* – goes beyond the observed cases: by comparing the cases, the researcher can formulate propositions which can be applied, with the appropriate caution, to other similar cases (Rihoux and Lobe 2009).

The configurational approach and QCA in network research

This section presents four empirical examples which demonstrate how QCA can be used to analyse networks in public sector settings, and how the process described in the previous section may develop based on the decisions taken by the researcher at key relevant moments. We do not aim at a comprehensive description of these studies but rather at exemplifying the implementation of the QCA procedure through its main components.

A first deserving example is represented by the study by Verweij et al. (2013), who look at the conditions that contribute to satisfactory outcomes of decision-making processes in governance networks. Based on a study of fourteen Dutch spatial planning projects, they used fsQCA to explore what combinations of three conditions – network complexity, network management and stakeholder involvement – are necessary or sufficient to achieve stakeholder satisfaction in governance networks.

As far as case selection and data collection is concerned, the authors note that the fourteen projects cover a variety of issues and conflicts: they generally take place in settings where different environmental functions are represented by separate organizations that try to influence the policy process. All cases were researched through document analyses, interviews and direct observation; they had also been studied for a number of years, thereby allowing a longitudinal view on their course.

The fsQCA procedure required the operationalization of the conditions and of the outcome, to be followed by their calibration. Verweij et al. (2013) opted for giving them a membership score of 1.00, 0.67, 0.33 or 0.00 after an iterative dialogue between theoretical and substantive knowledge, to obtain the raw data matrix.

In order to proceed with the QCA procedure, the total scores covering the three conditions and the outcome were combined into a raw data matrix. This matrix was first tested for necessary conditions for the outcome, and also for the negation of such conditions, so as to explore whether the presence or absence of each of the conditions was necessary to produce the outcome. No necessary conditions, meeting or exceeding the 0.9 consistency threshold, were found. The truth table generated with the fsQCA software (Ragin et al. 2006) shows the distribution of the fourteen cases across all logically possible configurations: seven of eight logically possible configurations were found to be empirically present. Because of the low number of cases, the frequency threshold was set at one, and the single configuration with no cases was thus removed.

This study provides an interesting example of how the consistency cut-off can be set by the researcher based on the characteristics of the data, as opposed to reliance on a commonly accepted threshold. The consistency value of the first four configurations was found to be 1.00, indicating that all networks with those configurations of conditions displayed high stakeholder satisfaction. The three remaining configurations obtained less than perfect consistency scores because of contradictions (i.e. the same configuration of conditions leading the different outcomes) in the fifth and sixth configurations (consistency equal to 0.90 and 0.89 respectively) which could not be solved. The seventh configuration shows a PRI (proportional reduction in consistency) value equal to 0.00 even if consistency (0.83) is relatively high: a low PRI indicates that something is wrong, for instance when a condition or a configuration appears to be sufficient for both the outcome and its absence (Schwellnus 2013). The truth table (see Table 10.2) therefore shows a gap in consistency between 1.00 and 0.90, which coincides with the logical contradictions and the low PRI consistency value. Hence, the consistency cut-off point was set by the authors at 0.90: the cases corresponding to the last three 'troublesome' configurations (i.e. WAAL, GOUW, LENT, SCHEL and WIER) were thus removed from the truth table (Ragin 2008) and not included in the minimization process.

The subsequent analysis and minimization of the truth table resulted in the following complex solution:

COMPLEXITY * MANAGEMENT + STAKEHOLDER

INVOLVEMENT * MANAGEMENT + complexity

* stakeholder involvement * management => OUTCOME

The analysis, in other words, highlights three paths that produce significant stakeholder satisfaction, that is, that are sufficient for the outcome: the first

Table 10.2 Truth table from a study of fourteen Dutch spatial planning projects

Conditions					Consistency	
Network complexity	*Stakeholder involvement*	*Network management*	*N*	*Outcome*	*Raw*	*PRI*
1	1	1	5	1	1.00	1.00
0	1	1	1	1	1.00	1.00
1	0	1	2	1	1.00	1.00
0	0	0	1	1	1.00	1.00
0	1	0	2	C	0.90	0.50
1	1	0	2	C	0.89	0.50
1	0	0	1	0	0.83	0.00

Source: Verweij et al. 2013

Note: the C in the column 'outcome' indicates a contradictory row (i.e. two cases with the same configuration of conditions lead to different outcomes)

configuration involves a combination of high network complexity and adaptive network management, the second one involves a combination of high stakeholder involvement and adaptive network management, and the third involves low network complexity combined with low stakeholder involvement and a closed style of management. The main conclusion drawn by the authors is that at least a certain level of adaptive network management is needed, notwithstanding the level of complexity. This adaptive style, as defined by Verweij et al. (2013), resembles the literature on network management, and calls for an open management orientation that includes shared goal searching and the facilitation of interactions by putting organizational arrangements in place. An adaptive style is needed especially when stakeholder involvement is deep, and thus a variety of stakes and perspectives are present.

A second example is provided by Raab, Mannak and Cambré (2015), who explored how network structure, context and governance modes relate to network effectiveness. Based on Provan and Milward's (1995) model on the effectiveness of designed and goal-directed inter-organizational networks, the authors analysed thirty-nine crime-prevention networks, so called Safety Houses (SH), in the Netherlands. They relied on csQCA to test hypotheses on the combined effects of age, network structure (network integration), network context (resource munificence and stability) and formal mode of governance on network effectiveness.

Starting from a review of the relevant extant theory, the authors developed five hypotheses about each of the following five network conditions being a necessary, but not sufficient, condition for network effectiveness: age (three years, as this threshold appeared to be important during the authors' exploratory research), system stability, resource munificence, centralized integration and being governed by a network administrative organization (NAO). One additional hypothesis combines the presence of all these conditions as leading to effectiveness.

As an example of how the outcome variable may be defined and operationalized, Raab, Mannak and Cambré (2015) chose the following path to define *network effectiveness*. The authors looked at effectiveness at the community level (Provan and Milward 2001) by first asking respondents whether their SH had achieved a 5.8 per cent reduction in recidivism in a two-year period, corresponding to a twenty-five per cent reduction in seven years (both percentages were set as nationwide targets by the Dutch Ministry of Justice). Respondents usually stated either that they could not show any reduction (yet) (coded as not effective, 0) or that the reduction was significantly higher than the 5.8 per cent (effective, 1). If there was evidence of a reduction, respondents were asked to elaborate for the four themes in which SHs were expected to be active: youth, habitual offenders, domestic violence and probation. If an SH was effective in at least three of the four themes, and therefore had a score of 3 out of 4, it was considered as being overall effective (threshold) and coded as 1.

Case selection did not require a specific approach, as the entire population of SHs in the Netherlands at that time was included in the analysis. Two rounds of data collection were carried out, involving document reviews, semi-structured and group interviews, observations, and administration of a questionnaire.

In order to test the hypotheses, Raab, Mannak and Cambré (2015) applied csQCA, which implied the categorization of cases for each condition either as present (1) or absent (0). The researchers noted that several conditions proved binary; for instance, system stability was either disturbed because of drop-out of an important partner, or undisturbed. The scores were either clearly low or high for most conditions, thereby producing bi-modal distributions which highlighted a single threshold.

Once all the conditions were operationalized and coded, the software Tosmana 1.3.1 was used to perform the csQCA analysis and to identify the configurations for network effectiveness:

AGE * STABILITY * INTEGRATION * RESOURCE

MUNIFICENCE + AGE * STABILITY * INTEGRATION *

NETWORK GOVERNANCE => NETWORK EFFECTIVENESS

The formula identifies two paths that lead to high network effectiveness: one that combines age (three-year existence) with high levels of system stability and centralized integration and high resource munificence; and a second one combining a three-year existence with high levels of system stability, centralized integration and NAO governance. This solution was reached without logical remainders; that is, without the configurations that are not empirically observed (complex solution). There was no need to set a consistency threshold because the truth table showed no contradictions in the combinations of configurations leading to an effective outcome, with the implication that the consistency was equal to 1.0. Raab, Mannak and Cambré (2015) decided to assess the strength of these two pathways to network effectiveness by also investigating the possible pathways that lead to network ineffectiveness. They found that network effectiveness can be hindered either by young network age (less than three years), a lack of centralized integration or a lack of resource munificence in combination with no NAO governance. The overall solution coverage was 1.0, since all cases were included in a configuration either leading to the outcome 0 (ineffective) or 1 (effective).

As for the interpretation of these results, the authors concluded that age, system stability and centralized integration are necessary, but not sufficient, conditions for the effectiveness of SHs, and that two sufficient paths exist with these three conditions. In terms of the original hypotheses, three were confirmed (those proposing that age, system stability and centralized integration are necessary, but not sufficient, conditions for network effectiveness), two were not (resource munificence and being governed by a NAO are not such conditions), and the last one was only partly confirmed. Especially for those hypotheses that were not confirmed, the authors noted that resources and governance mode indeed play an important role, but in a more differentiated way than originally imagined. Additionally, the results show that financial resources can, to some extent, be substituted by administrative resources in the form of a neutral facilitating institution.

As a third example, Cristofoli and Markovic (2016) further develop the analysis carried out by Raab, Mannak and Cambré (2015) by looking at how resource munificence, centralization of the network structure, formalization of coordination mechanisms and network management combine to affect network performance. They used fsQCA to compare twelve Swiss home care networks (Spitex), along with their performance and the combinations of the above-mentioned factors, and to identify the different paths that lead to network success.

As far as case selection is concerned, this study provides an interesting example of how the twelve networks were purposefully chosen in order to give sufficient variation in the causal and outcome conditions (Rihoux and Ragin 2009). The criteria included a catchment area of at least 25,000 people and the fact of being located in different cantons, with varying public funding (resource munificence) and different structural characteristics (modes of network governance). Lastly, in order to provide variation in the outcome conditions, six successful and six unsuccessful cases were chosen (based on the authors' definition of performance). Data collection was carried out first through a national survey distributed to the directors of all the focal Spitex organizations operating in Switzerland, with a response rate of about fifty per cent. The next steps involved analysing information provided by network members on their websites, annual reports and official information on government sites of every level, followed by semi-structured interviews with the directors, other executives of each Spitex organization and the heads of public and private organizations in the networks.

The four determinants of network performance (resource munificence, centralization of the network structures, formalization of coordination mechanisms and network management) were identified based on previous literature and operationalized; the criteria for calibration were drawn from other studies – such as Provan and Milward (1995), Provan and Sebastian (1998), Provan and Kenis (2008) and Herranz (2010) – or derived from knowledge gained through the research process. As for the analysis, Tosmana 1.3.1 was used to obtain the truth table and identify the sets of conditions leading to high network performance. The consistency threshold was set at 0.75, and logical remainders were taken into consideration. The application of the Boolean minimization process then allowed the extraction of the following minimal formula:

RESOURCE MUNIFICENCE (R) * CENTRALLY GOVERNED

NETWORK STRUCTURE(G) * NETWORK MANAGEMENT(M) +

RESOURCE MUNIFICENCE (R) * centrally governed network

structures(g) * FORMALIZED COORDINATION MECHANISMS (F)

*network management (m) => HIGH NETWORK PERFORMANCE

In other words, two paths leading to high network performance were identified, both featuring a resource-munificent context together with, respectively:
(1) the presence of centrally governed network structures combined with the
presence of network management, and (2) the absence of centrally governed
network structures combined with formalized coordination mechanisms and
the absence of distinct network management. The analysis of necessity showed
that no condition exceeded the consistency threshold of 0.9 (i.e. no condition
was identified as necessary for high network performance), but the authors were
able to identify resource munificence as an INUS condition, meaning that the
condition is an insufficient but necessary part of causal paths which are themselves unnecessary but sufficient.

The last example differs from the previous ones, as Wang (2016) employed
a mixed-methods approach to study the determinants of the effectiveness of
governance networks, based on the analysis of twenty-two neighbourhood governance networks in Beijing, with each network consisting of public, business
and civic organizations. The author used linear regression analysis to identify the
independent variables that exert statistically significant influence over network
effectiveness, and fsQCA to investigate the interactions between explanatory
variables.

As far as case selection and data collection are concerned, the author relied
on purposeful sampling: a Beijing non-profit organization specializing in home-
owners' advocacy helped to contact the first six neighbourhoods; the author
subsequently asked interviewees to introduce him to new neighbourhoods that
exhibited combinations of network effectiveness and causal conditions that he
had not covered. He stopped at twenty-two cases, once he had begun to come
across similar cases and could not identify new patterns. Semi-structured interviews were used as the major approach to collecting data.

Following the author's mixed-methods approach, ordinary least squares
regression was first employed to study the relationships between variables, by
relying on the bootstrap approach to mitigate the problems posed by the small
sample size for regression analysis. Adjusting for the influence of other independent variables, a first regression analysis showed that network stability was
positively related to effectiveness and network centralization was negatively
related to effectiveness; a second regression analysis showed that network density
was positively related to network effectiveness.

The fsQCA analysis was subsequently employed, with the usual requirements
for calibration of raw data in order to be analysed by the fsQCA software. The
calibration was mainly based on substantive knowledge of each network. The
analysis conducted without consideration of logical remainders produced two
causal paths, expressed through the following minimal formula:

RESOURCE MUNIFICENCE * NEIGHBOURHOOD SES *

network centralization + RESOURCE MUNIFICENCE *

NETWORK STABILITY => NETWORK EFFECTIVENESS.

The first causal path combines high resource munificence, high neighbourhood SES and low network centralization. The second one combines resource munificence and network stability. The overall solution coverage was 0.74, showing that these two paths could explain seventy-four per cent of all the effective networks, and the solution consistency was 0.80, indicating that eighty per cent of the networks with the two configurations were effective.

To test the impact of network density on network effectiveness, the author subsequently replaced network centralization with density and ran the procedure again, resulting in two causal recipes:

RESOURCE MUNIFICENCE * NETWORK STABILITY

+ RESOURCE MUNIFICENCE * NEIGHBOURHOOD SES

* NETWORK DENSITY => NETWORK EFFECTIVENESS.

The first causal path combines resource munificence and network stability, as in the previous analysis. The second path combines resource munificence, network density and high neighbourhood SES, with network stability being in this case irrelevant. The overall solution coverage here was 0.67, and the solution consistency 0.81. Lastly, the author also conducted analysis of configurations of factors leading to network ineffectiveness. One configuration was obtained, as a combination of low membership scores in three sets: network density, network stability and neighbourhood SES. If a network is unstable, lacks cooperation between organizations and has a low SES then it is very likely to be ineffective. Eighty-two per cent of the networks with this configuration were ineffective, and this configuration alone could explain fifty per cent of all ineffective networks.

As for the interpretation of these results, the first fsQCA analysis revealed the interesting impact of network centralization on effectiveness. In this context, a network is very likely to be effective if it has sufficient resources, high SES and low centralization, and this is also consistent with the regression analysis in that a lower level of network centralization is favourable for effectiveness. This finding, however, conflicts with other studies that suggest a positive relationship between centralization and effectiveness (Jennings and Ewalt 1998; Provan and Milward 1995), including the study by Raab, Mannak and Cambré (2015) described earlier. According to these studies, central organizations can better coordinate other organizations to overcome fragmentation and increase efficiency. The author, however, notes that the negative relationship between centralization and effectiveness does not necessarily invalidate previous findings, but rather calls for a re-examination of the relationship. The size of networks may be an important factor to moderate the relationship (Provan and Kenis 2008; Provan and Milward 1995; Provan and Sebastian 1998): the governance networks under study are small, so organizations have little problem with handling all possible links. The type of networks – and the policy domain where they operate – may also moderate the relationship between network integration and effectiveness. Previous studies, including Raab, Mannak and Cambré (2015), have focused mainly on service-providing networks, and specifically on crime-prevention networks in the case of Raab, Mannak and Cambré. Another important piece of interpretation relates to the fact that a common causal path identified by the two fsQCA analyses is the combination of network stability and resource munificence. With this configuration, neither density-based integration nor centralized integration was relevant; this suggests that the combination of resource and stability can offset some negative effects deriving from a lack of dense collaborative relationships.

Opportunities and challenges of QCA in network research: the path forward

In light of the above-mentioned considerations, it is clear how configurational thinking and the QCA method can help to move forward our understanding of public networks. As the above-mentioned study by Wang (2016) shows, QCA may also be fruitfully used in combination with other techniques for those scholars wishing to adopt a mixed-methods approach. For instance, Fischer (2011) notes the benefits from combining QCA with Social Network Analysis (SNA) (Chapter 9 in this volume): quantitative social network data on individual cases and their relations at the micro-level can be used to describe the structure of the network that these cases constitute at the macro-level; different network structures can then be compared by using QCA. This approach allows to add a component of causal explanation to SNA, while SNA indicators allow for a systematic description of the cases to be analysed through QCA. As the papers we analysed in the previous section show, it is, in particular, the shift toward a new concept of causality that helps in enhancing theoretical and empirical knowledge on public networks, as QCA allows researchers to look at the following important questions in network research from a different perspective.

Which combinations of factors can lead to network success?

Since the beginning of the 1990s, network scholars have been committed to finding the predictors of network success. Factors related to network context, structure, functioning and management have been identified. Recently, scholars have started to think that those factors can operate in conjunction, and that different managerial factors can be necessary to achieve network success in different structural and contextual network settings. The principle of *conjunctional causation* helps to shed light on these aspects.

Which alternative paths can lead to network success?

The principle 'one size does fit all' is increasingly being challenged by both scholars and practitioners. They are increasingly convinced that different factors can be equally able to lead to network success under different circumstances, and that factors leading to success are not necessarily the opposite of those leading to failure. The principles of equifinality and asymmetric causation help in this endeavour.

How do personal relationships among people working for partner organizations combine with relationships at the network or subnetwork level to achieve network success? Networks are constellations of factors at multiple levels of analysis. Scholars are increasingly convinced that the functioning of relationships among organizations is influenced by personal relationships among people working for those organizations. The principle of multiple conjunctional causation allows to look for answers to these questions. An example of such integration of factors at different levels is the study by Bensaou and Venkatraman (1995), who relied on cluster analysis to uncover configurations of inter-organizational relationships in the United States and Japanese car industries. Here the authors considered, among other variables, uncertainty at the environmental, partnership and task level. Similar studies can be conducted also in public settings by using QCA or a mixed-methods approach.

On top of this, set-theoretic methods and QCA allow to put forward network research with new research designs. Case study research can be conducted in a way that is both methodologically rigorous and also able to offer new insights relative to traditional methods. Set theoretic methods can be used to analyse quantitative data as well as qualitative evidence contained in the narratives that often accompany case studies; QCA can also be relied upon as a meta-analysis tool to examine case studies (Fiss 2009). As a method, it was born to treat intermediate-n samples (five to fifty cases), but researchers increasingly use it also for large-n studies (Ragin and Fiss 2007; Raab, Lemaire and Provan 2013) or as part of a mixed-methods approach to complement traditional variable-based analysis (Wang 2016).

An important way forward lies in the study of configurations across levels of analysis (Fiss 2009), reaching across the individual, organizational and supra-organizational levels. Networks especially, combine features, actions and relations that take place at these different levels and which jointly contribute to the production of outcomes. As described earlier, several recent studies explore the determinants of network outcomes, such as performance and effectiveness. Future efforts could focus attention on more specific outcomes that may be of particular interest to policy-makers and public administrators, such as knowledge transfer, innovation, equity and so on. These outcomes could be fruitfully explained not through models of singular causation, but through configurations of variables, which assume complex causation.

Finally, future directions for network studies may also benefit from certain considerations that have been proposed for organizations in general (Fiss 2009). Many organizational phenomena are constituted by configurations of configurations; this is especially true within networks, with their entanglements of individuals and organizations and their relations at multiple levels that may also lead to sub-groups within the wider network. This phenomenon where a whole takes the same form as its parts is called self-similarity in complexity theory; configurations of conditions at the level of individual organizations may resemble configurations of network-level conditions, for example when they relate to relations, interactions, governance forms and so on. Possible connections between network and organization theory, on one hand, and complexity theory (Koliba et al. 2016), on the other, could be explored through case studies analysed through a configurational approach. Lastly, most existing research focuses on static rather than dynamic configurations. A few studies of public sector networks based on a configurational approach actually try to capture certain dynamic dimensions, for instance when they measure network *stability* by looking at the entrance or exit of important organizations to and from the network, the permanence of network coordination and the impact of internal or external changes on the network (Raab, Mannak and Cambré 2015). The additional step of tracking configurations over time would be challenging, but it would also increase our understanding of organizational phenomena in and around networks and organizations.

Notes

1 We will mainly rely on csQCA, as this sequence is similar for the other techniques (fsQCA and mvQCA); specificities that pertain to the other two techniques can be found, for instance, in Cronqvist and Berg-Schlosser 2009, Rihoux and De Meur 2009 and Ragin 2009.
2 For an overview of all the software used in QCA visit the COMPASSs website: www.compasss.org.
3 Some studies use the tilde sign (~) to indicate negation or absence of a condition, but we have adopted the same approach across all the examples to facilitate readability.

References

Bensaou, M. and N. Venkatraman. 1995. "Configurations of interorganizational relationships: A comparison between US and Japanese automakers." *Management Science* 41 (9): 1471–1492.

Cristofoli, D. and J. Markovic. 2016. "How to make public networks really work: A Qualitative Comparative Analysis." *Public Administration* 94: 89–110.

Cronqvist, L. and D. Berg-Schlosser. (2009). "Multi-value QCA (mvQCA)." *Configurational Comparative Methods: Qualitative Comparative Analysis (QCA) and Related Techniques* 51: 69–86.

Fischer, M. 2011. "Social network analysis and Qualitative Comparative Analysis: Their mutual benefit for the explanation of policy network structures." *Methodological Innovations Online* 6 (2): 27–51.

Fiss, P.C. 2007. "A set-theoretic approach to organizational configurations." *The Academy of Management Review* 32 (4): 1180–1198.

Fiss, P.C. 2009. "Case studies and the configurational analysis of organizational phenomena." In *The SAGE handbook of case-based methods*, edited by D. Byrne and C.C. Ragin. London: Sage Publications.

Fiss, P.C. 2011. "Building better causal theories: A fuzzy set approach to typologies in organization research." *Academy of Management Journal* 54 (2): 393–420.

Fiss, P.C., A. Marx and B. Cambré. 2013. "Configurational theory and methods in organizational research: Introduction." In *Configurational theory and methods in organizational research*

(Research in the sociology of organizations), Vol. 38, edited by A. Marx, B. Cambre, and P.C. Fiss, 1–22. Bingley, UK: Emerald.

Greckhamer, T., V.F. Misangyi, H. Elms, and R. Lacey. 2008. "Using Qualitative Comparative Analysis in strategic management research: An examination of combinations of industry, corporate, and business-unit effects." *Organizational Research Methods* 11: 695–726.

Greckhamer, T., V.F. Misangyi, and P.C. Fiss. 2013. "The two QCAs: From a small-N to a large-N set theoretic approach." In *Configurational theory and methods in organizational research (Research in the sociology of organizations)*, Vol. 38, edited by A. Marx, B. Cambre, and P.C. Fiss, 49–75. Bingley, UK: Emerald.

Herranz Jr, J. 2010. "Multilevel performance indicators for multisectoral networks and management." *The American Review of Public Administration* 40 (4): 445–460.

Jennings Jr, E.T. and J.A.G. Ewalt. 1998. "Interorganizational coordination, administrative consolidation, and policy performance." *Public Administration Review* 58 (5): 417–428.

Keast, R. and M.P. Mandell. 2013. "Network performance: A complex interplay of form and action." *International Review of Public Administration* 18 (2): 27–45.

Kitchener, M., M. Beynon, and C. Harrington. 2002. "Qualitative Comparative Analysis and public services research: Lessons from an early application." *Public Management Review* 4 (4): 485–504.

Koliba, C., L. Gerrts, M-L. Rhodes, and J. Meek. 2016. "Complexity theory, networks and systems analysis." *Handbook on theories of governance*, edited by C. Ansell and F. Torfing, 364–379. Cheltenham, UK: Edward Elgar Publishing.

Marx, A. 2010. "Crisp-Set Qualitative Comparative Analysis (csQCA) and model specification: Benchmarks for future csQCA applications." *International Journal of Multiple Research Approaches* 4: 138–158.

Meyer, A.D., A.S. Tsui, and C.R. Hinings. 1993. "Configurational approaches to organizational analysis." *Academy of Management Journal* 36 (6): 1175–1195.

Provan, K.G. and P. Kenis. 2008. "Modes of network governance: Structure, management, and effectiveness." *Journal of Public Administration Research and Theory* 18 (2): 229–252.

Provan, K.G. and B.H. Milward. 1995. "A preliminary theory of interorganizational network effectiveness: A comparative study of four community mental health systems." *Administrative Science Quarterly* 40 (1): 1–33.

Provan, K.G. and B.H. Milward. 2001. "Do networks really work? A framework for evaluating public sector organizational networks." *Public Administration Review* 61: 414–423.

Provan, K.G. and J.G. Sebastian. 1998. "Networks within networks: Service link overlap, organizational cliques, and network effectiveness." *Academy of Management Journal* 41 (4): 453–463.

Raab, J., R.H. Lemaire, and K.G. Provan. 2013. "The configurational approach in organizational network research." In *Configurational theory and methods in organizational research (research in the sociology of organizations)*, Vol. 38, edited by A. Marx, B. Cambre, and P.C. Fiss, 225–253. Bingley, UK: Emerald.

Raab, J., R.S. Mannak, and B. Cambré. 2015. "Combining structure, governance, and context: A configurational approach to network effectiveness." *Journal of Public Administration Research Theory* 25 (2): 479–511.

Ragin, C. 1987. *The comparative method: Moving beyond qualitative and quantitative strategies.* Berkeley: The University of California Press.

Ragin, C. 2000. *Fuzzy-set social science.* Chicago, IL: University of Chicago Press.

Ragin, C. 2006. "Set relations in social research: Evaluating their consistency and coverage." *Political Analysis* 14: 291–310.

Ragin, C. 2008. *Redesigning social inquiry: Fuzzy sets and beyond.* Chicago, IL: University of Chicago Press.

Ragin, C. 2009. *Redesigning social inquiry: Fuzzy sets and beyond.* Chicago: University of Chicago Press.

Ragin, C. and P.C. Fiss. 2007. *Fuzzy set policy analysis.* Tucson, Arizona: University of Arizona.

Ragin, C., K.A. Drass, and S. Davey. 2006. *Fuzzy-Set/Qualitative Comparative Analysis 2.0.* Tucson, Arizona: Department of Sociology, University of Arizona.

Rihoux, B. and B. Lobe. 2009. "The case for Qualitative Comparative Analysis (QCA): Adding leverage for thick cross-case comparison." In *The SAGE handbook of case-based methods,* edited by D. Byrne and C.C. Ragin. London: Sage Publications.

Rihoux, B. and C. Ragin. 2009. *Configurational comparative methods: Qualitative Comparative Analysis (QCA) and related techniques.* Los Angeles, CA: Sage Publications.

Rihoux, B. and G. De Meur. (2009). Crisp-set Qualitative Comparative Analysis (csQCA). *Configurational Comparative Methods: Qualitative Comparative Analysis (QCA) and Related Techniques* 51: 33–68.

Schneider, C.Q. and C. Wagemann. 2010. "Standards of good practice in Qualitative Comparative Analysis (QCA) and fuzzy-sets." *Comparative Sociology* 9 (3): 397–418.

Schwellnus, G. 2013. "Eliminating the influence of irrelevant cases on the consistency and coverage of necessary and sufficient conditions in fuzzy-set QCA." Paper presented at the 7th ECPR General Conference, Bordeaux, 4–7 September 2013.

Urueña, A. and A. Hidalgo. 2016. "Successful loyalty in e-complaints: FsQCA and structural equation modeling analyses." *Journal of Business Research* 69 (4): 1384–1389.

Verweij, S., E.-H. Klijn, J. Edelenbos, and A. Van Buuren. 2013. "What makes governance networks work? A fuzzy set Qualitative Comparative Analysis of 14 Dutch spatial planning projects." *Public Administration* 91: 1035–1055.

Wang, W. 2016. "Exploring the determinants of network effectiveness: The case of neighborhood governance networks in Beijing." *Journal of Public Administration Research Theory* 26 (2): 375–388.

11 Using agent-based models to study network and collaborative governance

Christopher Koliba, Asim Zia and Scott Merrill

Introduction

The use of computational models to study the relationship between networks, collaboration, policy outcomes and performance will continue to gain traction in the coming years. Although a variety of computational modelling approaches have been used in these regards (including social network models, system dynamics (SD) models and dynamic discrete-event models), we focus on the use of agent-based modelling in this chapter. Beginning with some background on the origins and early applications of agent-based models (ABMs) to study social phenomena, we pay particular attention to the uses of ABMs to study the emergence of the kind of collaborative and network governance phenomena that are the focus of this book. Although there are many computational modelling platforms to choose from, ABMs are particularly interesting because they enable us to generate the emergent phenomena resulting from networks and collaborations from the bottom-up interactions of agents.

Agent-based models are computer models that allow autonomous agents, such as individuals, groups or organizational actors to act and interact with each other and their wider environments. As a result, networks of agents are simulated to create experiments to study the internal and external drivers of change and stability. When applied to matters of public policy and public administration, ABMs are particularly well-suited to study how networks of individuals and institutions interact to address particular governance designs, public policy analysis, public service delivery or common-pool resource management problems and needs. The ability to model agents as non-social actors (planned projects, built and natural infrastructure, etc.), as well, adds an additional capacity, allowing for models in which social actors engage with, and are shaped by, non-social objects. The non-social objects can be physically presented, like buildings and facilities, projects, segments of infrastructure, parcels of land and ecological features. Moreover, ABMs allow us to undertake empirically derived pattern validation (Grimm et al. 2005), in which model behaviours are evaluated in relation to patterns of behaviour observed in actual social-ecological-technical systems.

Origins and early uses of ABMs

ABMs are a class of computer simulation models that broadly fall under 'objected-oriented programming' domains. The first computer simulation models that served as the precursor of contemporary ABMs were developed during World War II as part of the race to develop nuclear weapons. In order to simulate what was a difficult, if not impossible at the time, task to conduct live field experiments, Jon Von Neumann and Stanislaw Ulam used computer models to study the behaviour of neutrons using 'cellular automata' theory in a simulated setting. With the successful employment of computational modelling to simulate physical phenomena, like subatomic particles, industry, business and academia eventually caught on to the use of computer-aided models to conduct simulated 'experiments' on subject matter that was not easily manipulated or controlled, or too complex, or ethically or practically inaccessible for simple field experiments.

Widespread adoption of computer simulations took a number of decades to materialize. It was not until the 1960s when the first batch computer systems were advanced using punch cards that large-scale and faster processing of data made it feasible for businesses, industry and academia to consider using simulations as a viable method for planning, research and development. Those early batch-system simulations were pioneered by IBM and focused on weather prediction for aviation. Thomas Schelling presented one of the first applications of dynamic modelling in his classic 1971 article looking at racial segregation, demonstrating the power of simulations to uncover dynamic patterns of social arrangements that, in this case, highlighted the underlying inequities of systemic operation. It was not until the 1990s that the ability to build and run simulations became widespread.

Although many interesting and important ABMs have been developed that have not been parameterized or calibrated using empirical data, most notably Axelrod's (1997a) early prisoner's dilemma simulations and Joshua Epstein and Rob Axtell's (1996) Sugarscape model, we focus here on a certain class of ABMs, namely 'empirically based' ABMs (Janssen and Ostrom 2006), which are calibrated to empirically derived data sources.

Since the earliest applications of questions of public policy and public administration, ABMs have been used to advance theory (Axelrod and Hamilton 1984; Epstein and Axtell 1996; Dean et al. 2006) and specific policy objectives (Schelling 1971). Axelrod first conducted a simulation experiment using the prisoner's dilemma framework (see his classic *Evolution of Cooperation;* Axelrod and Hamilton 1984). By testing what had been historically a one-shot prisoner's game as an 'iterated' game of multiple interactions between agents, Axelrod uncovered an important pattern of interaction – the 'tit-for-tat' strategy – that has since formed a basic tenet of cooperation and negotiation theory and practice. Commenting on the value of Axelrod's contribution to cooperation theory, Martinez-Coll and Hirshleifer observed that, "the simple reciprocity behavior known as tit-for-tat is a best strategy not only in the particular environment modelled by Axelrod's simulations but quite generally. Or still more sweepingly, that tit-for-tat can provide the basis for co-operation in complex social interaction among humans" (1997a: 37).

Lansing and Kremer (1993) constructed an ABM to simulate the governance of Balinese irrigation systems. Their model included a set of agents physically located on the empirically observed landscape comprised of catchment basin weirs, subaks (parcels of rice-paddy production) and water temples (regional coordination institutions). These structures were spatially situated and linked together through the observed network of rivers, streams and canals. Water temples served as regional coordinating mechanisms and were a common form of irrigation system governance in the observed regions. A basic hydrology model to simulate the flow of water was attached to the geospatial two-dimensional grid. Lansing and Kremer calibrated their model to observed, actual harvest rates, yielding a Pearson's product–moment correlation $r = .90$ (Lansing and Kremer 1993). With the model calibrated, scenarios were generated using several different scales of social coordination – ranging from whole watershed level, to water temple (sub-watershed) levels, to subak (parcel); that is, the name associated with water management for paddy fields – levels of coordination. Lansing and Kremer concluded that if each subak acted on its own self-interest (e.g. to maximize their own water use during critical moments of paddy production), the whole system responds chaotically: the governance of the common-pool resource (water) falls apart. The persistence of 'water temple networks' (which are subwatershed-level coordinating institutions), was viewed as serving as the critical element in keeping the whole system at the watershed level in some form of equilibrium, even during periods of water scarcity. In essence, the institutions for collective action to have emerged in ancient Balinese societies to coordinate irrigation systems likely emerged as a latent property of self-organization. The policy implications drawn from Lansing and Kremer's model are particularly compelling. Steve Lansing drew on the results of the model to support efforts to declare the Balinesian Water Temple System a UNESCO World Heritage Site in 2013.

Axelrod (1997b) later created an ABM to study globalization, concluding that local convergences among culturally approximate states can lead to global polarizations. In this model, the agents in the model are artificial nation-states that possess specific cultural characteristics. The resulting social influence model has been an important step in modelling of social contagion applied at larger, institutional and national scales.

Epstein and Axtell's (1996) 'Sugarscape' ABM was designed to study the relationship between the basic needs and utility of social agents, and their production and consumption of 'sugar' and 'spice', arranged in an unequally distributed two-dimensional geospatial grid. Their model built upon one of the most widely regarded modelling configurations in agent-based modelling: cellular automata. Dean et al.'s (2006) ABM of the evolution of the Anasazi culture from 900 to 1300 AD is one of the most famous ABMs developed by social scientists. Agents in this model were household agents capable of making planting and harvesting decisions, possessive of fertility rates, grain storage capacities and age. The model was calibrated to archaeological data known about the stages of development of the Anasazi culture within one geographically explicit 'Long House Valley'. The model provides one of the earliest robust and calibrated ABMs, illustrating the interactions between social agents with specific demographics, environmental factors and processes of sociocultural stability, variation and change (Dean et al. 2006: 113).

These early examples of ABMs applied to the study of social systems demonstrated the promise and potential of the method. This potential exists because ABMs, 'allow explicit consideration of changes in the behavior of individual actors that arise from perceived changes in the natural or social environment. ABMs have the advantage that social and institutional relations between human actors can be represented at different scales' (Schlüter and Pahl-Wostl 2007: 2). Epstein observes that ABMs, 'permit one to study how rules of individual behavior give rise – or "map to" – the macroscopic regularities and organizations' (2006: 4). ABM is currently 'the only technique available today to formalize models based on micro-foundations, such as agents' beliefs and behavior and social interactions, all aspects that we know are of a certain importance to understand macro outcomes' (Squazzoni and Boero 2010: 6), particularly in relation to policy issues. The discovery of the emergent properties of larger networks from the micro-level interactions of individual nodes continues to serve as the holy grail for agent-based modellers. While, more practically, agent-based modelling now has an established history of providing insights into decision-making across many scales and types of social actors (Eckerd 2013: 285).

Modelling the 'emergent' patterns of networks

Miller and Page (2007) describe modelling as an, 'attempt to reduce the world to a fundamental set of elements (equivalent classes) and laws (transition functions), and on this basis . . . understand and predict key aspects of the world' (40). They go on to add that, 'Modeling proceeds by deciding what simplifications to impose on the underlying entities and then, based on those abstractions, uncovering their implications' (65). The effort to translate a conceptual model into an adequate simulation of real-world phenomenon ultimately requires grounding model development, parameterization and calibration in some observed phenomenon, preferably using empirically validated data to set model parameters and test the efficacy of model outputs against observed patterns (Grimm et al. 2005; Janssen and Ostrom 2006). Parameterization occurs when specific classes of critical elements of the system are defined into parameters (often represented as algorithms). Parameters can be understood as the variables used to construct a 'strategy space' in which agents interact with each other. Such strategy spaces have been described as the game board or multidimensional grid of a simulation. Calibration occurs when the measured values and outputs of the simulation are compared to some empirically observable data or validated statistical model.

Parametric calibration occurs when empirical data are used to validate specific parametric patterns.

As a form of object-oriented modelling, the first major feature of all ABMs are 'agents' that may be construed as social actors (individuals, animals, groups of individuals, organizations), physical or natural objects (atoms, buildings, commodities, built and natural infrastructure, stars and galaxies) or socially constructed, but reified objects of organized activities (programs, projects or processes). Agent behaviours are parameterized using fixed-variable values. Clusters of fixed sets of parameters form the basis of certain classes of agents in which agents of similar type will possess specific common characteristics. Social agents may be endowed with certain gender, age, ethnicity, wealth and so on. Organizational agents may possess certain human resource capacity, financial resources, missions, objectives, sectorial characteristics and so on. Project agents may possess fixed resources or resource needs. Physical or natural agents, such as buildings and facilities or parcels of land, may carry specific physical or natural characteristics. Agent parameters may also be variable and subject to manipulation by the modeller to render specific scenarios. For instance, a social agent may possess more or less risk-aversion, more or less social affinity, more or less propensity to maximize utility and so on. These varying behaviours lead to decisions that, in turn, have an effect on other agents and other aspects of the modelled environment. Under certain circumstances, agents may grow in size and influence, lose power and influence, 'die,' 'end,' change form or properties. Computationally, each agent possesses its own set of attributes (often produced from an excel or batch file), as well as a 'state chart' – similar to a flow chart that lays out the scope and sequence of decision-making and process flows. Agent behaviour may be programmed to exhibit memory, path-dependence and hysteresis, non-Markovian behaviour or temporal corrections, including learning and adapting (Bonabeau 2002: 7280).

A second major feature of an ABM is that agents interact with each other. These relationships often take the form of network ties or through some kind of spatial proximities – meaning that if an agent is adjacent or linked to another agent it may exert some measure of influence over that agent. The actions of one agent can serve as inputs into the decision or actions of another agent, sometimes directly and most likely at a larger, aggregated scale. In this manner, '[a]gent interactions are heterogeneous and can generate network effects' (Bonabeau 2002: 7280). These network effects are shaped tie characteristics (e.g. administrative arrangements, the types of capital resource flowing across tied and accountability structures).

A third major feature of an ABM lies in the ability to run scenarios or experiments that are generated through changes made to specific parameters or entire suites of parameters. The parameters may appear as 'sliders' in a user interface that can be fashioned as 'dashboards' for undertaking scenario development. Simulation 'experiments' may be run to ascertain the impact that changes to certain parameters play in shaping model outputs. By running and comparing these 'what if' scenarios as experiments, interesting policy analysis, theory testing and theory tuning may take place (Koliba and Zia 2015).

Contemporary examples of governance and policy-focused ABMs

Although there is a growing body of literature employing empirically-based ABMs to study public policy, service delivery systems and common-pool resource governance, we highlight several models for deeper examination in this chapter. These examples include models looking at the governance of water resources (Lansing and Kremer 1993; Janssen 2007; Schlüter and Pahl-Wostl 2007); environmental hazard mitigation and economic justice (Eckerd 2013; Eckerd et al. 2012), school choice and institutional capacity (Maroulis 2016); patterns of fraud in public service delivery networks (Kim, Zhong and Chun 2013); and the impact of equity and resource scarcity and flux on transportation project prioritization in intergovernmental settings (Zia and Koliba 2013). Each model possesses networked agents operating at different scales, parameterized using at least some empirical data, and poses a number of scenarios to build understanding of important public policy or common-pool resource management issues.

Schluter and Pahl-Wostl's model of the governance of water resources in the Amu Darya river basin

Another ABM built to study the governance of water resources was Schlüter and Pahl-Wostl's (2007) effort to simulate the resilience of different water-management institutions to changes in environmental conditions in a semi-arid Amu Darya river basin in Central Asia. This model is partitioned into subsystems: social, water resource, irrigation and aquatic ecosystems. The irrigation and aquatic ecosystems are geospatially explicit hydrological models that simulate the flow of water across the observed aquafer. The hydrology model takes into account the role that irrigation infrastructure plays in managing the flow of water in the region. The hydrology portion of the model was calibrated with historic water flow data. The agents in this model are land owners and land managers (construed as farmers in the model) who are influenced by, but not dictated by, water resource allocation decisions from a national authority 'government' agent. As is the case in most AMBs of social actors, the decision heuristics of the farmer agents and the government agent are developed from assumptions derived from decision theory (particularly Simon's (1955) notion of bounded rationality and utility maximization common in neo-classical micro economics). Schluter and Pahl-Wostl then ran several 'centralized' and 'decentralized' scenarios in which farmer water resource management decisions are more or less influenced by 'national authority' agents (see Figure 11.1). In this manner, their ABM offers another operationalization of complex, common-pool resource dynamics. In the centralization scenarios the national authority possessed a system-level knowledge of water resources and used this information

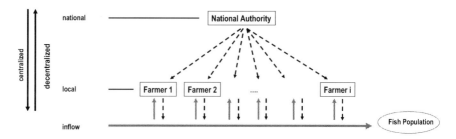

Figure 11.1 Modelling centralized and decentralized decision-making

Source: Schlüter and Pahl-Wostl 2007; reprinted ith permission

to influence farmer irrigation decisions. While in the decentralized scenarios farmers make decisions based on only their 'local' knowledge.

Their model demonstrates the impact that the decision-making architecture of a prevailing network has in mitigating water resource scarcities, with them concluding that, '[m]odel outputs suggest that the governance structure expressed in the two governance regimes: centralization and decentralization, has a significant effect on the resilience of the coupled [human-natural] system' (Schlüter and Pahl-Wostl 2007: 17).

Eckerd et al.'s model of hazardous waste remediation

ABMs have been constructed to examine the relationship between structural inequities, racial injustice and environmental degradation. Eckerd, Campbell and Kim (2012) and Eckerd (2013) developed an ABM to study equity in relation to hazardous-site remediation. Their model examines the environmental justice consequences of decision-making around the selection of hazardous sites for remediation. In their model a population of residents possess similar preferences for living in close proximities to people like themselves. Another key parameter in the model is the use of location preferences for placing high-polluting industries near minority populations and a series of choices for prioritizing hazardous sites for remediation. Hazardous waste sites are objects in the ABM. In this manner they modelled the relationship between clusters of residential patterns, location of hazardous waste sites and the selection of sites for remediation project prioritization. Policy scenarios using three different priority decisions were run based on the variable influence of economic pressure, environmental justice and risk-elimination preferences. The results of the ABM provided new insights into the persistent patterns of placement of hazardous waste sites near minority populations – and types of equity – efficiency trade-offs that are likely to recur unless targeted policies are directed at remediating sites near high-minority population areas. In this manner, Eckerd, Campbell and Kim's model demonstrates how the physical distribution of populations and hazardous waste is related to the types of decisions made by policy-makers and public administrators with resource allocation discretion. In another use of the model, Kim, Campbell and Eckerd (2014) focused on experimentation with population mobility and racial segregation in relation to the placement of hazardous-waste sites. In this context, their model simulates the geospatial proximity of residents and hazardous-waste sites, in what we may construe as networks, which are shaped by policy and resource-allocation decisions. In this model those decision-making bodies were treated as exogenous features of the model.

Maroulis' model of public and private school district governance in Chicago

ABMs have also been used to study the institutional capacity of public service delivery networks. Maroulis (2016) constructed an ABM of school choice treatment effects using data from the Chicago Public School District. This study follows in a line of ABMs used to simulate school district-level outcomes using the 'micro-level' behaviours of students and parents (Maroulis et al. 2010; Maroulis et al. 2014). Key parameters in this study were the preference functions of students, who rated schools by geographic proximity and student achievement levels. Students and schools were distributed to represent the geography of the city of Chicago and were simulated as agents in the model. Maroulis ran a series of policy scenarios to determine the extent to which allowing for students to choose schools, limiting student choice through lottery systems, or simply allowing for students to attend the nearest school. The individual student 'mean achievement' was tracked over time, as the model simulates the flow of students between schools of varying proclivities to foster student achievement. Drawing on data from Chicago public schools, real student achievement scores were used to calibrate the model. Maroulis was able present a more complex understanding of the relationship between student choice and student achievement by considering the capacity of the educational infrastructure to sustain and support an educational system built to enable student choice. This would require the ability to open and close schools based on the 'market' of students. In this manner, he was able to run experiments regarding what he labels 'district capacity' (which could alternatively be labelled as institutional design). He was able to compare optimal district capacity and current district capacity and concluded that the initial conditions of the existing capacity are likely to have a big impact on the relative success of school-choice programs. Specifically, he found this to be the case when lottery treatment mechanisms were used to ration students to higher-performing private schools. In a network context, Maroulis' model draws on a geospatially configured set of network relationships between students and schools modelled after the Chicago school district.

Kim et al.'s governance of fraudulent exchange model

Tackling the problem of fraudulent benefit exchanges in public service delivery networks, Kim (2007) and Kim, Zhong and Chun (2013) created an ABM to simulate the relationship between public agencies, third parties, contracted

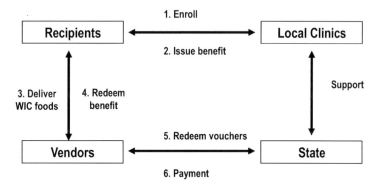

Figure 11.2 Operation of the Ohio WIC program

Source: Kim 2012; reprinted with permission

service venders and recipients. The model was parameterized with fixed variables regarding the number of public agencies, vendors and recipients (see Figure 11.2), with variable 'risk propensities' of venders and recipients as variable parameters of the model, in addition to a range of percentage of fraudulent venders and variable speed with which venders are sanctioned by the public agency. 'Fraudulent exchanges' of public benefits occur in the model when both vender and recipient want to exchange benefits fraudulently. The model is able to simulate the role that sanction rates (from 0% to 10% of fraudulent venders sanctioned), and variability of when, across a time series, sanctions are issued. The simulated environment covered a two-dimensional 201 x 201 grid.

Kim et al. found that even modest sanction levels improved deterrent rates of fraudulent behaviour (2013), justifying the value of deterrence theory in reproach to criminal activity (Cooter and Ulen 2007). The network structure of this ABM included a network of venders, public agencies and recipients. Although this ABM is not calibrated to empirical data, this model does shed new light into the roles that specific governance and regulatory actors can play in bringing about stronger legal compliance.

Zia and Koliba's intergovernmental transportation project prioritization model

In an ABM of the transportation prioritization process used by a state Agency of Transportation (AOT), regional planning organizations and local municipalities, Zia and Koliba (2013) modelled the decision-making process of the network agents responsible for prioritizing roadway construction projects. This ABM modelled the intergovernmental network of institutional actors responsible for making transportation project prioritization (TPP) decisions. Specific roadway project proposals were identified as agents as well, and parameterized using construction and planning costs, and evaluation standards rendered by state and

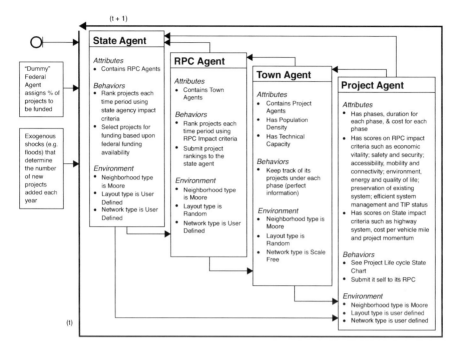

Figure 11.3 Nested structure of intergovernmental model

Source: Zia and Koliba 2013; reprinted with permission

regional agents. This model was designed to test specific institutional designs using data from the observed multi-criteria objective functions used by the transportation prioritization network. The ABM was organized as a series of nested agents (see Figure 11.3), with municipal agents nested in regional agents that were, in turn, nested in the state agent.

Historical data from the state AOT were used to calibrate the model. Drawing on the scoring data of all transportation roadway project prioritization over a period of ten years, a state chart of the decision-making process used to prioritize projects was constructed (see Figure 11.4). The actual state-level and regional-level decision-making criteria, as scored in their asset management programs, were used to calibrate the model. Regional priority, cost per vehicle mile and highway management criteria were scored and weighted to determine the type and location of roadway projects.

Each project has its own 'state chart', a flow chart illustrating the sequence of decision-making that each project undertakes (see Figure 11.4).

The decision heuristics of the state and regional agents used in Zia and Koliba (2013) were parameterized using the breakdown of weighted criteria found in Table 11.1. The parameters listed in the left-hand column are those employed by the state AOT agent. The regional priority parameter is, itself, informed by

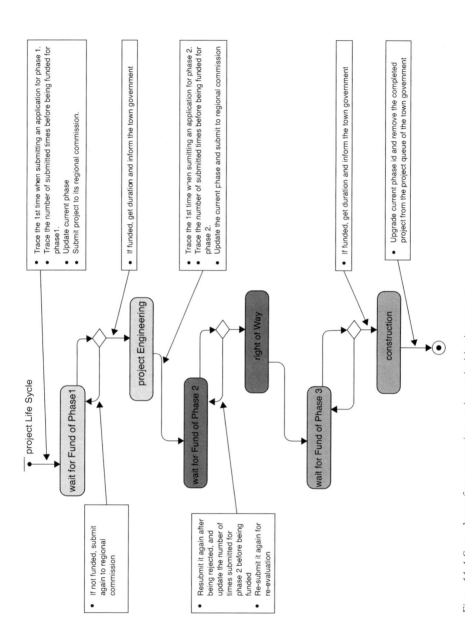

Figure 11.4 State chart of transportation project prioritization process

Source: Zia and Koliba 2013; reprinted with permission

Table 11.1 Parametric values for six alternative scenarios

Parameter	Scenario 1 (Baseline)	Scenario 2 (Regionalization)	Scenario 3 (Cost-effective)	Scenario 4 (Funding flux)	Scenario 5 (Sequestration)	Scenario 6 (Sequestration with shocks)
Weight on regional proximity	0.2	0.5	0.2	0.2	0.2	0.2
Weight on highway system	0.4	0.1	0.1	0.4	0.4	0.4
Weight on cost per vehicle mile	0.2	0.2	0.5	0.2	0.2	0.2
Weight on project momentum	0.2	0.2	0.2	0.2	0.2	0.2
% of projects funded each year	0.1 (10%)	0.1 (10%)	0.1 (10%)	0.3 (30%)	0.05 (5%)	0.05 (5%)
Number of new projects added each year	30	30	30	30	30	40

*Source:*Zia and Koliba 2013

the scoring preferences of regional and local government agents. Scenarios 1 through 6 present the different weighting schemes that presume a baseline, regionalization, cost-effective, funding flux, sequestration and sequestration and shock scenarios.

The availability of resources was structured as an exogenous feature of the model, with monies flowing into the state AOT from an outside (federal) source. The availability of these funds could be varied to simulate funding flux, sequestration, and sequestration and shock scenarios. Scenarios were also run by increasing the levels of influence of regional and local actors (see Table 11.1). Inequities in the distribution of resources across regions were apparent. A 'dashboard' interface used in the model was constructed to allow stakeholders and researchers to play with the model.

The sample of ABMs reviewed here provides insights into the different ways that ABMs have been developed to study collaborative and network governance arrangements. The ABMs highlighted here focus on a variety of different policy domains: watershed management, the citing and remediation of hazardous-waste sites, school district capacity to deliver education, fraud across social service delivery networks, and TPP – all of which require collaborative and network governance. Across these examples we find agents defined as water managers and government regulators (Schlüter and Pahl-Wostl 2007), residents and hazardous-waste sites (Eckerd et al. 2012), schools and students (Maroulis et al., 2010; Maroulis et al. 2014), service delivery agencies and contractors (Kim 2012), and transportation projects and intergovernmental actors (Zia and Koliba 2013). All of these models demonstrate the ability of well-constructed ABMs to examine how the interactions of heterogeneous agents generate larger scales of emergent patterns. Across these models, agent interactions form the basis of governance dynamics that, in turn, contribute to the performance or outputs of the system.

Methodological considerations

Over the last several decades, greater standardization of ABM development has emerged. The most robust approach to formatting and describing these models is Grimm et al.'s (2006) Overview, Design concepts, Details protocol (ODD). Their ODD template is organized by: purpose, entities, state variables and scales, process overview and scheduling, design concepts, initialization, input data and submodels. Müller et al. (2013) have added an additional 'D' – decision-making – to form the ODD+D protocol. The ODD + D approach provides a consistent framework to the process of building (and, as noted in the previous section, rebuilding) an ABM. Starting with an overview of the project, including the purpose for writing the model, followed by the entities and state variables of interest, and the scale at which the problem will be examined. The overview section is concluded with an overview of the process and notes about scheduling. The next major section of the ODD is design concepts, which starts with the theoretical and empirical background. This section provides many of the details necessary for writing an ABM, such as individual decision-making, learning, sensing, agent prediction, how agents are interacting, details about collectives, how variability (both through heterogeneity and stochasticity) is incorporated and, lastly, how data are observed. The last major section of the ODD is the details section, which explicitly details implementation, initialization and required input data. Thus, the ODD+D approach provides a standardized methodology allowing for scientific repeatability of the project, details of required assumptions, and thus provides a robust framework for analysis.

The process of modelling generally follows the sequence of creating an abstract or 'scoping' model of the phenomena observed. Process-tracing approaches, as found in Keast's Chapter 8 of this volume, can be used to develop initial conceptual models that can eventually lead to the construction of an ABM. The conceptualization of the initial model, particularly in the kinds of contexts and settings used to study network governance, collaboration, problem definitions, thesis statements and hypothesis testing, all feed into the setting of the *model boundaries* and *model parameters*. Very often these kinds of 'system mapping' exercises and visualizations can be used to aid modellers and stakeholders to envision the structure of the system being modelled.

In the context of empirically-based ABMs, both boundary-setting and parameterization decisions are best informed through the triangulation of many data sources, including findings from social science research, qualitative observations, surveys, focus groups, experimental games, interviews and content analysis that are integrated into the initial model design, the determination of parameters available, and the construction of a model as a series of functions between those parameters. Axelrod (2006), for one, has been a strong advocate of the uses of ABMs to bridge between disciplines. He notes how ABMs can facilitate interdisciplinary collaboration, with the modelling process and the model itself serving as a boundary object around which disciplinary frameworks combine. We have also noted earlier how ABMs are particularly amendable to integrating quantitative data drawn from more traditional methodologies. In this way, ABMs are particularly amendable to 'methodological' and 'theoretical pluralism'.

The complexity of the systems modelled by ABMs often requires the triangulation of many data sources that are both quantitative and qualitative in nature. Some modellers use initial in-depth case study analysis to determine the structures and functions of the ABM (Lansing and Kremer 1993; Schlüter and Pahl-Wostl 2007; and Zia and Koliba 2013). As Ming and Voets note in Chapter 3 of this volume, case study analysis is often used to capture the contextual complexity of systems. If critical elements of this complexity are ignored in the architecture of an ABM, the models will lose important face validity. Surveys can be used to calibrate the decision rules of actors within ABMs. For instance, Tsai et al. (2015) used farmer perception data drawn from a panel survey to calibrate a land-use governance ABM. In this manner, the types of survey methods discussed in van Meerkerk, Edelenbos and Klijn's Chapter 4 of this volume can be extremely useful in developing ABMs. Social network analysis (SNA) methods, like those outlined in Lemaire and Raab's Chapter 9 of this volume, can be used to build the foundational structures of governance of an ABM. Maroulis' (2016) ABM of the Chicago public and private school system possesses a complex network structure underlying it that relies on SNA to initialize the business-as-usual scenario of the model. We have already noted earlier in this chapter how Qualitative Comparative Analysis or QCA (see Cepiku, Cristofoli and Trivellato's Chapter 10 of this volume) and process tracing (see Keast's Chapter 8 of this volume) can be implicated in the design of governance ABMs. In sum, construction of computer simulation models will often require the use of other data sources collected using many of the methods outlined in this volume.

Issues relating to model validation

A very common adage used by modellers is the caveat that all models are wrong, but some are useful (Box 1979). That all models are some approximation of observed reality calls for us to acknowledge the major analytical challenges facing those employing ABMs to study collaborative and network governance. For example, are input variables and parameters empirically relevant and meaningful, and rendered at the appropriate scale? Are the modelled processes calibrated to a scale that is appropriate for the study? 'Are the model outputs capable of generating reasonably accurate forecasts or predictions?'

Many of these challenges can be overcome in pattern-oriented and empirically validated ABMs with the integration of quality data, both for initial parameterization and for model validation. Empirically based ABMs are 'data hungry'. Deep consideration needs to be given to the data used to initialize ABMs and to calibrate them. In some cases, parameter ranges and baseline levels and rates are inferred through qualitative observations, expert opinions or other indirect approaches to account for parameters that lack empirical grounding. When data is lacking or incomplete, the validity of the ABM suffers.

However, we should note that ABMs that have not been empirically based (commonly referred to as 'toy' models), have yielded very important findings. Take, for instance, Axelrod's iterated prisoner's dilemma model. Axelrod and Hamilton's agents were generated through game theory logic (1984), yet universal patterns of tit-for-tat emerged from the micro-level decisions of simulated agents. Similarly, social contagion and cellular automata agent behaviours are inferred based on the prevailing theoretical assumptions.

Louie and Carley (2008) discuss validity issues in ABMs and discuss a useful schematic to differentiate between types of validity. 'Real-world systems', the types of empirically observed systems the subject of traditional social science methods, are best described and analysed with valid sources of and approaches to the analysis of data. In the context of empirically based ABMs, conceptual (scoping) and computational models are also validated through the collection and analysis of data. As we consider the relationship to the real system, the conceptual model and the computational model, additional types of validity may be considered.

The relationship between the real–world system and the conceptual model is described by Louie and Carley (2008) as 'conceptual model validity'. The main question driving this form of validity is: 'How closely does the conceptual model describe the basic component parts and relationship between the component parts of the system?' Conceptual model validity may be demonstrated through the use of widely accepted theoretical frameworks, as in the case of using cellular automata theory in Eckerd et al.'s (2012) model of Hazard Waste Site Remediation and in Kim's (2012) model of fraudulent public service delivery networks. Conceptual model validity may also be found in the 'thick description' of the system that is created after extensive study of the system in question, as was the case in Lansing and Kremer's (1993) Irrigation Management system and Zia and Koliba's (2013) transportation project prioritization model. In the latter case, the conceptual model was 'ground truthed' by stakeholder experts during focus groups.

Computerized model verification, or computerized model validity is rendered at the intersection of the computer and conceptual model. In empirically-based ABMs, this type of validity is achieved when a model is said to be calibrated. 'Calibration appeals to the principle that a theory is better supported when it is validated using information that is not used in it[s] formulation' (Fagiolo, Windrum and Moneta 2006:14). A calibrated model is achieved when the computer and conceptual model align with empirical data drawn from the real-world system. The internal assumptions driving the computer model (as often spelled out in state charts and relational diagrams of the conceptual model) must be computationally rendered accurately to achieve calibration. The algorithms and parameters used to model the interactions of agents must adequately generate results that are validated through empirical observation.

Fagiolo, Windrum and Moneta (2006: 7–13) identify several challenges that agent-based modellers face when attempting to empirically validate ABMs. They frame these challenges as a trade-off between analytical solvability and descriptive accuracy:

> [T]he more accurate and consistent is our knowledge about reality with respect to assumptions, and the more numerous the number of parameters in a model, the higher is the risk of failing to analytically solve the model. By contrast, the more abstract and simplified the model, the more analytically tractable it is.
>
> (10)

In this manner, ABMs have much in common with some of the kinds of more traditional methods discussed in this volume, most particularly in relation to qualitative methods. The specificity, context and contingency of models and the data needed to provide it butt up against the need to generate some generalizability through ABMs.

A key challenge in modelling human decision-making in ABMs concerns the ability to model 'creative-' and 'innovative-' thinking processes. Zia, Kauffman and Niiranen (2012) elaborate upon four specific limits of ABMs in simulating creative-thinking processes: (1) the decision rule and strategy space assignment problem; (2) the 'framing' or 'affordances' problem; (3) the problem of translation between higher level and base (Boolean) languages; and, finally, (4) the problem of choosing appropriate space-time scales for assigning decision rules to intelligent agents. To address these limitations, they propose future development of non-algorithmic information-processing systems, derived from genetic algorithms and learning classifier systems on the one hand, and Neurosciences and Neurobiology on the other hand, to simulate creative decision-making.

An additional challenge is not a conceptual or empirical one, but rather a pragmatic one. The quantitative sophistication of computer-simulation models is of critical importance to resolving the challenges of model validation. The ability to code in complex computer programming languages, coupled with the need to understand matrix algebra, differential equations and so on, can present significant barriers to the use of ABMs. However, the advancement of software programs, such as NETLOGO, MASON and ANYLOGIC, all provide more user-friendly applications to developing ABMs. In these cases, some knowledge of object-oriented programming languages, such as JAVA, is required to customize features of the model.

Improvements in ABM methodology will likely increase as new software applications and computational power increases. Improvements in graphical user interfaces with less reliance on pure programming (e.g. JAVA) should increase accessibility to a broader scientific community, which should feedback to enhance ABM methods. New versions of modelling software are coming out at regular intervals, particularly as more and more users employ the approach. With the application of neural network algorithms to model creative decision-making, learning and autocatalytic set theory, we believe we may eventually be able to anticipate how empirically observed, meso-scale collaborative and network governance systems evolve over time as a result of emergent behaviours, self-organization and adaptation. To build such models, better access to governmental and agency databases will be necessary.

Using ABMs to develop situational awareness of complex and stochastic governance systems

We argue that approaching the study of any public policy, public service delivery or common-pool resource problem through the lens of agent-based modelling presents an ontological breakthrough relative to the kinds of questions that may be posed. Instead of approaching a governance or collaborative system through a lens of reductionism (e.g. making attempts to isolate the interaction effects of specific variables, or letting oneself off the hook of needing to offer generalizations by falling back on the unique characteristics brought on by specific contexts and contingencies), approaching a complex social system through an agent-based modelling lens allows a researcher, modeller, theorist or practitioner to 'see' the system as a dynamic whole. Using ABMs we may be able to actually observe how, as the Aristotelian adage goes: 'the whole is greater than the sum of all of the parts'. The value of constructing ABMs can be found in the manifestation of the role of 'autonomous' decision-making by agents in governance networks, which can neither be aggregated in a concise empirical measure of the network, nor ignored in an accurate representation of a network. Only by explicitly representing the decision-making rules of autonomous agents can the emergent patterns of resource dynamics, and so forth, be explained. This is a hallmark of generative social science, which is assumed away in traditional empirical social science (e.g. see Epstein 2006).

A 'cognitive' turn in the ABM community is a frontier research interest. Another non-algorithmic information-processing approach could be the use of 'autocatalytic set theory' (e.g. Kauffman 1995) that could be used to develop ABMs for modelling the governance of social-ecological systems with explicit incorporation of co-evolution and resource constraints among agents in both social and ecological systems (for more details on this idea see Zia et al. 2014). As an example, Padgett, Lee and Collier (2003) developed an ABM called 'Hypercycle,' which used autocatalytic set theory to model the emergence of complex market structures from simple firm interactions, representing market competition and their coevolution in the technology sector.

ABMs may be used to consider the stochasticity of human behaviour and decision-making as they relate to networked relationships. Stochastic systems are shaped by seemingly random behaviours of particular components of, or actors in, systems. Social systems are inherently stochastic because of the existence of human agency and 'free will'. Since the early consideration of human behaviour, to the mid-twentieth century exploration of bounded rationality (Simon 1955) and incrementalism (Lindblom 1959), social scientists, and increasingly policy-makers and public managers, have been forced to consider the 'irrational' behaviours of citizens, customers and even fellow policy-makers when crafting and implementing public policies. Epstein (2006), in particular, believes that ABMs may provide an avenue for taking such 'non-rationality' into consideration. He suggests that, '[p]erhaps the main issue is not how much rationality there is (at the micro level), but how little is enough to generate the macro equilibrium' (22). Epstein goes on to add, 'in passing,' that 'fad creation' may 'be far more effective' than evidence-based decision-making, education and other attempts at making decisions rationally:

> Often, the aim is not to equip target populations with the data and analytical tools needed to make rational choices; rather, one displays exemplars and then presses for mindless imitation. . . . The manipulation of uncritical imitative impulses may be more effective in getting to a desired macro equilibrium than policies based on individual rationality. The social problem, of course, is that populations of uncritical imitators are also easy fodder for lynch mobs, witch hunts, Nazi parties, and so forth.
>
> (22)

They are also, we might add, likely to be influenced by marketing, priming and anchoring effects (Tversky and Kahneman 1981), all potential features of the propagation of information and ideas across networks. To address such complexities, ABMs that capture contagion and diffusion of innovation phenomena are needed, particularly in the current rise of nationalistic and populist leaders and political movements.

Toward the later stages of her career, Nobel Laurent, Elinor Ostrom, came to this very conclusion. Writing in 2010, she observed that:

> Scholars are slowly shifting from positing simple systems to using more complex frameworks, theories, and models to understand the diversity of puzzles and problems facing humans interacting in contemporary societies. The humans we study have complex motivational structures and establish diverse private-for-profit, governmental, and community institutional arrangements that operate at multiple scales to generate productive and innovative as well as destructive and perverse outcomes.
>
> (Ostrom 2010: 641)

Having spent several decades studying the 'polycentric' characteristics of the governance of common-pool resources, she called for the use of ABMs and game theory to explore what are likely to be the substantial relationships between institutional rule structures and individual behaviours and decisions (Ostrom 2010). She concluded that due to this complexity, we need to develop more configural approaches to the study of factors that enhance or detract from the emergence and robustness of self-organized efforts within multilevel, polycentric systems. (We should note here as well that other approaches, such as QCA, described in Cepiku, Cristofoli and Trivellato's Chapter 10 in this volume, offer other ways of studying the configural approaches to governance networks.) Ostrom advocated for the development of a common set of structural elements to develop structured coding forms for data collection and analysis. Her vision was for a community of researchers and modellers to 'design experiments using a common set of variables for many situations of interest to political economists and then examine why particular behavior and outcomes occur in some situations and not in others' (2010: 647). In one of her last publications, she concluded that agent-based modelling is a viable analytical tool to undertake this, since it enables one to examine the pattern of likely outcomes over time when agents, who have limited information, are making choices over time (Janssen 2007),' (Ostrom 2014: 25).

In addition to possessing the potential to advance our understanding of institutional and governance design, ABMs are increasingly being used as a tool to broaden the situational awareness of policy-makers, public managers and the like. Squazzoni and Boero (2010) suggest that '. . . the challenges for policy in a complex world is not to predict the future state of a given system, but to understand the system's properties and dissect its generative mechanisms and processes, so that policy decisions can be better informed and embedded within the system's behaviour, thus becoming part of it' (3). By building the capacity to undertake different policy scenarios we may possess the capacity to consider policy choices as design parameters of an ABM: 'Once viewed as something that is embedded within the system, rather than taking place before and off-line, policy starts to be practiced as a crucial component that interacts with other components in a constitutive process' (Squazzoni and Boero 2010: 3).

Fagiolo, Windrum and Moneta note that ABMs, 'are useful, either for increasing our understanding of the world or of a theory, or because they provide the kind of information that allows us to intervene in the world, or both' (Fagiolo, Windrum and Moneta 2006: 10). ABMs can be used 'when policy makers need to *learn from science* about the complexity of systems where their decision is needed', as well as 'when policy makers need to *find and negotiate certain concrete ad hoc solutions,* so that policy becomes part of a complex process of management that is internal to the system itself' (Squazzoni and Boero 2010: 6; Italic added). Thus, knowledge and information regarding network governance and collaborative processes may be fed into the communication systems of the network (Guney and Cresswell 2010), facilitating system-wide learning, adaptation and the emergence of new strategies.

Recommended reading

The following texts are recommended for further reading:

- Bonabeau, E. 2002. "Agent-based modeling: Methods and techniques for simulating human systems." *Proceedings of the National Academy of Sciences* 99 (suppl. 3): 7280–7287.
- Grimm, V., E. Revilla, U. Berger, F. Jeltsch, W.M. Mooij, S.F. Railsback . . . DeAngelis, D.L. (2005). "Pattern-oriented modeling of agent-based complex systems: Lessons from ecology." *Science* 310 (5750): 987–991.
- Miller, J.H. and S.E. Page. 2007. *Complex adaptive systems: An introduction to computational models of social life*. Princeton, NJ: Princeton University Press.
- North, M.J. and C.M. Macal. 2007. *Managing business complexity: Discovering strategic solutions with agent-based modeling and simulation*. Oxford: Oxford University Press.
- Wilensky, U. and W. Rand. 2015. *An introduction to agent-based modeling: Modeling natural, social, and engineered complex systems with NetLogo*. Cambridge, MA: MIT Press.

References

Axelrod, R.M. 1997a. *The complexity of cooperation: Agent-based models of competition and collaboration*. Princeton, NJ: Princeton University Press.

Axelrod, R.M. 1997b. "The dissemination of culture a model with local convergence and global polarization." *Journal of Conflict Resolution* 41 (2): 203–226.

Axelrod, R.M. 2006. "Agent-based modeling as a bridge between disciplines." In *Handbook of computational economics:Volume 2 agent-based computational economics*, edited by L. Tesfatsion and K. Judd, 1566–1583. Amsterdam: Elsevier.

Axelrod, R., & Hamilton, W. D. 1984. *The evolution of cooperation*. Basic Books, New York.

Bonabeau, E. 2002. "Agent-based modeling: Methods and techniques for simulating human-systems." *Proceedings of the National Academy of Sciences* 99 (suppl. 3): 7280–7287.

Box, G.E.P. 1979. "Robustness in the strategy of scientific model building." In Robustness in Statistics, edited by R.L. Launer and G. N. Wilkinson, 201–236. Atlanta, GA: Academic Press.

Cooter, R. and T. Ulen. 2007. *Introduction to law and economics*. Berkley, CA: Berkley Law Books.

Dean, J.S., G.J. Gumerman, J.M. Epstein, R.L. Axtell, A.C. Swedlund, M.T. Parker, and S. McCaroll. 2006. "Understanding Anasazi culture change through agent-based modeling." In *Generative Social Science: Studies in Agent-Based Computational Modeling*, edited by J. M. Eppstein, 90–116. Princeton, NJ: Princeton University Press.

Eckerd, A. 2013. "Policy alternatives in adaptive communities: Simulating the environmental justice consequences of hazardous site remediation strategies." *Review of Policy Research* 30 (3): 281–301.

Eckerd, A., H. Campbell and Y. Kim. 2012. "Helping those like us or harming those unlike us: Illuminating social processes leading to environmental injustice." *Environment and Planning B: Planning and Design* 39 (5): 945–964.

Eckerd, A., Y. Kim, and H.E. Campbell. 2017. "Community privilege and environmental justice: An agent-based analysis." *Review of Policy Research* 34 (2): 144–167.

Epstein, J.M. 2006. *Generative social science: Studies in agent-based computational modeling*. Princeton, NJ: Princeton University Press.

Epstein, J. M. and R. Axtell. (1996). *Growing artificial societies: Social science from the bottom up*. Washington, DC: Brookings Institution Press.

Fagiolo, G., P. Windrum, and A. Moneta. 2006. "Empirical validation of agent-based models: A critical survey." *ILEM Papers Series* 14: 1–45.

Grimm, V., U. Berger, F. Bastiansen, S. Eliassen, V. Ginot, J. Giske . . . and A. Huth. 2006. "A standard protocol for describing individual-based and agent-based models." *Ecological Modelling* 198 (1): 115–126.

Grimm, V., E. Revilla, U. Berger, F. Jeltsch, W.M. Mooij, S.F. Railsback . . . and D.L. DeAngelis. 2005. "Pattern-oriented modeling of agent-based complex systems: Lessons from ecology." *Science* 310 (5750): 987–991.

Guney, S. and A.M. Cresswell. (2010, January). "IT governance as organizing: Playing the Game." In *43rd Hawaii International Conference on Systems Science (HICSS-43 2010), Proceedings*, 1–10, 5–8 January 2010, Koloa, Kauai, HI, USA. IEEE.

Janssen, M.A. 2007. "Coordination in irrigation systems: An analysis of the Lansing: Kremer model of Bali." *Agricultural Systems* 93 (1–3): 170–190.

Janssen, M.A. and E. Ostrom. 2006. "Empirically based, agent-based models." *Ecology and Society* 11 (2): 37.

Kauffman, S. (1995). "Random chemistry." *Perspectives in Drug Discovery and Design* 2 (2): 319–326.

Kim, Y. 2007. "Using spatial analysis for monitoring fraud in a public delivery program." *Social Science Computer Review* 25 (3): 287–301.

Kim, Y. 2012. "Simulating a fraud mechanism in public service delivery." In *Simulation for Policy Inquiry*, edited by A. Desai, 121–138. New York: Springer.

Kim, Y., H. Campbell, and A. Eckerd. 2014. "Residential choice constraints and environmental justice." *Social Science Quarterly* 95 (1): 40–56.

Kim, Y., W. Zhong, and Y. Chun. 2013. "Modeling sanction choices on fraudulent benefit exchanges in public service delivery." *Journal of Artificial Societies and Social Simulation* 16 (2): 8. http://jasss.soc.surrey.ac.uk/16/2/8.html. doi: 10.18564/jasss.2175.

Koliba, C. and A. Zia. 2015. "Educating public managers and policy analysts in an era of informatics." In *Policy practice and digital science*, edited by M. Janssen, M.A. Wimmer, and A. Deljoo, 15–34. Berlin: Springer.

Lansing, J.S. and J.N. Kremer. 1993. "Emergent properties of Balinese water temple networks: Coadaptation on a rugged fitness landscape." *American Anthropologist* 95 (1): 97–114.

Lindblom, C.E. 1959. "The science of 'muddling through'." *Public Administration Review* 19 (2): 79–88.

Louie, M.A. and K.M. Carley. 2008. "Balancing the criticisms: Validating multi-agent models of social systems." *Simulation Modelling Practice and Theory* 16 (2): 242–256.

Maroulis, S. 2016. "Interpreting school choice treatment effects: Results and implications from computational experiments." *Journal of Artificial Societies and Social Simulation* 19 (1): 7.

Maroulis, S., E. Bakshy, L. Gomez, and U. Wilensky. 2014. "Modelling the transition to public school choice." *Journal of Artificial Societies and Social Simulation* 17 (2): 3.

Maroulis, S., R. Guimera, H. Petry, M.J. Stringer, L.M. Gomez, L.A.N. Amaral, and U. Wilensky. 2010. "Complex systems view of educational policy research." *Science* 330 (6000): 38–39.

Martinez-Coll, J. and J. Hirshleifer. 1991. "The limits of reciprocity." *Rationality and Society* 3: 35–64.

Miller, J.H. and S.E. Page. 2007. *Complex adaptive systems: An introduction to computational models of social life*. Princeton, NJ: Princeton University Press.

Müller, B., F. Bohn, G. Dreíler, J. Groeneveld, C. Klassert, R. Martin, M. Schlüter, J. Schulze, H. Weise, and N. Schwarz. 2013. "Describing human decisions in agent-based models: ODD + D, an extension of the ODD protocol." *Environmental Modelling & Software* 48 (October 2013): 37–48. https://doi.org/10.1016/j.envsoft.2013.06.003.

North, M.J. and C.M. Macal. 2007. *Managing business complexity: Discovering strategic solutions with agent-based modeling and simulation.* Oxford University Press.

Ostrom, E. 2010. "Beyond markets and states: Polycentric governance of complex economic systems." *American Economic Review* 100 (3): 641–672.

Ostrom, E. 2014. "Do institutions for collective action evolve?" *Journal of Bioeconomics* 16 (1): 3–30.

Padgett, J.F., D. Lee, and N. Collier. 2003. "Economic production as chemistry." *Industrial and Corporate Change* 12 (4): 843–877.

Schelling, T.C. 1971. "Dynamic models of segregation." *Journal of Mathematical Sociology* 1 (2): 143–186.

Schlüter, M. and C. Pahl-Wostl. 2007. "Mechanisms of resilience in common-pool resource management systems: An agent-based model of water use in a river basin." *Ecology and Society* 12 (2): 4.

Simon, H.A. 1955. "A behavioral model of rational choice." *The Quarterly Journal of Economics* 69 (1): 99–118.

Squazzoni, F. and R. Boero. 2010. *Complexity-friendly policy modelling.* London: Routledge.

Tsai, Y., A. Zia, C. Koliba, J. Guilbert, G. Bucini, and B. Beckage. 2015. "An Interactive Land Use Transition Agent-Based Model (ILUTABM): Endogenizing human-environment interactions at watershed scales." *Land Use Policy* 49: 161–176.

Tversky, A. and D. Kahneman. 1981. "The framing of decisions and the psychology of choice." *Science* 211 (4481): 453–458.

Wilensky, U. and W. Rand. 2015. *An introduction to agent-based modeling: Modeling natural, social, and engineered complex systems with NetLogo.* Cambridge, MA: MIT Press.

Zia, A., S. Kauffman, and S. Niiranen. 2012. "The prospects and limits of algorithms in simulating creative decision making." *Emergence: Complexity and Organization (E:CO): An International Transdisciplinary Journal of Complex Social Systems* 14 (3): 89–109.

Zia, A., S. Kauffman, C. Koliba, B. Beckage, G. Vattay, and A. Bomblies. 2014. "From the habit of control to institutional enablement: Re-envisioning the governance of social-ecological systems from the perspective of complexity sciences." *Complexity, Governance and Networks* 1 (1): 79–88. doi: 10.7564/14-CGN4.

Zia, A. and C. Koliba. 2013. "The emergence of attractors under multi-level institutional designs: Agent-based modeling of intergovernmental decision making for funding transportation projects." *AI & Society: Knowledge, Culture and Communication* 30: 315–331. doi: 10.1007/s00146-013-0527-2.

12 Practitioners

What do they want to know?

John M. Kamensky

Introduction

The 2002 classic how-to handbook, *The Tools of Government: A Guide to the New Governance*, by Lester Salamon, shows just how much government has evolved in the past seventeen years. It makes scant mention of networks and collaborative arrangements, obliquely described as 'indirect' or 'third-party' government. There is no mention of communities of practice, shared services, social network analysis (SNA) or other tools of collaborative governance that have grown in prominence in intervening years. Donald Kettl's 2009 book, *The Next Government of the United States*, presages the shift underway in American Government, toward a greater reliance on collaborative networks in delivering services and results. Nevertheless, while the world of public administrators has changed significantly in recent years, there has been no real roadmap on how to best proceed.

Background

In the United States (US) and in other countries, governments have moved from a 'single operating system' – the traditional hierarchical set of organizations and programs with clear reporting and funding structures – to a dual operating system. This dual operating system includes the traditional hierarchy but running parallel to it is a growing web of collaborative networks, both within and across public organizations, and increasingly with other sectors of society. Some of these networks are formal, while others are informal, having risen organically. How to manage this dual operating system is increasingly a challenge for public administrators. But their first step is to understand it, its tools and mores, and how to best use them to operate in this new world.

The trend toward the growing use of collaborative networks is not just a public-sector phenomenon. They are growing in the private, non-profit and civic worlds as well. This growth can probably be attributed to the evolving role of technology and its associated tools. As a result, large corporations are internally facing the same 'dual operating system' conundrum as the public sector (Hecksher 2007). However, there is a growing number of cases where the use of collaborative networks – often called 'platforms' in the tech world – has become the dominant operating system, where a network is the foundation of a company or non-profit's business model. Examples include Facebook, Uber, AirBnB, GoFundMe and more. And in a number of cases, these private and non-profit networks are blurring into the public sector, such as city governments hosting a Facebook page for their citizens. For the rest of this chapter, however, the focus will be on public-sector uses.

What are the key elements of a collaborative network?

Most public-sector practitioners at the managerial level have been trained in traditional public administration practices – a single operating system. They got where they are by understanding how hierarchies work, how programs get implemented, how government is funded, held accountable and is responsive to stakeholders. But for the most part, little of this experience is relevant in collaborative networks, which tend to be peer-based, not agency-based, and tend to be focused on results and services, not programs.

Practitioners can see the value of collaborative networks, but being naturally cautious and risk-adverse, they have many questions about differences among networks, their structure, their value, when to use them and so on. This is complicated by the fact that there are different definitions of networks, different uses, different models and a wide range of tools. In addition, public sector networks are difficult to assess as to whether they are effective in achieving results. As Donald Kettl (personal communication 7 August 2018) notes: 'collaboration is not an easy answer to hard problems, but rather it is a hard answer to hard problems.'

But first things first: what do we mean by 'collaborative network?' They can go by different names: alliances, partnerships, networks, communities, coalitions, consortiums and more (see Croppers et al. 2008; Keast 2016). In general, traditional hierarchical governance approaches assume stability, linearity, defined boundaries and clear authority from above. In contrast, networks assume fluidity, multi-linearity, are boundary-less and seek permission of peers to operate. Ansell and Gash (2018) define it as a 'high intensity mode of interaction that nurtures mutual interdependence while preserving the autonomy of collaborating parties'. Kettl (2009) more colourfully describes this approach to government as a shift from a 'vending machine' model to a 'barn raising' model.

What are some of the key questions in the minds of practitioners?

There tends to be a fairly robust body of literature about specific tools and methods for managing and assessing collaborative networks, but practitioners tend to be less interested in the tools and methods and are more interested in the questions they have, and the answers. In many cases, there has been very useful research providing insightful answers for practitioners, but this research is either not widely known in practitioner circles or it is not couched in terms that are readily digestible by busy readers. Following are some questions that practitioners have raised, along with some useful research that helps answer them. The chapter ends with questions that have been insufficiently researched that practitioners would likely want to know more about.

Question 1: when is the use of networks and collaboration most useful in addressing public challenges?

In a dual operating system world, when should the traditional hierarchical model be used and when might a collaborative network be more effective? There is a robust literature describing the varieties of collaborative networks (Agranoff 2003; Kaiser 2011; Kotter 2012; Popp et al. 2014). For the most part, the different business models depend on purposes, duration and scope:

*   Service delivery networks, such as Service Canada's single point of delivery of social services across a range of agencies (Langford and Roy 2008), Los Angeles' network of social services agencies (Thoennes and Pearson 2008) and improving public safety (Fedorowicz and Sawyer 2012).
*   Information diffusion networks, such as the Safe Cities and 21st Century Skills communities of practice (Briggs and Snyder 2003) and the food safety network (Greis and Nogueira 2010).
*   Problem-solving networks, such as the New Zealand 'Results Programme' to improve performance in ten specific policy areas by jointly solving problems such as recidivism and high school dropouts (Scott and Boyd 2017), or reducing the impact of natural disasters by improving construction standards (Waugh 2002).
*   Community capacity building networks, such as creating the White House Leadership Development Program (Kamensky 2016) and better engaging citizens in co-creating and delivering programs (Sirianni 2009).

These different kinds of networks can be used to solve problems, act jointly, share resources or provide technical assistance. They can be large-scale catalysts for action; for example, the cross-agency network created to implement the 2009 *Recovery Act* was managed out of the White House and involved more than a dozen agencies managing nearly 200 programs and more than US$787 billion (DeSeve 2011). Or they can be much more targeted networks, focused on specific watersheds to improve the quality of a river (Imperial 2004).

Question 2: what competencies, skills and experiences should leaders and participants have in order for networks to be effective?

A collateral question is whether these skills and competencies differ depending on the roles of individuals within a network. Again, there is a growing body of literature providing useful insights for practitioners that provides a framework of the competencies needed, such as planning, communicating and negotiating, as well as skills such as analytic, strategic thinking and use of technology (Policy Consensus Initiative 2011; O'Leary and Gerard 2012; Jang, Valero and Jung 2016; US Government Accountability Office (GAO) 2010b). There is also useful literature on the differences in roles of network participants – sponsors, champions, leaders, members and stakeholders (Milward and Provan 2006) – and on managing conflict within a network (Bingham and O'Leary 2007).

In networks, individuals may perform different roles, and these roles may change over time. For example, in the management of legitimacy in a network, Milward and Provan (2006: 19) write: 'Legitimacy isn't asserted; it is externally conferred . . . it is based on reputation and social acceptance.' In this case, network managers would be responsible for attracting positive publicity and demonstrating tangible successes to stakeholders, while a network member would have the role of demonstrating the value of network participation to others. Similarly, there are managerial roles for accountability, conflict management, network design, and developing and maintaining levels of commitment.

Question 3: what kinds of processes, tools and technologies are used to form and to manage networks?

The starting point is the need for a network and for collaboration. This can come from a top-down policy decision, or a bottom-up organic need. A top-down example is the statutory creation of federal cross-agency priority goals, whereby the US Office of Management and Budget designates specific policy issues as interagency in nature and designates a goal leader responsible for developing a four-year plan of action with quarterly progress reviews in areas such as improving cybersecurity or customer service (Fountain 2013; Kamensky 2017). An example of bottom-up collaboration is the creation of informal employee networks in the private sector (Bryan, Matson and Weiss 2007) and the efforts of employees in intelligence agencies to work across boundaries (Treverton 2016).

Whether top-down or bottom-up, these networks share common processes such as the creation of a common vision among participants, information sharing, the development of trust and the use of various collaboration processes and tools, such as

- the use of Cross-Agency Priority Goals and the use of National Strategies as top-down organizing constructs (Kamensky 2017; US GAO 2004);
- the use of communities of practice and SNA (Briggs and Snyder 2003; Ryan and Pole 2009);
- the use of heterarchy and incident command system approaches for networks that form to respond to a specific incident, such as a pandemic, and then revert to their traditional hierarchical form (Reihlen 1996; Gerberding 2004; Moynihan 2007);
- the use of platforms and crowdsourcing (Ansell and Gash 2018; McAfee and Brynjolfsson 2017; Brabham 2013); and

- the development of dispute resolution mechanisms since there are always differences in perspective in any large-scale endeavour (Bingham and O'Leary 2007).

The types of tools and methods that researchers might use to help inform public managers about these different models and tools will vary, depending on the types of questions facing practitioners. These include the development of descriptive, ethnographic case studies that suggest when, where and why different tools are used. Sometimes theory-based models help inform the best business model to use (Fountain 2017; Friedman and Foster 2011; Alberts, Garstka and Stein 1999; Bryan and Joyce 2005; Goldsmith and Eggers 2004; Popp et al. 2014).

Question 4: what kinds of network and governance structures help ensure the effectiveness of networks?

There are the different design options for a network. For example, some networks are 'closed' to those who are invited, while others are 'open' to any who choose to be members, such as Facebook. Some are informal and self-organizing, for example, criminal network-based tax-evasion schemes involving partnerships, trusts and corporations (US GAO 2010a).

Other networks are event-based, such as the Decennial Census, where a network of neighbours accompany census-takers to assure their neighbours that it is okay to participate in the census (Kamensky and Burlin 2004), and in response to emergencies, such as pandemics, forest fires and other disasters (Moynihan 2007).

And yet other networks are formal, long-term efforts, such as the US Department of Labor's hub-spoke networks of job training in each state, that connect with community-based private industry councils, Virginia's No Wrong Door provision of mental health services, or San Diego's 'Live Well' social services program that connects programs and services across a range of county agencies. Other examples include the Minneapolis-St. Paul traffic congestion network (Stone et al. 2009) and the cross-agency priority goals, mentioned earlier (Kamensky 2017).

In the case of the event-based and longer-term networks, governance structures are put in place. These structures involve the designation of roles, defining the prerogatives of the role-players, developing communication patterns and specifying the decision rights of the role-players, in order to allocate resources or coordinate or control activities (Fountain 2013, 2017; US GAO 2007, 2012, 2014).

Question 5: how do networks obtain resources necessary to achieve their objectives?

Probably the biggest challenge for networks is leveraging the resources needed to accomplish objectives. Typically, the central network has a small amount of funding, since its role is largely planning, coordination and oversight – not the direct delivery of services. The performance partnership pilots program in

2014 allowed, for the first time, 'blending' funding streams from seven different federal departments into a single, locally-based program for at-risk youth. The pilots allowed localities to request waivers from various federal requirements and to report progress to a single entity, the Department of Education, instead of to each of the different granting agencies (Lester 2016). While this funding approach is still a pilot, it offers insight into a different method of funding collaborative ventures.

In the case of the cross-agency priority goals, the Office of Management and Budget received authority to create a small US$15 million fund to support the strategic management of the cross-agency goals. This fund supported both small staff leads for individual goal leaders as well as websites, such as the one-stop website for consolidating various infrastructure permits and reviews.

Question 6: how do we know if a network is working?

How can public administrators find out if a network is internally healthy and whether it is making a difference for its intended target audience? According to a literature review by Popp et al. (2014), 'Evaluating "how" results are achieved may be just as important (if not more important in the longer term) as looking at "what" results are achieved.' They suggest that multilevel analysis may be needed to assess how a network operates – at the individual, organizational, network and community levels.

Evaluations of networks in the US have been conducted, but typically not on a systematic basis. Examples include the federal response to Hurricane Katrina, and the coordination of service delivery in social service networks in Los Angeles and in Brazos Valley, Texas (Popp et al. 2014). There are more examples in other countries, such as the evaluations undertaken of New Zealand's 'Results Programme' initiative in 2015–2016 (Scott and Boyd 2017).

There is some promise for an increased emphasis on evaluation at the federal level, given the 2016 report and recommendations by the Commission on Evidence-Based Policymaking and subsequent legislation that will regularize evaluations and the collection of data across agencies. The Office of Management and Budget continues to be supportive of such efforts.

What else do practitioners want to know?

The questions posed in the last section are but a small handful of those that practitioners tend to ask, especially when facing policy and program management decisions and trade-offs. But these questions at least have a body of research behind them! In other cases, there is little research available to help inform answers. These include topics and questions such as the following:

- How can managers create or ensure accountability in a hierarchical/ dual operating system (Koliba, Mills and Zia 2011; Romzek, LeRoux and Blackmar 2012)?

- What is the role of open data, transparency, crowd sourcing/funding? These are important elements in the creation of platforms (such as openstreetmap. org) in the private and non-profit sectors, but little research seems to be available in the public sector (McAfee and Brynjolfsson 2017).
- What is the role of private, non-profit platforms and the use of co-production approaches, such as the coding of census and weather data (Nambisan and Nambisan 2013)? Given that many of these platforms are in the private sector, how does this blur the lines between the public vs. the private sector in terms of their respective roles?
- What is the role of social capital, trust and legitimacy in the formation, health and sustainability of networks (Briggs and Snyder 2003; Alberts and Hayes 2003; Kamensky and Burlin 2004; Popp et al. 2014)?
- What is the role of complex adaptive system approaches in understanding the operation of networks (Alberts, Garstka and Stein 1999; Witzel 2012)?

While these are but some of the important questions being asked, there will clearly be more as the field matures and evolves in years to come.

Conclusion

The future of collaborative networks in government seems bright, and the role of social networking tools supporting the development and assessment of these networks is also promising. We can look forward to the use of real-time assessments with pulse surveys of networks and understand changes in stakeholder perceptions via the use of sentiment analysis of social media. At least at the federal level, there will be increased legitimacy in the use of collaborative networks as a governance model, with the maturing of the statutory authority for the creation and use of cross-agency priority goals. Still, for practitioners, there will always be opportunities to learn to better create the capacity to manage, sustain and evaluate the effectiveness of networks. That's where researchers can make their contributions.

References

Alberts, D.S., J.J. Garstka, and F.P. Stein. 1999. *Network centric warfare: Developing and leveraging information superiority*, 2nd ed. (Revised). Washington, DC: CCRP Publication Series.
Alberts, D.S. and R.E. Hayes. 2003. *Power to the edge: Command, control in the information age.* Washington, DC: CCRP Publication Series.
Agranoff, R. 2003. *Leveraging networks: A guide for public managers working across organizations.* Washington, DC: IBM Center for the Business of Government. www.businessofgovernment. org/sites/default/files/LeveragingNetworks.pdf.
Ansell, C. and A. Gash. 2018. "Collaborative platforms as a governance strategy." *Journal of Public Administration Research and Theory* 28 (1): 16–32.
Bingham, L.B. and R. O'Leary. 2007. *A manager's guide to resolving conflicts in collaborative networks.* Washington, DC: IBM Center for the Business of Government. www.business ofgovernment.org/sites/default/files/ConflictsCollaborativeNetworks.pdf.

Brabham, D.C. 2013. *Using crowdsourcing in government.* Washington, DC: IBM Center for the Business of Government. www.businessofgovernment.org/sites/default/files/Using%20 Crowdsourcing%20In%20Government.pdf.

Briggs, X.D.S and W.M. Snyder. 2003. *Communities of practice: A new tool for government managers.* Washington, DC: IBM Center for the Business of Government. www.businessof government.org/sites/default/files/Communities%20of%20Practices.odf_.pdf.

Bryan, L.L. and C. Joyce. 2005. "The 21st-century organization: Big corporations must make sweeping organizational changes to get the best from their professionals." *The McKinsey Quarterly,* No. 3.

Bryan, L.L., E. Matson, and L.M. Weiss. 2007. "Harnessing the power of informal employee networks." *The McKinsey Quarterly* 4: 1–11.

Croppers, S., M. Ebers, C. Huxham, and P. Smith Ring, eds. 2008. "Introducing inter-organizational relations." In *The Oxford handbook of inter-organizational relations,* 3–21. Oxford: Oxford University Press.

DeSeve, G.E. 2011. *Managing recovery: An insider's view.* Washington, DC: IBM Center for the Business of Government. www.businessofgovernment.org/sites/default/files/Managing %20Recovery.pdf.

Fedorowicz, J. and S. Sawyer. 2012. *Designing collaborative networks: Lessons learned from public safety.* Washington, DC: IBM Center for the Business of Government. www.businessof government.org/sites/default/files/Designing%20Collaborative%20Networks.pdf.

Fountain, J. 2013. *Implementing cross-agency collaboration: A guide for federal managers.* Washington, DC: IBM Center for the Business of Government. www.businessofgovernment.org/ sites/default/files/Implementing%20Cross%20Agency%20Collaboration.pdf.

Fountain, J. 2017. *Building an enterprise government: Creating an ecosystem for cross-agency collaboration in in the next administration.* A Joint Publication of the Partnership for Public Service and the IBM Center for the Business of Government. www.businessofgovernment.org/ sites/default/files/Building%20An%20Enterprise%20Government_0.pdf.

Friedman, K.B. and K. Foster. 2011. *Environmental collaboration: Lessons learned about cross-boundary collaborations.* Washington, DC: IBM Center for the Business of Government. www.businessofgovernment.org/sites/default/files/Environmental%20Collaboration.pdf.

Gerberding, J. 2004. "Director, Centers for Disease Control and Prevention." *Webb Lecture.* Washington, DC: National Academy of Public Administration.

Goldsmith, S. and W.D. Eggers. 2004. *Governing by network: The new shape of the public sector.* Washington, DC: Deloitte Research and Brookings Institution.

Greis, N.P. and M.L. Nogueira. 2010. *Food safety: Emerging public-private approaches: A perspective for local, state, and federal government leaders.* Washington, DC: IBM Center for the Business of Government. www.businessofgovernment.org/sites/default/files/Food%20 Safety.pdf.

Hecksher, C. 2007. *The collaborative enterprise: Managing speed and complexity in knowledge-based business.* New Haven, CT: Yale University Press.

Imperial, M. 2004. *Collaboration and performance management in network settings: Lessons from three watershed governance efforts.* Washington, DC: IBM Center for the Business of Government. www.businessofgovernment.org/sites/default/files/Governance%20Efforts.pdf.

Jang, H.S., J.N. Valero, and K. Jung. 2016. *Effective leadership in network collaboration: Lessons learned from continuum of care homeless programs.* Washington, DC: IBM Center for the Business of Government. www.businessofgovernment.org/sites/default/files/Effective%20 Leadership%20in%20Network%20Collaboration.pdf.

Kaiser, F.M. 2011. *Interagency collaborative arrangements and activities: Types, rationales, considerations.* Washington, DC: Congressional Research Service. Report #R41803.

Kamensky, J.M. 2016. "Creating a cadre of enterprise-wide leaders: Fledgling efforts underway to create cross-agency, career level capacity building." In *Business of Government* (Summer), 88–91. Washington, DC: IBM Center for the Business of Government.

Kamensky, J.M. 2017. *Cross-agency collaboration: A case study of cross-agency priority goals.* Washington, DC: IBM Center for the Business of Government. http://businessofgovernment. org/sites/default/files/Cross-Agency%20Collaboration.pdf.

Kamensky, J.M. and T.J. Burlin, eds. 2004. "Chapter one: Networks and partnerships: Collaborating to achieve results no one can achieve alone." In *Collaboration: Using networks and partnerships*, 3–20. Lanham, MD: Roman & Littlefield Publishers, Inc.

Keast, R. 2016. "Integration terms: Same or different." In *Grass roots to government: Joined-up working in Australia*, edited by G. Carey, 25–46. Melbourne: Melbourne University Press.

Kettl, D.F. 2009. *The next government of the United States: Why our institutions fail us and how to fix them.* New York: W.W. Norton & Co.

Koliba, C.J., R. Mills, and A. Zia. 2011. "Accountability in governance networks: An assessment of public, private, and nonprofit emergency management practices following Hurricane Katrina." *Public Administration Review* 71 (2): 210–220.

Kotter, J.P. 2012. "Accelerate." *Harvard Business Review*, November. https://hbr.org/2012/11/ accelerate.

Langford, J. and J. Roy. 2008. *Integrating Service delivery across levels of government: Case studies of Canada and other countries.* Washington, DC: IBM Center for the Business of Government. www.businessofgovernment.org/sites/default/files/RoyLangfordReport.pdf.

Lester, P. 2016. *Performance partnership pilots: Increasing program flexibility to improve outcomes.* Washington, DC: IBM Center for the Business of Government. http://businessof government.org/sites/default/files/Performance%20Partnership%20Pilots_0.pdf.

McAfee, A. and E. Brynjolfsson. 2017. *Machine, platform, crowd: Harnessing our digital future.* New York: W.W. Norton & Co.

Milward, H.B. and K.G. Provan. 2006. *A manager's guide to choosing and using collaborative networks.* Washington, DC: IBM Center for the Business of Government. www. businessofgovernment.org/sites/default/files/CollaborativeNetworks.pdf.

Moynihan, D. 2007. *From forest fires to Hurricane Katrina: Case studies of incident command systems.* Washington, DC: IBM Center for the Business of Government. www.businessof government.org/sites/default/files/MoynihanKatrina.pdf.

Nambisan, S. and P. Nambisan. 2013. *Engaging citizens in co-creation in public services: Lessons learned and best practices.* Washington, DC: IBM Center for the Business of Government. www.businessofgovernment.org/sites/default/files/Engaging%20Citizens%20in%20Co-Creation%20in%20Public%20Service.pdf.

O'Leary, R. and C. Gerard. 2012. *Collaboration across boundaries: Insights and tips from senior federal executives.* Washington, DC: IBM Center for the Business of Government. www. businessofgovernment.org/sites/default/files/Collaboration%20Across%20Boundaries.pdf.

Policy Consensus Initiative. 2011. *UNCG guide to collaborative competencies.* Chapel Hill, NC: University Network for Collaborative Governance.

Popp, J., H.B. Milward, G. MacKean, A. Casebeer, and R. Lindstrom. 2014. *Inter-organizational networks: A review of the literature to inform practice.* Washington, DC: IBM Center for the Business of Government. www.businessofgovernment.org/sites/default/files/Inter-Organizational %20Networks_0.pdf.

Reihlen, M. 1996. "The logic of heterarchies: Making organizations competitive for knowledge-based competition." Working Paper No. 91. Universität zu Köln.

Romzek, B.S., K. LeRoux, and J.M. Blackmar. 2012. "A preliminary theory of informal accountability among network organizational actors." *Public Administration Review* 72 (3): 442–453.

Ryan, R.A. and N. Pole. 2009. "Enabling a collaborative organization using social networking: Capturing social networks for business performance." IBM Research Paper.

Salamon, L., ed. 2002. *The tools of government: A guide to the new governance.* New York: Oxford University Press.

Scott, R. and R. Boyd. 2017. *Interagency performance targets: A case study of New Zealand's results programme.* Washington, DC: IBM Center for the Business of Government. www.businessof government.org/sites/default/files/Interagency%20Performance%20Targets.pdf.

Sirianni, C. 2009. *Investing in democracy: Engaging citizens in collaborative governance.* Washington, DC: Brookings Institution.

Stone, M.M., E.O. Saunoi-Sandgren, J.M. Bryson, and B.C. Crosby. 2009. *Designing and managing cross-sector collaboration: A case study in reducing traffic congestion.* Washington, DC: IBM Center for the Business of Government. www.businessofgovernment.org/sites/default/files/Designing%20and%20Managing.pdf.

Thoennes, N. and J. Pearson. 2008. *Inter-agency collaboration among social services agencies in Los Angeles County.* Washington, DC: IBM Center for the Business of Government. www.businessofgovernment.org/sites/default/files/Inter-Agency.pdf.

Treverton, G. 2016. *New tools for collaboration: The experience of the intelligence community.* Washington, DC: IBM Center for the Business of Government. www.businessofgovernment.org/sites/default/files/New%20Tools%20for%20Collaboration.pdf.

US Government Accountability Office (GAO). 2004. *Homeland security: Observations on the national security strategies related to terrorism.* Washington, DC: U.S. Government Printing Office. GAO-04-1075T.

US Government Accountability Office (GAO). 2007. *DHS multi-agency operation centers would benefit from taking further steps to enhance collaboration and coordination.* Washington, DC: U.S. Government Printing Office. GAO-07-686R.

US Government Accountability Office (GAO). 2010a. *Tax gap: IRS can improve efforts to address tax evasion by networks of businesses and related entities.* Washington, DC: U.S. Government Printing Office. GAO-10-968.

US Government Accountability Office (GAO). 2010b. *National security: An overview of professional development activities intended to improve interagency collaboration.* Washington, DC: U.S. Government Printing Office. GAO-11-108.

US Government Accountability Office (GAO). 2012. *Managing for results: Key considerations for implementing interagency collaborative mechanisms.* Washington, DC: U.S. Government Printing Office. GAO-12-1022.

US Government Accountability Office (GAO). 2014. *Managing for results: Implementation approaches used to enhance collaboration in interagency groups.* Washington, DC: U.S. Government Printing Office. GAO-14-220.

Waugh, W. 2002. *Leveraging networks to meet national goals: FEMA and the safe construction networks.* Washington, DC: IBM Center for the Business of Government. www.businessofgovernment.org/sites/default/files/Leveraging%20Networks%20to%20Meet%20National%20Goals.pdf.

Witzel, D. 2012. *Designing open projects: Lessons from internet pioneers.* Washington, DC: IBM Center for the Business of Government. http://businessofgovernment.org/sites/default/files/Designing%20Open%20Projects.pdf.

13 Network and collaboration research futures

Dan Chamberlain and Ben Farr-Wharton

Introduction

Collaboration and social network research have a long history together and will likely be entwined for a long time yet. Collaborative and networked arrangements are vital to the public sector, allowing the knowledge and resources of multiple organizations to come together and address intractable problems that are beyond the ability of any single organization to address independently. Social network research, with its focus on relationships and relational analysis, is a natural fit for understanding how both networks and collaborations function, and for exploring ways to make them more efficient, effective and economical. The growing demands for measuring outcomes and impacts of networks and collaborations is driving the research into good network practice and good collaborative practice, much of which is covered in the earlier chapters of this book. Out of these demands has come a confluence of qualitative and quantitative approaches; quantitative researchers are recognizing that network research cannot rely solely on positivist approaches, and qualitative researchers are increasingly incorporating quantitative tools, such as qualitative comparative analysis.

This chapter looks at this confluence from the perspectives of two early career researchers with different research backgrounds. Farr–Wharton has a background in public administration (PA) and management, with a quantitative focus; his PhD research was in creative communities and networks, looking at labour precarity and employment insecurity in the arts. The research evolved to include an analysis of how network structures could help or hinder artists in securing regular, paid, creative work using social network analysis (SNA). Chamberlain has a background in sociology and social network methodology. His PhD research looked at emerging adulthood in Australia, initially as an innovation of egocentric social network methods, before broadening it to include a more substantial qualitative analysis. Chamberlain also works as a consultant, providing methodological expertise in social network research design and analysis. Through this work, he has been involved in numerous research projects examining collaborations and networks in the public sector, including in academia, social services and public health.

Drawing on their backgrounds and knowledge of public sector and social network research, Chamberlain and Farr–Wharton offer this chapter as a

speculation on the future opportunities and challenges that confront researchers examining collaboration and collaborative networks. With a background
in PA and management, Farr-Wharton has been interested in the difficult, and
sometimes intractable, issues of collaboration and looking at how networks can
be better used to understand and address these problems. As a network method-
ologist, Chamberlain has been interested in applying the vast array of methods
available to research into collaborations, to quantify their structures, processes
and impact, and in so doing to unpack collaborative practices. This chapter
outlines many of the opportunities and issues that are expected to confront
future researchers examining collaborations, particularly in the study of network
structures, networking behaviours and network governance.

The presentation of ideas, as they appear in this chapter, were assembled
through an extended dialogue between Chamberlain and Farr-Wharton. The
dialogue was initiated in 2015, when the pair submitted the original proposal
for this chapter. At the time, both Chamberlain and Farr-Wharton were in the
process of accepting their first postdoctoral academic positions, and both moved
to separate states of Australia to take up these postings. From this time, the formative discussion around the ideas presented herein went 'mobile', whereupon
emails and phone conversations became the primary forum of deliberation.
What emerged through the drawn-out discourse (over many months) was a
consensus and shared understanding around several emerging themes related to
the future of network and collaboration research (particularly as it pertains to
PA and public-sector management). These themes form subheadings over the
remainder of the chapter, which act to guide the reader in exploring the foundations and trajectory of 'movements' in network and collaboration research.

Drawing on our backgrounds and knowledge of public sector networks
and social network research being conducted across many fields, this chapter
speculates on the future opportunities and challenges facing research into collaboration and collaborative networks. Evoking images of a high-tech future,
where algorithms and big data are increasingly used to inform public policy
and management, the first section begins by examining the trend of 'improved
statistical analysis' as it applies to network research. Keeping to the theme, quantitative method advances in multilevel analysis pertaining to the examination
of network and collaboration research are examined. This is followed by an
exploration of emerging trends in laboratory and network intervention research
and, finally, a discussion as to the implications of the democratization of SNA.

Improved statistical analysis

Certain methods bring with them an inherent power of association, and irrespec-
tive of the emergence of a more pragmatic and balanced discourse in recent times
concerning the value of both qualitative and quantitative methods, the latter car-
ries with it a traditional air of dominance and supremacy. Yet, specifically in the
context of network and collaboration research, the application of statistical analysis
to network phenomena has not been as wide-spread and carte blanche as in other

fields. A key reason for this is that traditional methods of statistical analysis are limited by the number of variables that can be computed in models, so that results are meaningful and robust. For example, statistical equations using more than five variables will start to suffer from small deviations in normality, which begin to erode 'model fit' and therefore the reliability of the results.

Network phenomena, encompassing the behaviour of nodes, and groups of nodes, and the different kinds of relationships that connect them, as one can imagine, involves many, many variables. Making matters worse is the problem that observations (i.e. relationships) are not independent, 'A's' relationship to 'B' is not independent of 'B's' relationship to 'A'. Traditionally then, conclusions derived from quantitative methods in the field of network and collaboration research have been met with a degree of scepticism (and rightly so). However, with the advent of new methods, including exponential random graph models (ERGMs) (also discussed in Chapter 9) and stochastic actor-oriented models (SAOMs), the robustness of statistical methods applied to the examination of networks and collaborations has been radically enhanced in recent times.

ERGMs seek to account for the interdependence of nodes, and the ties that connect them, in any given network (Wasserman and Faust 1994). As network structures become more complex it is difficult to account for the effect of structural properties on actors using traditional linear methods (i.e. because there are simply too many connections and nodes to account for accurately). ERGMs overcome this by accounting for all possible structures between nodes within a complex network. Understandably, the computational requirements for ERGMs are very high, and the mathematics behind network statistics are complicated by the relational nature of networks. This is formalized in the work of Frank and Strauss (1986) and Wasserman and Pattison (1996), who proposed Markov random graphs as a method for estimating the social structures of networks. The $p^{\star}$ model allows the approximation of logistic regressions, which can be used to draw inferences and make predictions about the function of the network structure in quantitative analysis (Lusher, Koskinen and Robins 2013). Building from this, SAOMs (Snijders 2011; Snijders, van de Bunt and Steglich 2010) push the analytical possibilities of ERGMs further by allowing longitudinal analysis of networks. SAOMs assume that the actors in a network are the driving force behind its structure, and that the network will co-evolve depending on both the existing network structure and the actions of the actors.

ERGMs and SAOMs allow a far greater understanding of collaboration, by modelling how individuals working collectively can shape networks purposefully. Their emergence can be attributed to advances in computing and the work of dedicated theorists with significant mathematical acumen. As ERGM and SAOM analytics becomes more widespread, the field of network and collaboration research is likely to benefit from empirical advances and meta-level conclusions regarding the statistical likelihood of certain outcomes resulting from networks behaviour and structure. These will likely be highly complementary to existing qualitative (and quantitative) theorizing, ushering in a more comprehensive and connected theory of networks that is multidisciplinary in nature. However, ERGM and SAOM analysis, as it has been referred to here, is largely situated with a single-network context. What is perhaps even more exciting, is the possibility of deploying these kinds of analytical models in multilevel and multinetwork contexts.

Multilevel analysis

People rarely belong to only one network (Latour 1987). Furthermore, membership in one network may impact the way that a person interacts in another network. Inter-organizational networks overlap with interpersonal networks, as relationships between people are fundamental to relationships between organizations. Yet, the reductionist nature of statistical reasoning has made it difficult to conceive of multiple network membership simultaneously (in analysis), and this is particularly important in this current age of online social networks. When researchers collect psychometric or ego network data from a person, the data typically pertain to only one network setting or context (e.g. in public management research, subjects are usually asked to indicate if they belong to a service delivery network). Yet, a person may belong to a variety of networks, and may occupy different positions in each of those networks. Analytically, this situates a person in an individual *uber-network* (a network of networks), yet without sufficient data on an *uber-network*, and methods to compute such data, statistical reasoning regarding a particular network membership is difficult to generalize outside of the context that the study is situated in, thereby limiting comprehensive theorizing. When data and analysis methods are not available to compute the impact of multiple network membership on either a person within a network or the network itself, it is impossible to rule out the unmeasured impact multiple network membership might have.

While ERGMs and SAOMs have been possible for the last decade, more recent advances in mathematical theory and statistical reasoning allow for multilevel network analysis using ERGMs (Klein and Kozlowski 2000; Wang et al. 2013; Wang et al. 2015). These multilevel models have different types of actors at different levels, and different types of relations across and between levels. Bodin and Tengö (2012), for example, used a multilevel ERGM to model the social-ecological systems in southern Madagascar, showing the interactions between inhabitants and forest areas, and in the common-pool management of resources. Multilevel network analysis can identify why different parts of a network, which seem to be identical, function differently or have different results by showing that the interactions with other levels of the network have different influences. Both ERGMs and SAOMs are accessible using free software; for example, SIENA (Ripley et al. 2017) and Statnet (Handcock et al. 2015) are software packages integrated with the statistical software R, PNet (Wang, Robins and Pattison 2009), which is purpose-built for ERGMs, and MPNet, which is designed for multilevel networks.

The promise of these predictive statistical models lies in empirically verifying the decades of research and theorizing into network research, particularly around inter- and intra-organizational structures, and the outcomes that they produce. The effectiveness of an inter-agency network at facilitating collaboration or collaborative relationships, for instance, will be a complex product of the network's structure, the context and the attributes of individual members and their interpersonal networks. Being able to model multilevel structures and attributes opens up the possibility of better understanding the role of context in shaping behavioural and network outcomes. Multilevel network analysis in particular opens up the possibility of understanding how external networks can relate to an organization or collaboration's network structure, and either impede or facilitate its effectiveness. Alternately, multilevel network analysis could be used to model inter-organizational and interpersonal ties and their interactions simultaneously. This will radically advance predictive network modelling and network-optimization processes in practice.

Laboratory experiments

Laboratory conditions are ideal for testing many of the theories around network formation, particularly those of interest to collaborations, such as social selection, social influence and leadership. There is a long history of network experimentation, dating from the social psychology experiments of the early 1950s on communication flows, to experiments based in game theory and on economic network formation (Jackson 2008; Kosfeld 2003). The ability to control the environment makes a laboratory setting ideal for isolating and understanding network effects or interactions which are otherwise difficult to observe, or which cannot be guaranteed to occur. Controlled conditions do not have to be restricted to laboratories; for example, experiments have been conducted incorporating control groups using artificially structured online communities, which demonstrated that social reinforcement from multiple neighbours encouraged the spread of health behaviours (Centola 2010).

There are a number of questions important to the study of collaborations which could be addressed through future laboratory experiments, particularly around the effect of network structures on individual behaviour, and vice versa. The relationship between cognition and network structure is one area that requires rigorous study (Kilduff and Krackhardt 2008), as there are plenty of unanswered questions regarding how individual personalities influence perceptions of a network, networking behaviour, the dynamics of a network, and how network structures can affect individual perceptions, behaviours and relationships. The enormous field of social capital research would also benefit from laboratory experiments, potentially answering questions such as how social capital is accrued and accessed. These areas have substantial bodies of theoretical and observational research behind them, but lack compelling empirical foundations, which are important for intervening in real-world networks. Laboratory experiments are one important way to test the many variables involved independently and empirically, and present future researchers with a rich platform to make meaningful improvements to theory and practice.

Interventions in social networks

Interventions into collaborations and collaborative networks is fast becoming a new domain of practice for consultants and researchers. The ability to influence real-world networks and intervene in order to effect positive change are important goals, particularly in collaborations, where optimal efficiency is highly desirable. Identifying leaders, influencers and bottlenecks within networks are common aims of many network studies, often with the explicit purpose of using them to alter the existing network or exploit the network to produce a particular outcome (Valente 2010, 2012). Network interventions can take numerous forms, including identifying individuals by virtue of their network position, working with groups to alter established behaviours, and altering network structure through removing links or people from the network, or through creating links between nodes. Such approaches have been successful at reducing conflicts in schools (Paluck, Sherpherd and Aronow 2016), encouraging the spread of positive health behaviours (Centola 2010), identifying opinion leaders to affect behavioural change (Valente and Pumpuang 2007), but have also shown how difficult it is to change behaviours at the community level (Fortmann et al. 1995; Valente 2010).

In the public sector there is a strong need to consider interventions at the whole network level, as programs often have structural implications, in that they can affect the structure of relationships within the network, or their efficacy is affected by the networks structure, dynamics and context (Hawe, Shiell and Riley 2009; Rychetnik et al. 2002). There are numerous important questions that should be asked before embarking on a network intervention: 'What is the mechanism through which the intervention will affect network structure?', 'What is the intended outcome of the intervention?' (i.e. is it behavioural change or structural change or both?) and 'Who stands to benefit most from an intervention, and how do you plan for unintended consequences?' These questions do not always have clear answers in terms of the cause and effect of network change, in what an effective network structure actually looks like or in how to deal with the ethical issues that arise.

Interventions into collaborations and collaborative networks are likely to employ both individual- and network-level approaches, aimed at a number of outcomes, including better communication, cross-fertilization of ideas or expertise, more efficient use of resources and so on. There is a preponderance of theory on what makes good collaboration, but manufacturing collaborations are, as yet, impossible. Adding to the complexity of intervening is the need for efficiency in both the network structure produced as a result, and the effort required to produce the result. For example, a completely connected network might ensure excellent communication, but it is hardly efficient, extremely difficult to achieve and does not guarantee collaboration. Interventions in networks is an area that will greatly benefit from the increased use of both statistical analysis and experimentation into network structures. In this way, the advances in statistical computational methods and multilevel analysis provide a fertile pathway to further evidence-based interventions. Coupled with this is an exponential increase in the sheer amount of network data available, otherwise known as 'big data'.

Big data analysis

'Big data', the massive data sets that have accrued thanks to the increased use of electronic interaction and surveillance, offer unprecedented opportunities to analyse social networks at the micro and macro levels. Already there are numerous articles using Facebook and Twitter data (among others) to map trends and patterns in social behaviours. These studies include the diffusion of information through weak ties in a social network of 100s of millions of people (Bakshy et al. 2012), accessing social capital (Bohn et al. 2014), the intersection of cultural tastes and social relationships (Lewis et al. 2008), and political communication and information diffusion on Twitter (Maireder et al. 2017) to name a few. Yet, the computational requirements of sorting through and applying analytical methods to big data are immense, and it is far simpler to collect the data and store it than to analyse it. However, there are techniques being developed to circumvent these issues, and this will allow individual researchers with desktop computers to conduct analysis on big data (Jia et al. 2015). A more difficult problem to address is the need to develop social theory that works at the massive scale and complexity of the data (Lazer et al. 2009; Robins 2015). Concomitant with that is the need to be able to analyse the data in ways that are sensible, and that produce conclusions which are significant and meaningful.

Big data analysis and data mining are inevitably a part of future research in the public sector and in collaborative networks; there are simply too many companies and government organizations collecting this kind of data without clear ideas on how to handle it. The question that underpins all big data, but seems to be rarely asked, is: 'Why are the data being collected?' Primarily it is because big data is cheap to collect, rather than it has a specific purpose in mind. The opportunities for researchers in this space is in access to data, which would otherwise be impossible for them to collect. In return, researchers can offer guidance in how to make sense of the data, and to make the process more efficient by identifying what is useful information to have and what is extraneous. At a practical level, however, collaborations involving governments (at all levels) and university researchers (individually or in teams) can be fraught with conflict and competing values (and are often stimulus for meaningful research in their own right). Thus, establishing the kinds of collaborations needed to extract utility from big data is no small feat.

Yet, it is also important to persist in embracing big data. The key reason for this is that today, more than ever before, we are confronted with 'big networks' (i.e. massive, global, interconnected, multilevel, multi-actor networks), and the ability to observe trends and test theories against such models has enormous potential. In the field of PA, recent discussion in the developed world has turned to the need for a more connected, democratic public decision-making system

(Brun-Martos and Lapsley 2017). Traditionally, we have conceived the public sector to be a hierarchy but, with a connected-governance model powered through effective management of big data, new forms of social service delivery and democratic actions are plausible – the prospects of which will have a transformational effect for society.

Better software tools for data collection and analysis

There have been computer programs designed for SNA available for decades, with a wide range of tools for visualization and/or analysis. Several of the classic handbooks of SNA devote chapters or appendices to listing various software packages, including long-running programs such as UCInet and Pajek (e.g. Huisman and van Duijn 2005; Wasserman and Faust 1994). However, these lists include only a fraction of what is available, and quickly become out of date. There are now scores of network analysis and/or visualization packages available, many of which are fit-for-purpose, or designed for comprehensive network analysis.

The programs have a range of purposes, often trading ease of use for functionality. Programs such as UCInet (Borgatti, Everett and Freeman 2002) and Pajek (Batagelj and Mrvar 2003) range from easily accessible to impenetrable for novices with little training, often requiring data file construction in other programs, but are powerful applications capable of almost all network procedures, including Quadratic Assignment Procedures and hypothesis testing. Gephi (Bastian, Heymann and Jacomy 2009) and NodeXL (Smith et al. 2010) are more accessible, with data file editors as part of the program, but offer limited functionality. Other network software incorporate data collection procedures, such as ONASurveys (www.onasurveys.com), which is designed for creating online network surveys, or VOSviewer (Van Eck and Waltman 2010), which scrapes journal databases for bibliometric data.

Ultimately, these applications will become more prevalent on handheld devices, using cloud-based computing to handle the analysis, to be more portable tools for field work. The use of networks constructed by respondents as part of the research process have been demonstrated to be useful as prompts for researchers to qualitatively follow up with participants about their networks, and for participants to reflect on their network's structure and their position within it (Molina, Maya-Jariego and McCarty 2014). Ideally, network survey instruments will be easy to set up within these mobile tools, able to have data inputted graphically (visually creating the network of the respondent as they are interviewed), link related interviewees' networks, and provide robust statistics and visualizations to the researcher over the course of the interview.

Easily portable tools which merge data entry, analysis and visualization would greatly improve the ability to conduct high-quality research, lowering the barriers to using network software, particularly around the need to construct and manipulate data files, and making them accessible to non-specialist researchers. More specifically, tools of these kind would allow for more focused research into collaborations, as participants will be able to update their networks through syncing with email and calendar apps, and by providing regular updates on their networks over the course of weeks and months. Such detailed data would be invaluable for researchers looking to map the evolution of collaborations, or to measure the effect of changes and interventions to the network. Herein, the perpetual improvements of software and network analysis technology has a democratic and empowering value not only for researchers, but also for novices – network actors in public and organizational contexts. Through a reduction in the complexity of network analysis and visualization, the application and future of network and collaboration can become more widespread – and even take on co-designed properties, where participants and researchers have a shared understanding of the significance of any network membership. Yet, this democratization of network research also poses challenges to ensure that the complexities of network theorizing remain suitably nuanced (and useful).

Appropriation of social network research

The inevitable consequence of social network research becoming more accessible, well-known and formulaic is that it will be incorporated into the practices of organizations and governments. In a prediction that predated social media, Valente (1995) highlighted the potential for mass media campaigns to target influential individuals to borrow their influence. These practices have made their way into all aspects of internet advertising, particularly Instagram, where people with large numbers of followers are paid to advertise products, and YouTube, where videos with a large number of views share in the advertising revenue generated. Similarly, Twitter has become an important vehicle for political communication, playing significant roles in recent Presidential elections (Kreiss 2016; Enli 2017) and Australian federal elections (Bruns 2017) and, more worryingly, as sources of news and information.

The dramatic rise in information communication technologies has changed the way in which organizations are physically organized, making it possible for employees to work remotely, and organizational groups to be spread across hemispheres. At the turn of the century, social network researchers were looking to the possibilities in peer-to-peer online networks, and new forms of networked organizing (Rice 1994; Monge and Contractor 2003). There is a considerable body of research showing that networked forms of organizing provide numerous benefits for employees and organizations, including greater flexibility, cross-communication, better skill development, greater creativity and better understanding of organizations' goals (Rainie and Wellman 2012). While there are disadvantages to working this way, there is a definite trend toward networked organizing, and traditional barriers such as workplace culture and strong preference for clear hierarchical structures are tumbling. Extending upon these principles, SNA has the potential to be incorporated into Human Resource processes using key performance indicators and communication logs already being collected, assessing the network positions of employees and managers as a measure of performance, or in determining whether someone is essential or redundant to the organization's network structure. Of course, the incorporation of such (reductionist) SNA data into representations of employee performance metrics raises a number of ethical considerations that require more extensive consideration and critique than is provided here.

Corporations and governments have access to vast reserves of big data, including on social relationships, and there are few controls, if any, over how they are collected or used. Concerns have been raised that the use of social network data intended to uncover terrorist or criminal networks ('dark' networks) could lead to significant harm, including the death, of innocents who are tangentially or mistakenly connected to the targets of these operations (Everton 2012). For those who work with corporations on intra-organizational networks there are considerable concerns about the conduct of the research, the impact and influence of managers and employers on participation in research, and the potential use of identified network members in research results to make management decisions (Borgatti and Molina 2003, 2005; Kadushin 2012). The 'echo chamber' effects of social media such as Facebook and Twitter lead to communities polarized around particular viewpoints, which are reinforced through preferentially seeing links and articles that are similar or closely related to those previously viewed/liked and reducing the amount of heterogeneous perspectives people are exposed to (Jacobson, Myung and Johnson 2016; Quattrociocchi 2017). More sinisterly, China's proposed 'Social Credit System' includes rating individuals based on their social and political activity in person, and on sites such as Twitter and Facebook, with potential for the ratings of individuals to be affected by the ratings of the people they associate with (Jones 2016).

While the examples and issues listed here may seem removed from the work of many researchers, they should be areas of concern and ethical enquiry more broadly. There is vast potential for the research on social networks, collaborative structures, networking behaviours and network governance to be used to manipulate communities and populations. Social engineering by governments and corporations may seem to be more the realm of the dystopic science fiction of Orwell and Huxley, but it is not inconceivable the tools currently being developed could be used perversely. While such issues are impossible to avoid, there are at least two things that should be done to minimize the issues that might arise, both of which are in nascent stages. The first is the development and exploration of ethical issues specific to SNA, in areas such as the use of network relationships as measures of performance or impact, how profiles are created of people using network data, and the algorithms that determine what content people see in social media. The second is a program of systematic review of government and corporate uses of SNA, with the aim of providing the oversight and transparency that would come about through Institutional Review Boards or Higher Research Ethics Committees in a university setting, and in translating these reviews for the broader population.

Notwithstanding the ethical challenges that are emerging as a result of the democratization of SNA, there are some positives. At the individual level, network actors have more information available to them regarding how they might alter their behaviour and position to achieve social good and generate public value. This kind of value-laden work attitude is not an uncommon psychological driver for those working in the public and social services sector (where it falls under the banner of public service motivation), and when equipped with evidence generated through user-friendly network analysis, those who generate public value will have increased potential to do so. In moving forward, however, the key opportunity is for network and collaboration researchers to remain ahead of the game – moving from a position of a knowledge and theory distributor, to a group of people who empower and advance appropriate and ethical practice. In this way, researchers are a key stakeholder in the future of a networked society, as they are equipped with the requisite knowledge and experience and use robust ethical review practice, in the context of network reasoning, to help guide appropriate practice.

The future

The technological advances in computing, software and modelling will likely see rapid advances in translating the qualitative explorations of social networks into empirically supported predictive models. Apart from making this research methodology more accessible to non-specialists, there is (and will be) greater opportunity for larger-scale programs of research into how networks form and function, and how this translates into outcomes. There is a wide array of areas where network interventions and network research are attempting to measure, assess and improve inter-agency networks and collaborations, particularly in the social services sector and public health, where the problems being addressed are of such complexity that they cannot be addressed by a single organization, or by organizations working alone. However, the issues that are being addressed in these areas have far wider applications, and it is far too difficult to predict exactly where and when SNA will find its next home. The ethical challenges created by advances in network analysis are surmountable and warrant an ongoing commitment from enthusiastic researchers to help steer collaborative and network practices to where they can generate the most meaningful and significant public good, as well as deter those practices that are dubious, perverse and dangerous.

At this final point, it is worth noting that, while the study of networks and collaborations has come a very long way in a very short while, there are still fundamental gaps in our knowledge. Theories about what makes a good networker, a good team, a good collaborator, a good collaboration and a great network are still conjectural, owing to incomplete evidence. Many great advances have occurred which enable researchers and practitioners to make meaningful contributions to network practice and theory, based on our current (but incomplete) body of knowledge, but the future brings with it hopes of a more robust understanding and resultant effective practice. The call posited herein, is for a rich combination of both tenacity and optimism on the part of emerging and established scholars. As scholars, we have much to examine, share and critically comment on, as the unveiling of a networked future is constantly presented, changed and re-presented.

References

Bakshy, E., I. Rosenn, C. Marlow, and L. Adamic. 2012. "The role of social networks in information diffusion." *International World Wide Web Conference Committee*, 16–20 April, Lyon.

Bastian, M., S. Heymann, and M. Jacomy. 2009. "Gephi: An open source software for exploring and manipulating networks." *International AAAI Conference on Weblogs and Social Media*.

Batagelj, V. and A. Mrvar. 2003. *Pajek: Program for large network analysis*. http://vlado.fmf. uni-lj.si/pub/networks/pajek/.

Bodin, Ö. and M. Tengö. 2012. "Disentangling intangible social-ecological systems." *Global Environmental Change* 22 (2): 430–439.

Bohn, A., C. Buchta, K. Hornik, and P. Mair. 2014. "Making friends and communicating on Facebook: Implications for the access to social capital." *Social Networks* 37: 29–41.

Borgatti, S.P., M.G. Everett, and L.C. Freeman. 2002. *Ucinet 6 for windows: Software for social network analysis*. Harvard, MA: Analytic Technologies.

Borgatti, S.P. and J.-L. Molina. 2003. "Ethical and strategic issues in organizational social network analysis." *The Journal of Applied Behavioral Science* 39 (3): 337–349.

Borgatti, S.P. and J.-L. Molina. 2005. "Toward ethical guidelines for network research in organizations." *Social Networks* 27: 107–117.

Brun-Martos, M.I. and I. Lapsley. 2017. "Democracy, governmentality and transparency: Participatory budgeting in action." *Public Management Review* 19 (7): 1006–1021.

Bruns, A. 2017. "Tweeting to save the furniture: The 2013 Australian election campaign on Twitter." *Media International Australia* 162 (1): 49–64.

Centola, D. 2010. "The spread of behavior in an online social network experiment." *Science* 329 (5996): 1194–1197.

Enli, G. 2017. "Twitter as arena for the authentic outsider: Exploring the social media campaigns of Trump and Clinton in the 2016 US presidential election." *European Journal of Communication* 32 (1): 50–61.

Everton, S.F. 2012. *Disrupting dark networks*. New York: Cambridge University Press.

Fortmann, S.P., J.A. Flora, M.A. Winkleby, C. Schooler, C.B. Taylor, and J.W. Farquhar. 1995. "Community intervention trials: Reflections on the Stanford five-city project experience." *American Journal of Epidemiology* 142 (6): 576–586.

Frank, O. and D. Strauss. 1986. "Markov graphs." *Journal of the American Statistical Association* 81 (395): 832–842.

Handcock, M., D. Hunter, C. Butts, S. Goodreau, P. Krivitsky, S. Bender-deMoll, and M. Morris. 2015. *Statnet: Software tools for the statistical analysis of network data*. The Statnet Project. www.statnet.org.

Hawe, P., A. Shiell, and T. Riley. 2009. "Theorising interventions as events in systems." *American Journal of Community Psychology* 42: 267–276.

Huisman, M. and M.A.J. van Duijn. 2005. "Software for social network analysis." In *Models and methods in social network analysis*, edited by P.J. Carrington, J. Scott, and S. Wasserman. New York: Cambridge University Press.

Jackson, M.O. 2008. *Social and economic networks*. Princeton, NJ: Princeton University Press.

Jacobson, S., E. Myung, and S.L. Johnson. 2016. "Open media or echo chamber: The use of links in audience discussions on the Facebook pages of partisan news organizations." *Information, Communication & Society* 19 (7): 875–891.

Jia, M., H. Xu, J. Wang, Y. Bai, B. Liu, and J. Wang. 2015. "Handling big data of online social networks on a small machine." *Computational Social Networks* 2 (1): 5–16.

Jones, S. 2016. "Big data meet big brother: China invents the digital totalitarian state." *The Economist*, December 17. www.economist.com/news/briefing/21711902-worrying-implications-its-social-credit-project-china-invents-digital-totalitarian.

Kadushin, C. 2012. *Understanding social networks.* New York: Oxford University Press.

Kilduff, M. and D. Krackhardt. 2008. *Interpersonal networks in organizations: Cognition, personality, dynamics, and culture.* New York: Cambridge University Press.

Klein, K. J. and S. W. J. Kozlowski. 2000. *Multilevel theory, research and methods in organizations: Foundations, extensions, and new directions.* San Francisco, CA: Jossey-Bass.

Kosfeld, M. 2003. "Network experiments." Working Paper No. 152, Institute for Empirical Research in Economics, University of Zurich.

Kreiss, D. 2016. "Seizing the moment: The presidential campaigns' use of Twitter during the 2012 electoral cycle." *New Media & Society* 18 (8): 1473–1490.

Latour, B. 1987. *Science in action.* Cambridge: Harvard University Press.

Lazer, D., A. Pentland, L. Adamic, S. Aral, A. Barabási, D. Brewer, N. Christakis, N. Contractor, J. Fowler, M. Gutmann, T. Jebara, G. King, M. Macy, D. Roy, and M. Van Alstyne. 2009. "Computation social science." *Science* 323 (5915): 721–723.

Lewis, K., J. Kaufman, M. Gonzalez, A. Wimmer, and N. Chistakis. 2008. "Tastes, ties, and time: A new social network dataset using Facebook.com." *Social Networks* 30: 330–342.

Lusher, D., J. Koskinen, and G. Robins, eds. 2013. *Exponential random graph models for social networks: Theory, methods, and applications.* Cambridge: Cambridge University Press.

Maireder, A., B.E. Weeks, H. Gil de Zúñiga, and S. Schlögl. 2017. "Big data and political social networks: Introducing audience diversity and communication connector bridging measures in social network theory." *Social Science Computer Review* 35 (1): 126–141.

Molina, J.L., I. Maya-Jariego, and C. McCarty. 2014. "Giving meaning to social networks: Methodology for conducting and analyzing interviews based on personal network visualisations." In *Mixed methods social networks research: Design and applications*, edited by S. Domínguez, and B. Hollstein. New York: Cambridge University Press.

Monge, P.R. and N.S. Contractor. 2003. *Theories of communication networks.* Oxford: Oxford University Press.

Paluck, E.L., H. Shepherd, and P.M. Aronow. 2016. "Changing climates of conflict: A social network experiment in 56 schools." *PNAS* 113 (3): 566–571.

Quattrociocchi, W. 2017. "Inside the echo chamber: Computational social scientists are studying how conspiracy theories spread online- and what, if anything, can be done to stop them." *Scientific American*, April, 316: 60–63.

Rainie, L. and B. Wellman. 2012. *Networked: The new social operating system.* Cambridge, MA: The MIT Press.

Rice, R.E. 1994. "Network analysis and computer-mediated communication systems." In *Advance in social network analysis: Research in the social and behavioral sciences*, edited by S.E. Wasserman and J. Galaskiewicz. Thousand Oaks: Sage Publications.

Ripley, R.M., T.A.B. Snijders, Z. Boda, A. Vörös, and P. Preciado. 2017. *Manual for SIENA version 4.0 (version February 16, 2017).* Oxford: University of Oxford, Department of Statistics; Nuffield College. www.stats.ox.ac.uk/siena/.

Robins, G. 2015. *Doing social network research: Network-based research design for social scientists.* Los Angeles: Sage Publications.

Rychetnik, L., M. Frommer, P. Hawe, and A. Shiell. 2002. "Criteria for evaluating evidence on public health interventions." *Journal of Epidemiology and Community Health* 56: 119–127.

Smith, M., A. Ceni, N. Milic-Frayling, B. Shneiderman, E. Mendes Rodrigues, J. Leskovec, and C. Dunne. 2010. *NodeXL: A free and open network overview, discovery and exploration add-in for Excel 2007/2010/2013/2016.* Social Media Research Foundation. http://nodexl. codeplex.com/.

Snijders, T. 2011. "Statistical models for social networks." *Annual Review of Sociology* 37: 131–153.

Snijders, T., G.G. van de Bunt, and C.E.G. Steglich. 2010. "Introduction to stochastic actor-based models for network dynamics." *Social Networks* 32 (1): 44–60.

Valente, T.W. 1995. *Network models of the diffusion of innovations.* New Jersey: Hampton Press Inc.

Valente, T.W. 2010. *Social networks and health: Models, methods, and applications.* New York: Oxford University Press.

Valente, T.W. 2012. "Network interventions." *Science* 337 (6090): 49–53.

Valente, T.W. and P. Pumpuang. 2007. "Identifying opinion leaders to promote behavior change." *Health Education & Behavior* 34 (6): 881–896.

Van Eck, N.J. and L. Waltman. 2010. "Software survey: VOSviewer, a computer program for bibliometric mapping." *Scientometrics* 84 (2): 523–538.

Wang, P., G. Robins, and P. Pattison. 2009. *PNet: Program for the simulation and estimation of exponential random graph models.* Melbourne: School of Psychological Sciences and The University of Melbourne.

Wang, P., G. Robins, P. Pattison, and E. Lazega. 2013. "Exponential random graph models for multilevel networks." *Social Networks* 35 (1): 96–115.

Wang, P., G. Robins, P. Pattison, and E. Lazega. 2015. "Social selection models for multilevel networks." *Social Networks* 44: 346–362.

Wasserman, S. and K. Faust. 1994. *Social network analysis: Methods and applications.* New York: Cambridge University Press.

Wasserman, S. and P. Pattison. 1996. "Logit models and logistic regressions for social networks: I. An introduction to markov graphs and $p\star$." *Psychometrika* 61 (3): 401–425.

14 Cross-cutting themes and opportunities for network and collaboration research

Robyn Keast, Christopher Koliba and Joris Voets

In this concluding chapter, the volume editors summarize and reflect on some of the key overarching themes and considerations that emerge from a comprehensive review of the chapters. These themes relate to questions of qualitative-quantitative and mixed-methods approaches, advances in computational capacity, big data, artificial intelligence (AI) and experimentation, stakeholder engagement, ethical and normative considerations, and adaptive and reflective capacity. This chapter considers these themes relative to the future directions of a research program for networks and collaboratives.

Bridging the qualitative/quantitative divide?

Public-sector research has a long tradition of drawing on qualitative research, and this preference has largely transferred across to research on networks and collaborations. Recently, however, quantitative techniques are increasingly being applied in public administration (PA) research generally, and as useful means for uncovering and testing overall properties of network and collaboration functioning such as, for example, management and leadership characteristics (O'Toole and Meier 2004; O'Leary, Choi and Gerard 2012) and facilitated processes (Thomas and Perry 2006). This developing methodological shift is highlighted in Chapter 4 by van Meerkerk, Edelenbos and Klijn and supported by both Groeneveld et al. (2015) and Kapucu, Hu and Khosa (2017), the latter particularly discussing quantitative approaches to network studies.

Despite an apparent 'quantitative turn', a strong theme across many chapters within this volume, as well as the vast body of research undertaken on public sector networks and collaborations, is the continued appreciation of and reliance on qualitative approaches and associated methodologies, methods and techniques. Chapter authors stress the value of qualitative approaches for uncovering the contexts in which network and collaborative forms operate, highlighting the complexity of structures and process mechanisms, as well as providing a means for drawing out and describing the everyday experiences of participants. The chapters by Vangen (Chapter 7) and Dodge, Saz-Carranza and Ospina (Chapter 5) are illustrative of the unique value that qualitative methods provide to multiparty research and multilevel analysis that enable researchers to drill down into the work practices of network and collaboration members, while at the same time accounting for the overall context of their operations. Vangen's chapter on RO-AR, which is embedded within an action-research approach, re-enforces the importance of understanding the role of context and people in the study of multiparty initiatives and offers a way to distil the behaviours and actions of participants that are not easily extracted by other research approaches. Dodge, Saz-Carranza and Ospina's chapter draws upon and extends the qualitative tradition in public sector network research with their narrative contribution enabling a more nuanced and layered understanding to emerge from collective-working phenomena, thus accommodating the renewed interest in micro-processes, such as the language, behaviours, motivations and social identity of participants (see Gray 1989; Innes and Booher 2010; Keast 2016; Mandell, Keast and Chamberlain 2016; Stout and Love 2017) as well as how these relationships are facilitated (Flynn, published 2019) and the role of small wins in retaining commitment for collective effort (Termeer and Dewulf 2018).

It is the case study, however, that is most closely aligned with the qualitative approach in PA, having been somewhat of a 'fail safe' mode for many network/ collaboration research studies (see as exemplars, Innes and Booher 2010; Klijn and Koppenjan 2016). Not surprisingly then, the case study approach was well represented within the chapters; pointing to continued confidence in its utility to the PA field, especially given its ability to tackle an assortment of research questions as well as take a variety of forms. Cheng and Voets' chapter (Chapter 3) highlighted the different perspectives and types of case study approaches (thus illustrating the versatility of the case study, while at the same time noting some of the debates and considerations that need to be addressed). It is worth noting here though that, while often depicted as qualitative, case studies can assume quantitative forms or be constructed based on combinations of both methodologies, depending on the phenomena being examined, the research questions to be answered and the data available (Yin 2014). Following this line, Cheng and Voets contend that the case study approach is less a method and more of a research design that specifies and contextualizes what is to be studied, while providing a framework that could potentially incorporate several data collection methods.

Process tracing and Qualitative Comparative Analysis (QCA) are also case-oriented methods that have come into their own, partly in response to growing practitioner expectation and demands and academic interest for evidence of causality within public sector networks and collaborations (Emerson, Nabatchi and Balogh 2012). Demonstrating causality is an increasingly relevant issue given public financial and personal investment in networks and the often-complex nature of their operations, with sub-elements that vary across time and space, as well as the contexts within which they operate (Koliba et al. 2018) making it difficult to assign 'certainty' between action and outcome. This ability to isolate and distil causal relations is increasingly relevant to those involved in the design and management of networks and collaborations, especially in providing evidence needed to re-configure structures and processes to enhance positive and limit suboptimal outcomes (Glass et al. 2013: 61; see also Chiolero 2018). The survey and Q-methodology contributions, Chapters 5 and 6 respectively, are also useful means by which to ascertain causality (see as an example Jeffares and Skelcher 2011). Although the search for causality in networks and collaborative arrangements is not new (see Dorien 2001) it does present as a potentially viable and fruitful direction for future network research. However, as Fafchamps, Kebede and Zizzo (2015) warn, there are still practical and methodological obstacles to overcome, including clarifying the differences between correlation and causality that continue to befuddle many researchers, a point we return to when we discuss big data.

As noted earlier, even though categorized as inherently 'qualitative,' methods such as QCA, Q methodology and process tracing have the capacity to combine and synthesize qualitative and quantitative information. For example, although QCA 'aims to achieve thick description of complex cases' (Hudson and Kühner 2013: 280; see also Berg-Schlosser et al. 2009), as Cepiku, Christofoli and Trivellato (Chapter 11) stress, it can do so by mixing qualitative insights with quantitative statistical measures to identify the sets of configuring factors that explain collective phenomena and, as a secondary benefit, supplement limited or unreliable data sets. Similarly, as Kivits notes in his chapter (Chapter 6) Q methodology applies quantitative analysis to qualitatively derived data to examine and understand complex subjective items, such as the personal opinions, attitudes and values that shape network formation and collaborative practices. Although Agranoff and Kolpakov's chapter (Chapter 2) on sequential explanatory design focuses on the role of mixed methods, they do advocate a prominent role for qualitative data acquisition as a key feature of building a grounded approach to theory development. This approach seeks to use qualitative data in data analysis software to build theory and draw inferences. A similar approach to using qualitative data is suggested in Koliba, Zia and Merrill's chapter on agent-based modelling (Chapter 11). The discussions taking place within these chapters, and reflected more generally across the field, are leading to more reciprocal understandings of the different approaches and how they might be best re-configured to address the complex problems besetting the public sector.

Representing the traditional quantitative element, Chapter 4 by Van Meerkerk, Edelenbos and Klijn demonstrates the contribution that survey approaches bring to capturing and confirming the detailed elements of network and collaboration behaviour, operation and performance, such as for example trust, managerial roles and impact – all of which provide essential information to public sector workers charged with the design, management and evaluation of these entities. These authors also point to a growing maturity of the field and practice of survey analysis, describing how it has been 'extended and refined' over time, partly through its willingness to leverage from qualitative insights from, for example, case studies and partly through advances in computational techniques, and they identify multilevel analysis as an important future development for survey investigations of networks. Similarly, Agranoff and Kolpakov

(Chapter 2) note that the combination of grounded theory and survey analysis by way of sequential explanatory design is pushing and extending the traditional mixed-methodology approach, while adding to the knowledge set for network operation. As these chapters and other studies attest, the introduction of quantitative modes and techniques into previously qualitative approaches and vice versa has resulted in the formation of new methods and techniques that have pushed boundaries and afforded new, or at least different, insights into the workings of networks and collaborative arrangements. Yet, despite these benefits, the current quantitative turn in PA has been received less positively by some, at least partially, as undermining qualitative research through efforts to make it more rigorous so that it can be taken more seriously (Sale, Lohfeld and Brazil 2002). It could be argued, however, that this situation is somewhat ironic and even a little disappointing, given that qualitative researchers have worked hard to have the value of this approach acknowledged and accepted as 'legitimate', and in doing so have overcome what has been viewed as a privileging of quantitative position (see for example Clarke 1999). Smith and Heshusius (1986: 10) sounded an early warning that still appears relevant:

> Pressure is being exerted from the quantitative call for qualitative research to 'measure up' to its standards without understanding the basic premises of qualitative research. Proponents of the qualitative paradigm need to address this pressure, but without 'slipping on the mantle' of quantitative inquiry.

In the thirty years since the publication of this sentiment, questions have emerged about the ability of the quantitative approach, including the survey mode, to capture 'accurate, fully textured, and nuanced data at multiple levels of social reality' (Kertzer and Frinke 1997). This doubt has occurred alongside a growing appreciation of the added value that qualitative research brings, particularly in terms of the rich descriptions it affords of networked phenomena, experiences and operations, which in turn can generate new questions to be answered (Toye et al. 2016).

However, these research approaches or paradigms need not be exclusive or competitive – forcing one or the other methodology decisions, and instead could be more complementary considering each of the underpinning assumptions while studying different phenomena (Sale, Lohfeld and Brazil 2002). To overcome or at least partially address the long-standing qualitative/quantitative binary and harness their benefits, mixed-methodology approaches are argued to be a 'distinct third methodological movement' (Tashakkori and Teddlie 2003: 24). For Cresswell and Plano Clark (2007: 5) mixed methodology is a 'research design with philosophical assumptions as well as methods of inquiry'. Mertens et al. (2016: 4) provide further clarification calling for the 'use of more than one method, methodology, technique, approach, theoretical or paradigmatic framework and the integration of those different components'; that is, it is more than the inclusion of qualitative or quantitative methods in a study, its strength lays in the integration of qualitative and quantitative methods in the analysis and results to generate enhanced findings. Following Miles and Huberman (1984), a mixed-methods approach has always been driven somewhat by this pragmatic rationale. Here Carey's (1993: 234) argument that 'qualitative and quantitative techniques are merely tools; integrating them allows us to answer questions of substantial importance,' seems to retain its relevance. Indeed, Mertens et al. (2016), in their five-year projection for mixed-methods research, reiterate that questions are not necessarily aligned with a particular method, although they do acknowledge some methods are more appropriate to answer certain types of questions (6) (see also Tashakkori and Cresswell 2007). These authors go on to stress the danger in pre-determining the research methodology based on existing skills or practices, noting that it can prevent the uptake of alternative or new approaches that could generate different data to answer questions (Mertens et al. 2016: 6); that is, it is not the method but the question that provides the starting point.

This volume has shown research on networks and collaborations has available to it a diversity of options: theories, concepts, designs, methodologies and techniques. At the same time, the authors are pointing to a more pluralist approach, one that breaks down the paradigm and provides avenues for new methodological discussions and configurations.

Mixed methods and beyond

As the discussion in the previous section indicates, the blurring of the quantitative/qualitative divide and the greater acceptance of mixed research approaches has become a growing trend in public sector network research. Overall, the pull toward mixed methods is consistent with the broader network research field, which for some time now has been calling for research that integrates quantitative methods with qualitative methods (Berry et al. 2004; Isett et al. 2011; Lecy et al. 2014; Provan, Fisher and Sydow 2007; Provan and Lemaire 2012; Robinson 2006). Many recent studies have heeded this call, resulting in various configurations and mixtures of methods utilized to answer a diverse array of questions (Haugen Gausdal, Svare and Möllering 2016). For instance, Ulibarri and Scott (2017) drew on network analysis, documentary review, interview and survey in their study of governance. Kapucu, Hu and Khosa's (2017) recent meta-analysis re-affirms this growing practice of using mixed methods of data collection in network research.

Indeed, many chapters in this volume, especially those focusing on QCA, process tracing, sequential explanatory design, agent-based modelling and survey, re-enforce this practice, providing a strong argument that the structure, processes, interactions and motivations of networks and collaborations are so complex, dynamic and emergent that a single quantitative or qualitative approach is insufficient and inadequate to answer all questions or capture their problem-solving nuances. The chapter authors share the sentiment that different methodological approaches attend to diverse elements of a research problem, and therefore provide new avenues for posing research questions that are more likely to generate unique insights that add value to findings.

The chapters in this volume that identify the virtue of mixed methods build on earlier mixed-methods models, such as that proposed by Creswell (2003). The 'traditional' mixed-methods approach to social research follows a set sequence, often with qualitative data analysis employed first to identify and refine issues for further quantification. The Agranoff and Kolpakov contribution (Chapter 2), promoting the benefit of combining grounded theory and surveys to tap into the use of qualitative methods to elicit 'deep meanings' within an expanded multistage of perspectives on governances networks and collaboratives, provides a good example of an alternative mode for sequential mixed methods. Their approach begins with basic understandings of data, using some deductive reasoning drawn from assumptions identified out of quantitatively derived coding schemes. By contrast, QCA, as highlighted in Cepiku, Cristofoli and Trivellato's Chapter 10, begins with a set of variables deduced from theory or prior research to build truth tables through which Bayesian analysis is rendered.

As well as advancing research outcomes, the use of mixed methods can lead to greater efficiencies in data analysis. Mertens et al. (2016: 8) for example, noted that the combination of survey and field work data can be more efficient than ethnography, which requires more time and engagement with respondents. Furthermore, the synergies created by the coming together of methods can lead to methodological innovation and development that are better able to address emergent as well as persistent problems. One such development is Qualitative Network Analysis, which arises from the synthesis of SNA and the advancement of computational models that draw on network and collaborative frameworks, and qualitative methods such as focus groups, interviews and documentary analysis (Aherns 2018).

These advantages aside, advancing mixed-methods approaches for the study of networks and collaborations remains largely a nascent practice at present. Further work is needed to develop some methods integration guidelines, as well as build new skills sets that extend methodological repertoires, including those that incorporate emergent technologies, for the most effective use of mixed-methods approaches. The implications for this methodological development are discussed in the final paragraph of this chapter.

Computational advances, big data, AI and experimentation

The amplified use of quantitative methods and the associated prominence of mixed-methods approaches and related techniques has been facilitated by the enormous advancements made in computational power allowing for the interrogation of large data sets and more sophisticated statistical analyses as well as complex visualization outputs (see for example, Koliba, Zia and Merrill's Chapter 11 on agent-based models (ABMs) and Chamberlain and Farr-Wharton's Chapter 13 focusing on the frontiers of research in our field). Chamberlain and Farr-Wharton point out how these developments have already shaped, and will continue to shape, the current thinking about research approaches and offer predictions for the future, while Koliba et al. (Chapter 11) discuss one type of approach to computational modelling that allows for scenario development, theory testing and theory tuning. Other methodologies and methods benefiting substantially from advancements in user friendly technology and software advancements include SNA (as discussed in Lemaire and Raab's Chapter 9, QCA in Chapter 10 by Cepiku, Cristofoli and Trivellato, Q methodology in Kivit's Chapter 6 and van Meerkerk et al.'s Chapter 4 on survey methodology). As indicated in all these chapters, these new technologies and platforms for data collection, transfer, mining and visualization have contributed to the development of new and often novel ways to uncover and represent the dynamic nature of networks and collaborative activities, which is important for sharing and engaging with practitioners.

Alongside these computational advances, is the exponential growth in the digitization of data made available through the internet. The resulting big data sets are an important and growing source of information and therefore an effective medium for research, providing a range of new opportunities for collecting information, networking, conducting research and disseminating research results across many sectors (Nunan and Di Domenico 2017). In a 2016 article published in *Public Administration Review*, Mergel, Rethemeyer and Isett (2016) explored the impact of big data on PA. They noted that big data is closely related to 'data analytics' and 'data science' and assert that all these terms refer to 'the amount of data, computational practices used to harvest large-scale data sets from multiple sources, and analytical strategies that manipulate these data in real time' (2016: 929). Writing about the development of advanced data-mining tools and techniques to the study of governance networks, Koliba et al. (2018: 431) observe, 'As our capacity to undertake data mining of textual and narrative data expands, the opportunities to understand the phenomenological traces of nuanced network interactions intensifies. These advancements will deepen our capacity to develop finer and finer grained analysis of governance networks.'

At the same time, the noticeable increase in data-mining approaches by policy analysts and practicing public administrators has raised a cautionary flag. For example, Mergel et al. (2016), in their excellent review of the topic of big data in public management, echoed already expressed concerns that the big data revolution could signal an end to theory and, more importantly, lead to policy and administrative analysis that 'ends with correlation' falling short on ascribing underlying meaning and deeper explanations of causality (see page 933 for this discussion). In other words, if we take big data and data analytics too far we will fall into the trap of seeing correlation as causation. Thankfully, the methodologies surveyed in this volume seek to integrate data analytics with theory construction, scenario testing and causation.

Extending beyond big data and data analytics, and with the potential to change both the public sector and public sector research, is AI. The English Oxford Living Dictionary defines AI as 'The theory and development of computer systems able to perform tasks normally requiring human intelligence, such as visual perception, speech recognition, decision-making, and translation between languages'. The application of computer-simulation modelling to address the kinds of questions of concern to the PA field has begun to emerge, such as assessing welfare payments and immigration decisions, detecting fraud, planning new infrastructure projects, answering citizen queries, triaging health care cases (Kim, Zhong and Chun 2103; Eggers, Schatsky and Viechniki 2017; Martinho-Truswell 2018). Applied to a network or collaborative context, AI is increasingly being used to model or simulate the actions of inter-organizational networks. As noted in the chapter by Koliba, Zia and Merrill (Chapter 11), ABMs of collaborative governance networks have been constructed and combined with game theory to yield studies that examine some of the fundamental tenets guiding the establishment of voluntary ties (Axelrod and Cohen 1999), with specific inferences drawn to administrative practice (Knott, Miller and Verkuilen 2003). There is also a growing body of research that is focused on 'pattern-oriented' (Grimm et al. 2005) computer-simulation models that employ ABMs to study complex governance networks carrying on specific policy functions. These examples include models looking at: the governance of water resources (Lansing and Kremer 1993; Janssen and Ostrom 2006; Schlüter and Pahl-Wostl 2007); environmental hazard mitigation and economic justice (Eckerd 2013), school choice and institutional capacity (Maroulis et al. 2010; Maroulis 2016); patterns of fraud in public service delivery networks (Kim, Zhong and Chun 2103); and the impact of equity and resource scarcity and flux on transportation project prioritization in intergovernmental settings (Zia, Koliba and Tian 2013). These models are being used to run experiments using scenario-based approaches, often in concert with stakeholders.

In their chapter as early career network researchers, Farr-Wharton and Chamberlain also point to the growing use of and potential for experimentation in network and collaboration research, especially given the increasing computational capacity being made available and cloud-computing technologies (as noted previously). Experimental research has been long considered a 'gold standard' method of inquiry for its ability to test for causality (Provan and Sydow 2008; Anderson and Edwards 2015), but has been largely underutilized in the public sector because it has been seen as too time-consuming, too costly, ethically problematic and difficult to control (Clarke 1999, cited in Provan and Sydow 2008; Anderson and Edwards 2015). In 2011 Margetts lamented that '[T]here is as yet little evidence that experimental research is penetrating the mainstream of public management' (195). Much has changed since then. The combination of increased computational capacity and growing interest in the behavioural aspects of PA (Grimmelikhuijsen, Tummers and Pandey 2017) has led to an interest in the application of experimental research methods within public sector research generally (Baekgaard et al. 2015), but also for inter-organizational and collective modes (Shirado and Christakis 2017). A recent article by James, Jilke and Van Ryzin (2017) highlights the potential of experimental research approaches to detect the micro-perspectives of individual and network behaviour, as well as isolate causal effects to inform policy and practice, test intervention theories and establish generalization. Experimental research also meets the growing need and demand for research that is replicable; that is, research that can be re-executed, either in existing or modified forms, to enable comparisons with prior outcomes. Like Chamberlain and Farr-Wharton (Chapter 13), these authors also forecast laboratory experimental design approaches, such as simulations and games, as new and intriguing avenues with which to study networks and collaboratives, offering safe, ethical ways to manipulate alternative circumstances not possible in real-world situations.

The progression of big data, AI, experimentation and simulation as viable research options will demand both personal and organizational research adjustments, not the least of which are the need to respond to new and expanded ethical challenges (discussed later) (Morozov 2011). One emerging shift for researchers is the requirement by funding bodies and journals for more transparency of research procedures and raw data, which could be perceived as a loss of sole control of their research. Mooney and Newton (2012) suggest this perceived loss of control could be tempered easily by allocating scholarly credit for the creation and sharing of reusable data sets; although they also acknowledged a lack of consensus as to how this might best be implemented. Similarly, organizations are now obligated to create and regulate administrative procedures and implementation mechanisms that allow those processes and data to be made available for replication (OECD Principles and Guidelines for Access to Research Data from Public Funding, 2007; the Australian Research Council Funding Guidelines www.arc.gov.au/research-data-management).

Co-design, co-production, collaborative research

Several chapters (for example, those of Dodge, Saz-Carranza and Ospina; Vangen; Kamensky; Agranoff and Kolpakov; Lemaire and Raab; and Koliba, Zia and Merrill) deliver an important reminder that research, and especially research on networks and other collective/multiparty arrangements, is rarely a solitary undertaking, and instead is often crafted through various negotiated interactions and joint arrangements between researchers, the 'researched', their organizations, commissioning bodies and other related parties.

These chapter authors re-enforce well-held views that research is enhanced through the inclusion of the lived experiences and real-world insights of participants and, further, as Lemaire and Raab (Chapter 9), Vangen (Chapter 4) and Kamensky (Chapter 12) especially argue, any research should be constructed in such a way that participants are able to garner some benefit from their involvement and/or contribution. Through their chapter contributions these authors have offered methodological and practical ways forward for researchers for more genuine involvement of industry partners, government officials and community members in research design, implementation and interpretation, through various levels from partial involvement; for example, the early sharing of results with respondents for sense making; see Lemaire and Raab), to participatory modelling approaches (see Koliba, Zia and Merrill) and full-blown engagement as highlighted within the Vangen chapter.

The regular inclusion of terms such as 'engaged scholarship' (van de Ven 2007), 'co-design' and 'co-creation' (Griffin, Hamburg and Lundgren 2013; Voorberg, Bekkers and Tummers 2015) in research proposals and designs signals a significant and essential shift away from 'expert' research to the enactment of a collaborative element (see Ansell and Torfing 2014) that not only looks to leverage the different knowledges, experiences, skills and insights that different stakeholders can bring to a problem, but also aims to strengthen the capacity of the people involved in the research projects to interpret and implement findings to their projects as well as commission future research. As such, Heron's (1982: 19) description retains its relevance for contemporary researchers:

> In the new paradigm, this separation of roles is dissolved. Those involved in the research are co-researchers and co-subjects. They devise, manage and draw conclusions from the research; and they also undergo the experiences and perform the actions that are being researched.

Alongside of the types of academic-community research partnerships noted earlier has been a noticeable rhetoric and growth in the development of academic/industry alliances and research collaborations, leading to the funding and formation of dedicated research institutes, such as: in the Australian context Cooperative Research Centres; the US National Science Corp Program Research and Development Collaboration; the European Joint Research Centre (EU Science Hub); virtual international research networks (see for instance the Canadian Institute of Health Researchers, which includes a PA focus); and communities of practice, such as special interest groups like those formed within the International Research Society for Public Sector Management.

With goals of creating innovative and applied solutions and enhanced knowledge pathways (Van de Ven 2007; Jull, Giles and Graham 2017), these participatory and partnership modes are advanced by genuinely involving their partners in the design, implementation and interpretation modes of research. This orientation to practice presents a viable response to criticisms that research is 'elitist', undertaken on 'the studied' (Heron 1982), is not 'relevant' to practitioners (Jull, Giles and Graham 2017) or is unable to adequately measure and demonstrate its 'social impact' (O'Flynn and Barnett 2017).

Despite the increased appreciation for and undertaking of collaborative research, there remains what has been described elsewhere as a 'knowing – doing gap' (Hughes, O'Reagon and Wornham n.d.), where governments and not-for-profits practitioners searching for insights and strategies to address their work problems frequently overlook academic research as a knowledge source (Beer 2001), and instead seem to prefer the advice offered by consultants. This, it is argued, is often due to the style of academic writing, the availability of findings and the perceived academic preference to address assertoric theoretic questions over practical issues (Charles and Keast 2016). It is through genuine academic-industry interaction that thorny practical problems are brought to the fore, often providing researchers with new research avenues to pursue. Kamensky's chapter aptly picks up on this disconnect and outlines a set of questions that challenge practitioners in their every-day work, inviting researchers to engage with these questions and practitioners to advance both knowledge and practice. Readers of this volume would do well to prioritize the reading of Kamensky's chapter, particularly if they are looking to mount research studies that will have salience with policy-makers and practicing public administrators.

So, what does a participatory, co-created research agenda mean for future research on networks and collaborative arrangements? For the contributors to this volume there is a clear consensus that genuine engagement with research members in all their forms (participants, practitioners, partners and procurers) will lead to enhanced relationships, more accurate understandings of both the research issues and context, and as a result will deliver relevant research outcomes. Overall, the chapters in this volume reflect this collaborative ethos, urging the use of collective approaches and designs, where relevant and appropriate, as well as the uptake of emergent as well as existing alternative tools not covered in this volume, including, for example, video ethnography and reflective ethnographic interviewing (for a review of several alternative contemporary collaborative research methodologies see Gremillion 2013).

It is also worth mentioning that, although notions of co-created research are not new, it nonetheless remains out of the scope of normal practice for many researchers and research bodies, with the consequence that many personal and institutional research practices and structures do not adequately support this style of research. Research on networked and collaborative research models and processes has delivered many important insights that have been applied to enhance the operation and performance of these collective entities (Van de Ven 2007; Noble, Charles and Keast 2017; Griffin, Hamburg and Lundgren 2013). These insights notwithstanding, there remain many practice gaps and underexamined elements of research collaboration, including optimal infrastructures, incentives and expanded skill-sets as well as more attention to the micro-relational processes, such as emotions, motivations and social identity, needed to work in collaborative ways (Griffin, Branstrom-Oham and Kalman 2013).

Ethical considerations (especially for new approaches and tools)

Consideration of the additional ethical requirements in network research is long-standing. Quite early on, researchers of networks, collaborations and other multiparty and inter-organizational arrangements realized that the traditional principles of research ethics, such as informed consent and anonymity, were difficult to ensure due to the relational nature of the data and, for network analysis especially, the visual power of the network map that could be generated (Borgatti and Molina 2003, 2005). The SNA chapter by Lemaire and Raab in this volume reiterates the ethical challenges as well as raises some contemporary issues, and stresses the importance of adopting strong ethical standards in network research. Concerns around participant consent and privacy (especially for people nominated in network survey responses who are themselves not respondents), the growing use of secondary data, data sharing and data storage are emerging as key items that researchers will have to be extra mindful of in their design and implementation.

In particular, Lemaire and Raab (Chapter 9) remind current and future researchers of the visual power of SNA (and other visually oriented research outputs), which they note, without sufficient and suitable safeguards, can be used by unethical or ill-informed research sponsors to divert findings for political, fiscal and other pragmatic but nonetheless questionable rationales. For this type of research method, which shows relational connections, even apparently neutral data outcomes and maps can be potentially discriminatory, thereby compounding social inequities and undermining social justice outcomes (Boyd, Keller and Tijerna 2016; Casilli and Tubaro 2017). Furthermore, as Tene and Polonetsky (2014) demonstrated, when new technology pushes ahead of social norms it can be perceived by individuals as 'creepy', even when it does not violate data-protection regulations or privacy laws.

As noted earlier, many chapters raised the evolving technology theme, including its provision of access to previously unavailable public and personal data sets, as well as the ability to 'scrape' or 'mine' this data, for example from Facebook or Twitter, to interrogate relational links and personal attributes. Alongside these advantages are real concerns that current ethical and best practice codes and data regulations are no longer adequate, and personal information will increasingly be accessed and used for unintended or even nefarious purposes (Mertens and Wilson 2012; Nunan and Di Domenico 2017). Furthermore, there are genuine concerns that new directions in AI may take these data sets in unknown directions (Nunan and Di Domenico 2017). As responsible and ethical researchers we are required to be open to new ideas, technologies and approaches, while at the same time ever diligent to the new ethical challenges these developments may bring. As Tijerna (2016: 48) warns:

> New and complex data sets raise challenging ethical questions about risk to individuals that are not sufficiently covered by computer science training, ethics codes, or Institutional Review Boards (IRBs). The use of publicly available, corporate, and government data sets in research projects may reveal human practices, behaviours, and interactions in unintended ways, creating the need for new kinds of ethical support.

Failing to take these new challenges into account will lead to ethical breaches, with Boyd's (2016) account of the Facebook emotional contagion study showing evidence of a disconnect between research and those being researched, with people expressing their discomfort with both the study's use of 'personal' data and Facebook's underlying data practices. The more recent Cambridge Analytical debacle further stresses the need to take ethics in the new data age even more seriously.

There is also the matter of normative values and their place in research. Although networks and collaborations may be a viable means for leveraging human, social, political and cultural capital and, as we will argue, building demo-cratic anchorage, they can also be an ineffective means for delivering public goods and services. In the worst-case scenarios, networks and collaboration can lead to decidedly undemocratic practices. We must account for the possibility that in the worst cases, networks and collaboration structures and practices can result in groupthink or collusion: a togetherness mentality lacking intelligent debate or a plotting together toward an unethical end.

Taken together, the chapters in this volume serve as a timely and important reminder to both researchers and research procurers to be cognisant of the ethical requirements involved in undertaking, sourcing and utilizing network research. Moreover, they point to the need for more and deeper thinking and action as well as research to develop appropriate ethical mechanisms that will advance network research, particularly to support participatory processes in this field (see for example, Australian Council for International Development 2017). Casilli and Tubaro (2017) make a call to action, arguing that researchers and those being researched ought to be actively involved in the 'co-production' of appropriate ethical frameworks.

Where to from here and how? On the importance of adaptation and reflection

Two concluding themes have emerged from within the broader network and collaboration literature and are re-iterated in the previous chapters – adaptation and reflection. Combined, these themes point to the types of actions needed to deftly navigate the diverse array of methodological approaches available with which to address the array of problems and issues confronting PA as well as shape future practices in this sphere.

The problems and choices faced by those responsible for the development and management of effective PA outcomes are real, complex and challenging, and so too must be the research response. We are cautiously optimistic that the advances in research methodologies highlighted in this volume are 'up to the challenge'. It is clear though, that as the complexity of wicked policy and public service problems persist, we also need to evolve methodologies that are capable of explaining and critically evaluating policy and administrative experimenta-tion. The chapters herein reflect this complexity as, although each focuses on a particular method, there is also acknowledgement of the plurality of approaches and methods available to researchers and the potential value that cross-overs may bring for triangulation of findings and also to the creation of new knowledge and questions. The contemporary research context is one of continuing change: shifting problem and funding contexts, expansions of research forms and sites, rapid technological advances that not only provide extended computational capacity but also continually spin off new methods and techniques with which to conduct research. For researchers to stay relevant and offer value to their field as well as avoid professional obsolesce they must be able to adapt to these chal-lenges and opportunities as they arise – and even foresee changes.

This is, of course, easier said than done. As individual methods such as those discussed in this book continue to advance, being able to learn and master them and keep up with those developments, as well as judiciously combine them, is already challenging and time-consuming for network researchers. Now more than ever life-long learning in terms of research methods applies to network and collaboration researchers: mastering one method and excelling in its application is only a starting point in a research career, as several authors in this volume have pointed out in their contributions. It goes without saying that, in an era of collaboration, team efforts can help to ensure the right methodological mix and rigour, rather than only assuming super-method powers for individual researchers.

This brings us to the notion of reflection. Successfully working in a changing and often uncertain context and undertaking the multitude of tasks associated with crafting novel yet manageable research projects, often with multiple partners with multiple approaches to knowledge, requires that researchers be 'reflective practitioners' (Cravens et al. 2014). This is a position also held by Schon (1983), who argues that research relies on the development of personal insight and learning through critical examination and deliberations, as well as theoretical engagement with their actions: 'We may also consider science as a process in which scientists grapple with uncertainties and display arts of inquiry akin to the uncertainties and arts of practice' (49). By becoming reflective practitioners, reviewing and critically analysing their research practice and examining how it relates to their operating environment, researchers will not only be able to advance their professional practice, but also have a greater capacity to adapt and adjust to these conditions (or adjust their goals).

As the final set of chapters in this volume from emerging researchers Chamberlain and Farr-Wharton and an experienced practitioner John M. Kamensky, who serve as key boundary-spanners between academics and practitioners, remind us: the quality of our research enterprises is only as good as the research questions we ask. To ask 'good questions' we must be adaptive and reflective. We must be 'good listeners' and we must be able to take our research cues and shape our methodology from these questions, the voices of our respondents as well as the context in which they exist. And, interestingly, and not without a touch of irony, we must be mindful that quality research requires the development and maintenance of efficacious networks and collaborative endeavours. This is something at which, as scholars of networks and collaboratives, we as a community should excel. It is our sincere hope that this volume serves as a useful aid in these endeavours.

References

Aherns, P. 2018. "Qualitative network analysis: A useful tool for investigating policy networks in transnational settings?" *Methodological Innovations* 11 (1): article first published online: April 18, 2018.

Anderson, D. and B. Edwards. 2015. "Unfulfilled promises: Laboratory experiments in public management research." *Public Management Review* 17 (10): 1518–1542.

Ansell, C. and J. Torfing. 2014. *Public innovation through collaboration and design.* Abingdon, UK: Routledge.

Australian Council for International Development. 2017. *Research for development: Principles and guidelines for ethics research in development.* https://acfid.asn.au/sites/site.acfid/files/resource_document/ACFID_RDI%20Principles%20and%20Guidelines%20for%20ethical%20research12-07-2017.pdf.

Axelrod, R. and M. Cohen. 1999. *Harnessing complexity: Organizational implications of a scientific frontier.* New York: Free Press.

Baekgaard, M., C. Baethge, J. Blom-Hansen, C. Dunlop, M. Esteve, M. Jakobsen, B. Kisida, J. Marvel, A. Moseley, S. Serritzlew, P. Patrick Stewart, M. Kjaergaard Thomsen, and P. J. Wolf. 2015. "Conducting experiments in public management research: A practical guide." *International Public Management Journal* 18 (2): 323–342. doi: 10.1080/10967494.2015.1024905.

Beer, M. 2001. "Why management research findings are unimplementable: An action science perspective." *Reflections* 2 (3): 58–63.

Berg-Schlosser, D., G. De Meur, B. Rihoux, and C. Ragin. 2009. "Qualitative Comparative Analysis (QCA) as an approach." In *Configurational comparative methods: Qualitative Comparative Analysis (QCA) and related techniques,* edited by B. Rihoux and C.C. Ragin. London: Sage Publications.

Berry, F., R. Brower, S. Choi, W. Goa, H. Jang, M. Kwon, and J. Word. (2004). "Three traditions in network research: What the public management research agenda can learn from other research communities." *Public Administration Review* 64 (5): 539–552.

Borgatti, S.P. and J.-L. Molina. 2003. "Ethical and strategic issues in organizational network analysis." *Journal of Applied Behavioral Science* 39 (3): 337–349.

Borgatti, S.P. and J.-L. Molina. 2005. "Toward ethical guidelines for network research in organizations." *Social Networks* 27: 107–117.

Boyd, D. 2016. "Untangling research and practice: What Facebook's 'emotional contagion' study teaches us." *Research Ethics* 12 (1): 4–13.

Boyd, D., E. Keller, and B. Tijerna. 2016. "Supporting ethical data research: An exploratory study of emerging issues in big data and technology research, data & society research." Working Paper 08.04.2016. www.datasociety.nct/pubs/sedr/SupportingEthicsDataResearch_Sept2016.pdf.

Bressers, H.T.A. and L.J.J. O'Toole. 2005. "Instrument selection and implementation in a networked context." In *Designing governance: From instruments to governance,* edited by P. Eliadis, M.M. Hill, and M. Howlett. Montreal: McGill-Queen's University Press.

Carey, J.W. 1993. "Linking qualitative and quantitative methods: Integrating cultural factors into public health." *Qualitative Health Research* 3: 298–318.

Casilli, A. and P. Tubaro. 2017. "Rethinking ethics in social-network research." *The Conversation,* December 12. http://theconversation.com/rethinking-ethics-in-social-network-research-88988.

Charles, M. and R. Keast. 2016. "Publish and perish: Why academia needs to accept other ways of showing impact in industry-based projects." *Power to Persuade,* June 8. www.powertopersuade.org.au/blog/publish-and-perish-why-academia-needs-to-accept-other-ways-of-showing-impact-in-industry-based-research-projects/8/6/2016.

Chiolero, A. 2018. "Data are not enough: Hurray for causality." *American Journal of Public Health* 108 (5): 622.

Clarke, A. 1999. *Evaluation research: An introduction to principles, methods and practice.* London: Sage Publications.

Cravens, A.E., N. Ulibarri, M. Cornelius, A. Royalty, and A.S. Nabergoj. 2014. "Reflecting, iterating, and tolerating ambiguity: Highlighting the creative process of scientific and scholarly research for doctoral education." *International Journal of Doctoral Studies* 9: 229–247.

Creswell, J.W. 2003. *Research design: Qualitative and quantitative and mixed method approaches.* Thousand Oaks, CA: Sage Publications.

Cresswell, J.W. and V. Plano Clark. 2007. *Designing and conducting mixed methods research.* Thousand Oaks, CA: Sage Publications.

Dorien, P. 2001. *Causality in social network analysis, sociological methods and research.* Thousand Oaks, CA: Sage Publications.

Eckerd, A. 2013. "Policy alternatives in adaptive communities: Simulating the environmental justice consequences of hazardous site remediation strategies." *Review of Policy Research* 30 (3): 281–301.

Eggers, W., D. Schatsky, and P. Viechniki. 2017. "AI augmented government: Using cognitive technology to redesign public sector work." *Deloitte Insight.* https://www2.deloitte.com/insights/us/en/focus/cognitive-technologies/artificial-intelligence-government.html.

Emerson, K., T. Nabatchi, and S. Balogh. 2012. "An integrative framework for collaborative governance." *Journal of Public Administration Research and Theory* 22 (1): 1–29.

Fafchamps, M., D. Kebede, and D. Zizzo. 2015. "Keep up with the winners: Experimental evidence on risk taking, asset integration and peer effects." *European Economic Review* 79: 59–79.

Flynn, C. 2019. "The craft challenge." In *Crossing boundaries in public policy and management: Tackling the critical challenges*, edited by H. Dickenson, L. Craven, and G. Carey. London: Palgrave.

Glass, T., S. Goodman, M. Hernan, and J. Samet. 2013. "Causal inference in public health." *Annual Review of Public Health* 34: 61–75.

Gray, B. 1989. *Collaborating: Finding common ground for multiparty problems.* San Francisco: Jossey-Bass.

Gremillion, H. 2013. "Developing a collaborative methodology for research with community groups." *New Zealand Journal of Social Sciences* 8 (1–2): 74–78.

Griffin, G., A. Branstrom-Oham, and H. Kalman. 2013. *The emotional politics of research collaboration.* New York: Routledge.

Griffin, G., K. Hamburg, and B. Lundgren, eds. 2013. *The social politics of research collaboration.* New York: Routledge.

Grimm, V., E. Revilla, U. Berger, F. Jeltsch, W.M. Mooij, S.F. Railsback, H-H. Thulke, J. Weiner, T. Wiegand, and D.L. DeAngelis. 2005. "Pattern-oriented modeling of agent-based complex systems: Lessons from ecology." *Science* 310 (5750): 987–991.

Grimmelikhuijsen, S., L. Tummers, and S.K. Pandey. 2017. "Promoting state-of-the-art methods in public management research." *International Public Management Journal* 20 (1): 7–13.

Groeneveld, S., L. Tummers, B. Bronkhorst, T. Ashikali, and S. van Thoel. 2015. "Quantitative methods in public administration: Their use and development through time." *International Public Management Journal* 18 (1): 61–85.

Haugen Gausdal, A., H. Svare, and G. Möllering. 2016. "Why don't all high-trust networks achieve strong network benefits? A case-based exploration of cooperation in Norwegian SME networks." *Journal of Trust Research* 6 (2): 194–212.

Heron, J. 1982. *Empirical validity in experiential research.* London: Sage Publications.

Hudson, J. and S. Kühner. 2013. "Qualitative Comparative Analysis: New applications of innovative methods." *Policy & Society* 32: 379–281.

Hughes, T., N. O'Reagon, and D. Wornham. n.d. *The knowing-doing gap: Academic/practitioner engagement in strategic management.* file:///C:/Users/PC%20User/Downloads/Strategic%20Management%20Findings%20strat.pdf

Innes, J.E. and D.E. Booher. 2010. *Planning with complexity: An introduction to collaborative rationality for public policy.* New York: Routledge.

Isett, K.R., I.A. Mergel, K. LeRoux, P.A. Mischen, and R.K. Rethemeyer. 2011. "Networks in public administration scholarship: Understanding where we are and where we need to go." *Journal of Public Administration Research and Theory* 21 (suppl. 1): i157–i173.

James, O., S. Jilke, and G. Van Ryzin. 2017. "Behavioural and experimental public administration: Emerging contributions and new directions." *Public Administration* 95: 865–873.

Janssen, M.A. and E. Ostrom. 2006. "Chapter 30: Governing social-ecological systems." *Handbook of Computational Economics* 2: 1465–1509.

Jeffares, S. and C. Skelcher. 2011. "Democratic subjectivity in network governance: A Q-methodology study of English and Dutch public administration managers." *Public Administration* 89 (4): 1253–1273.

Jull, J., A. Giles, and I. Graham. 2017. "Community based knowledge translation: Advancing the co-creation of knowledge." *Implementation Science* 12: 150–159. https://implementation science.biomedcentral.com/track/pdf/10.1186/s13012-017-0696-3.

Kapucu, N., Q. Hu, and S. Khosa. 2017. "The state of network research in public administration." *Administration & Society* 49 (8): 1087–1120.

Keast, R. 2016. "Shining a light into the black box of collaboration: Mapping the prerequisites for cross sector working." In *The three sector solution: Delivering public policy in collaboration with not-for-profits and business,* edited by J. Butcher and D. Gilcrest, 157–180. Canberra, Australia: ANZSOG, ANU Press.

Kertzer, D. and T. Frinke. 1997. *Anthropological demography: Toward a new synthesis.* Chicago: University of Chicago Press.

Kim, Y., W. Zhong, and Y. Chun. 2013. "Modeling sanction choices on fraudulent benefit exchanges in public service delivery." *Journal of Artificial Societies and Social Simulation* 16 (2): 8. doi: 10.18564/jasss.2175.

Klijn, E.-H. and J. Koopenjan. 2016. *Governance networks in the public sector.* Abingdon, UK: Routledge.

Knott, J.H., G.J. Miller, and J. Verkuilen. 2003. "Adaptive incrementalism and complexity: Experiments with two-person cooperative signalling games." *Journal of Public Administration Research and Theory* 13 (3): 341–365.

Koliba, C., J. Meek, A. Zia, and R. Mills. 2018. *Governance networks in public administration and public policy,* 2nd ed. New York: Routledge Press.

Lansing, J.S. and J.N. Kremer. 1993. "Emergent properties of Balinese water temple networks: Coadaptation on a rugged fitness landscape." *American Anthropologist* 95 (1): 97–114.

Lecy, J., I. Merger, and H.-P. Smitz. 2014. "Networks in public administration: Current scholarship in review." *Public Management Review* 16 (5): 649–665.

Mandell, M., R. Keast, and D. Chamberlain. 2016. "Collaborative networks and the need for a new management language." *Public Management Review* 20 (7): 326–341.

Margetts, H.Z. 2011. "Experiments for public management research." *Public Management Review* 13 (2): 189–208.

Maroulis, S. 2016. "Interpreting school choice treatment effects: Results and implications from computational experiments." *Journal of Artificial Societies and Social Simulation* 19 (1): 7.

Maroulis, S., R. Guimera, H. Petry, M.J. Stringer, L.M. Gomez, L.A.N. Amaral, and U. Wilensky. 2010. "Complex systems view of educational policy research." *Science* 330 (6000): 38–39.

Martinho-Truswell, E. 2018. "How AI could help the public sector." *Harvard Business Review*, Jan 26. https://hbr.org/2018/01/how-ai-could-help-the-public-sector.

Mergel, I., R.K. Rethemeyer, and K. Isett. 2016. "Big data in public affairs." *Public Administration Review* 76 (6): 928–937.

Mertens, D., P. Bazeley, L. Bowleg, N. Fielding, J. Maxwell, J. Molina-Azorin, and K. Niglas. 2016. *The future of mixed methods: A five year projections to 2020: Mixed Methods International Research Association (MMIRA) task force report.* https://mmira.wildapricot.org/resources/Documents/MMIRA%20task%20force%20report%20Jan2016%20final.pdf.

Mertens, D. and A. Wilson. 2012. *Program evaluation theory and practice.* New York: Guilford Press.

Miles, M.B. and A.M. Huberman. 1984. *Qualitative data analysis.* London: Sage Publications.

Mooney, H. and M.P. Newton. 2012. "The anatomy of a data citation: Discovery, reuse, and credit." *Journal of Librarianship and Scholarly Communication* 1 (1): eP1035. http://dx.doi.org/10.7710/2162-3309.1035.

Morozov, E. 2011. *The net delusion: The dark side of internet freedom.* New York: Public Affairs.

Noble, D., M. Charles, and R. Keast. 2017. "Towards a collaborative competency framework to enhance public value in university: Industry collaboration." *Public Management and Money* 37 (5): 373–377.

Nunan, D. and M. Di Domenico. 2017. "Big data: A normal accident waiting to happen." *Journal of Business Ethics* 145: 481–491.

OECD. 2007. *Principles and guidelines for access to research data from public funding, 2007.* www.oecd.org/sti/sci-tech/38500813.pdf.

O'Flynn, P. and C. Barnett. 2017. *Evaluation and impact investing: A review of methodologies to assess social impact.* IDS Evidence Report No. 222. Brighton, UK: Institute of Development Studies, University of Sussex.

O'Leary, R., Y. Choi, and C. Gerard. 2012. "The skill set of the successful collaborator." *Public Administration Review* 72 (S1): 70–83.

O'Toole, L. and K. Meier. 2004. "Public management in intergovernmental networks: Matching structural networks and managerial networking." *Journal of Public Administration Research and Theory* 14 (4): 469–494.

Provan, K.G., A. Fisher, and J. Sydow. 2007. "Interorganizational networks at the network level: A review of empirical literature on whole networks." *Journal of Management* 33 (6): 479–516.

Provan, K.G. and R.H. Lemaire. 2012. "Core concepts and key ideas for understanding public sector organizational networks: Using research to inform scholarship and practice." *Public Administration Review* 72 (5): 638–648.

Provan, K.G. and J. Sydow. 2008. "Evaluating inter-organizational relationships." In *The Oxford handbook of inter-organizational relations,* edited by S. Cropper, M. Ebers, C. Huxham, and P. Smith-Ring, 691–716. Oxford: Oxford University Press.

Robinson, S. 2006. "A decade of taking networks seriously." *Policy Studies Journal* 34 (5): 569–589.

Sale, J., L. Lohfeld, and K. Brazil. 2002. "Revisiting the qualitative-quantitative debate: Implications for mixed methods research." *Quality and Quantity* 36 (1): 43–53.

Schlüter, M. and C. Pahl-Wostl. 2007. "Mechanisms of resilience in common-pool resource management systems: An agent-based model of water use in a river basin." *Ecology and Society* 12 (2): 4.

Schon, D. 1983. *The reflective practitioner: How professionals think in action.* New York: Basic Books.

Shirado, H. and N. Christakis. 2017. "Locally noisy autonomous agents improve global human coordination in network experiments." *Nature* 545 (May): 370–374.

Smith, J.K. and L. Heshusius. 1986. "Closing down the conversation: The end of the quantitative-qualitative debate among educational researchers." *Educational Researcher* 15 (1): 4–12.

Stout, M. and J. Love. 2017. "A method for fruitful public encounters." *American Review of Public Administration* 47 (1): 130–147.

Tashakkori, A. and J. Cresswell. 2007. "Editorial: Exploring the nature of research questions in mixed methods research." *Journal of Mixed Methods Research* 1: 207–211.

Tashakkori, A. and C. Teddlie. 2003. *Handbook of mixed methods in social & behavioral research.* Thousand Oaks: Sage Publications.

Tene, O. and J. Polonetsky. 2014. "A theory of creepy: Technology, privacy, and shifting social norms." *Yale Journal of Law and Technology* 16 (1): Article 2. http://digitalcommons.law. yale.edu/yjolt/vol16/iss1/2.

Termeer, C. and Dewulf, A. 2018. "A small wins framework to overcome the evaluation paradox of governing wicked problems." *Policy and Society.* https://doi.org/10.1080/144 94035.2018.1497933.

Thomas, A.-M. and J. Perry. 2006. "Collaboration processes: Inside the black box." (Special Issue) *Public Administration Review* 66: 19–32.

Tijerna, B. 2016. "Campus support systems for technical researchers: Navigating big data ethics." *EDUCAUSEreview,* June 27. https://er.educause.edu/articles/2016/6/ campus-support-systems-for-technical-researchers-navigating-big-data-ethics.

Toye, F., E. Williamson, A. Williams, J. Fairbank, and S. Lamb. 2016. "What value can qualitative research add to quantitative research design? An example from an adolescent idiopathic scoliosis trial feasibility study." *Qualitative Health Research* 26 (13): 1838–1850. www.ncbi.nlm.nih.gov/pubmed/27509903.

Ulibarri, N. and T. Scott. 2017. "Linking network structure to collaborative governance." *Journal of Public Administration Research and Theory* 27 (1): 163–181.

Van de Ven, A. 2007. *Engaged scholarship: A guide for organizational and social research.* Oxford: Oxford University Press.

Voorberg, W., V. Bekkers, and L. Tummers. 2015. "A systematic review of co-creation and co-production: Embarking on the social innovation." *Journey Public Administration Review* 17 (9): 333–1357.

Yin, R. 2014. *Case study research,* 5th Ed. Thousand Oaks, CA: Sage Publications.

Zia, A., C. Koliba, and Y. Tian. 2013. "Governance network analysis: Experimental simulations of alternate institutional designs for intergovernmental project prioritization processes." In *Compact I: Public administration in complexity,* edited by L. Gerrits and P.K. Marks. Litchfield Park, AZ: Emergent Publications.

Index

Note: Page numbers in *italic* indicate a figure and page numbers in **bold** indicate a table on the corresponding page. An "n" following a page number indicates a note on that page.

pattern-oriented computer-simulation models 263
PCA (Principal Components Factor Analysis) 117
performance measurements, rise of 2
performance of networks 3
performance partnership pilots program 236–237
phenomenology 10, 125–127, 134, 136–137, 262
p*model 12, 180, 244
PNet software 245
policy discourse 108–109, 112
positive ties 168–169
PQMethod 116–118
practice-oriented agenda, RO-AR and 127–128, 132
practice-oriented research, theorizing 134
practice-oriented theory 129, 132, 135–136
practitioner questions 233–238, 266; accountability 237; competencies, skills and experiences of leaders and participants 234–235; effectiveness, kinds of networks and governance structures for 236; evaluating networks 237; processes, tools and technologies used to form and manage networks 235–236; resources, obtaining 236–237; role of complex adaptive systems 236; role of co-production approaches 236; role of open data, transparency, crowd sourcing/funding 236; role of private, non-profit platforms 236; role of social capital, trust, and legitimacy 236; when to use networks and collaboration 234
primary data, in network analysis 169
Principal Components Factor Analysis (PCA) 117
prisoner dilemma simulations 211–212
privacy 267
private, non-profit platforms, role of 236
probabilistic approach to study of mechanisms 145
problem-solving networks 234
process, definition of 148
process mapping *144–145,* 146, 149
process theory 21
process tracing 11, 257–258; agent-based models (ABMs) and 14, 222; benefits and limitations 151–153; case study 51–52; combining and synthesizing qualitative and quantitative information 258; further reading on 154; future of

153–154; limitations of 11; relevance to public sector networks and collaborative arrangements 147–149
program desk audits 21, 38, *39*
proportional reduction in consistency (PRI) 199
public administration 1, 4, 6, 9; agent-based models and 210–211; big data and 262; case study and 45–46; narrative inquiry and 82, 84–85; process mapping 146; process tracing and 146, 151; recent application of quantitative techniques 256; single operating system 233; surveys and 64–65; typology of study of networks in 84–85
pulse surveys 15

Q analysis 116–118, 117n2, 121
QAP (Quadratic Assignment Procedure) 12, 180, 249
QCA *see* qualitative comparative analysis (QCA)
Q methodology 9–10, 107–122, 258, 261; application 111–118; combining and synthesizing qualitative and quantitative information 258; Dryzek's classification of environmental discourses 107, *108*; evaluating 118–120; frames of reference 108–111, 115–120; future of 120–121; introduction to 107–108; limitations of 119–120; relevance of 108–111; resources 120–122; R methodology compared 115; standard survey methods compared to 118–119; statistical analysis 115–116; strengths of 9, 119
Q sort 111, 113–116, 118–121
Q-sort grid *113,* 113–115
Q study stages 10, 111–116; concourse establishment 111–112; concourse management 112–113; Q survey *113,* 113–115; statistical analysis 115–116
Q survey 113–115
Quadratic Assignment Procedure (QAP) 12, 180, 249
qualitative analysis: agent-based models (ABMs) 223; bridging the qualitative/quantitative divide 256–260; building theory 22–27; process tracing and 151; software 112
qualitative comparative analysis (QCA) 189–207, 257–258, 261; agent-based models (ABMs) and 223; analysis of necessary and sufficient conditions

Made in the USA
Middletown, DE
15 September 2021